The Los Angeles
Angels of the
Pacific Coast League

LOS ANGELES BASEBALL CLUB OFFICES

435 E. 42nd Place, Los Angeles, Calif.

Box Office	ADams 4107—4108
Business Office	ADams 8966
Publicity-Promotion	ADams 0949

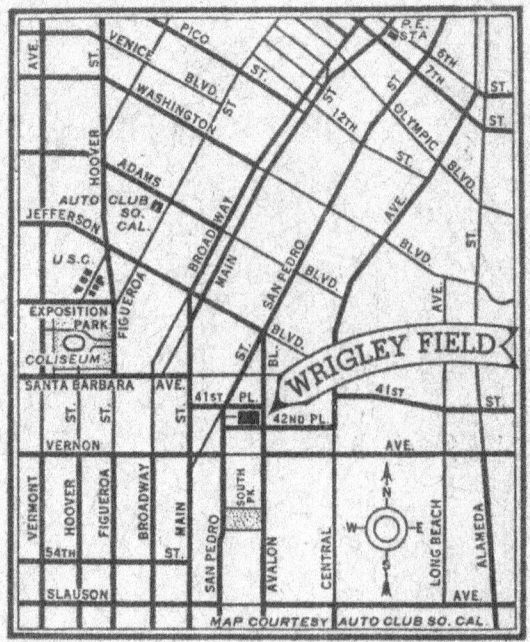

The Los Angeles Angels of the Pacific Coast League
A History, 1903–1957

RICHARD BEVERAGE

McFarland & Company, Inc., Publishers
Jefferson, North Carolina, and London

Frontispiece: These maps were given to members of the
Auto Club of Southern California (courtesy Dick Dobbins).

LIBRARY OF CONGRESS CATALOGUING-IN-PUBLICATION DATA

Beverage, Richard E.
The Los Angeles Angels of the Pacific Coast League :
a history, 1903–1957 / Richard Beverage.
       p.   cm.
Includes bibliographical references and index.

ISBN 978-0-7864-6520-0
softcover : 50# alkaline paper ∞

1. Los Angeles Angels (Baseball team)— History.
2. Pacific Coast League — History.
I. Title.
GV875.A6B484 2011   796.357′640979494 — dc23   2011033872

BRITISH LIBRARY CATALOGUING DATA ARE AVAILABLE

© 2011 Richard Beverage. All rights reserved

*No part of this book may be reproduced or transmitted in any form
or by any means, electronic or mechanical, including photocopying
or recording, or by any information storage and retrieval system,
without permission in writing from the publisher.*

Front cover: The 1926 Angels. Front row (left to right): Les Holmes,
Rube Yarrison, Bert Read, Jigger Statz, Ray Dwyer, Ray Jacobs.
Middle row: Batboy, Whitey Glazner, Wally Hood, Gale Staley,
Marty Krug, Clyde "Pea Ridge" Day, Johnny Mitchell (holding
Russell Krug), Frank Brazill. Back row: Moe Genser, Wayne
Wright, Ralph Stroud, Art Jahn, Elmer Jacobs, Art Weis, Truck
Hannah, Gus Sandberg (courtesy Mark Macrae);
cover design by David K. Landis (Shake It Loose Graphics)

Manufactured in the United States of America

*McFarland & Company, Inc., Publishers
Box 611, Jefferson, North Carolina 28640
www.mcfarlandpub.com*

To the memory of my dear son, Jerry Beverage,
who left this world on April 8, 2011.
We were privileged to have him
for as long as we did.

Table of Contents

Preface	1
1. The Early Years of the Pacific Coast League	5
2. A New Ball Park and New Owners	7
3. World War I and Another Angels Championship	10
4. The War Is Over and the Tigers Win Twice	12
5. An Angels Pennant and a New Owner	19
6. A New Management Team Takes Over as Red Leaves	22
7. A New Ballpark and a Pennant to Follow	30
8. A Collapse and the Angels Rebuild	39
9. Night Baseball Is Introduced as the Depression Begins	48
10. Depression Baseball	57
11. The Yankees of the West	61
12. The Streak Is Broken and the Stars Leave Town	74
13. Truck Hannah Takes the Helm	83
14. Hannah Is Out and Statz Is In	91
15. As World War II Beckons, the Angels Flounder	101
16. Disaster in Sacramento	107
17. Wartime Baseball and Two Pennants	112
18. A Third Major League? Meanwhile, the Angels Win Another Pennant	123
19. Decline and Fall	135
20. The Angels Fall to the Bottom	142
21. Smilin' Stan in Charge	153
22. Bill Sweeney Is Back in Town	166
23. Sgt. Bilko and His Gang	171
24. Dodger Blue	183

Epilogue	188
Appendix A: All-Time Los Angeles Angeles Roster	191
Appendix B: Team Batting, Fielding and Pitching	200
Appendix C: Individual Batting and Pitching, by Season and Career	207
Appendix D: Managers and Their Records	239
Appendix E: Paid Attendance	240
Bibliography	241
Index	243

Preface

As these words are written, it is difficult to imagine the thriving cities of the Pacific Coast without major league baseball. The territory was first opened to the National League when the Brooklyn Dodgers and New York Giants migrated west in 1958. They settled in Los Angeles and San Francisco, respectively, and were soon followed by other major league clubs in Oakland, Los Angeles, San Diego and Seattle. A generation of baseball fans has grown up knowing only these teams and the National and American Leagues. They can be excused for thinking that there is nothing else in the baseball spectrum. But once upon a time the world of the national pastime was very different.

Long before the arrival of the two Eastern teams made our national game truly national, professional baseball was thriving in the West in the form of the Pacific Coast League (PCL). While only a minor league in name, the PCL was anything but that in reality. During its prime years, the league featured future members of the National Baseball Hall of Fame in Joe DiMaggio, Ted Williams, Paul and Lloyd Waner, Tony Lazzeri, Ernie Lombardi, Earl Averill, Bobby Doerr and Joe Gordon. Each of these players made his professional debut in the Pacific Coast League. Other major league stars—Dom DiMaggio, Wally Berger, Lefty O'Doul, Willie Kamm, and Bob and Irish Meusel, among others—were developed in the PCL as well. The quality of play was also enhanced by veteran major leaguers who were in the twilight of their careers. Sam Crawford, for instance, played three years in the Coast League after a long Hall of Fame career with Cincinnati and Detroit. And then there were the local legends—men who did not enjoy long major league careers but were superb players nevertheless, such as Buzz Arlett, Jigger Statz and Frank Shellenback. You will find their names in this book, and you will see the names of many more, men whose names might be unfamiliar to you. They all contributed to making the Pacific Coast League the great league that it was.

The PCL featured intense rivalries that were the equal of anything the major leagues had to offer. Competition between the Los Angeles Angels and Hollywood Stars and the Oakland Oaks and San Francisco Seals was every bit as fierce as the legendary Giant-Dodger confrontations in the East. Other mainstays of the league were the Seattle Rainiers, Portland Beavers, Sacramento Solons and, after 1935, the San Diego Padres. The arrival of the major league clubs and the ones that followed merely continued the fine baseball that Coast League fans were used to and had enjoyed in the past.

This book tells the story of what was perhaps the premier franchise in the Pacific Coast League, the Los Angeles Angels. It focuses on the glory years of the league, 1919 through

1957, the last year of the Angels' existence, with a summary review of the league's early years, beginning in 1903. The league did not take modern form until 1919, when at the end of World War I it first expanded to eight clubs. That season proved pivotal in baseball history, as the events of that year led to major changes in the way the game was played and administered. Babe Ruth was first recognized as a dominant power hitter, for instance; his performance led to a renewed emphasis on the offensive part of the game. And the so-called Black Sox scandal in the World Series led to the creation of the commissioner's office and tighter control of off-the-field activities.

The Angels won the pennant in 1903 and won 13 more during their existence. They were an exciting team that regularly finished in the first division and, even when they were not the team to beat, made themselves a factor in the pennant race. Wrigley Field, where the Angels played from 1925 on, added to the team's character and class. It was a wonderful park, in its day one of the finest in the United States. Wrigley was a hitter's park, and games played there generally gave the customer his or her money's worth in terms of excitement.

A history of this sort wouldn't be complete without statistics, and I have provided an abundance of them. All-time records in the major hitting and pitching categories are included, and I have presented the basic roster and lineup for each year. As a general rule, if a player batted 100 times or pitched 45 innings, his record will be included. The opening day lineup for each year, 1919–57, and the attendance for each of those years is part of the appendix, along with a listing of home runs by each player in each park in those years. The complete all-time roster of Angels players who appeared in at least one game from 1903 to 1957 is included as well.

From the league's inception, PCL clubs were owned and operated by local interests. They signed their own players, developed them to the point where the best of them were ready to play in the major leagues, and would then sell them to the highest bidder. Those that didn't make it to the majors might stay with the local club for a number of years. This pattern created a large degree of stability during this period. Things began to change during the '30s when the major league clubs began to purchase minor league clubs and use them for development of their own talent. Although few PCL clubs became the property of the major leagues, they could no longer compete with them for the young talent. Beginning shortly before World War II, there would be more players coming and going; in some years there was no clear-cut regular at a position. Two or more names will be shown in those instances. In virtually every season more than one catcher is shown, as the duty was split between two or more men. In 1903–04, Heinie Spies caught 359 games, an incredible iron-man performance, while Bob Collins caught 162 of the 178 games the Angels played in 1937. Those are the only exceptions.

I was fortunate to be able to speak to and correspond with many former Angels during my research. Specifically, Wally Berger, Bruce Cunningham, Carl Dittmar, Charlie English, George Goodale, Clarence Maddern, Hugh McMullen, Eddie Malone, Bill Schuster, Jigger Statz, Ken Raffensberger, Max West, Fay Thomas and Art Weis contributed memories of their playing days, and in some cases provided materials to use. Umpire Cece Carlucci filled me in on the great riot of 1953 at Gilmore Field. Bill Schroeder of the Helms Athletic Foundation allowed me to spend many hours in his library, as did Chuck Stevens, the longtime secretary of the Association of Professional Ballplayers of America, and a veteran of many Coast League years himself. Sadly, almost all of these men have since died. It was a privilege to share their insights and memories.

A shorter version of this book was published in 1981, but since then much more information on the Angels and the PCL in general has become available, leading to this expanded and completely revised version. Many have encouraged me to complete this task and have shared with me their insights. My wife, Rae, deserves special credit; it was her original idea to do this work. In no particular order, Jerry Mezerow, Helen Hannah Campbell, Jay Berman, Bob Hoie, Dick Dobbins, John Spalding, Doug McWilliams, Mark Macrae, Carlos Bauer, Vic Pallos, Jeff Tillies and Grover Coleman contributed to this effort.

In recent years there have been several significant additions to the literature of the PCL, and there are more on the way. It appears that interest in the league has never been greater. In 1987 the Pacific Coast League Historical Society was founded as an outlet for this increased interest, and the organization has grown to almost 700 members. Some of this attention is no doubt attributable to nostalgia, but much of it is a result of curiosity about how the game of baseball developed in the West over the years. Baseball is a wonderful part of our heritage, after all. If this history provides some answers and satisfies some of that curiosity that exists, I will be very pleased indeed.

1

The Early Years of the Pacific Coast League

The Pacific Coast League (PCL) was officially founded in 1903, but in reality it had its origins in the California State League of 1899. That league was a serious league, consisting of six teams with a moderate schedule of 90 games. By 1902 the league had shrunk to four strong teams in Oakland, San Francisco, Sacramento and Los Angeles. Its schedule had increased to 168 games, and shortly after the season ended in November, interest began to develop in expanding the league to the Pacific Northwest to include the cities of Portland and Seattle. Accordingly, those two cities were added, and on December 29, the new Pacific Coast League was formed with a projected schedule of over 200 games.

This was not the beginning of professional baseball in the West, of course. West Coast baseball as we know it dates to at least 1860, when the first organized game was played in San Francisco. From then on until the first edition of the California State League began play in 1886, there were many professional teams, some of which were no more than town teams. John Spalding has captured much of the flavor of this era in his fine book, *Always on Sunday,* while Dick Dobbins has done the same in his *Nuggets on the Diamond,* a history of baseball in the San Francisco Bay Area. Clearly, by the end of the nineteenth century, baseball was a thriving enterprise on the Pacific Coast.

The first professional game in Los Angeles was played in 1886, and in 1893 the city had its first professional league team when it joined the California State League. That experience was short-lived as the league folded after that season. Los Angeles did not have a professional team again until 1901, when it replaced Stockton in the revived California State League. This club was known as the Loo-Loos.

The PCL began play on March 26, 1903. It was an "outlaw" league during that first season — working against the attempt to control professional baseball and the movement of players. During this year the Coast League did not honor contracts signed by players with National Association member clubs. However, under the guidance of league president Eugene F. Bert, the PCL became a full-fledged member of the Association.

Los Angeles was an immediate factor in the Pacific Coast League, winning the first championship in 1903 with 133 victories and finishing 27½ games ahead of second-place Sacramento, which finished at .500. No other team won half of its games that year. The Angels/Loo-Loos were led by manager Cap Dillon, who hit .364, an incredibly high average in that deadball year. Future National League star Gavvy Cravath led the team with seven home runs, while third baseman Jud Smith was a stalwart player, leading the league in assists and total chances. The pitching staff was led by Rusty Hall and Doc Newton, each of whom won over 30 games while pitching over 400 innings, an incredible total compared to the workload of present day pitchers.

The domination of the Loo-Loos in 1903 caused the PCL to split the season in 1904. Los Angeles did not do so well under this arrangement. The new Tacoma club, which had replaced Sacramento, won the first half by seven games and tied with the Loo-Loos for the second-half crown. In a best-of-nine-game playoff between the two clubs, Tacoma won the league championship, five games to four. The Loo-Loos, now known mostly as the Angels, missed the big bat of Dillon, who played in the major leagues with Brooklyn that year. His replacement, Hal Chase, hit .279 but displayed a remarkable fielding talent that would soon carry him to the majors. Cravath increased his home run total to 13 while hitting .270, and Curt Bernard led the hitting attack with a .308 average. Yet, Angels pitching was not at the same level as 1903. Hall suffered a relapse, winning only 16 games while showing the effect of pitching 468 innings in 1903. Doc Newton carried the club, winning 39 games with 11 shutouts.

Dillon was back in 1905, replacing Chase at first base, and the Angels thrived under his leadership. Once again the schedule was split, but this would be the last time this would happen until 1928. This time Tacoma won the first-half season, but the Angels rebounded to win the second half and defeated the Tigers in the championship playoffs. Shortstop Kitty Brashear won the batting championship in 1905 with a .303 average, not particularly high, but a good mark as overall hitting began to decline, a trend that would continue until 1911. Angels pitching was just average that year, and the club would not have won the second-half season without the fine performance of young pitcher/outfielder Walter Nagel. "The Judge," as he would come to be known, came up late in the season and won 11 games without a loss.

The Angels fell to third place in 1906 in a season in which events were dominated by the effects of the great San Francisco earthquake in April. But they bounced back in 1907 to win their third pennant in a season that saw the league shrink to four clubs. Oakland, Portland and San Francisco remained along with the Angels, who won again in 1908. The team was almost completely rebuilt by this time, with Dillon and Kitty Brashear the only remaining regulars from the early championship years. Pitcher Dolly Gray had become the ace of the staff with back-to-back seasons of 34 and 26 wins in his last years with the Angels.

During the first five years of the PCL's existence, the league battled with a new, outlaw California State League for supremacy in the West. There were teams from each league in some of the cities, but by 1909 the Coast League had won the war, and it remained the dominant baseball organization in the West before the National League moved to California after the 1957 season. In 1909, two new teams were added in Sacramento and Vernon, a small industrial city bordering Los Angeles. The Vernon franchise was owned by Fred and Edward Maier, who owned a brewery in Los Angeles. Although there was a ballpark in Vernon, the club arranged to play most of its games at Chutes Park, which it shared with the Angels. Now there would be a ball game every day in Los Angeles. The stage was set for a new rivalry.

2

A New Ballpark and New Owners

The Angels' fortunes began to decline in 1909, when they finished in third place. There were no .300 hitters on the club, and pitcher Bill Tozer was the star of the team with a 30–12 record. The club fell to fifth place in 1910, as they lost more games then they won for the first time in their history. Walter Nagle was the outstanding player of the team, pitching 401 innings and winning 25 games. Hitting was approaching an all-time low, with outfielder Pete Daley leading the team with a record low of .262. And 1911 was even worse. The Angels finished dead last, 39½ games behind the champion Portland Beavers. The only bright spot on the field was outfielder Heinie Heitmuller, who was acquired from Baltimore of the Eastern League in mid-season. He had previously played at Oakland and Seattle, and was a fine hitter. In 78 games, Heitmuller hit .343. He was even better in 1912, when he hit .335 with 15 home runs before contracting typhoid fever in late September. In those days that was a deadly disease, and Heitmuller died on October 8, several weeks before the season ended. He was leading the league in hitting when he departed, and remained in front for the balance of the season, the only posthumous batting champion in league history.

The Angels moved into a new ballpark in 1911. Chutes Park was demolished during the winter, and the new facility was partially built on its site, located near the corner of Washington Boulevard and Hill Street near downtown Los Angeles. Washington Park, as it was known, was a wooden structure, seating approximately 8,000 when it opened, and later expanded with the addition of bleacher seats down the lines and extending into right field. The later capacity was said to be approximately 12,000.

The dimensions of Washington Park were 353 feet at the left field corner and 335 feet in right field, increasing in the power alleys to 460 feet in right-center and 420 feet in left-center. It was very favorable to the pitchers, and home runs were at a premium there. The park was home to both of the Southern California clubs through the 1925 season, and given that both the Angels and the Vernon Tigers played the bulk of their home games there during the lengthy PCL schedules, close to 4,000 professional games were played in Washington Park.

The fine hitting of Heitmuller and improved pitching in 1912 helped Los Angeles jump to third place that year, only ten games behind the champion Oakland Oaks. The ball was livelier that year, and this was reflected in higher batting averages. Cap Dillon, who seemed to be on the decline during the previous three years, had one of his better seasons, hitting

The 1913 Angels (left to right). *Top row:* Ivan Howard, Walt Slagle, Bill Tozer, Pol Perritt, Cap Dillon, Charlie Chech, Charley Jackson, Charlie Moore, Roy Crabb, George Metzger. *Middle row:* Brownie Rodgers, Rube Ellis, Dutch Hoffman, Jack Ryan, Mike Wotell, Harl Maggert. *Front row:* Warren Gill, Clarence Brooks, Ty Lober, Walter Boles, Ernie Johnson, Howard Fahey, Billy Page.

.293. Pete Daley finished close to Heimuller's league-leading mark, hitting .332, and Ivan Howard, Billy Page, Charlie Moore, Clarence Brooks and John Core all hit over. 280. The pitching staff was unspectacular but solid. Charlie Chech and Walt Leverenz led the way with records of 25–14 and 23–13, respectively.

The Angels fell back below .500 and finished in fifth place in 1913. The loss of Heitmuller was offset by the acquisition of Harl Maggert, who hit .313 with 13 home runs, and the return of Rube Ellis after a four-year stint in the major leagues. Cap Dillon was no longer an active player, although he continued as the club's manager. Disappointing as 1913 had been, the Angels were soon on the rebound. They finished in second place in 1914, only 3½ games behind the Portland Beavers. New players that year were outfielder Harry Wolter and first baseman Bill Abstein. Wolter finished second in the batting race, hitting .328, while both Abstein and Rube Ellis were .300 hitters. Earned Run Average (ERA) was calculated for the pitchers for the first time in 1914, with the Angels featuring the league leader in Jack Ryan, who had a 24–11 record to go along with a fine ERA of 1.84.

The Angels fell to third place in 1915, 8½ games behind first-place San Francisco and 3½ games behind Salt Lake City, which had taken over the Sacramento franchise. Wolter had his finest season, hitting .359 to win the PCL batting championship. Slim Love led the league with a 1.95 ERA and 23 wins, while Jack Ryan saw his ERA increase by almost a run a game, although he posted a 26–21 record.

At the close of the 1915 season, the Angels had a major change in ownership. Henry Berry, who had taken over the franchise from James Morley in 1906, sold his interests to a group headed by John Powers, which included the former manager of the Chicago Cubs and future Hall of Fame member, Frank Chance. With his arrival, it meant the end of Cap Dillon's tenure as Angels manager. He served the longest of any Angels manager with an overall record of 1,311–1,154.

Chance took the Angels helm in 1916, and for the first time since 1908 Los Angeles was the champion of the PCL. The Angels finished eight games ahead of the Vernon Tigers and had control of the pennant race through most of the season. The team won with outstanding pitching, for its hitting was decidedly average and the defense finished near the bottom of the league. Jack Ryan had the best year of his career with a 29–10 record and 2.19 ERA. Pete Standridge, at 20–10, and Brad Hogg, at 16–9, were major contributors. A late-season trade brought Otis "Doc" Crandall over from Oakland. He posted only a 5–5 record with the Angels, but would become a major factor for the club in the years ahead. No Angels player finished among the batting leaders, though young catcher Johnny Bassler did lead the way at .304. This was the beginning of his long and successful career in the Coast League.

3

World War I and Another Angels Championship

The Angels dropped to second place in 1917, and Chance did not complete the season, leaving his post on July 4. He was replaced by Wade "Red" Killefer, an outfielder who had been acquired earlier that year from Louisville of the American Association. The Angels had a 43–44 record when Killefer took charge, and he seemed to be the spark that the club needed. The Angels were soon in the thick of what was a very tight pennant race, with all clubs except Vernon in contention. Gradually, Los Angeles and San Francisco pulled away, and the two clubs were tied for the lead, entering the last week of the season. But San Francisco nosed ahead of the Angels and clinched the pennant on the season's last day, finishing two games ahead.

The Angels were stronger defensively in 1917 with several new players in the infield. First baseman Jack Fournier was purchased from the Chicago White Sox, and he was joined by second baseman Duke Kenworthy and shortstop Zeb Terry. Terry was the best shortstop in the league, and all of the newcomers hit better than the men they replaced. Fournier hit .305 while leading the club with seven home runs, and Kenworthy hit .302. New outfielder Irish Meusel led the way with a .311 average, and player-manager Killefer wasn't far behind at .295. The club could have won the pennant easily had Ryan and Standridge been close to their 1916 performances. But Ryan was a disappointing 12–11 and Standridge was even worse at 10–13. Neither man ever pitched for the Angels again. Brad Hogg, at 27–13, and Doc Crandall, at 26–15, were more than adequate replacements, but the club fell just short of the championship.

Although there was a very exciting pennant race in 1917, it was not a successful year at the box office. The United States had entered World War I in April, and for a time it was thought that the league would not finish the season. Attendance fell off significantly early in the year and did not improve to any great extent until late September during the climax of the race. But no PCL club was thought to have made a profit for the year, and at the end of the season the Portland club was shifted to Sacramento.

The war began to have a greater impact on the PCL when the 1918 season began. More players were drafted into the military. Gone from the 1917 Angels were Duke Kenworthy, Johnny Bassler and Maurice Schick. Other clubs were similarly affected. Nevertheless, the league planned for a full schedule and opened play on April 3. The early pennant race was very exciting, with the Angels and Vernon the strongest contenders. Attendance had increased over the previous year through April and May, but then in early June, Provost Marshall General Crowder issued his famous "work or fight" order. All men of draft age would be forced to either enlist in the military or find work in an essential industry; baseball was declared as a non-essential industry. All professional leagues were given a month to put their affairs in order before they would be forced to close down.

All of the minor leagues, with the exception of the International League, ended play in the middle of July. The PCL ended its season on July 14 with Vernon leading Los Angeles by two games. Because of the closeness of the race, the PCL directors directed those two clubs to play an additional series to determine the champion. The series would be a best-of-nine playoff with all games to be played at Washington Park. The Angels won the series, five games to two and were recognized as champions of the PCL for that season. They won the series because of their strong pitching. Doc Crandall, Curly Brown and Bill Pertica had fine years, and each would have won 20 games had the season not ended so abruptly. The hitters were led by Jack Fournier, who hit .325, and manager Killefer, who hit .295 while playing second base as the replacement for Kenworthy. A notable addition to the 1918 club was outfielder Sam Crawford. He had finished his great career with Detroit in 1917. A lifetime .309 hitter, Crawford was destined for a place in baseball's Hall of Fame. He was 38 years old when he joined the Angels, and not much was expected from him, for he had hit .173 in his last season with the Tigers. But Crawford took over right field and hit a solid .289 in 96 games. There would be more to come in the next two years.

4

The War Is Over and the Tigers Win Twice

Peace at last! The Great War finally came to a victorious conclusion on November 11, 1918, as Germany sued for peace and an armistice was declared on that day. There would be a period of time before the United States returned to normal, but baseball would be back in 1919 as it was before the war. The Pacific Coast League restored its usual lengthy schedule and added clubs in Seattle and Portland. It was now an eight-team league for the first time in its history.

There was some concern among the other club owners about the wisdom of expansion and the additional travel costs involved, but the two Northwest cities eventually proved that they could support Coast League baseball. There were plenty of players available for all of the clubs with the armed forces releasing men from military duty.

The Angels were generally considered to be the favorite to win the 1919 pennant, with Vernon once again to be their stiffest competition. Los Angeles had the nucleus of its 1918 roster in place. Jack Fournier was back for his third year with the club, but he complained about the contract he was offered; those matters would not be resolved until late in the training period. Manager Wade Killefer returned at second base, with Paddy Driscoll at shortstop and Duke Kenworthy back from the military at third base.

The outfield was very experienced with Rube Ellis in left field, Claude Cooper in center field and Sam Crawford in right. Ellis was beginning his eleventh season with the Angels. He had first played with the club in 1905, and save for a four-year period with the St. Louis Cardinals, had spent his entire career in the PCL. He was a fine fielder but at this late stage of his career was merely an average hitter with little speed. Cooper had spent most of 1918 in the Navy and didn't remain long in Los Angeles. He was sent to Oakland when Killefer installed Maurice Schick in center field. Finally, Crawford had played well in 1918 despite his age and looked good in spring training.

The Angels had their 1918 catchers back; Walter Boles had been the regular since 1914 and Pete Lapan had been a good back-up. Johnny Bassler was still in the military when the season began, and he would take over the regular spot when he returned.

The pitching staff looked to be the best in the league. The leader was spitballer Otis "Doc" Crandall. He had joined the club late in the 1916 season and had a fine season in 1917, winning 26 games. He had been one of the game's first relief specialists during his years with the New York Giants, from 1910 to 1913, and acquired his nickname when writer

Damon Runyon labeled him as "the doctor of ball games" for his outstanding work out of the bullpen. In the PCL, however, Crandall was a starting pitcher of the workhorse type. He could be counted on to go the distance in most of his starts.

The other starters were Curly Brown, Bill Pertica, Paul Fittery and Vic Aldridge. All except Aldridge had been with the Angels in 1918. He and Pertica were the younger members of the staff, and it was only a matter of time before they would return to the major leagues, where they had pitched briefly before joining Los Angeles. Brown had won 18 games in 1917 while Fittery had shown promise during the short 1918 season. All of these pitchers were very durable, never missing a turn on the mound and rarely needing relief.

In 1919 the Pacific Coast League began its season on April 8, well before the major leagues opened their season. This was customary during most of the years that Los Angeles was in the league. The favorable weather conditions in California enabled the PCL to begin its season early, and play continued well into October, sometimes after the World Series had ended. With the addition of two teams, the league began to schedule weeks of play, rather than a balanced number of games between each team. Each week consisted of a seven-game series, beginning on Tuesday and topped off with a Sunday doubleheader. Monday was a travel day, and sometimes the clubs were not able to arrive at their destination until late Tuesday. In those cases a doubleheader would be scheduled for Wednesday. There were occasional Monday games to make up for rainouts, and doubleheaders were always played on Memorial Day, Independence Day, and Labor Day, and in California, Admission Day (September 9). In 1919 a 26-week schedule was arranged. This was increased to 28 weeks for most of the 1920s so that the teams were playing around 200 games each year.

Opening Day was always a gala event in PCL cities. Usually, the festivities opened with a parade featuring many of the local dignitaries and celebrities. In 1919 the Los Angeles parade assembled at Washington Park at one o'clock. The group headed by players of both the Portland and Los Angeles teams proceeded to Main Street, then to 5th Street downtown. The parade then turned left to Broadway and went back to the ballpark. The flag was unfurled in all of its glory, the first ball was thrown out and another baseball season was underway.

The Angels started out with a furious rush, winning 16 of their first 20 games. They boasted a very strong batting order with Crawford, Fournier and Lapan each hitting over .360 and new center fielder Maurice Schick over .330 during the month of April. The pitching was consistently strong with Brown and Crandall virtually unbeatable in their early starts. San Francisco and Salt Lake City were also playing very well, but Vernon started very slowly, losing six of its first seven games with the Angels and quickly falling nine games behind. It looked to be a runaway to an easy pennant for Los Angeles.

Unfortunately, there were some troublesome spots on this team, and they began to manifest themselves in May. Paddy Driscoll, who would later earn a reputation as a star professional football player and became a member of the Pro Football Hall of Fame, did not appear to be an adequate shortstop. He did not have enough range in the field, and his throwing was hindered by the development of a sore arm as well. Wade Killefer was not a natural second baseman and had limited range, while Duke Kenworthy seemed out of position at third. Too many balls were getting through this infield; in the Dead Ball year of 1919, a good fielding infield was essential.

After the Angels lost a series to the Seals in mid–May, Killefer made several changes. Maurice Schick, who had replaced Claude Cooper in center field, cooled off after his hot start, and the Angels sent him to San Francisco. Bert Niehoff was brought in from Seattle to play third base with Kenworthy moving back to second and Killefer taking over center field. Driscoll was benched, and rookie Fred Haney was given the first opportunity at shortstop. He wasn't ready for PCL play, and the Angels purchased Bunny Fabrique from Seattle to replace him. Later in the month, Johnny Bassler returned from military service and replaced Pete Lapan, who was sent to Seattle.

These changes seemed to help; the club played out of its slump and took an 8½-game lead over the second-place Seals. Fabrique tightened the infield with his play at shortstop, although he was a very light hitter. Once again it seemed that Los Angeles was on its way to the championship.

The club went on the road for a four-week stretch beginning in late June, and when the Angels returned to Washington Park, the Vernon Tigers had begun to stir and were closing fast. Angels pitchers began to struggle for the first time all year. Doc Crandall suffered a mid-season slump, losing as often as he won, and Vic Aldridge missed several starts because of arm problems. The hitting had fallen off drastically with only Crawford providing a consistent threat. To add strength to the attack, business manager Jim Morley unveiled a wire fence in front of the permanent bleachers in right field at the beginning of the homestand. This cut down the home run distance by 20 feet, but as often happens when changes like this are made, the opposition took advantage of the reduced distance as often as the Angels, and the fence came down when the Seraphs went back on the road.

Vernon went on a winning streak during the Angels doldrums and took over first place during the last week of July. The real pennant race began at that point, with the two clubs alternating in the lead through August and much of September. The infield problems that had plagued the Angels through much of the season were finally solved on September 1, when Los Angeles acquired second baseman Karl Crandall from San Francisco. He replaced Kenworthy, who had been a major disappointment. Much had been expected from him upon his return from military service, but the veteran was no longer making the plays in the field and was hitting .222 when he was released to Seattle. Immediately, the Angels began to play better and moved back into the lead on September 16. They enjoyed a successful two weeks on the road in Portland and Seattle and were 2½ games ahead when they returned home to face the Tigers in the final series of the season.

The stage was set for an exciting climax to the season, and the Angels fully expected to emerge as champions. They had dominated the season series with Vernon, winning 15 of the 22 games already played, and they needed three wins to clinch the flag. The clubs split the first two games, leaving Los Angeles still 2½ games ahead with only five games to go.

Alas, the Angels were to win no more in 1919. Wheezer Dell, the ace of the Vernon staff, beat the Angels, 3–2, on Thursday; Byron Houck was the winner on Friday, beating Paul Fittery, 4–3. That shrank the lead to half a game, and the Tigers moved into first place on Saturday with a 3–1 win over Vic Aldridge. The Sunday doubleheader would decide the season.

The largest crowd in Washington Park history gathered on Sunday to see the finish. Ticket lines began forming before nine o'clock that morning, and by game time over 22,000 fans were squeezed into the park, with an estimated 5,000 cranks surrounding the park and unable to get in. The Tiger would clinch the pennant if they won the first game, and manager Bill Essick called on Dell again, even though he had enjoyed only two days rest. The Angels countered with their best, Curly Brown, who was seeking his 26th win. The game was scoreless through five innings, but the Tigers broke through for two runs in the sixth, scored another in the seventh and enjoyed a 3–0 lead going into the last of the eighth. The Angels broke their scoring drought with one run in that frame and then scored again in the ninth. Then with two out and Rube Ellis representing the tying run at first, Bert Niehoff hit a high chopper to the left of the mound. Dell's throw to first was too late, and Ellis, pausing only slightly as he rounded second, raced all the way to third. But Rube didn't slide, and overran the bag, and that proved to be fatal to the Angels cause. First baseman Frank Eddington rifled a throw to third to catch him for the final out. Vernon became the champion of the Pacific Coast League.

The second game was now meaningless, and it had to be called when the angry Angels fans rioted and filled the infield with their rented seat cushions. It was a bitter defeat for the Angels, who had led for so much of the year, only to lose out at the end. Without question the erratic infield play cost the Angels the pennant. The shifting of players from position to position early in the season cost the club a number of games that could have been won. Not until Karl Crandall arrived in September did the Angels have a steady infield.

Many players had fine performances that year. Sam Crawford showed the same form that had served him so well during his brilliant major league career by hitting .360 with 14 home runs. These were very impressive numbers in the Dead Ball era of 1919, especially for a club playing in a very large ballpark. Crawford finished a close second in the race for the batting title, losing by only two points to Bill Rumler of Salt Lake City. Jack Fournier had his second fine year in a row, hitting .328 in his final Coast League season. Manager Killefer was right behind him at .320. This trio provided the bulk of the Angels offense, for no other regular hit better than .273.

Curly Brown and Doc Crandall were the best pitchers. Crandall won 28 games, the most among the league's pitchers, while Brown's 25–8 record was the best percentage-wise, and his 2.03 ERA was the lowest in the league. They were two solid veteran pitchers, each of whom pitched over 300 innings, and they walked a total of 87 batters combined. Paul Fittery and Bill Pertica also pitched over 300 innings, but they were not nearly as effective, each man losing 20 games. Vic Aldridge pitched 221 innings with a 15–10 record in 31 games. There was not much need for additional pitchers with this durable group.

The Angels were bitterly disappointed with their failure to win the 1919 pennant, but the club expected to be right in the thick of the pennant race again. Vernon remained relatively intact from the previous year and was the consensus favorite, but both owner Johnny Powers and manager Killefer thought the Angels would give the Tigers a strong battle and perhaps overtake them.

The infield situation was the most serious Angels weakness in 1919, and Killefer took steps to address that issue. In those days, farm systems and working agreements with major league clubs did not exist in the manner that later became so prevalent. The personal relationships that club personnel had with major league management usually provided the basis for player activity, and Killefer had such a relationship with the St. Louis Cardinals. The Redbirds wanted to improve their offense, and Jack Fournier was the player they wanted. To get him, St. Louis was willing to pay a high price; that winter the Cardinals gave Los Angeles four players for him and Bunny Fabrique—first baseman Art Griggs, shortstop Jim "Ike" McAuley, pitcher Claude Thomas and catcher Grover Hartley.

Hartley was of little use to the club and was released during spring training. There was no need for him with Johnny Bassler on hand and Pete Lapan returning from loan to Seattle. But the other three players proved to be extremely valuable. Although Griggs was seven years older than Fournier and was past his prime, he was still a good hitter who had batted .288 for Sacramento in 1919. As the ball became more lively during the 1920s, Griggs was able to take advantage of it and became a major power source for the Angels. The left-handed Thomas had experienced an off-year with Seattle but still managed 10 wins with that last-place team. He would be a major factor for the Angels in 1920.

The key to the trade was McAuley. He had enjoyed a fine season with Kansas City in the American Association in 1919, hitting .273, and was generally considered the best shortstop in that league before his acquisition by St. Louis. Killefer had been after him for three years now and was pleased to get him. An excellent fielder, McAuley was just a fair hitter with the Angels and later became somewhat injury prone. But he gave Los Angeles the stability in the middle infield that had been lacking all throughout 1919.

The play at the third base position had also not been to Killefer's liking in 1919, so he secured Tex McDonald, a veteran of the Federal League, to fill the gap. This move did not work out so well. McDonald had hit .317 with Nashville in the Southern Association in 1919, but he hit a weak .226 in 48 games with the Angels and was barely adequate in the field. McDonald appeared in only 35 games at third base before breaking a leg in June and missing the balance of the season. Bert Niehoff had to take over that position as he had in 1919, but the results were no better.

The outfield was intact from the previous year, and of the pitchers, only Paul Fittery was absent, having been sent to Sacramento during the off season. He would not be missed with the addition of Thomas and Ray Keating, a right-hander picked up from the Boston Braves after several years with the Yankees. Additional depth was provided by Tom Hughes, another National League veteran who was signed as a free agent. This was a strong experienced pitching staff thought by some observers to be the best in the league.

The enthusiasm shown by the fans in 1919 convinced the PCL owners that prosperity was here to stay after the war years, and they bravely added another two weeks to the schedule. This increased the length of the season to 28 weeks, which meant that each team would play about 200 games. For the rest of the 1920s that would be the standard length of the schedule. Each year would begin on the first Tuesday in April and would last until mid-October, a long time indeed. Whether this was a wise approach is open to some question, since interest declined rapidly after Labor Day, especially in those cities whose clubs were hopelessly out of the pennant race. The league tried to cope with the problem later in the 1920s by splitting the season and creating post-season championship playoffs, but this plan had only mixed success.

Unlike in the previous season, when the Angels were the hottest team in the league at the beginning of the year, the 1920 club started very slowly. Part of the problem was caused by Ike McAuley, who did not originally want to come to Los Angeles and held out until April 20, when the season was two weeks old. Fred Haney opened at shortstop but hit an anemic .144 and was sent to Omaha in the Western League after McAuley arrived. The team began to show improvement after he settled into the job and showed flashes of brilliance in the field.

Injuries plagued Los Angeles in 1920. Griggs started well at first base but was injured in early May and was in and out of the lineup for the balance of the year. He managed to hit .306, but did not play half the schedule, appearing in only 94 games. Rollie Zeider and Red Killefer filled in for Griggs, but neither had ever played the position to any extent, and their lack of experience proved costly at times.

Neither Red Killefer nor Sam Crawford played as well as he had in 1919. Killefer's average fell to .286, and although he stole 56 bases, he suffered a number of minor ailments that limited his productivity. Crawford led the club with a .332 average and 12 home runs, a bit below his 1919 performance, and at times he showed his age in the field. Overall, the Angels offense was a problem; the team batting average was .262, sixth in the league. Only Crawford, Griggs and Johnny Bassler were above .300, and there was very little power. The team hit only 27 home runs all year, just four of them in Washington Park. If there was a lively ball in 1920, Angels fans saw no evidence of it.

It was up to the pitchers to carry the team to the pennant, but they were not up to the task. Curly Brown fell off tremendously from his fine 1919 season, winning only seven games, while Doc Crandall was not as effective as he had been during the previous three seasons. He missed several turns because of minor injuries, and his 15–13 record was well below his usual performance. Some of the slack was picked up by Claude Thomas, who started slowly but came on strong in August and September to finish with 21 wins. Ray Keating was another important addition, winning 18 games.

The Angels spent most of April and May in sixth place as San Francisco and Salt Lake City took turns in the lead. Los Angeles then had a fine June that saw the club rise to third place, where it remained through July. Vernon occupied the fourth position just behind the Angels, while the Seals and Bees fought for first place.

Then in August the long investigation into PCL gambling incidents finally culminated with the expulsion of several players from the league. President William McCarthy had conducted a year-long investigation into the rumors that several games in a crucial Vernon–Salt Lake series in 1919 might have been influenced by gamblers. Baseball in general was infested with gambling incidents during the first two decades of the 20th century. Gamblers were very visible at ball games, and the problem seemed to be getting worse. The Vernon club had been thought to be the major offender in 1919, with the greatest attention directed towards first baseman Babe Borton, who had supposedly offered bribes to several Salt Lake players. The details of those gambling incidents extend beyond the scope of this book. Suffice it to say that gambling was a growing problem in the Coast League, and it was to McCarthy's credit that he confronted it. Ultimately, outfielders Harl Maggert and Bill Rumler of Salt Lake City, pitchers Tom Seaton, Casey Smith of San Francisco, Jean Dale of Salt Lake City and Borton were all expelled from the PCL.

The loss of sluggers Maggert and Rumler, which took place in August, proved to be a fatal blow to Salt Lake pennant hopes, and the Bees plunged to fifth place. Although the Seals had lost Seaton and Smith in May, their fortunes took a nose dive in August as well, and San Francisco fell out of contention. The Vernon Tigers took advantage of the others' misfortunes, and even with the loss of Borton, who was their leading slugger, they surged by the Angels into first place. The Angels rallied to within five games of the lead in mid–September, but they could never get any closer. After Vernon clinched the flag, the Angels lost interest and slumped to third place, a fraction of a percentage point ahead of San Francisco, as Seattle passed them during the last week of the season.

An Angels star of the future made his debut in 1920. Arnold "Jigger" Statz was acquired from the Red Sox after a very short stay in Boston. He was 22 years old and had been signed by the Giants off the Holy Cross campus in 1919, only to be exiled to Boston after a very brief look. Statz was a remarkable outfielder. This was evident from the very beginning of his professional career. Jigger hit .236 while filling in for Killefer in center field during the last half of the season. He and Red provided virtually the only speed on what had become a slow veteran team.

Another Angels legend-to-be made a cameo appearance in the last game of the 1920 season. Jimmie Reese, who had served as Angels batboy for several years, accompanied the team on its final road trip of the season to Sacramento. With the Senators holding a firm lead in the season finale, Reese played the eighth inning at second base and handled his only chance. Reese would be voted to the all-time PCL All-Star team in 1956, along with 1920 teammates Bassler and Statz. He was the epitome of a baseball "lifer," playing, managing or coaching until his death in July, 1994, and still active to the end as a coach for the California Angels of the American League.

5

An Angels Pennant and a New Owner

Nineteen twenty-one was a very eventful year in Angels history. On the field, the ball club came from 12½ games behind late in the year to overtake the first-place San Francisco Seals and win its sixth pennant, the first since 1916. Off the field, William Wrigley, Jr., the president of the Wrigley Gum Company, purchased the controlling interest in the club from John F. Powers. Thus began the long relationship between the Wrigley family and the Angels, which did not end until 1957.

Los Angeles did not appear to be a likely contender for the pennant when the team began spring training at Elsinore. There was a noticeable lack of team speed, and three regular positions were held down by veterans who were nearing the end of their careers — Art Griggs, 38, at first base; Bert Niehoff, 37, at second base; and Sam Crawford, 41, in right field. During the winter Johnny Bassler had been sold to Detroit for cash and 37-year-old Oscar Stanage took over the catching duties. Other off-season deals saw Bill Pertica go to the St. Louis Cardinals for outfielders Dixie Carroll and Ed Bogart, and pitcher Art Reinhart. Infielder Howard Lindimore came to Los Angeles by way of Detroit. These were good moves. Carroll added considerable speed to the outfield and led the PCL with 22 triples as he replaced Rube Ellis in left field, while Lindimore became the regular at third base. Reinhart was a vital addition to the pitching staff, which had become a bit long of tooth. He started fast by winning ten of his first 12 decisions and was the Angels' best pitcher during the mid-season doldrums.

The Angels looked sharp in defeating Seattle, 8–1, in the season opener behind Doc Crandall. But for the first half of the year Los Angeles was essentially a .500 club. There was little offense; other than Crawford, no one was hitting above .300. Griggs and Killefer were hitting well below their normal levels. Although Griggs picked up the pace during the stretch run and finished at .294, Killefer began to use Jigger Statz more and more as his replacement. Finally, on June 8, Statz was inserted into the lineup in the lead-off position, and Carroll took the manager's place in the lineup. The club played much better after that move, and Killefer was never again more than a part-time player.

The pitching was much improved over 1920. Crandall rebounded after his mediocre 1920 season and was pitching with the same skill he showed in 1919. Vic Aldridge started slowly and became the ace of the staff, winning 20 games and leading the PCL with a 2.16 ERA. By July Killefer was using a five-man rotation of Crandall, Aldridge, Reinhart, Tom

Hughes (a veteran who had been used infrequently the previous year), and George Lyons, another acquisition from the Cardinals. Rookie Nick Dumovich and veteran spitballer Claude Thomas were used in spot starts, while Dumovich also saw some relief duty.

The year 1921 saw the PCL follow the lead of the major leagues in limiting the use of trick pitches and restricted the use of the spitball to those men who had previously used it. Of the ten Coast Leaguers who were allowed to use the pitch, three wore a Los Angeles uniform — Crandall, Aldridge and Thomas. This gave the other clubs something more to think about when they faced the Angels and undoubtedly contributed to the success of the staff.

The PCL had a peculiar balance in 1921, with two terrible teams — Salt Lake City and Portland — and the rest of the clubs bunched closely together. The Angels were in the back of the pack from early May, and by June 10 were 10½ games behind the first-place Seals, in sixth place. San Francisco was getting fine pitching from Johnny Couch, Lefty O'Doul and "Death Valley" Scott, and was led at bat by Jimmy O'Connell, Bert Ellison and Willie Kamm. The race appeared to be a two-team affair between the Seals and Sacramento; the Angels stayed nine to ten games back through mid–August before reaching their low point of the season on August 15. On that day they fell victim to a 6–0 pasting by Frank Shellenback of the Vernon Tigers, while the first place Seals were winning. The Angels were now 12½ games behind, in fourth place.

Then in one of the many ebbs and flows during the long PCL season, the San Francisco pitching staff began to go sour. Scott lost his early season effectiveness, leaving the Seals with only O'Doul and Couch as dependable pitchers. That was not enough to win a PCL pennant, and concurrently, Crandall and Aldridge began to win almost every time out. The Seals lost five straight to Vernon while the Angels were beating Sacramento. In a week's time, Los Angeles had moved into third place and reduced the lead to 7½ games.

A quirk in the schedule then gave a decided advantage to the Angels. San Francisco had built its early lead by beating up on Portland, which that year was one of the worst PCL teams of all time. Now it was the Angels' turn to feast on the Beavers. Twenty-one of their final 51 games were to be with Portland, and the Angels would win 16 of those games. A 13-game set, the longest series in PCL history, began on August 29 at Washington Park, and the Angels won ten of the games, including the last seven in a row, cutting the Seals' lead to four games. Los Angeles was ready and waiting when San Francisco made its final appearance of the year at Washington Park for an eight-game series.

The Angels had momentum on their side. They were scorching and took six of the eight games from the slumping Seals. On September 6, Vic Aldridge defeated Herb McQuaid, 5–3. The next day Tom Hughes was an easy winner, 11–2, cutting the lead to two games. Thursday was the critical day, with Crandall scheduled to go against Scott. The Doc had early inning troubles, but held on to beat the Seals, 4–3, in 12 innings. The Seals were done. On the next day, the Angels swept the Admission Day doubleheader when George Lyons beat Johnny Couch, 4–3, in the first game and Art Reinhart threw an 8–0 masterpiece for their twelfth win in a row. The Angels were now in first place.

The winning streak came to an end the next day, but a split in the Sunday doubleheader kept the Angels in the lead by percentage points as the Seals left town. That was it! Although the race remained close until the end of the season, Los Angeles stayed in first place for the rest of the year. The club was only one-half game ahead when the final series of the year began in Portland, but the Angels took four of the first five games. Once again San Francisco pitching faltered as the Seals lost three straight at Seattle. But the pennant was not clinched until the first game of the season-ending doubleheader, when Aldridge was an easy 12–3 winner over the Beavers, his 20th win.

This was one of the tightest races in Coast League history with only 11 games separating sixth-place Vernon from first place. The Angels margin of victory was 1½ games over Sacramento and two games ahead of the Seals. Sacramento played three fewer games than the Angels, and that was the difference between the teams. In those days the league did not play postponed games after a club finished its season's activity with another. Today those games would be made up, and perhaps the results would have been different.

How did this Angels team win the pennant? The club finished seventh in team batting and was last in home runs with only 42. Their defense at second and third was only average, as was the catching staff of Oscar Stanage and Earl Baldwin. But the club had a fine shortstop in Ike McAuley and a vastly improved outfield defense once Carroll and Statz were given regular work in June. They added greatly to the overall team speed as well. Statz hit .310 with 52 stolen bases, while Carroll almost matched him at .292 and 45 steals. Bill McCabe was a speedy utility man who could play anywhere in the infield and outfield. And the Angels had the deepest pitching staff in the league with six experienced starters. In a pennant race as close as the 1921 season was, strong pitching at the right time was enough to create a winner. During the last six weeks of the season, Crandall and Aldridge provided the best one-two pitching punch in the league.

The Angels' drive to the pennant almost obscured the purchase of the majority interest in the club by Wrigley. The transaction had been under consideration by both parties for some time and was finally completed on August 24. Wrigley was given an option by Powers to purchase from him a controlling interest in the Angel City Baseball Association, the corporation that was the actual owner of the ball club. Wrigley exercised that option on August 30, when he delivered a check for $75,000 to Powers for 55 percent of the stock. Wrigley later acquired virtually all of the remaining shares, a total of 2,309 and a half shares at a net price per share of $57.50, making the total transaction worth about $133,000.

Mr. Wrigley had a strong Southern California connection, owning a home in Pasadena as well as majority interest in the Santa Catalina Island Company, along with many other local business interests. He was, of course, the majority stockholder in the Chicago Cubs, then one of the premier franchises of the major leagues, but he made it clear that the Angels were not to be a farm club of the Cubs. Nevertheless, the fans thought that the relationship would provide the Angels with a plentiful supply of good players. At times, it did just that, but not quite to the extent that had been hoped. Minority interests in both franchises meant that every transaction between the two had to satisfy those interests. Occasionally, a fine Angels prospect wound up in another organization, and the Angels did not always get the choicest Cub material.

The Wrigley purchase was a landmark transaction in the PCL. Although Cleveland had a relationship with Portland during the 1910s, this was the first time that a major league organization had such a close interest in a Coast League club. Wrigley himself did not participate in the day-to-day operations of the Angels, leaving those tasks to Joe Patrick, who was appointed as president, and Oscar Reichow, a former Chicago sportswriter, as business manager. Boots Weber, the only holdover from the Powers era, served as secretary of the Angels. These three men formed the visible management of the ballclub, with Mr. Wrigley remaining in the background while establishing club policy.

6

A New Management Team Takes Over as Red Leaves

In the first year of the Wrigley era, the Angels were unable to defend their championship. San Francisco won its first of two consecutive pennants in 1922 under new manager Jack "Dots" Miller. The Angels were never really a contender as the Seals and Vernon Tigers battled for the lead most of the season. Unlike the previous year when six clubs finished over .500, only the top three teams won more than they lost. The Angels finished a distant third, and after the first two weeks of the season were never any higher than that.

During the off-season Chicago reaped the first of many dividends from its Angels connection by acquiring Jigger Statz and Vic Aldridge for five players—outfielder Clarence "Babe" Twombly, third baseman Charlie Deal, pitchers Elmer Ponder and Jim York, and catcher Tom Daly. This was not a bad exchange for Los Angeles, either. Twombly would be a useful player for the next four years as the regular right fielder. He was a good hitter for average, never falling below .300, but he had little power. Deal was bitter about the demotion from Chicago and spent much of the spring training period at his Pasadena home before coming to terms with the Angels. He was still a fine hitter; in his two years with the Angels, he would hit .331 and .315 while performing adequately at third. Ponder started well before a serious injury put him out of action for most of the 1922 season, while York soon departed from the scene, and Daly served a year as the regular catcher.

The beginning of the season was almost a repeat of 1921. Once again, San Francisco jumped out to an early lead, with the Angels lagging well behind the leaders in fourth place, losing as often as they won. However, there would be no repeat of the stretch drive this year. The club was limited in power as only Art Griggs reached double figures in home runs. Part of the power vacuum was caused by Sam Crawford's decision to retire during spring training. Although he was almost 42 years old, Crawford was still a very potent hitter and was counted on to provide some of the power that had been lacking in 1921. Killefer replaced Crawford in right field with Clarence Twombly, where he was flanked by Dixie Carroll in center field and Bill McCabe in left field. This outfield was marginal, to say the least.

Twombly had a good arm but did not cover much ground in right field, and many balls that should have been caught dropped safely. Carroll, who had played well in left field, quickly demonstrated that he was not a good center fielder, so Killefer moved him back to left field where he was more comfortable. McCabe took over in center field, and while he was adequate in that position, he was not nearly the fielder that Statz had been.

Angels pitching was actually better than in the previous year. However, any hopes the Angels had of catching San Francisco were dealt a severe blow when pitcher Elmer Ponder dislocated his shoulder during batting practice on June 22. The shoulder was later found to be broken, and Ponder was effectively through for the year. The ace of the staff at 10–2 when he was injured, Ponder pitched only three more innings the rest of the season. Nick Dumovich moved into the starting rotation to replace him and pitched more than adequately, finishing with 20 victories. The rest of the staff was handicapped by the shoddy defense. Tom Hughes, at 17–9, and Claude Thomas, at 18–11, were workhorses on the mound, but Doc Crandall suffered one of his worst years at 17–19 and found it very difficult to win during the last two months of the season. George Lyons pitched well throughout the season, but was given little run support by the club and was frequently victimized by the erratic defense. His 17–17 record should have been much better.

Art Griggs provided the bulk of the offense, hitting .338 with 20 home runs, and Charlie Deal finished right behind him at .331. The club tried to compensate for its lack of power by running whenever possible, but the Angels lacked the speed to compete with the Seals, who were one of the best teams in PCL history. Los Angeles was in fifth place through early July, before winning 14 straight games to advance to third place by the end of the month. The Angels were only nine games out of first place when August began, and they played well during that month, cutting the Seals' lead to seven games by Labor Day. But that was as close as they would come. San Francisco and Vernon waged a torrid battle in September, with the Seals finally prevailing by four games. The Angels drifted back, finishing 16 games behind the leaders, in third place.

Of great importance for the future was the announcement on August 8 that the Angels had taken an option on property bounded by 39th Street, South Park Avenue and 41st Street (in what was then the southern outskirts of Los Angeles), for the purpose of building a new ballpark. The decision was in keeping with Mr. Wrigley's desire to provide "the best possible surroundings for Los Angeles fans to watch a ball game." The proposed park was to seat 21,000 fans and would be double decked from the left field wall all the way around to right field. The walls would be screened with trees and flowers, with ample parking to be located to the west of the park. That provision proved to be inaccurate, for no one could foresee the tremendous dependence that Los Angeles would have on the automobile. The announcement was greeted with great approval by the fans, for Washington Park was beginning to show signs of deterioration. The Vernon club did not look upon the decision with much favor, however. The Maier brothers expressed no interest in locating at the new park, nor were they asked to do so. Eventually, the building of the new facility would bring an end to the Vernon franchise. But that was several years away.

The 1923 season began inauspiciously during spring training. An announcement was made on March 20 that Red Killefer, along with former Angels business manager Charlie Lockhardt had purchased part of the Seattle Indians' franchise. Where did Killefer get the money to make this investment? That was what everyone wanted to know. Immediate speculation centered on William Wrigley. Did Mr. Wrigley lend Killefer the money, and by so doing maintain some control over the Seattle club? No one answered this question satisfactorily, but the issue was discussed throughout the summer and provided some interest during what was essentially a boring pennant race.

Marty Krug was appointed as the new Angels manager. He had been the regular third baseman for the Cubs in 1922, but had been sent to Los Angeles along with pitcher Percy Jones for Nick Dumovich. He was 34 years old and was expected to hold down the second base position, in addition to his new managerial duties. Krug had played in the PCL previously with Salt Lake City and Portland. He would remain at the Angels helm until the middle of the 1929 season. As a manager, Krug's greatest skill was that of a teacher. In an era when young players were expected to learn the game with little assistance from management, Krug was an exception to the rule and spent much time with the younger players.

Krug thought the 1923 Angels had some promise, but in reality it was a transition team from one era to another. The game was changing dramatically, from one with an emphasis on defense and conservative play to a new type of high-powered offense. The so-called "Lively Ball" era began in earnest that year. The Angels hit .289 as a team, their highest yet, but five teams had higher averages. A few years earlier that mark would have easily led the league. Los Angeles finished last in scoring, however, even though the club doubled its home run production over the previous year. The roster was about the same as in 1922, with outfielder Wally Hood the most significant addition. He had been acquired from Seattle by way of Brooklyn when the Cubs sent outfielder Turner Barber to the Robins. Hood was a fine player who would enjoy six excellent years in Los Angeles. He was pleased to be in Los Angeles, having been raised in suburban Whittier, and hit .340 with 21 home runs. Hood took over center field and led the PCL with 45 assists that year. With his addition, McCabe returned to left field with Clarence Twombly back in right field, and the outfield defense was much better.

Krug's optimism of the spring was not well founded as the Angels finished in sixth place. Once again, San Francisco was the league champion, overcoming the early death of manager Dots Miller in September, with Sacramento the only other contender for the crown. The Angels were never a factor in the race, spending most of the year in the second division. They were plagued by various injuries during the year, including some to the infield. Art Griggs was back for what would be his final season in Los Angeles, with Krug, Jimmy McAuley and Charlie Deal rounding out the infield. But Griggs and Krug missed a signifi-

Wally Hood. One of the great Angels hitters of the 1920s, he posted a .318 average during his six years with the club (courtesy Dick Dobbins).

cant number of games, and Krug was not especially effective when he did play. Howard Lindimore filled in for him and had his best season. He emerged as the best fielding second baseman in the league, and when he was in the lineup, the Angels defense was exceptional.

The pitching was the great weakness of the 1923 Angels. The veteran Doc Crandall, who was thought to be nearing the end of his illustrious career, experienced a tender arm during spring training and did not make his first start until May. But after a slow beginning, he reversed his pattern of 1922 and finished strongly with 17 victories. Elmer Ponder was not so fortunate. The shoulder injury of the previous year had not healed, and he struggled to win seven games. Never again would Ponder be the pitcher he had appeared to be during the first two months of 1922.

George Lyons was steady once again, leading the club with 18 wins, but Claude Thomas and Tom Hughes declined badly. Thomas won only nine games, and Hughes finished at 14–16, missing several starts because of arm problems. Percy Jones was a good addition to the staff, finishing at 16–17, but he, too, was out of action for several weeks.

At the beginning of September, it looked as if the Los Angeles and Vernon teams would finish at the bottom of the league, but the Angels rallied to finish two games ahead of Oakland in sixth place and actually made a brief run at fourth-place Seattle. Vernon collapsed during this period and finished deep in last place for the first time in that club's history. For the first time there was speculation that the Vernon club might move from the city. It was no secret that owner Edward Maier wanted to sell, and he certainly wanted no part of the high rent that he would have to pay the Angels when Wrigley Field was completed.

President Joe Patrick recognized early that the Angels needed a drastic overhaul, and he decided to make changes before the 1923 season was complete. In August, the Angels sent third baseman Charlie Deal to Vernon in exchange for the Tigers' third baseman, Red Smith. This trade did not seem to make any sense, for Smith was also a veteran player who had seen better days, and he was re-routed to Atlanta in the Southern Association in December. At the same time, the Angels sent Bill McCabe and Elmer Ponder to Atlanta and released Percy Jones and Red Baldwin to Seattle. They then acquired Ray Jacobs, a young infielder from Salt Lake City. Jacobs would play a major role in Angels fortunes during the next several years.

The Angels continued to clear the roster during the winter; no fewer than 11 new faces were on hand when the club assembled for spring training in Long Beach, a new site after several years at Elsinore. Also missing was the long time baseball writer of *The Los Angeles Times*, Harry Williams. In a surprising turn of events during the league winter meetings, the PCL owners voted not to renew the contract of President Bill McCarthy and replaced him with Williams after a bitterly contested vote. This was an important event in the history of the Coast League. The tenure of McCarthy was filled with controversy, including gambling scandals and the ongoing war with the National Association concerning the player draft.

In addition, McCarthy had alienated several of the owners, leading to a divided organization in which it was difficult to accomplish anything of substance. That era was now at an end, and the owners could focus their attention on improving the conditions in the league. Williams held the post of secretary as well through his term of office, which ended in 1931, and he later served as secretary for an additional 16 years, until his death in 1953. His greatest contribution as president was to end the animosity that had existed between the northern and southern cities of the league, and he created a strong administrative staff within the PCL office where none had existed previously.

The Angels were a considerably different team from the one that had ended the 1923 season. Only Jimmy McAuley and Marty Krug returned as infield regulars. Art Griggs had embarked on a managerial career with Omaha in the Western League, and in his place was Walter Golvin, obtained from St. Paul of the American Association. Ray Jacobs was installed at third base, and a young infielder from Gardena, Clyde Beck, made the club in a utility role after an impressive showing in spring training.

The outfield appeared to be much stronger. Babe Twombly returned to his position in right field, but Wally Hood was installed in left field to make room for the new centerfielder, Cedric Durst, acquired from the St. Louis Browns on option. He was a part-time player for the Browns in 1923 and was sent to Los Angeles as part of a trade for pitcher George Lyons. Durst blossomed as a player in Los Angeles in 1924, beginning a journey that eventually led him to the Yankees. But he was unable to break into the Ruth-Meusel-Combs outfield combination of the great New York teams of the 1920s, and when he finally had his chance to play regularly after a trade to the Red Sox in 1930, he was past his prime. Later on, he returned to the PCL as a player and manager for the San Diego Padres.

Catching had become a chronic problem for the Angels after Johnny Bassler had gone to the major leagues, and the situation was no different during the spring of 1924. Some resolution of the problem finally took place after the season was two months old, when the club purchased the experienced Joe Jenkins from Salt Lake City. He was not a great catcher by any means, but he did provide some stability behind the plate, and the pitchers seemed to improve after Jenkins joined the club.

Much had been expected of the staff when the season began. Only Doc Crandall returned from the 1923 starting staff, and he seemed ready to rebound from an unsatisfactory season. Newcomers George Payne, a 24-game winner at Oklahoma City in 1924, and Charlie Root both looked impressive during training, and the Angels filled out the staff when they traded Howard Lindimore and Elmer Ponder, who had been returned by Atlanta, to Salt Lake City for Elmer Myers. Myers had experienced two bad years in a row at Salt Lake, but Marty Krug was doubtful that Ponder would ever recover from his shoulder injury of 1922. He guessed right on this one, for Ponder was never again an effective starting pitcher, and he gambled that Myers would have a better year.

Root had come to Los Angeles from the Browns along with Durst and outfielder Bill Whaley. He had not done well in a brief trial with St. Louis, and the Browns could not wait for a young pitcher to develop after they had come so close to the American League pennant in 1922. They sent him to Los Angeles as part of the trade to acquire George Lyons, a more experienced pitcher who was expected to provide immediate help. But it was a terrible mistake by the Browns. Lyons won only three games during his lone year in St. Louis, in what proved to be his last appearance in the major leagues. Meanwhile, Root turned in two fine years with the Angels before joining the Cubs in 1926. He would spend 16 years in Chicago, ending his career with 201 major league victories.

Just before the season began, the club rounded out the pitching staff when Chicago returned Nick Dumovich to Los Angeles. There were high hopes for the team, which appeared to have greatly improved, but after a good month of April the Angels reverted to their mediocre play of the previous year and fell into last place on May 15. The offense was much weaker than expected. Walter Golvin at first base was barely hitting .200, while Durst did not immediately adjust to Coast League pitching. Only Hood and Babe Twombly were hitting with any consistency. As luck would have it, they collided in the outfield while going for a routine fly ball on May 11, and Twombly was forced out of the lineup for three weeks.

Bill Whaley was an able replacement for him, and when Twombly returned, Whaley moved to third base for a period, replacing a slumping Ray Jacobs.

The 1924 season was one of the most exciting in PCL history, with all clubs closely bunched. Even in last place the Angels were only 11 games out of the lead at the end of May, and it seemed that any one of the eight teams could win the pennant. San Francisco, which had been so dominant the previous two years, did not appear as strong this year, and the surprising Seattle Indians under Red Killefer soon moved into contention. The Indians were enjoying tremendous years from ancient pitcher Vean Gregg and centerfielder Brick Eldred. The efforts of these two, more than anything else, kept Seattle close to first place.

The disappointing Golvin was finally benched when Los Angeles bought Walton Cruise from the Boston Braves. Although a good hitter, Cruise was not a first baseman and was eventually used strictly as a utility outfielder. Then in July, the Cubs sent first baseman Ray Grimes to the Angels, a move that seemed to provide the necessary spark to turn the team around. A serious back problem had limited his productivity in the National League, but once recovered, Grimes was a far better hitter than Golvin and was also tough in the clutch. The club played better through August before moving out of the basement during the last week of the month. The Angels reached the heights of fifth place, although still well below .500 as the month closed. Another week of shoddy play left them in sixth place, 15½ games behind on September 8. Then things began to happen.

The Angels concluded a series in Salt Lake City by routing the Bees, 21–2, and then proceeded to take seven out of eight games from San Francisco in a series that ultimately would cost the Seals the championship. Los Angeles had now become a solid ballclub. Cedric Durst had recovered from his early season woes and was pounding the ball, and the combination of Grimes, Hood and Durst in the middle of the lineup became very formidable indeed. The Angels seemed inspired and went on to win 16 of the next 20 games. With two weeks to go, they moved into third place, only six games behind the first-place Seals and a game behind Seattle, this after taking five straight from the Indians. The Angels then beat up on Portland, winning six straight from the Beavers at Washington Park while San Francisco was being manhandled in Seattle. On the morning of October 13, the Angels were only one-half game from the lead, now held by Seattle, as the last week of the season began. Additionally, the Seals were only percentage points behind the Angels, and anyone of the three clubs could win the pennant.

But that was as close as Los Angeles would come to the top. The Angels returned to Washington Park to play the arch-rival Vernon Tigers in the final series, while Seattle had the opportunity to feast on a slumping Portland. The Tigers took a doubleheader from the Angels on Wednesday, while Seattle was winning two at home against the Beavers, dropping Los Angeles 2½ games behind the leaders. That was too much of a deficit to make up that late in the season, although the Angels did put pressure on the Indians by sweeping the remaining games with the Tigers. But Seattle was winning four more from Portland, thereby clinching the pennant on the last day of the season. The Angels finished in second place, 1½ games behind.

The hitting down the stretch kept the Angels in the pennant race. Durst and Hood had marvelous years, hitting .342 and .338, respectively. Hood set a club RBI record that was never exceeded, driving in 184 runners, only four behind league leader Bert Ellison of San Francisco. Durst had a 24-game hitting streak during his only year in Los Angeles, and he socked 17 home runs. That was second on the club to Hood's 22 round trippers, the most by an Angels player up to that time. The club hit 87 home runs in 1924, but only 23 at

Washington Park, where the dimensions did not lend themselves to power baseball. That situation would change in the new Wrigley Field, which was beginning to take shape for its grand opening in 1925.

As the hitting improved during the last two months of the season, so did the pitching, and by season's end the Angels had arguably the best staff in the league. Only Doc Crandall was able to win with any degree of consistency when the club was floundering in the basement, but during the last six weeks, Charlie Root and George Payne were almost unbeatable. Payne's record was 2–7 on June 12, but he was a completely different pitcher after that. His final mark was 21–13, and he walked only 42 men in 315 innings. Root won 12 of his last 14 decisions to finish at 21–16, and led the staff with four shutouts. Crandall added 19 victories to go along with an impressive 2.71 ERA. Tom Hughes and

Top: Doc Crandall. The best starting pitcher in Angels history, he won 230 games during his career (courtesy Dick Dobbins). *Bottom:* Wrigley Field at its opening on September 29, 1925 (courtesy Dick Dobbins).

Elmer Myers were effective at times, although neither won as many as he lost. The Angels probably would have won the pennant if Nick Dumovich performed the way he had in 1922. But he won only nine games, and his ERA of 6.15 was the worst on the staff. The Angels shipped him to Seattle that winter after those dismal results

President Joe Patrick was immensely pleased with his team, and to show his appreciation for their efforts, he gave each man a bonus of $100, a fine sum in those days. He could easily afford this gesture, for the Angels drew 355,480 fans to Washington Park, the highest attendance ever at that location and a figure not to be surpassed in Los Angeles for 20 years. Both Patrick and manager Marty Krug felt that very little was needed to make the Angels a team of champions. That would make for a perfect opening season for Wrigley Field.

7

A New Ballpark and a Pennant to Follow

As so often happened during their history, the Angels were unable to improve on their standing from one year to the next, and the club experienced a disappointing season in 1925, finishing in fourth place. The record in terms of games won and lost was not much worse than in 1924, but this time the Angels were chasing a team that was vastly superior to the rest of the league. The San Francisco Seals dominated the league from the second week of the season, when they began a 14 game winning streak that propelled them into the league lead, and they never trailed from that point Only the Salt Lake Bees gave them any competition, but they were never any closer than six games from the top. This Seals team was the finest in franchise history, and it ranks among the top two or three best clubs that ever played in the PCL. San Francisco was led by Paul Waner, who hit .401 that year, a great infield of Hal Rhyne, Pete Kilduff, Eddie Mulligan and Bert Ellison, and a very strong pitching staff. The final margin of victory was 12½ games over the second-place Bees, with Seattle a percentage point ahead of the Angels in third, both clubs 22½ games behind.

The Angels were only briefly in the race. They began the season impressively with six straight wins over Portland, but were caught in the middle of the Seals' winning streak and fell to third place. They alternated between third and fourth place for the balance of the year, always at a distance from the top two teams.

The Angels-Chicago connection was growing stronger with each passing year, and the winter of 1924-25 saw the Cubs purchase the contract of Charlie Root from the Angels. He might have made the big club that spring, but shortstop Rabbit Maranville broke his ankle in spring training, and the Cubs were left short of infielders. They returned Root to Los Angeles along with infielder Clarke Pittenger for Jimmy McAuley.

This was a fortunate turn of events for the Angels. Root followed up his fine 1924 season with an even more brilliant performance in what was to be his last year in the minor leagues until 1942. The right-hander developed a fine curve to go with his impressive fast ball and proceeded to win 25 games. At the end of the season he was returned to Chicago, where he began a career that saw him make his mark as one of the all-time great Cub pitchers. McAuley, on the other hand, could not hit big-league pitching and was returned to Los Angeles in June when Maranville returned to active duty.

With McAuley gone, the Angels opened the season with Pittenger at shortstop, but he lasted only four games before suffering a season-ending broken ankle. This forced Marty

Krug to move Ray Jacobs to shortstop, with the manager taking over at third base. While Jacobs was a satisfactory third baseman, he had very limited range as a shortstop, and the team's defense was severely weakened. Krug had no such worries at second base, where Clyde Beck had a fine season, both in the field and at bat where he hit a surprising 17 home runs. The infield was unsettled all season, with Krug, Bill Whaley and Jacobs spending time at third base. When McAuley returned from Chicago, he regained his shortstop position, but he didn't seem to be the player he had been, either in the field or at the plate. Grimes returned at first base, and a new catcher in the person of Gus Sandberg was on hand. Sandberg was purchased from Cincinnati and would prove to be a pretty good defensive catcher, although not much of a hitter. He would see much action for the club over the next five years before his tragic death in February, 1930.

The Angels began with an outfield of Hood, Twombly and Joe "Shags" Horan, who had been with the Yankees for part of 1924. Horan had a reputation as a power hitter, but there was little evidence of it in Los Angeles. He played regularly for the first month of the season, then was benched and released to Vernon in July. Bill Whaley played there until June, when the Cubs returned Jigger Statz to Los Angeles. Although his numbers were not bad, Statz was a disappointment in Chicago; Cub management expected him to hit better than he did. Jigger was not at all pleased with his return to the PCL and immediately held out for a better contract, threatening retirement if he didn't receive one. When he was finally satisfied, he assumed his old position in center field, with Twombly returning to right, and the outfield became immensely better.

As the Angels drifted through the season, everyone eagerly awaited the completion of Wrigley Field, which was originally expected to take place in August but was delayed until the last week of September. The park was finally finished, at a cost estimated at $1,300,000, and was ready for business on September 29. Before a crowd of 18,000, the Angels defeated the first-place Seals, 10–8, behind Doc Crandall on the mound. Jigger Statz was the star of the game, hitting the first Angels home run at the new park and adding a single, double and triple to complete the cycle. Paul Waner hit the very first home run in the first inning, a drive over the right field screen.

"Absolutely the very last word in baseball architecture," said PCL President Harry Williams at the opening, and it certainly was — at least, in 1925. The distinguishing feature was a 150-foot clock tower with eight floors of offices inside for the Angels officials and later, PCL offices as well. The tower could be seen for miles away. The structure was double-decked all the way around from the right field corner to left field and held approximately 18,650 seats. A 16-foot high brick wall surrounded the outfield. The distance to the left field wall, which faced East 41st Place, was 340 feet at the line; center field was 412 feet from home plate. A nine-foot high screen extended from the deepest point in center to the right field corner, where the distance was 339 feet. In right center field was an open section of bleachers that seated an estimated 2,000 fans, and behind them was an enormous scoreboard.

Although not as immense as those in Washington Park, the distances seemed adequate, with one major exception. The power alleys were only 345 feet away, a result of a design that turned the outfield walls slightly inward. Since left field followed the street plan and backed up on it, there was nothing that could be done to correct this problem, short of condemning the street itself. With a prevailing wind blowing towards right field much of the time, Wrigley was destined to be a hitter's delight. The effect of these dimensions was almost immediately apparent. The Angels played their last 21 games of 1925 in Wrigley

This flyer, announcing the opening of Wrigley Field, was distributed throughout the city of Los Angeles (courtesy Al Parnis).

Field, and in that three-week period, 28 home runs were hit, including 10 by the Seals. Only 51 homers had been hit at Washington Park in the 77 games played there earlier. The style of baseball in Los Angeles was about to change dramatically. Finally, the era of power baseball and the lively ball had arrived.

Wally Hood almost missed the Wrigley Field opening when he decided to take a few days off to be present at the birth of his son on September 24. When Hood took a few of his Angels friends to visit Mrs. Hood and the baby, he boasted proudly, "Did you ever see such long fingers on a baby? What a curve ball pitcher he'll make." A very good prediction by a proud father. A generation later, Wally Hood, Jr., became a star pitcher for the University of Southern California and pitched for several PCL clubs as well.

The season closed with the Angels playing out the string, and management was not pleased with the results. It was obvious that the Angels did not have the power to compete with the Seals and Bees. Hood was the only legitimate home run threat. His 27 homers, four of which were hit at Wrigley Field, easily led the club, and only Beck and Jacobs joined him in double figures. Babe Twombly hit .329 to lead the Angels, but he was basically a singles hitter with only one home run to his credit. With the new park showing signs of being a home run hitter's paradise, there would be no room for hitters like Twombly, who would soon be departing.

There was much activity off the field as 1925 came to an end. For years Bill Lane had threatened to move his ball club from Salt Lake City, where support for the Bees had been

It is January 15, 1926, and Wrigley Field is formally dedicated. Commissioner Kenesaw Mountain Landis is on the podium as the featured speaker. A plaque commemorating those who perished during World War I is behind him. It will soon be affixed to the clock tower, where it remained until the ballpark was razed in 1969. The plaque currently is located at a park on Catalina Island.

moderate at best. Now the opening of Wrigley Field provided an opportunity to do just that. He had forged a good relationship with Wrigley when the Chicago man came into the league, and an agreement was struck that would allow Lane's club to share quarters with the Angels, an arrangement that was not offered to the Vernon club. There were rumors that the Tigers would return to Maier Park in Vernon, but Ed Maier decided to sell his club instead. He found willing buyers in San Francisco, and despite the resistance of Oakland's Cal Ewing, the Vernon club moved to Northern California. It took up residence at Recreation Park in San Francisco, where it would be known as the Mission Club of San Francisco, to use its formal name. The new club was listed as Mission in the league standing, and it was no longer the Tigers. The Missions were called the Bears during their first year in the Bay Area and operated under a variety of nicknames during their years there.

Lane wanted his club to retain the name of Bees when he moved to Los Angeles, but when he appropriated the name of Hollywood to distinguish the team from the Angels, the press quickly began to refer to the team as the Stars, or more commonly in the early years, the Sheiks, after Hollywood High School's teams. Soon it was apparent that Lane and the Angels management team of Joe Patrick and Oscar Reichow were not getting along, and the stage was set for the long and bitter Angels-Hollywood rivalry that lasted as long as the ballclubs did.

No one outside of Salt Lake City was unhappy to see the Bees move. The league owners had advocated that move for years because of the high cost of travel to the Utah city. The pitchers were especially grateful for the change. The ball traveled farther in the high altitude, and the small dimensions of Bonneville Park meant that games in Salt Lake City were usually slugfests. Most of the PCL team and individual batting records were established by the Bees of this era, and many of them still stand today.

If the Angels were to contend during their first years in the new ballpark, the club would need a complete make-over, and Wrigley gave his complete approval to Patrick and Reichow to do just that. The entire infield was completely redone. Ray Grimes had slumped badly in 1925 after almost leading the Angels to the 1924 pennant, and he was released, along with shortstop McAuley, who had hit .205 and was erratic in the field in what was his last year in the PCL. Ray Jacobs moved from shortstop to replace Grimes at first base, a position where he seemed more comfortable. Krug acquired John Mitchell from the Cubs as his new shortstop. An all-star with the Vernon Tigers in 1919, Mitchell had played for Brooklyn as well as Chicago and was a natural shortstop, unlike Jacobs. The Angels had sent second baseman Clyde Beck to the Cubs, and to replace him, they purchased Ed Hemingway from the new Mission club. But he was moved to third base during spring training, with rookie Gale Staley getting the first opportunity at second.

The Angels were rich with outfielders that spring. The Beck trade had brought Art Weis and Art Jahn, who were quickly installed in right and left field, respectively. Statz was back in center field and had a great spring, portending a banner year for him. Wally Hood held out through most of the spring, but signed his contract just as the training session ended. His absence gave Jahn and Weis the opportunity to solidify their places in the outfield, and Hood became the odd man out. Although he was a three-year regular, Hood acted as a replacement when the others were out of action and also played 52 games at first base.

Angels catching had been inferior since Johnny Bassler had gone to Detroit, but they made a major improvement when they traded pitcher George Payne to Portland for Truck Hannah and pitcher Rube Yarrison. Hannah was one of the greatest catchers in PCL history. He first appeared in the league in 1914 with Sacramento and subsequently played with Salt

Art Weis — Part of the great outfield of 1926, along with Jigger Statz and Art Jahn (courtesy Dick Dobbins).

Lake City, Vernon and Portland, as well as three years with the Yankees. Although he was almost 37 years old and on the downside of his career, Hannah was still a fine catcher. He handled the pitchers well and had a great throwing arm. He and Gus Sandberg provided the best catching in the league in 1926, and this was reflected in the records of the pitching staff. Charlie Root and George Payne had been serious losses, but the club had adequate replacements on hand in Elmer Jacobs and Earl Hamilton. Jacobs had joined the Angels from the Cubs in August, 1925, and made an immediate impression by winning nine games over the last two months of the season. Hamilton, a free agent veteran of 14 years in the major leagues, earned a spot in the rotation with outstanding work in the spring. Doc Crandall was back for his eleventh and last full season in an Angels uniform. Jacobs, Hamilton and Crandall formed a fine nucleus, and each would be a 20-game winner. Other returning starters were Whitey Glazner and Wayne Wright.

But the club was still somewhat lacking in power, an important element in the more hitter-friendly Wrigley Field. Only Ray Jacobs and Wally Hood were recognized as home run threats. The Angels then partly filled that need on the day before the season opener, when they purchased all-star third baseman Frank Brazill from Seattle. Brazill had hit .394 for the Indians in 1925, but was a holdout and threatened to sit out the entire year. In desperation, the Indians offered him to Los Angeles, and he was eagerly accepted. Brazill was from Los Angeles and welcomed the opportunity to play in Southern California. Ed Hemingway was moved to second base to make room for Brazill, and Staley was sent out for more experience. Brazill was not a good fielder and would lead the PCL in errors in 1926, but his lively bat more than made up for his defensive shortcomings.

The Angels were ready to begin the season, but the worst April rains in over 40 years hit Los Angeles and delayed the opener for four days. When play began, a crowd of 15,550 watched Elmer Jacobs shut out Oakland, 4–0, with Brazill hitting a home run in the very first Wrigley Field opener. The club played at a .500 pace through most of the first month,

Truck Hannah—He was an important addition to the 1926 championship club. He would remain with the Angels through the 1938 season, serving as coach and manager after his playing days were over (courtesy Helen Hannah Campbell).

but broke out of the pack in earnest by winning 13 games in a row during a trip to Seattle and San Francisco to take over first place on May 15. By mid–June the Angels had extended their lead to 7½ games, effectively ending the pennant race. Sacramento and Oakland made brief runs at Los Angeles but never got any closer than six games. When the Angels crushed Oakland in a ten-game series at the end of September, they extended their lead to 16 games. Their final margin was 10½ games over the second-place Oaks. Mr. Wrigley had the pennant he so badly wanted.

Although the Angels finished second in team batting, it was pitching and defense that won that pennant. Hamilton led the staff with 24 wins to go along with his 2.48 ERA. Jacobs and Crandall each won 20, and each finished with an ERA of 2.20, the lowest in the league. That was a remarkable performance in an era of heavy hitting, and no pitcher would post a lower figure in the PCL for 16 years. Wayne Wright lost his first three decisions but later won 12 straight decisions and finished with a 19–7 record. Rube Yarrison helped early and finished at 13–8. The staff threw 21 shutouts and had 127 complete games, the most ever by the Angels.

The pitchers were helped by a league-leading defense that featured perhaps the finest fielding outfield in PCL history. The combination of Weis, Statz, and Jahn made only 13 errors all season. Weis went 125 games before making his only error of the season in late September, while Statz covered center field like a blanket with over 600 chances and only two errors. The infield featured the fine play of shortstop John Mitchell, who led the league in total chances and fielding percentage. And Hannah led all catchers as well.

Offensively, the club featured strength from top to bottom of the lineup. Jigger Statz had his finest year in Los Angeles. In his leadoff position, Statz hit .354 to finish fourth among PCL regulars. He had the remarkable total of 291 hits, an all-time Angels record, with 68 doubles and 18 triples, both league-leading figures. The late Bill Schroeder, the

The 1926 Angels. *Front row (left to right):* Les Holmes, Rube Yarrison, Bert Read, Jigger Statz, Ray Dwyer, Ray Jacobs. *Middle row:* Batboy, Whitey Glazner, Wally Hood, Gale Staley, Marty Krug, Clyde "Pea Ridge" Day, Johnny Mitchell (holding Russell Krug), Frank Brazill. *Back row:* Moe Genser, Wayne Wright, Ralph Stroud, Art Jahn, Elmer Jacobs, Art Weis, Truck Hannah, Gus Sandberg (courtesy Mark Macrae).

longtime managing director of the Helms Athletic Foundation and the foremost Pacific Coast League historian, rated Jigger's play in 1926 as one of the three best seasons a PCL outfielder ever had. He ranked the Statz performance on a par with Frank Demaree of Los Angeles in 1934 and Ike Boone of Mission in 1929. There was no recognized Most Valuable Player Award in 1926, but had there been, Statz most certainly would have won it. Brazill and Jahn hit .337 and .336 respectively, and Brazill also blasted 19 home runs. Jacobs led the club with 22 homers and Wally Hood hit 13 while splitting time between the outfield and first base. The Angels hit 82 home runs altogether, 46 of them at Wrigley Field.

Despite the fine play of this Angels team, attendance fell by over 20,000 in 1926. The first season in Wrigley Field saw only 273,202 paid admissions, to the dismay of Angels management. Part of the decline was attributable to the presence of the Hollywood club, which attracted 212,830 in its first year at Wrigley Field. The Sheiks were developing a strong core of loyal fans who would add more fuel to the rivalry between the teams.

At the end of the season, the Angels lost two of their important stars when Elmer Jacobs was drafted by the White Sox and Jigger Statz was sold to Brooklyn. The pitching staff was weakened when Doc Crandall left for Wichita as part owner. These losses would prove to be difficult to overcome in 1927, and the Angels would be forced to undergo a rebuilding program that would take several years. But Wrigley, Joe Patrick and Oscar Reichow were well satisfied in spite of the work ahead. They had done what they had planned to do — bring a pennant to Wrigley Field in its first year of operation.

8

A Collapse and the Angels Rebuild

Mr. Wrigley's delight with the 1926 pennant did not last long. In 1927, for the first time in their history, the Angels finished in last place. Los Angeles won only 80 games, had a miserable .408 winning percentage and finished 40½ games behind the champion Oakland Oaks. The Angels were never in contention for the lead, and after June 1 the Angels were never higher than seventh place. Not until 1949 would an Angels team play so poorly. It was clear that the rebuilding process that led to the 1926 championship would have to begin anew.

Although it was not anticipated that the Angels would finish at the bottom of the league when spring training began, no one should have expected another pennant. The club had lost too much talent during the off-season, especially its most important player, Jigger Statz. He was sent to Brooklyn in exchange for outfielder Dick Cox and pitcher George Boehler. This deal might have been satisfactory had Boehler been allowed to remain in Los Angeles. But he had been drafted from Oakland prior to the 1926 season, and the Oaks retained priority rights should he be returned to the Coast League. The Angels were forced to return the pitcher to Oakland, and he became a dominant pitcher there, winning 22 games with a fine 3.10 ERA. No Angels pitcher approached that record in 1927. Brooklyn sent pitcher Ray Moss to Los Angeles as a replacement, but he was an utter failure, winning only one game with a horrendous 8.10 ERA before the Angels released him in June.

Cox had a very good offensive year with the Angels, hitting .345 with 90 runs batted in, but defensively, it was another story. He was expected to replace Statz in center field, but within a month it was obvious that he was not suited to the position, and he was moved to right field, where he played most of the year. Cox was among the league leaders at the beginning of the season, but as the season wore on, his hitting began to decline and he saw less action. By the end of August, he was relegated to part-time action and was then released to Shreveport of the Texas League after the season.

For the first time since 1916, the Angels opened a season without Doc Crandall on hand. He was now at Wichita of the Western League as the manager and part-owner, along with former Angels player Art Griggs. The Doc was almost 40 years old now. He was the solid foundation of the Angels pitching staff for the past 11 years and would be sorely missed. Crandall won 230 games in the PCL, 207 of them while wearing an Angels uniform. That number is unsurpassed in Angels history, and only Frank Shellenback, Spider Baum, Harry Krause and Dick Barrett won more games in the league.

Crandall relied heavily on the spitball, as did Shellenback, and was in the minors when that pitch was outlawed in the major leagues. Although he toiled in the majors for the better part of ten years, he pitched his last game with the Boston Braves before he turned 30 years old. He was a very popular player in Los Angeles and made his home in Southern California after his playing days were over. In later years his son, Jimmy Crandall, would play in the Coast League as well.

Replacing Crandall and Elmer Jacobs on the pitching staff would be difficult, but the Angels thought they had done so with the addition of two youngsters, Bruce Cunningham and Earl "Tex" Weathersby, and the purchase of veteran Bill Piercy from the Cubs. Piercy had seen service with the Yankees earlier and was expected to be the leading pitcher on the staff. He pitched well at times and gave manager Marty Krug a number of innings, but his control was a problem and he was not nearly as reliable as Crandall and Jacobs had been. The left-handed Weathersby had been the best pitcher during spring training, and with returnees Wayne Wright and Earl Hamilton, the Angels thought they had the makings of another championship pitching staff. The local newspapermen agreed with that assessment, and many picked the Angels to repeat as pennant winners.

But it was not to be. The Angels started slowly and then began a gradual decline before finally falling into last place in early July. Across the league, the ball seemed much livelier in 1927 than ever before, and batting averages increased throughout the PCL. The Angels did their share of hitting, finishing with a team batting average of .295, their highest up to that time, and scored runs at a slightly greater clip than the previous year.

But the pitching turned out to be much worse than expected, and the vaunted defense of 1926 simply collapsed. Statz was sorely missed; neither Cox nor Art Weis could cover center field properly, and each made his share of errors that cost ball games. Jahn was no better in left field, and Krug tried Wally Hood as well as rookie Forrest "Woody" Jensen in center field but with little improvement. In 1926 the outfielders committed a combined total of 13 errors. Cox and Art Jahn each bettered that number by himself. The infield was a shambles as well. Mitchell, who was at the top of the league defensively in 1926, became very unreliable and was benched in mid-season in favor of rookie Jack Kahn. He was no better in the field nor was he able to hit PCL pitching, forcing Krug to restore Mitchell to the lineup. Krug watched him end up as the worst fielding shortstop in the league. Altogether, the Angels committed over 100 more errors than they had previously.

The pitching could not overcome such shoddy defense, but the staff was generally ineffective anyway. What games the Angels won were slugfests, it seemed. Only Wright seemed to be able to win with any consistency during the early months of the season. Hamilton appeared to be through; he was hit hard in almost every start. The league batted .339 against him, and his record showed it. Piercy had always had control issues during his career, and 1927 was no different. Weathersby showed his inexperience at the beginning of the season, although he improved considerably as the season wore on.

The Angels settled in seventh place during the first week of May, stayed there through most of June and ended that month only seven games below .500 and within reasonable distance of the first division. They then suffered a total collapse that lasted for the better part of two months. Los Angeles fell into last place to stay on July 10 and won only 17 games during July and August. The Angels lost 15 of 16 games during a two-week road trip to Portland and Oakland in August, removing all doubt about their eventual finish. They were fairly competitive at Wrigley Field, winning more than half of their home games, but they were an astounding 40 games below .500 on the road.

As the club continued to play poorly, Marty Krug began to shuffle his lineup and experiment with younger players. He released second baseman Ed Hemingway in August to make room for Gale Staley, who had seen some action the previous year. Staley hit .318 as a regular and showed promise for the years ahead. Earl Hamilton was released in early September, and Bruce Cunningham replaced him as a regular starter. He looked especially good as the season drew to a close and pitched an impressive one-hitter against the first-place Oaks in one of his last starts.

The Angels had entered into a modified working agreement with the Pocatello club of the Utah-Idaho League, which allowed them to acquire outfielders Walter "Wally" Berger and Woody Jensen. Jensen first came up in June and saw extended play for two weeks before returning to Idaho for the balance of the season. He came back to Los Angeles with Berger in September, and these youngsters, along with Wes Schulmerich, saw most of the outfield duty in the remaining few weeks of the season. Schulmerich joined the Angels after a collegiate career at Oregon State. All three would have successful careers in the National League after their PCL service. Glen Gabler, a hard-throwing right-hander from Long Beach who was only 18 years old, also made his debut in September and pitched impressively in several of his outings. The club played surprisingly well in September considering the presence of so many rookies in the lineup.

The last-place finish of 1927 was an embarrassment to Angels management, and the triumvirate of Patrick, Reichow and Krug was determined that it not happen again in 1928. A wholesale turnover of personnel took place during the winter, and this would become an annual occurrence over the next several years as the Angels sought a return to championship status. The only returning regulars from the cellar dwellers were Wally Hood, Gale Staley and the two catchers, Truck Hannah and Gus Sandberg. Tex Weathersby, Bruce Cunningham, Wayne Wright and Will Peters were the only pitchers to return.

The infield was brand new with the exception of Staley, who retained his second base position, and was considerably stronger on the whole. The new shortstop was Carl Dittmar, acquired from San Francisco. He had been a regular for the Seals in 1927, but when Hal Rhyne was returned to San Francisco by the Pirates, Dittmar became expendable. Although he did not have great speed, he had a terrific arm and knew how to play the hitters. He would only get better over time and would contribute greatly to Angels pennants in the future. At third base was Bobby Jones, a veteran of nine years with the Detroit Tigers, who had played with the Missions in 1927. He was obtained along with pitcher Clyde Barfoot in a trade for Frank Brazill and Art Weis. Although Jones was now 38 years old, he was still a much better defensive third baseman than Brazill. He was not as powerful a hitter however.

Before spring training was over the Cubs assigned Charlie "Slug" Tolson to the Angels to fill the first base position left vacant by the promotion of Ray Jacobs to Chicago. Tolson was a powerful right-handed hitter who would be a mainstay of the Angels offense during the next two years. In the outfield, Krug planned to use the two youngsters, Berger and Schulmerich, alongside the reliable Hood, with veteran Carson Bigbee and Woody Jensen in reserve.

The pitching staff seemed stronger with the addition of Barfoot and Norm Plitt, a sinkerballer purchased from the New York Giants. Barfoot was 36, a veteran of 14 seasons who had won 15 games for the Missions in 1927 and regularly pitched over 250 innings each year. He was thought to be near the end of his career, but he quickly became the ace of the staff and won 20 games in 1928. A very good hitting pitcher as well, Barfoot had a beautiful change of pace and taught it to several of the younger Angels pitchers that summer. Plitt joined Barfoot, Cunningham, Peters and Weathersby as regular starters, with Wayne

Wright and Glen Gabler as spot starters and relief. This was a much improved group over the dismal aggregation of 1927, but it was not at the high quality level of San Francisco and Sacramento, the two strongest clubs in the league. The Angels were recognized as being slightly improved though not a pennant contender, and the consensus was that they would finish in sixth place.

Nineteen twenty-eight marked the first year that the PCL would play a split season. In the days before the Shaughnessy playoff system became so popular in the minor leagues, splitting the season was designed to sustain interest throughout the year. Attendance would generally fall dramatically in the last half of a season when one team had taken a commanding lead. The Coast League had experienced that problem in 1927, when Oakland had won the pennant by a wide margin and was never challenged by the other clubs. The 1928 schedule called for 27 weeks of play with the second half to begin on July 3. The PCL directors were mostly skeptical of the plan but voted to try it for one year with an evaluation of the results before a new schedule was planned. Although no one particularly liked a split season, this scheme became the norm for the next several years.

The Angels opened the season at home with an 11–5 win over Portland, featuring two homers by Slug Tolson and a solo blast by Wally Berger. The club played at a .500 level through the middle of May and then stepped up the pace for the next month, reaching third place with one week to go in the first half. The Angels were only five games behind first-place San Francisco at that point, facing a series with the Seals. A sweep of the games would give the first-half championship to Los Angeles, but the Angels were not up to the challenge, losing six of the seven games and dropping to fifth place when the first half ended.

Stars of the first half were Tolson and Berger, who formed a ferocious one-two punch and were ably supported by Wes Schulmerich and Wally Hood. But the Angels may have played over their heads. They slumped badly after July 15, and after a nine game losing streak in the middle of August, the Angels fell into seventh place, where they remained. Only Seattle played worse than Los Angeles during the second half.

Clyde Barfoot — He gave the Angels two solid years as a starting pitcher after being acquired from the Missions in 1928 (courtesy Dick Dobbins).

The Sacramento Senators won the second-half season after a fierce fight with the Seals, but then lost to San Francisco, four games to two in the league championship series. The Angels assisted the Seals in their quest for the pennant by losing 20 of the 24 games played between the two, the worst showing a Los Angeles club ever had against another PCL opponent.

A controversy developed in 1928 over the Angels' "Ladies Day" policy. The Cubs had developed the concept in Chicago, setting aside certain days of the week when female fans could enter the ballpark at no charge, and the Angels decided to follow suit in 1925. The policy seemed to stimulate attendance, and Mr. Wrigley decided to go one step further in 1928. Every day was Ladies Day at Wrigley Field, not only for Angels games but for Hollywood games as well. The other club owners protested vigorously over the loss of all the revenue from games played in Los Angeles. Hollywood owner Bill Lane revolted against the Wrigley policy and cancelled Ladies Day on June 3. But the Angels continued to open the gates to women at any time, and finally, Wrigley agreed to pay the league and the visiting clubs their share of the lost revenue for games played on Tuesday, Saturday and Sunday. It was estimated that this decision cost Wrigley in excess of $50,000 for the 1928 season. He recovered some of that loss when paid attendance increased by 89,000 over 1927, much of that attributed to the influx of women and their escorts. Ironically, Hollywood attendance increased by over 200,000. Whatever accounted for these higher numbers, there is no doubt that Ladies Day at Wrigley Field popularized the game of baseball with the women of Southern California.

Angels management was satisfied with the team's performance and the development of young talent in 1928. Angels hitting was much improved over the previous year, but the entire PCL was becoming a hitter's paradise. The league batted .290 as a whole. The Angels average of .281 was only good for sixth place. Tolson led the club with a .351 average and socked 28 home runs, but those were only middling performances in 1928. Smead Jolley of San Francisco led the PCL with a .404 average and smashed a league-leading 45 home runs. More slugging was to come during the next two years.

Berger hit .327 and Schulmerich .317; both men looked to be future stars. Dittmar and Jones tightened the defense on the left side of the infield, with Bobby hitting a surprisingly high .296. Of the pitchers, Barfoot led the way, and young Bruce Cunningham was right behind him at 17–13. Will Peters was the staff leader during the first half and finished 14–11 with a team leading 3.62 ERA.

The Angels were better in 1929, winning more than half of their games for the first time in three years. During the off-season management made it a priority to improve the pitching staff, and brought in Augie Walsh and Russ Miller from the Phillies, Carl Holling from the Red Sox, Red Roberts from Wichita. Miller was of little value and was soon let go, but the others all contributed to what was essentially a brand new staff. Only Clyde Barfoot, Will Peters and Norm Plitt were left from the 1928 group. The many moves helped somewhat, but at the finish, Angels pitching was no better than the previous year.

In fairness to the hurlers, 1929 was not a good year to pitch in the PCL. The league batted .302 as the Missions set the pace at .319, the highest mark since Salt Lake City was a member. The Angels took part in the heavy bombardment of pitchers, batting .303, a club record. In most years this figure would have led the league, but in 1929 it was merely good for fourth place. Los Angeles scored almost six runs a game and pounded out 180 home runs, a team record that lasted until the Steve Bilko-led Angels of 1956 hit 202.

As was usual in those years, the Angels roster was considerably different from the one that ended the previous season. The Cubs provided Los Angeles with some of their surplus, sending outfielder Earl Webb and shortstop Johnny Butler to Wrigley Field. Webb was a great addition. He took over the right field position and had a fine year, hitting .357 with 37 home runs to earn another major league opportunity. Butler was another story, and one wonders what the Angels were expected to do with him. He was 36 years old that spring and had been the regular shortstop for Brooklyn for two years before the Cubs acquired him late in the 1928 season. Although Carl Dittmar was returning from a very impressive year and was seemingly entrenched in the position, Butler opened the season as the regular shortstop. He hit .441 during the first two weeks of the season, but quickly fell into a deep slump and was benched. Dittmar quietly re-established himself in the position, and Butler was released at the end of June. This scenario was replayed several times during Dittmar's 11-year career in Los Angeles.

One of the additions was not exactly a new face. Jigger Statz had been acquired from Brooklyn after two rather unhappy years with the Robins. He had been Brooklyn's regular centerfielder in 1927 but was relegated to part time play the next year, a role that he did not enjoy, and he made his feelings known to manager Wilbert Robinson. Statz was now 31, and his once-promising career seemed to be drawing to a close. Who could have predicted that Jigger would roam the Angels outfield for the next 14 years?

The Angels made room for Statz by sending Wally Hood to Seattle, and Gale Staley was sold to Portland, leaving second base in the hands of Ray Jacobs, returning from the Cubs by way of Minneapolis late in the 1928 season. The always optimistic Krug thought he had the makings of a very good team after all of these player moves, and the Angels did play well during the exhibition games. They continued their fine play during the early weeks of the season, winning 14 of their first 20 games, and hitting .341 as a team. But the much stronger Missions began to pull away from the rest of the league, and decline set in for the Angels. Although their hitting was spectacular, with all regulars except Dittmar hitting over .300 at the end of April, the pitching was not good. Only Walsh was a consistent winner, and that was more often the result of a large number of runs scored rather than good pitching. He received better run support than any of the other pitchers. Carl Holling pitched poorly and had to be taken out of the rotation, while Norm Plitt and Will Peters were much less effective than they had been in 1928. The Angels picked up George Boehler from Oakland in mid–May and hoped for a repeat of his 1927 season, but Boehler's control deserted him and he was soon released.

The 1929 season was originally scheduled as 28 weeks after the experiment with a split season in 1928, but the Missions appeared to be so strong that the owners were fearful again of a runaway pennant race and falling attendance. In an emergency meeting in the middle of June, the owners agreed to split the season once more and announced that the second half would begin play during the first week of July. This was good news for the Angels, who had fallen into sixth place when the announcement was made. They had remained in the first division until early June, when they dropped 12 of 13 games. Coincidentally, outfielder Wally Berger went out of the lineup at that time, and the club missed his big bat. Webb was ailing, too, and the club had lost the enthusiasm it had demonstrated earlier. The Angels ended the first-half season five games below .500 and in fifth place, and neither Joe Patrick nor Oscar Reichow were pleased with that performance.

When it was announced that Mr. Wrigley was paying a surprise visit to Los Angeles during the first week of July, there was much speculation about Marty Krug's future with the club. The suspicions were well founded, for on July 5 Krug resigned and was replaced by Jack Lelivelt, who had recently been released as manager of the Milwaukee club in the American Association. Krug had held the manager's job for six and a half years, longer than any other Angels pilot up to that time. He was extremely popular with his players, and his demise was regretted by most of them. Krug had a fine reputation as a teacher of young players as well. Many years later, Wally Berger recalled how Marty had worked with him to improve his fielding and also gave him much credit for helping him become a good outfielder. On the down side, Krug may have been a little too easy on his men. Sources within the Angels organization indicated that Patrick wanted a firmer hand in control.

Lelivelt featured a completely different type of personality. He had played in the American League and most recently had managed the Brewers for three years before being fired. Not a very demonstrative man, and one who handed out compliments sparingly, Lelivelt was a very intense manager who demanded much from his players. He had begun his managerial career at Omaha in the Western League in 1920, a city where, coincidentally, Marty Krug had also made his managerial debut. Lelivelt came to Los Angeles highly recommended by Cubs manager Joe McCarthy.

The Angels won seven of eight from Portland to begin the second half of the season, six of them in a row under interim manager Truck Hannah, who handled the club until Lelivelt arrived on July 11. The change in managers appeared to give the Angels a new lease on life. They played with much vigor and surged to an early lead before falling to third place in mid–August. The lineup had been improved with the purchase of Fred Haney from the St. Louis Cardinals. Haney did not have a regular position with the Angels, but he filled in at three infield positions, eventually playing in 150 games. Haney led off the batting order almost every day of the second-half season, and with Statz batting second, the Angels had a lot of baserunners for the big hitters—Tolson, Berger and Webb—to drive in. Haney's speed and versatility gave the Angels a weapon they had not had for several years. The club became much more aggressive on the basepaths. Haney led the PCL with 56 stolen

Fred Haney — The premier baserunner of his era, he led the PCL in stolen bases four times in his career (courtesy Dick Dobbins).

bases, Statz was not far behind with 37, and Los Angeles easily led the league with 193 steals.

Of equal importance was the signing of pitcher Ed Baecht after his release by Toledo. This was one of the most fortunate transactions of all time for Los Angeles. Baecht had opened the Coast League season at Portland but was sent to Toledo in May for a brief time. He won 14 games over the last half of the season with an ERA of 3.44, a full run less than any other Angels pitcher. Baecht would improve on the performance in 1930 and would bring high value on the player exchange market.

The addition of Baecht solidified the pitching staff, and Clyde Barfoot improved his work after a very slow start, giving the Angels some stability on the mound. Better pitching and the continued slugging of the outfielders kept them in contention for the second-half pennant through early September. But the club suffered a major blow when the Cubs were forced to bring up Charlie Tolson after their first baseman, Charlie Grimm, went down with an injury in the last week of August. Tolson was having an exceptional year, and his bat would be missed. Earl Webb was brought in from right field to replace him, and Wes Schulmerich, whose activity had been limited to part time duty this year, was given that outfield spot. The Cubs sent pitcher Berlyn Horne to Los Angeles as payment for Tolson. He contributed five wins down the stretch, but that did not make up for the loss of Tolson's big bat.

The Angels remained in striking distance for the last month of the season, but were unable to rise above third place. They finished four games behind arch-rival Hollywood, with a record of 57–46. The Sheiks nosed out the strong Missions by one game and then surprised them in the championship playoff series, winning four of the seven-game set.

The Angels lineup of 1929 was one of their greatest in history. The offense was paced by young Wally Berger, who led the club with 40 homers and 166 RBIs. Only 23 years old, Berger was the subject of season-long conjecture concerning which major league club would acquire his contract. It was assumed that he would be sold to the Cubs, but as it turned out, Berger went to the Boston Braves, not exactly the ideal destination for a player of his quality. Nevertheless, he prospered there while playing for a bad ball club most of the time, became the starting center fielder for the National League in the first All-Star game ever played in 1933, led the National League in home runs and RBIs in 1935, and hit .300 in a ten-year major league career. Berger thrived in Wrigley Field, and in a doubleheader sweep of Portland on July 4, he had one of the finest days that any Angels player ever had. He had seven hits in the two games, stole three bases, and scored nine runs. He hit two home runs that day, and his second-game blast was one of the longest in Wrigley Field history, soaring over the trees across East 41st Place, a distance that was estimated to be almost 500 feet.

Walt Berger — His great season of 1929 led to his purchase by the Boston Braves, where he soon became known as "Wally" Berger. He spent ten years in the National League and was a lifetime .300 hitter with 242 home runs before he returned to Los Angeles to finish his career in 1941.

Tolson and Webb also earned major league opportunities with their fine play that year. Webb had 37 home runs along with a .357 average, and he was drafted by Cincinnati at season's end. In 1931 while playing with the Boston Red Sox, he would set the major league record of 67 doubles, a mark that still stands. Tolson's Angels stay was cut short when he was promoted to Chicago in August. At the time he had 28 home runs while hitting .359, and probably would have approached 40 had he remained all season. Tolson never quite made the major league grade in spite of very fine minor league credentials. He was said to have very indifferent work habits, and that may have prevented him from having a good major league career.

Ray Jacobs hit 20 home runs to give the Angels four players with 20 or more, and Wes Schulmerich just missed the mark with 19. All of the regulars hit .300 or better, except for Bobby Jones and Gus Sandberg, and the catcher was close with a career high .289 mark. The hitting explosion caught the fancy of Los Angeles, and 341,173 spectators paid to watch an exciting team, along with an estimated 80,000 ladies admitted free of charge. This was the highest Angels attendance total at Wrigley Field so far, and it would not be surpassed until 1944.

Ray Jacobs — He enjoyed several fine seasons with the Angels and had a lifetime PCL average of .294 with 198 home runs over 14 years, but only appeared in two major league games. He died in an auto accident at age 50 in 1952 (courtesy Mark Macrae).

The Angels pitching staff as a whole was better in 1929, but most of the pitchers were average, and that prevented the club from taking full advantage of the high-powered offense that it had. The staff had an ERA of 4.78 with only Ed Baecht having a mark below 4.50. This might seem poor today, but in 1929 only 11 starting pitchers in the entire PCL gave up fewer than four runs a game. The Angels mark was right in the middle of the pack, and that is where the team finished. The starters pitched inconsistently all year long. During the first half, Augie Walsh was the big winner, but he tailed off after entering July with a 12–3 record and finished at 21–14. Barfoot won 18 games, but most of those were won in August and September. The Angels gave starts to 14 different pitchers as Krug and Lelivelt tried desperately to establish a rotation.

Baecht had a marvelous season, by any measure. His 3.44 ERA was second only to the 3.43 posted by Lefty Gomez of the Seals, and he pitched three shutouts over the second half, not an easy feat in 1929. He would perform even better in 1930. Yet, the club would need better pitching than it had featured to contend with the stronger Hollywood and Mission clubs.

9

Night Baseball Is Introduced as the Depression Begins

The season of 1930 was wonderful for the Los Angeles baseball fan. The hometown teams dominated the PCL that year, with the Angels winning the first half race and the Sheiks becoming the second-half champions. The two clubs met in a championship playoff for the first and only time in their history, and Hollywood marched off as the pennant winner for the year. In July a professional night game was played in Los Angeles for the first time, the spectacle delighting the city. While attendance at Wrigley Field was down a bit from 1929, it remained at a very high level, and for the first time ever, talk of Los Angeles becoming a major league city began to have some meaning. The Angels were expected to be a little weaker in 1930, having lost the power hitting of Berger, Tolson and Webb, and didn't figure to be a strong contender for the pennant. But a greatly improved defense led to better pitching, and the replacement hitters performed very well. This was the best balanced Angels team since 1926. The Angels batted .304, fourth place again in another year where the hitters dominated, and had the league's best defense. The pitching staff was led by Ed Baecht, who was the best pitcher in the league. He led in wins with 26, complete games with 32, and ERA at 3.23, and PCL hitters batted only .258 against him. Win "Old Pard" Ballou posted a record of 16–7, including wins in 11 of his last 12 decisions, and the staff had seven pitchers who won 12 or more games apiece.

An important development took place off the field. The Cubs had taken a part ownership in the Reading club of the International League, and over the winter, Bobby Jones, Norm Plitt and Red Roberts were sent to the Pennsylvania city. The move opened up third base for Fred Haney, who lacked a regular spot in 1929. Lelivelt moved Ray Jacobs to first base, replacing him with Frank Sigafoos, purchased from San Francisco. With Dittmar back at shortstop, the Angels now had the best infield in the PCL. Jacobs really could not play well at any position other than first base, his new spot, and the addition of Sigafoos filled a major hole in the infield. Haney was much faster than Jones, who had slowed considerably in 1929. And Dittmar was extremely sure handed, leading all PCL shortstops in fielding that year.

The outfield saw Jigger Statz returning to center field with Wes Schulmerich in left and George Harper opening in right field. Harper was one of the players who came from the Braves as part of the sale of Berger, and when the Cubs transferred Johnny Moore from Reading, Harper was scheduled to be a reserve. But various injuries throughout the season

The 1930 Angels. *Front row (left to right):* Art Delaney, Dallas Warren, Jigger Statz, Mascot Peterson, Johnny Moore, George Harper, Berlyn Horne. *Middle row:* Bill Skiff, Fred Haney, Carl Dittmar, Will Peters. *Back row:* Clyde Barfoot, Wes Schulmerich, Frank Sigafoos, Art Jacobs, Carroll Yerkes, Ed Baecht, Art Parker, manager Jack Lelivelt, coach Truck Hannah (courtesy Mark Macrae).

kept Harper in the lineup most of the time, and he appeared in 160 games. Moore was an exceptional player who led the Angels in home runs before a broken hand sidelined him in early September.

Unfortunately, the catching situation was very unsettled. The Angels suffered a tragic loss when the popular Gus Sandberg was killed in a freak accident in February. He and his wife had entertained former manager Marty Krug at their home in Los Angeles. When Krug went to leave that evening, he noticed that his car was almost out of gas. Sandberg offered to siphon gasoline out of his own car and foolishly lit a match near the gas tank to see how much was there. The ensuing explosion caused severe burns that proved fatal. Gus was only 33 at the time of his death.

Bill Skiff was purchased from Reading as a replacement for Sandberg, but he did not like the contract the Angels offered before eventually signing it, and he arrived late in spring training as a result. Then he was injured during the first week of the season and was able to play in only 62 games all season. In desperation Lelivelt turned to the venerable Truck Hannah. The long-time PCL catcher was now 40 years old and was beginning his 14th season in the league. He had caught 67 games in 1929, mostly in the second games of doubleheaders, and had planned to confine most of his duties to coaching in 1930. But with

Skiff out of action most of the time and Dallas Warren not up to PCL standards, Hannah was forced to catch most of the games. The large catcher responded with a .267 average in 125 games and handled the pitching staff with the consummate skill developed during his many years of experience in the league. At season's end, both Lelivelt and Baecht gave much of the credit for the pitchers' fine year to Hannah.

The Angels began the season well and led the league through most of April, but they fell behind when the Sacramento Senators made a rush to the top. But Los Angeles was never very far behind, and the club returned to the lead in late June. The Angels won ten of 12 games on the road in Seattle and Portland, while the Senators were losing seven straight at Hollywood, and they were never headed after that. The first-half championship was clinched on July 12 with an 8–3 win over Seattle behind Clyde Barfoot. The Angels finished 3½ games ahead of Hollywood, which had moved past Sacramento after the series sweep.

The coming of night baseball was the premier event in Los Angeles that season. After the stock market crash in October, 1929, and the first signs of what was to become the Great Depression in early 1930, there was an ominous decline in minor league attendance across the country. Night baseball, which had been dismissed as a viable activity for many years, was now looked upon as a possible salvation for the game itself. Lee Keyser, owner of the Des Moines club of the Western League, sought and received permission from his league to play night games at his park, and on May 2 the first regularly scheduled after-dark game in the history of Organized Baseball was played. It was a rousing success. Over 10,000 fans were present, including a number of minor league club owners, and there seemed to be no difference in the quality of play under the lights. Within weeks, light towers were installed in minor league parks in such places as Indianapolis, Omaha, San Antonio and Jersey City with similar results. The first night game in the PCL was played in Sacramento on May 22. Shortly thereafter, all clubs except the two in San Francisco announced their plans to play night games during the

Gus Sandberg — His life was cut short in 1930. He suffered fatal burns when a fire broke out while he was checking the gasoline tank in his car (courtesy Mark Macrae).

1930 season. Mr. Wrigley was enthusiastic over the opportunity and boasted that he would install "the best incandescent lighting money can buy" at Wrigley Field.

The first night game in Los Angeles was played on July 22 before 12,653 paying fans. The Angels defeated Sacramento, 5–4, in 11 innings, with Carroll Yerkes the winning pitcher. The crowd was probably five times the size of an average weekday crowd at Wrigley Field. The Angels played the next four games at night, with crowds exceeding 7,000 on each occasion. When only 2,100 fans showed up for the Saturday afternoon game and 5,900 for the Sunday doubleheader, Oscar Reichow announced that all weekday games for the rest of the year would be played at night.

The fans were more excited about this news than the players. Generally, the Angels felt that they could see well enough at night, but they preferred to play in the daytime. Johnny Moore was one Angels player who took exception to that view. He hit the first home run in a night game and crashed three more at night before the week was out. Coincidentally, Moore would play in the first major league night game as a member of the Phillies at Crosley Field in Cincinnati in 1935.

The Angels played about as well in the second half as they had in the first, but they never took the lead. Hollywood had become a far more formidable team by adding outfielder Dave Barbee to its roster in June. His hitting stroke was made for Wrigley Field. He socked seven home runs during his first two weeks in Los Angeles, and his presence simply added another threat to an already powerful team. The Angels could not improve their pace and gradually dropped well behind Hollywood. They were 6½ games behind when the two teams began what was the biggest series of the year on September 9. Eight games were scheduled, and the Angels needed to win at least six of them. A 3–1 win in the first game of the "Admission Day" doubleheader gave the club some hope, but Will Peters was pounded in the second game, and Hollywood won the next two games to all but end the Angels threat. The series ended in a split of the eight games, and the Angels would never get any closer, finishing eight games behind in second place. A total of 79,341 fans attended the games, including 28,000 ladies, the largest attendance for a single week's play in PCL history up to that time.

The Angels were a tired team as the long season drew to a close on October 19, an extremely late date for even the PCL. The club had been troubled with injuries during the last six weeks. Moore broke a bone in his hand and missed most of September, and Dittmar, Haney and Sigafoos were hurting as well. Los Angeles had dominated Hollywood in regular season play, winning the season series, 18 games to 12, but the Angels were not given much of a chance in the playoff. Hollywood showed the experts to be right by winning the best-of-seven series in five games. The crowds were very disappointing, averaging just over 5,000 per game, and it was thought that the length of the season had dampened the fans' interest.

The series was exciting, nevertheless. It featured hitting and more hitting. Hollywood won the first two games: 9–8 in 10 innings, in a game that saw five Angels home runs, and then a comeback from six runs down to beat the Angels, 14–12, behind two homers by Dave Barbee and one by pitcher Frank Shellenback. The next day it was the Sheiks' turn to blow a lead as the Angels rallied late to win, 11–10. But that was the high point of the series for Los Angeles. The Angels were slaughtered, 22–4, in Game Four with Baecht routed early and a parade of pitchers unable to control the Hollywood bats. The series came to a merciful end on Sunday, when Frank Shellenback pitched the only complete game of the series for either team, winning 8–4. The Sheiks batted .360 for the series, and the Angels were not far behind at .335. Barbee had 12 hits in the five games, including four home runs, and the two teams combined to hit 24 home runs.

The playoff was a disappointment, but president Joe Patrick and Oscar Reichow were very pleased with the Angels of 1930. Wes Schulmerich led the regulars at bat with a .380 average and 28 home runs. He was the team leader during the first half, hitting .410 in the first 100 games. In the final week of the season, it was announced that his contract had been sold to the Braves for $40,000 and outfielder Jimmy Welsh. Boston thought that Schulmerich might become another Wally Berger, but the ex–Oregon State football star did not live up to expectations and lasted only two years at Braves Field. Johnny Moore had the first of many fine years in Los Angeles, hitting .342 with 26 home runs before his recall to the Cubs at the end of the season. Jigger Statz had an exceptional year at .360 with 37 stolen bases, and he showed his versatility by filling in at third base when Fred Haney was injured. Haney again led the PCL with 52 steals, and the Angels as a team stole a league-leading 184 bases. Jack Lelivelt liked to play the running game, a feature of Angels clubs as long as he was the manager.

With a little more pitching, the Angels would have been undisputed PCL champions. Ed Baecht was the stopper, twice winning seven straight decisions, and Ballou matched him during the last two months of the season. Art Delaney started fast, winning five of his first six decisions, but he was ineffective after June and was taken out of the regular rotation. Carroll Yerkes, a good acquisition from Portland in May, won 12 games, and Berlyn Horne won 13 after replacing Delaney as a starter. The club could have used a return to their form of 1929 by Clyde Barfoot and Augie Walsh. Barfoot started strongly, but arm problems kept him out of action for much of the second half, and he won only two games after July. Walsh was sent down by the Cubs late in spring training, but he had limited success for the Angels, finishing at 6–4 with a horrendous 6.99 ERA. At year's end, the Angels disposed of their two

Ed Baecht — He was the best pitcher in the Coast League in 1930, but the 364 innings he pitched that year took a toll on him as he never pitched as well again (courtesy Doug McWilliams).

veterans, sending Walsh to Baltimore of the International League and Barfoot to Chattanooga of the Southern Association.

Baecht's great year made him an attractive commodity, and he was sent to Chicago for five players, with two more to follow in the spring. Pitchers Malcolm Moss, Lynn Nelson and Al Shealy, infielder Eddie "Doc" Farrell and catcher John Schulte would report to Catalina with the Angels in the spring.

But times were becoming difficult. The great economic collapse of the 1930s that had been heralded by the stock market crash of 1929 was now fully affecting the nation and beginning to have its effect on baseball. Although the advent of night baseball in July 1930 created much fan interest in Los Angeles and caused an early spurt in attendance, the crowds were rapidly shrinking by September. When the final attendance figures for 1930 were announced, it was learned that Los Angeles had suffered an absolute decline in paid admissions from the previous year. Earlier, the Angels had proudly boasted that more than 400,000 fans had passed through the Wrigley Field turnstiles. But more than one-third of them were women, who were now admitted free to every weekday game, including the night games. The Angels lost over 26,000 paying customers in 1930, and the PCL as a whole suffered a decline of 13 percent. It would be many years before the Coast League would return to the attendance levels of 1929.

In player news, the Cubs completed the transaction for Ed Baecht by sending outfielder Vince Barton and catcher Gilly Campbell to Los Angeles in the spring of 1931. The seven new players represented quite a haul for the Angels, who had acquired Baecht for virtually nothing less than two years earlier. It was ironic that Cub manager Rogers Hornsby approved this deal, for several years before he had the opportunity to sign Baecht to his first contract at no cost. The Alton, Illinois, youth appeared in Sportsman's Park in St. Louis one day in the summer of 1925 and asked Hornsby, then the manager of the Cardinals, for a tryout. After watching him throw a few pitches, the great Rajah, in his usual brusque manner, told Baecht, "Go on home, kid. Get out of here. You'll never be a pitcher." If Hornsby had any regrets over this decision, he did not make them known when Baecht joined the Cubs in 1931. There were high expectations for him, but the pitcher was a great disappointment in Chicago, winning only two games. He was back in Los Angeles in 1932 and never won another game in the major leagues.

Of the seven players obtained by the Angels, Vince Barton became the regular right fielder, Doc Farrell won the second base job (replacing Sigafoos, who was drafted by Cincinnati) and Campbell became the regular catcher. There would be no need for Truck Hannah to catch 125 games this year. Malcolm Moss, Leroy Herrmann and Lynn Nelson joined Win Ballou, the only holdover, and 38-year-old Jess Petty as starting pitchers. The infield would have Jacobs, Dittmar and Haney back from the 1930 club, while Barton and Homer Summa, picked up from the Missions in exchange for Jimmy Welsh, would flank Jigger Statz in the outfield. Summa was a veteran of several American League seasons and had hit .341 at Portland in 1930. On paper this club looked to be a pennant contender.

Then disaster struck. Fred Haney, who was so vital to the success of the team, suffered an attack of kidney stones shortly after spring training began, so severe that he eventually required an operation. He was unable to play in any of the exhibition games and clearly would not be ready for the regular season. Doc Farrell was moved to third base in his place, and Loris Baker, an infielder obtained from San Francisco for pitcher Art Delaney, replaced Farrell at second. The infield was left considerably weaker after these moves. Farrell lacked the quickness that made Haney such a good third baseman, and Baker could not cover the

The 1931 Angels. *Front row (left to right):* Trainer Frank Jacobs, Win Ballou, Art Parker, Gilly Campbell, Cecil Green, Ed DeCuir, Glen Gabler, Leroy Herrmann, Jigger Statz. *Middle row:* Lynn Nelson, John Schulte, Homer Summa, Carroll Yerkes, Loris Baker, Frank Sabella, Carl Dittmar, Will Peters, Charley Moncrief, Eddie "Doc" Farrell, George Harper. *Back row:* Boots Weber, Vince Barton, Jess Petty, Ray Jacobs, Truck Hannah, manager Jack Lelivelt, John Vusich, Malcolm Moss, Al Shealy, Oscar Reichow (courtesy Mark Macrae).

ground that Farrell did at second. Neither was the leadoff hitter that Haney was, and Lelivelt had built his offense around Haney's ability to get on base. Haney did not return to the Angels lineup until June 21 and appeared in only 85 games all year. His loss, more than any other factor, kept the Angels from reaching their potential that year.

Hollywood was the preseason favorite to repeat as league champions in 1931, largely because their lineup returned virtually intact. There was no split season planned when the schedules were announced in January, but that was always subject to review, especially given Hollywood's dominance. With pitcher Frank Shellenback having his finest year and Dave Barbee hitting home runs at a tremendous pace, the Sheiks jumped into the lead in the first week of May and began to pull away from the rest of the league. In the meantime, the Angels played at the .500 level through the middle of June, but then suffered through a wretched homestand, losing ten of 14 games to fall to sixth place by the end of the month.

By June 15 the Hollywood lead was so great that a pennant race of any kind appeared greatly in doubt. Attendance throughout the league had not been good since Opening Day, and with unemployment rising, there was danger that it would fall even further. The PCL directors did not want to revert to the split schedule again, but times were desperate. The league abruptly ended the first-half season on July 5 with Hollywood a comfortable five games ahead. The Angels rested in fifth place with a 43–47 mark, only 1½ games out of seventh place. The club was in shambles at that point. Only Ballou had pitched consistently well; Moss, Herrmann and Petty were no more than .500 pitchers; and Nelson had been so ineffective that he was relegated to bullpen duty. Vince Barton had provided some spark to the offense with 17 home runs, but the rest of the club had not been impressive. Haney's absence for most of the first-half season had cost the club a number of games.

Things began to improve almost immediately in the second-half season. Haney was now fully recovered and back in the lineup on an everyday basis. And the Cubs recalled Vince Barton after his fine half season and sent Johnny Moore as a replacement. Once again, Cub management demonstrated faulty judgment, for Moore was a much better player than Barton, although without the same power. Moore replaced Barton in right field and batted cleanup, where in 80 games he hit .366 while driving in 69 runs.

Immediately after the first half ended, the Angels signed first baseman George Burns, after he had been released by the Missions. Burns was 38 years old and had hit .307 in a 16-year career in the major leagues with the Cleveland Indians and the Philadelphia Athletics. He had begun the 1931 season as the playing manager of the Mission club, which had played reasonably well during the first half, finishing in fourth place. Thus, it came as a surprise when he resigned his managerial post on July 3. That should have been the end of the matter, with Burns returning to the playing ranks exclusively, but he had an unusual contract in that he could receive his release as a player as well. He chose to exercise that option and immediately signed a contract with the Angels for the balance of the 1931 season at a salary of $1,000 a month, a very high figure for those times. It was unclear why Burns left the helm of the Missions. But the decision was a fortunate one for Los Angeles.

"Tioga George," as he was called, joined the Angels on July 5 and was immediately inserted into the lineup at first base, replacing Ray Jacobs. In spite of his advanced age, he remained a dangerous hitter. Batting in the fifth position behind Moore, he provided additional power for a lineup that badly needed it, and won several games with late-inning home runs. His arrival signaled the end of Ray Jacobs' tenure as a member of the Angels. Once predicted to become a star player in the major leagues, Jacobs never made the grade. In retrospect, it appears that he was primarily a Wrigley Field hitter. The park seemed to fit his swing perfectly, and he hit most of his home runs there, seldom connecting anywhere else. He saw no action at first base after Burns arrived, was used only as a pinch hitter for the next month, and filled in at third base in September when Haney was sidelined once again. Although Jacobs hit several key homers down the stretch to help the Angels into first place, he would be gone by the next spring.

Los Angeles started slowly in the second half, then gradually began to play better and moved into the lead on August 6. The second half was a very tight race with four clubs taking turns in the lead—Oakland, San Francisco, Hollywood and the Angels. Gradually, the Sheiks fell out of contention, leaving the two Bay Area clubs and the Angels as the primary rivals. A streak that saw Los Angeles win 12 of 14 games at Wrigley Field from Hollywood and Seattle propelled the club into the lead on September 10, but then a series with the Seals in San Francisco proved to be disastrous. The Angels could score only one run during the first three games, all of them losses, and San Francisco moved on top by one game. The rest of the series was split, leaving the Seals in first place by one game.

The lead increased to 1½ games when San Francisco came to Los Angeles the next week for a brief four-game series, one of the few times in this period that a split-week series was scheduled. After losing the first game, the Seals took three straight again and left town 3½ games in front. The first game of the Sunday doubleheader was especially frustrating. The Angels had several opportunities to put the Seals away, but the game went into extra innings before San Francisco won the slugfest, 14–11, with three runs in the twelfth inning. That effectively decided the race, with the Angels finishing four games behind the Seals.

The second-half performance was made possible by the pitching of Win Ballou and Leroy Herrmann, who enjoyed outstanding years. "Old Pard" had his finest year in Los Angeles, posting a 24–13 mark with a 3.71 ERA. Herrmann was 20–11 and won seven of his last eight decisions. Between them, these two claimed 24 of the 55 Angels victories. Malcolm Moss and Petty gave Los Angeles a lot of innings, but both were .500 pitchers.

Jess Petty posed an attitude problem for much of the year and was briefly suspended by Lelivelt in August. Petty thought he still belonged in the major leagues, did not want to be in Los Angeles, and publicly accused Lelivelt of taking him out of games too early to prevent him from earning a bonus for winning 20 games. The issue became moot, for Petty finished 15–16 and lost his last four decisions. Moss showed signs of brilliance at times, especially on June 12, when he pitched a no-hit game at Sacramento. It was not a perfect game by any means. The Angels won, 5–1, with the lone Senator run scoring after a walk, a wild pitch and two infield outs. The club received some good work in August and September from rookie Hal Stitzel and veteran Buzz Wetzel, who was signed after his release by Hollywood, but the Angels staff was not quite good enough to win a pennant.

Angels attendance was down again in 1931, to 256,416. After signs that the economy might be improving in late summer, the stock market suffered another precipitous decline in September, and the Depression began to worsen. More jobs were lost and general wage cuts were becoming common in all industry. Baseball would be no exception.

Jack Lelivelt—He had the highest winning percentage of all Angels managers. After he left at the end of the 1937 season, he was hired by Seattle, where he won pennants in 1939 and 1940 before his untimely death in January 1941 (courtesy Mark Macrae).

10

Depression Baseball

The Depression was felt fully in Organized Baseball by the end of 1931. At the winter meetings in December, the National Association attempted to establish a salary limit for all minor league teams, as well as prescribing a reduction in the playing rosters. This was a logical move in view of the grave economic conditions that had developed nationwide. But the Coast League vigorously fought this attempt at control by the organization. Joe Patrick of the Angels was the leader of the revolt, which ultimately succeeded. Patrick's position, and one adopted by the league itself, was that each club wanted to put the best team on the field that it possibly could afford, even if it meant paying higher salaries to some players. A winning team would lead to more revenue at the box office, which in turn would enable the club to afford the higher pay. Conversely, a reduced roster would have an adverse effect on the quality of play on the field, and that in turn would result in lower attendance. Patrick felt that by leaving the rules the way they were, the PCL would manage somehow.

The Coast League continued its roster limits of 20 veterans and five rookies for the 1932 season, with each club free to negotiate its own payroll. But by the beginning of spring training in February, that decision seemed to have been unwise. The economy was considerably worse, and the league was anticipating attendance to be much less than in 1931. Most clubs imposed a 20 percent reduction in salary when contracts were sent out to returning players. Events during the coming season would show that even such a drastic measure was not enough.

Despite the gloomy economic picture, there was considerable excitement in the Angels camp that year, mostly over two young players who were making their first appearance in the PCL. Outfielder George "Tuck" Stainback was signed out of Fairfax High School in Los Angeles in the spring of 1931 and had been sent to Bisbee in the Arizona-Texas League for seasoning. He debuted with a fine .315 mark in that circuit and was now trying to show that he was ready for Coast League competition. Third baseman Gene Lillard, a 19-year-old from Goleta, near Santa Barbara, had a rifle for an arm and swung a powerful bat. Both rookies were outstanding during the exhibition games, and Stainback earned a spot in the Angels outfield. But manager Jack Lelivelt still had Fred Haney available for third base play and decided to send Lillard to Wichita in the Western League for more seasoning, but he knew the stay in Kansas would not be long.

Another impressive young player that spring was outfielder Mike Kreevich. He was Cub property, having seen action in a few National League games at the end of the 1931 season after spending most of the year at Des Moines in the Western League. This would be Kreevich's third season in professional baseball, and he displayed a fine throwing arm and very good speed, although he was not quite the hitter that Stainback promised to be. Kreevich took over in right field where he was to have a fine season in what was to be his only year in Los Angeles.

As usual, there were many player moves during the off-season. Gone were Doc Farrell, sold to the Yankees, and George Burns, sent to Seattle along with pitcher Lynn Nelson. Catcher John Schulte and pitcher Jess Petty were released, along with first baseman Ray Jacobs, who would open the 1932 season at Portland. The new players on the right side of the infield were first baseman Earl Sheely and second baseman Clarence "Footsie" Blair. Sheely was not new to the PCL by any means. He had first appeared in the league in 1916 and ranked as one of its all-time great players, leading the league in home runs three years in a row at Salt Lake City and also twice in hitting, reaching a peak of .403 with San Francisco in 1930. He had spent 1931 as the regular first baseman for the Boston Braves. But Sheely was now 39 and somewhat slower in the field than he used to be. Although he still swung a good bat, the defense was weaker with him in the lineup. Blair had spent the previous three years in Chicago without great distinction and was sent to Los Angeles after the Cubs brought up Billy Herman.

The only new pitcher of note was left-hander Les Sweetland, sent down by the Cubs. He joined Win Ballou, Leroy Herrmann, Hal Stitzel and Malcolm Moss as candidates for the starting roles. Gilly Campbell was back to handle the bulk of the catching with Bill Cronin, purchased from the Braves during the winter as the back-up.

The Angels and Portland were listed as the most likely pennant winners as the season began, but it seemed odd that Los Angeles would be ranked so high with a suspect pitching staff and two rookies in the outfield. However, for the first two months of the season, this appeared to be an accurate prediction with both clubs at or near the lead. The Angels were ahead by two games on May 22, their high point of the season. But then the club lost 16 of the next 22 games to fall into fourth place on June 12. The Angels remained there for most of the next two months.

The team had begun to unravel a month earlier when second baseman Footsie Blair, who had been doing a creditable job in the field, suffered through a terrible afternoon at Wrigley Field. The Angels were being slaughtered, 19–4, by Sacramento in the first game of a Sunday doubleheader, and Blair contributed to the debacle by committing four errors. Naturally, the fans expressed their displeasure, and in anger Blair threw a ball into the stands behind first base. The Angels suspended Blair for his display of temper, and he never did get back in the lineup on a regular basis. He then jumped the club on June 19, returning to his home in Texas without approval, after which the Angels released him. Blair was hitting only .232 when he left. The club signed infielder Bernie DeViveiros, who had been released by Sacramento, to replace Blair on the roster.

A week later, the Angels experienced another blow when Tuck Stainback, who was becoming an exceptional player, was hit by a pitch from Oakland southpaw Roy Joiner and went down with a broken cheekbone. The injury kept him out of the lineup for over a month. Homer Summa filled in for Stainback but his lack of power weakened the offense considerably.

In Jack Lelivelt's long and successful managerial career, he repeatedly demonstrated his ability to handle a pitching staff, but 1932 was not one of those years. He opened the season with two very dependable starters in Leroy Herrmann and Pard Ballou and filled the other two slots with Moss and Sweetland. But when those two veterans faltered and Ballou suddenly began to have great difficulty getting anyone out, Lelivelt seemed indecisive in his use of his pitchers. He used Ballou frequently on two days' rest and also in relief in the hope that he would shake his slump, but the veteran seemed overworked by this approach. Sweetland was used both as a starter and reliever, but was ineffective in each role after May and was finally released in July. Moss was in action almost every other day in May and June, it seemed, but saw hardly any action for the next month. Only Herrmann pitched consistently well, and without him the Angels might have plunged deep into the second division. In desperation Lelivelt tried Hal Stitzel, Charlie Moncrief and Ed Baecht as starters with mixed success. Baecht had been returned by the Cubs in May, and although he gave the club some good efforts, he was not nearly the pitcher he had been in 1930, nor would he ever be again.

By the middle of July, Los Angeles was at the .500 mark, ten games behind first place Portland and seemingly out of the pennant race. Then the club got hot. The Angels won 22 of the next 29 games to vault into second place, only 3½ games behind the Beavers. The club's defense was better with Bernie DeViveiros at second base. Although he had never been a particularly good hitter, he was a fine infielder and contributed some timely hitting during the hot streak. The pitching had stabilized somewhat with Baecht and Stitzel pitching well and Ballou coming out of his slump. Then the club lost Herrmann to the Cubs on July 24, just after he won his 21st game and was on a pace to win 30. That seemed to be the end of the Angels pennant hopes, but Ballou won four straight decisions, and the club received some good work from Bob Fitzke, who had not played professional baseball for five years. He was a high school coach in Scranton, Pennsylvania, who had come to Los Angeles for the Olympic games that summer and asked the Angels for permission to work out with them to keep in shape. He was so impressive that the club signed him to a contract. Fitzke pitched well for five weeks, mostly in relief, and won four games before returning to his coaching job in September.

Earl Sheely had performed satisfactorily as the club's first baseman and was its top RBI man, but he had an expensive contract. As a result, the Angels decided to release him on August 1. That was one of many such moves that PCL clubs were forced to make for the sake of economy in 1932. Attendance had dwindled to virtually nothing as the season wore on, and several clubs were hard pressed to meet payroll. The Angels saw their attendance down by almost 40 percent from 1931, while crowds were virtually invisible at games in the Bay Area.

The Angels purchased Jim Oglesby from Des Moines as Sheely's replacement. He was 27 years old and had never played above Class A before. But he was a fine replacement for Sheely at a much lower price and would contribute much to Angels fortunes in the years just ahead. In his first week of play, Oglesby had nine hits, was agile in the field, and added some life to a club that was dominated by quiet veterans. In the last 64 games of the season, Oglesby drove in 61 runs to go along with his .323 average. Sheely's bat was never missed.

The Angels were never quite able to catch the Beavers after their spurt in July, and by the end of August they had skidded to third place. At that point Angels management essentially gave up on the season and reduced the payroll once more. Veterans Homer Summa, Fred Haney and Malcolm Moss were released on September 1. Gene Lillard and pitcher Dick Ward were recalled from Wichita, with Lillard taking Haney's old spot at third base. Byron Blackburn, a rookie who had been signed by the Angels at a July tryout camp, was given an opportunity in left field. The club promptly went into a tailspin, losing 20 of the next 29 games and falling into fifth place, where the Angels remained for the rest of the year. Whether the collapse was caused by the release of three popular veterans, one can only speculate.

The star of the 1932 Angels was Jigger Statz, who was chosen as the Most Valuable Player in the league. He hit over .400 well into June, led the league until late August, and in spite of a late September slump finished at .347 while driving in a career high 93 runs. As usual, his defensive play in center field was superb, and most observers felt that his performance was the primary reason why the Angels stayed in contention as long as they did. Stainback was also a defensive wizard and hit .356 with 91 RBIs. Catcher Gilly Campbell enjoyed a fine year, hitting .319 while catching 153 games. But the Angels were not as powerful as they had been in recent years, hitting only 76 home runs with all but 11 of them at Wrigley Field. The baseball of 1932 was not as lively as it had been in the power years of 1929–30, and only Portland and Seattle hit more than 100 home runs. The Angels led the league in runs scored, but the pitchers gave up almost as many, and that doomed the club to a second-division finish.

Los Angeles could have won the pennant in 1932 had the Cubs not recalled pitcher Leroy Herrmann. The 26-year-old right-hander had a relatively undistinguished career in the major leagues with the Cubs and later the Cincinnati Reds, but beginning in late 1931 until his recall he may have been the best pitcher in the PCL. His record of 28–8 during that period was certainly comparable to that of the great Frank Shellenback, who was at the peak of his career with the rival Hollywood Sheiks. Had Herrmann remained in Los Angeles through August, the Angels might have caught Portland and surely would not have dumped Haney and the others.

It was quite apparent that the Angels would need more pitching if they were to reach the top of the PCL in 1933. Fortunately, that need would be fulfilled beyond all expectations, and the Angels would embark on perhaps the two most glorious years in their history.

Leroy Herrmann — He was a 20-game winner in 1931 and 1932 and was on his way to a third such season before he was sold to the Cubs in July 1933 (courtesy Doug McWilliams).

11

The Yankees of the West

For the Los Angeles baseball fan, 1933 was the best of times and the worst of times. Economic conditions were at their poorest during the first half of that year. There were no available jobs to speak of. Banks were failing at a rate five times greater than in 1930. Building permits in Los Angeles County were virtually non-existent, and the unemployment rate in Southern California was as high as 41 percent in some industries. But the fans had a pleasant distraction from the tough times in an exciting pennant race that saw the Angels beat out the rival Hollywood Sheiks to win their first undisputed league championship since 1926.

The impact of the Depression was the most important concern of the PCL owners as they conducted their annual winter meetings in January 1933. The Seattle and Oakland franchises were in desperate financial condition, and San Francisco, saddled with the expense of the new Seals Stadium, was only slightly better off. Coast League attendance had fallen almost 50 percent since 1930, and in an attempt to draw more people to the ballpark, all clubs cut their ticket prices. In 1933 the Angels would charge 85 cents for a box seat, 60 cents for the grandstand and 25 cents for the bleachers. Officially, player rosters would remain as they had been in 1932, but in practice no club carried the full complement of 23 players in 1933, and some operated with no more than 20 players all season long. Expensive veteran players were let go, replaced by young players in their first or second years in professional baseball, simply to save in salary. Naturally, this led to a decline in the quality of play on the field.

The foundation for the Angels championship had been laid during September of 1932 when young players Gene Lillard and Jim Oglesby became regulars and Dick Ward began to take a regular turn on the mound. Loser of his first three decisions, Ward won his last four starts and looked ready to assume a starting role. Only 24 years old, he had an excellent fastball, and in the spring developed a brutal curve that was almost unhittable. He would become an important part of the improved pitching staff that the Angels were hoping to build.

At the winter meetings in December 1932, Los Angeles acquired additional pitching strength with the purchase of Fay Thomas from Brooklyn. He would contribute greatly to the club's success in the years to come, and his name ranks high in Angels pitching annals. Thomas was 29 years old in the spring of 1933 and had long ties to Los Angeles. His home was Chatsworth in the San Fernando Valley, and he had attended the University of Southern California, where he had been a starting tackle on the Trojan football team in 1923 and

The 1933 Angels. *Front row (left to right):* Hans Korndor, Hal Stitzel, Marv Gudat, Joe Kies, Win Ballou, Carl Dittmar, Mike Gazella, Bill Cronin, Jigger Statz. *Middle row:* Charles Lightfoot, Tuck Stainback, Jimmie Reese, Jim Oglesby, Gene Lillard, Hugh McMullen, Ivan Crawford, Red Miller. *Back row:* Trainer Frankie Jacobs, Fay Thomas, Emmett Nelson, Cliff Ograin, manager Jack Lelivelt, Oscar Reichow, Truck Hannah, Buck Newsom (courtesy Mark Macrae).

1924. He was also a standout on the baseball team, where his coach was former Angels player Sam Crawford. Thomas began his professional career in 1925 and had trials with the Giants, Indians and Brooklyn, apparently falling just short of major league performance. He was no stranger to the PCL, having pitched at Sacramento and Oakland before joining the Dodgers in 1932. A tall man who seldom smiled, Thomas could intimidate the hitter by his very appearance. He possessed a fast ball that was only a little better than average, but he relied extensively on a slider and fork ball. The fork ball was especially lethal in night games. "If he got that pitch over with two strikes on the hitter, it was an automatic strike out," said Hugh McMullen, his catcher, as he reminisced about that Angels club some 45 years later.

The final member of the pitching triumvirate that was to dominate the PCL in 1933 arrived in Los Angeles on option from the Cubs. He was perhaps the most memorable of the three. Louis N. "Buck" Newsom was a big, loud, extroverted right-hander who had been purchased by Chicago from Little Rock in the Southern Association in 1932. He was optioned to Albany of the International League, where the club was weak and Newsom was not very impressive. Nonetheless, Newsom had great confidence in his ability and was determined to show it to the fans of Los Angeles. The PCL had never seen anybody like Newsom before. A carbon copy of Dizzy Dean, who was coming to prominence at the time, Newsom did not hesitate to tell others how good he was. His best pitch was a high, rising fastball that frequently landed out of the strike zone. But that pitch was very difficult to see in night games, leading to many strikeouts.

The Angels were so pleased with the performance of Gene Lillard at third base that they thought a younger player could replace the incumbent Carl Dittmar at shortstop. The first opportunity was given to Henry Warren, with Dittmar moving into a utility role behind second baseman Jimmie Reese, purchased from the St. Louis Cardinals just as spring training opened. But Warren showed during the training period that he could not play — nor would he ever be able to — and Dittmar was back at shortstop for a while. Then the Angels signed Orv Mohler, another USC football hero, and he was installed as the shortstop with Dittmar going to the bench for opening day.

Mohler was the son of Kid Mohler, the great second baseman of the San Francisco Seals during the first decade of the century, and had just finished a football career as one of the great running backs in Trojan history. He swung a hot bat during the early weeks of the season, but had very limited range in the field.

Other new regulars that spring were left fielder Marv Gudat, sent to Los Angeles as part of the purchase price for Tuck Stainback, who would report to Chicago in 1934, and catcher Hugh McMullen, obtained from Minneapolis in the American Association for pitcher Ed Baecht. Gudat was a line drive hitter with limited power, but he had great speed and a terrific arm. He would be a fixture in the Angels outfield for the next several years. McMullen was a veteran catcher with some major league experience who was regarded as a good handler of pitchers. 1933 was the only year McMullen spent in Los Angeles, but he remembered it fondly. "Newsom was easy to catch because he threw that fastball so much of the time, but he was hard to handle, especially if the hitters were on to him. He wanted to knock everybody down after they got a hit off him. Thomas was the only pitcher in the league who could throw the fork ball even though many others tried it. Ward could have been a great pitcher if he hadn't hurt his arm...."

The Los Angeles writers were impressed with the new Angels players and picked the club to win the pennant, as they so often did. But the Angels did not start well and played sluggishly for the first two months of the season. Much had been expected from Jimmie Reese, but he suffered from kidney problems that kept him out of the lineup from time to time, and then a mild shoulder separation limited his play while he was in action. Dittmar filled in for Reese but had not played much second base before, and with the average play of Mohler at shortstop, the Angels infield defense was shaky at best. Newsom, who had won his first three games and boasted to the world about it, suffered a minor thumb fracture in May. While he didn't miss any starts, he was hit hard and lost six of his next seven decisions after the injury. Leroy Herrmann, returned by the Cubs once again, was the most effective starting pitcher during this early period.

In June the Angels signed infielder Mike Gazella, who had been released by Hollywood, and put him at second base, with Dittmar back at shortstop. Mohler then saw some duty at third base when Lillard missed a few games and then alternated with him for a few weeks. Finally, the uncertainty of the situation was removed when the Angels released Mohler outright on July 10. The Angels record was 56–41, and the club was four games out of first place. But from that point on, Los Angeles was the dominant team in the league. The Angels finally took over first place on August 12 and demolished second-place Sacramento in a series the next week. That eliminated the Senators from pennant contention, but then Hollywood made its big move. The Sheiks won two consecutive series from Portland and Oakland, and then in the last week of August, took seven of nine games at Sacramento to go past the Angels into first place on August 31. Hollywood remained in the lead by one full game through Labor Day, September 4. That set the stage for a crucial series between the clubs beginning on Wednesday, September 6.

The Angels were ready. A double header was scheduled for that evening, and Buck Newsom would be matched against Frank Shellenback in the first game. Long before the game began, all the seats in the grandstands were full. The official attendance was given as 24,695, but there were many standees, and those who were there thought that the crowd could have approached 27,000.

The game was a masterpiece. Both pitchers were at the top of their games, with no score until the seventh inning. Then with a cool dense fog settling in, Hollywood outfielder Cleo Carlyle lost sight of a fly ball and then committed an error on a ground ball, allowing the only two runs of the game to score. It was the seventh shutout of the season for Newsom. More importantly, the clubs were now tied for first place.

The second game could not be played because of the fog, so another doubleheader was scheduled for Thursday. The Sheiks won the first game, 11–8, but once again the second game was postponed as heavy fog set in for the second straight night. For the third straight day, a doubleheader was scheduled, and this time the Angels took both games, 3–1, behind Fay Thomas, and 4–0, behind Win Ballou. All of the runs in the nightcap came on a grand slam home run by Tuck Stainback, putting the Angels in first place by a game. On Saturday, the clubs split yet another doubleheader, and then on Sunday, the Angels finished Hollywood for the season. Newsom bested Shellenback in a repeat of the first game matchup, 9–1, and the Angels took the second game, 4–2, behind Dick Ward. The Angels were now three games ahead. Hollywood never threatened again. Los Angeles clinched the pennant on September 26 with a 9–6 win at San Francisco. The final margin was 6½ games over Portland, which snuck past Hollywood on the season's last day.

After years of mediocre pitching, the Angels enjoyed the finest staff in the league in 1933, and one which ranks among the very best in their history. Newsom had a glorious year, winning 30 games and leading the PCL with 212 strikeouts. As a money pitcher, he couldn't have been much better, winning seven straight decisions from Hollywood, the main competition; he won four of those games during the critical days of September. Newsom won 15 straight games during the last two months of the season, including five shutouts. At the end of the season he was voted the Most Valuable Player in the PCL. The trophy for that honor was proudly displayed in the Buck Newsom exhibit in his home town of Hartsville, South Carolina, 63 years later.

Dick Ward was almost as good, finishing with a 25–9 record and a 3.25 ERA. His 172 strikeouts were second only to Newsom, and enemy batters hit only .232 against him, the lowest in the league. During a stretch in July and August, Ward won 12 of 13 decisions. Fay Thomas finished at 20–14 to give the Angels three 20-game winners. He was not as spectacular as the other two, but finished strong by winning his last seven decisions. From August 1 through the remainder of the season, this trio had a combined record of 32–9. Leroy Herrmann posted a 16–9 mark and surely would have won 20 had he not suffered a hand injury in July that forced him to miss the balance of the year. The "Big Four" pitched an amazing total of 89 complete games between them. Jack Lelivelt did not need many additional pitchers with this group. Win Ballou saw the most action of the others, but it was an off-year for him. He lost his first five decisions as a starter and was then put into the bullpen for much of the season. When Herrmann was incapacitated, "Old Pard" took his spot in the rotation. He was fairly effective down the stretch, but finished at 12–19.

The offense was led by Gene Lillard, who hit 43 home runs to lead the league, and at 19, the youngest player to do so. He drove in 149 runs to go along with his .307 average. Stainback hit .335 in his last year before joining the Cubs and drove in 148 runs. Jim Oglesby was right behind them with 137 RBIs.

Nineteen thirty-three was the season in which Joe DiMaggio came into prominence when he hit safely in 61 consecutive games. This performance stimulated attendance throughout the league, especially in San Francisco, where the Seals had been drawing poorly with a bad team. Overlooked by most was a 44-game streak that Oglesby put together at the same time that DiMaggio was the center of attention. Oglesby's streak ended on July 22, four days before DiMaggio was stopped.

If there was one single event that led to the Angels pennant in 1933, it was the restoration of Carl Dittmar to his familiar position of shortstop in July. The fine fielding veteran was the best defensive player in the league during the last half of the year, repeatedly making spectacular plays to cut off opposing base hits and lending some stability that had previously been missing. It seemed clear that naming Mohler as the shortstop was a mistake. The decision led to a weaker defense and may have disrupted the team chemistry. Hugh McMullen offered his opinion on the subject: "Mohler was not a PCL shortstop. He was given a fair chance, but his fielding was simply not up to standards." Mohler signed with the Missions

Jim Oglesby—He spent four very productive years in Los Angeles and was a member of the 1933-34 champions. His 44-game hitting streak in 1933 is the third longest in PCL history. Oglesby had a trial with the Philadelphia Athletics in 1936 but suffered blood poisoning in spring training and was never the same player after that (courtesy Mark Macrae).

after his release by the Angels, but elected to be placed on the retired list in 1934 and went on to other things. He became a distinguished pilot during World War II and died in a military plane crash after the war at the early age of 40.

The Angels lost their best pitchers as the season closed. The Cubs purchased Ward's contract for 1934 and hoped to bring Newsom to Chicago as well. But the colorful pitcher was now out of options. He had to remain on the Los Angeles roster, and was selected by the St. Louis Browns in the annual player draft. Tuck Stainback was recalled to Chicago at the end of the season while Herrmann, McMullen and Ballou were sent to San Francisco as part of the price the Cubs paid for Augie Galan. Could another championship team be assembled despite these huge losses? Very unlikely, or so it seemed.

The Angels of 1934 dominated the PCL. There was no pennant race that year as the Angels won 137 games and claimed the first and second-half pennant races by a wide margin. They monopolized the offensive and defensive leadership of the league and concluded by defeating a team of PCL All-Stars in a playoff series. This Angels team was the greatest in the history of the Los Angeles franchise and quite likely the best that ever played in the PCL. It ranks as one of the very best minor league teams of all time, along with the 1937 Newark Bears, the 1921 Baltimore Orioles and the 1925 San Francisco Seals.

The club excelled in all phases of the game, finishing first in hitting with a .299 average, first in home runs with 127, and first in fielding while enjoying a pitching staff with seven regulars having an ERA below 3.00. The defense completed 212 double plays, complementing an offense that scored almost six runs a game. Los Angeles was almost unbeatable at Wrigley Field,

Tuck Stainback — A brilliant prospect who hit .335 for the 1933 champions, he was purchased by the Cubs and spent 12 years in the major leagues before returning in 1947 to Los Angeles, where he finished his career (courtesy Mark Macrae).

posting a record of 92–23, including the games when Hollywood was the home team. Rarely has a team destroyed its competition as the Angels did in 1934.

How could a team of that magnitude be put together after suffering such losses? The pitching had needed a major overhaul, while the infield had some question marks with Jimmie Reese ailing for much of 1933 and Carl Dittmar appearing to be on the downside of his career. The loss of Stainback created a big hole to fill in the outfield, and a new catcher was needed.

The club would also be operating under new executive management. Joe Patrick had resigned as president at the end of the 1933 season after serving the Wrigleys in this position since 1921. This was a major loss to both the franchise and the league. Patrick was widely respected throughout all of baseball and was well liked by the players. He was an extremely generous man for his era, with Angels salaries generally better than those of other PCL clubs. Art Weis, a member of the 1926 champions, remembered many years later: "At times when you made an outstanding play, Mr. Patrick would call you to his box seat. He would say, 'Art, go downtown and get yourself a suit of clothes or some shirts, something like that.' He was a wonderful guy."

His successor as president was Dave Fleming, who had been with the Angels as vice-president since 1932, after previous service within the Wrigley organization. Fleming was a strong administrator, and there was no basic change in the club's operations. Like William Wrigley, Fleming was a great advocate of attracting women fans to the ballpark, and he restored the practice of every day being Ladies Day at Wrigley Field early in the year. Fleming was also a firm believer in the advantages of radio broadcasting, and before long, the Angels were airing their home games throughout Southern California.

Given all of their talent needs, the Angels moved quickly to rebuild the team. During the winter meetings, the Cubs sent outfielder Frank Demaree and Jim Mosolf along with left-handed pitcher Roy Henshaw as payment for Dick Ward, and the Angels then dispatched Mosolf to the Kansas City Blues for pitcher Lou Garland. Two other pitchers were acquired from the International League when catcher Bill Cronin was sent to Jersey City for pitcher Mike Meola and pitcher Hal Stitzel went to Albany in exchange for J. Millard "Whitey" Campbell.

It appeared doubtful that the newcomers would restore Los Angeles to the championship level, for none was especially impressive in 1933. Only Fay Thomas was returning from the 1933 staff, and the apparent lack of pitching depth caused many observers to question whether the Angels could repeat as champions.

As spring training wore on, some of the important issues began to resolve themselves. Demaree took over Stainback's right field position and showed in the exhibition games that he would be more than an adequate replacement. Concerns that Jigger Statz might be slowing up were also put to rest. He seemed better than ever in the outfield and appeared to have recaptured his speed after a down year for him on the basepaths in 1933. Reese's health problems had disappeared over the winter, and the Angels got the catcher they needed when the Cubs returned Gilly Campbell. And the new pitchers performed better than anyone had anticipated.

During the early 1930s there was great controversy over the baseballs used in the major leagues and the high minors. After the offensive explosion of 1930s, most leagues adopted a ball with higher seams than before, and batting averages dropped considerably. But there was no universal standard for the ball, and there was notable difference between the various leagues. Finally, during the winter of 1933–34, the major leagues agreed to use identical baseballs produced within certain parameters, and the minor leagues followed suit. The PCL baseballs of 1933 may have been more resilient than the new standardized baseball of 1934, for offensive production throughout the league was significantly reduced. The league batting average dropped from .298 to .280, and the number of home runs declined by 28 percent.

The Angels opened the season in fine fashion, blasting Portland, 12–2, at Wrigley Field. The early schedule favored Los Angeles in 1934 with the club playing four straight weeks at their home grounds, and the Angels took full advantage. They won the Portland series, five games to two, then lost only one game in each of the next three series. When they went on the road for the first time, their record was 23–5 and they were in first place by six games. The pitchers had performed far above expectations, with the starter going the distance in all but two of the games. The infield was terrific, with 23 double plays in the first 23 games. Clearly, this Angels team was something special. After two weeks on the road, the team had improved to 32–10 on May 15, and there was a loud cry from the other seven clubs to reinstate the split season. By May 27 the Angels record was 44–12, and Los Angeles was 10 games in front.

When the Angels lead increased to 12 games early in June, the league decided to go to the split season. Attendance had fallen behind the pace of 1933, and once again the clubs were concerned about cash flow. Los Angeles continued to devastate the league by winning 20 of the next 24 games to increase the lead to 18½ games at the end of the first half on June 24. The Angels record was 66–18 at that point.

The second half began as if there might be a real pennant race. The Angels won six of their first seven games at Portland, then lost their first series in over a year playing in Seattle. They then played poorly when they returned to Wrigley Field for the only time all year, against Hollywood and Portland. At the end of July, the club was in third place at 23–13. Seattle and Hollywood took turns in the lead spot during the first two weeks of August, but then the Angels reasserted themselves. They took six of seven from the Missions in San Francisco, and for the rest of the year the Angels played at a .774 pace. They ended the season 12 games ahead of second-place Hollywood and clinched the second half race with two weeks to go in the season.

Since there would be no playoff, what with the Angels winning both halves of the season, the league arranged a series with the PCL All-Stars, selected by the fans. All games would be played at Wrigley Field, beginning on October 3. The All-Stars featured Smead Jolley of Hollywood, Oscar Eckhardt and Babe Dahlgren of the Missions, and Mike Hunt of Seattle, with a pitching staff that included Leroy Herrmann and Sam Gibson of San Francisco and Herman Pillette of Seattle. Perhaps the best player in the league that year, Joe DiMaggio of San Francisco, did not play because of injury.

The Angels lined up the same way they had for virtually every game during the season:

Jigger Statz	CF
Jimmie Reese	2B
Marv Gudat	LF
Frank Demaree	RF
Jim Oglesby	1B
Gilly Campbell	C
Gene Lillard	3B
Carl Dittmar	SS

The 1934 Angels. *Front row (left to right):* Mike Gazella, Roy Henshaw, Ivan Crawford, clubhouse man (unknown), Bobby Mattick, Jigger Statz. *Middle row:* Walt Goebel, Gilly Campbell, Marv Gudat, Jimmie Reese, Gene Lillard, Carl Dittmar, Mike Meola, coach Truck Hannah. *Back row:* Trainer Frankie Jacobs, Kenny Richardson, Whitey Campbell, Emmett Nelson, Art McDougall, Dick Ward, Fay Thomas, Lou Garland, Jim Oglesby, Frank Demaree, Oscar Reichow (courtesy Mark Macrae).

This was a far more impressive lineup than the All-Stars, at least in 1934.

The Angels showed their class by defeating the All-Stars, 4 games to 2. Los Angeles won the first game, 6–4, but then the All-Stars won the next two games, 5–2 and 9–7. In the fourth game the All-Stars held a 4–0 lead in the fourth inning, when Carl Dittmar hit a three-run homer. That changed the momentum of the series. The Angels won that game, 13–7, and followed up with a 3–0 victory behind Fay Thomas to take the lead in the series. They then won the deciding game, 4–3, on a Dittmar home run in the last of the ninth, an appropriate climax to a year in which the Angels consistently came from behind in the late innings to overwhelm the opposition.

There were many heroes on the ballclub. Frank Demaree had the most spectacular season, one of the very best in PCL history, and was selected as Most Valuable Player of the league. He took full advantage of the early start at Wrigley Field, and after five weeks was hitting .471 with 44 RBIs. He did not fall off much from that torrid pace and completed the season as the league leader in average, RBIs, runs scored, hits, home runs and total bases. The line on Demaree looked like this:

G	AB	R	H	2B	3B	HR	RBI	TB	AVG.
186	702	190	269	51	4	45	173	463	.383

The runs scored and total bases for Demaree represent all-time Angels club records for one season, and the 45 home runs broke Gene Lillard's record set the previous year. Demaree found Wrigley Field much to his liking as he hit 36 of his home runs there. But his record lasted only one year; Lillard came back from a year filled with injuries to hit 56 home runs in 1935.

It was an incredible year for Demaree, who had made his first appearance in the PCL with Sacramento in 1930. After two years there, he was purchased by the Cubs and played as a regular with Chicago in 1932 and 1933. But after the Cubs acquired Chuck Klein for the 1934 season, Demaree was the odd man out and was shipped to Los Angeles. He developed into a complete player in Wrigley Field that year, becoming much more aggressive at the plate and demonstrating excellent power. Demaree played only that one season in Los Angeles, rejoining the Cubs in 1935. He remained in the National League for 10 years, becoming a fine,

Frank Demaree — The Most Valuable Player in the PCL in 1934, he earned admission to the Pacific Coast League Hall of Fame with that incredible season (courtesy Mark Macrae).

dependable outfielder for the Cubs and later the New York Giants, and a consistent hitter as well, hitting .350 in his best year.

Fay Thomas finished fourth in the MVP voting. His 28–4 record set the all-time PCL standard, and he also led the league in strikeouts with 204. Thomas won his first 15 decisions of 1934 and finished one short of the PCL record of 16, set by Frank Browning of San Francisco in 1909. But in one of his few bad outings of the year, Thomas was hit hard by Seattle and lost, 12–9, on July 6. That stopped his two-year streak of 22 straight, for he had won

Lou Garland (left) and Fay Thomas — These two pitchers combined to win 49 games, as each enjoyed the greatest season of his career (courtesy Mark Macrae).

his last seven decisions of 1933. Thomas defeated every team in the league at least once, with his favorite victim the Missions, winning eight straight decisions from them. His great year led to another major league opportunity in 1935, this time with the St. Louis Browns, who selected Thomas as the first player in what is now known as the Rule 5 draft. But that club was probably the poorest of all situations for him. The Browns were terrible and played in Sportsman's Park, which had the worst infield in the major leagues. The Thomas fork ball produced many ground ball outs in Los Angeles, but in St. Louis those grounders skipped through on the rock-hard surface at Sportsman's Park. Not surprisingly, Thomas struggled to a 7–15 mark. In 1936 he would be back in the PCL to stay.

Thomas was not the only Angels pitcher to enjoy a career year. The club had two other 20-game winners in Mike Meola, who went 20–5, and Lou Garland, who finished 21–8; Whitey Campbell just missed at 19–15. Campbell was a workhorse, starting and relieving, and seeing action in 48 games with 243 innings pitched. He was 13–6 during the first half of the season, but the heavy workload wore him down as the season progressed, and he was only 6–9 during the second half. Garland's performance was a complete surprise as he had endured a very mediocre year at St. Paul and Kansas City in 1933 with a 9–10 record. But he was brilliant for the Angels after a slow start and won 12 straight decisions in June and July. Meola saw limited action during the early weeks of the season, but improved dramatically as the year wore on, and by season's end he might have been the club's best pitcher.

With these four stalwarts handling most of the work, opportunities for the other members of the staff were somewhat limited, but they performed well when called upon. Lefty Roy Henshaw was in only his second year of professional baseball; he joined the Angels in the spring and did well as a spot starter and reliever, winning 13 games. Emmett Nelson and Dick Ward saw limited action but were effective when used. Nelson had arm trouble early in the season but performed well in the second half with a 14–5 record. Ward had been a dominant pitcher for the Angels in 1933, and the Cubs were certain that he would become a major league star. But there were signs that he had some arm problems during the spring, and he was returned to Los Angeles in May. Although he posted a satisfactory 13–4 mark, he had lost much of the zip from his fastball. Ward never did make the grade with the Cubs and was included in a trade with St. Louis that brought Tex Carleton to the Cubs in November 1934. It is likely that he was the victim of overwork in 1933, when he pitched 285 innings at the young age of 24.

The key factor in the improved Angels defense in 1934 was a healthy Jimmie Reese. He had missed almost one-third of the 1933 season, but he was in the lineup almost every day in 1934. The double play combination of Reese and Carl Dittmar may have been the best in Angels history, although both were past their prime years. They were both experienced and intelligent players who knew just where to play the hitters. Many of the Thomas sinkers resulted in ground balls that led to a number of the 212 Angels double plays.

How good were the 1934 Angels? The club was certainly comparable to the 1921 Orioles and the 1937 Bears. Both of those clubs won their pennants by 20 games or more and featured players who went on to great success in the major leagues. The Orioles stars were Jack Bentley, Lefty Grove, Max Bishop and Joe Boley. The latter three men formed the nucleus of the great Philadelphia Athletic teams of 1929–31. The Orioles won 119 games and finished 20 games ahead of Rochester, but lost to Louisville of the American Association in the Junior World Series. The Bears won the International League pennant by 25½ games and then defeated Columbus in the Junior World Series, four games to three after losing the first three games. All of their 17 regular players, with the exception of pitcher Jack Fallon, played in the major leagues, and several were stars—including first baseman George McQuinn, second baseman Joe Gordon and outfielder Charlie Keller.

The Angels players did not have major league records similar to the star players on those two clubs, but of their 16 regulars, all except Carl Dittmar appeared in the major leagues. Frank Demaree and Jigger Statz had good careers, but others did not receive a real opportunity. Gene Lillard was not fast and could not beat out Stan Hack, who was one of the best third basemen of all time. Ultimately, the Cubs converted Lillard into a pitcher because of his great arm, but he was not effective in the major leagues. Lillard regretted the change, calling it "the worst mistake I ever made in baseball." Jim Oglesby had a chance to win the first base job with the Philadelphia Athletics in 1936, but he developed a case of blood poisoning during the spring and was never the same player again. Dick Ward's career was shortened by arm trouble,

Jigger Statz in an advertisement for Wheaties, 1935 (courtesy Dick Dobbins).

while Fay Thomas found himself in the wrong ballpark with the Browns. Many of the Angels were experienced veterans, 30 years of age or more, and players of that type simply did not receive many major league chances during the 1930s.

The Angels dominated their league early, as did the Bears and Orioles. Both the Angels and the Bears were ten games in front before 60 games were played. They both played in hitter-friendly parks where they crushed the opposition. The Bears and Orioles had seven regulars who hit .300 or better; the Angels had six. All three clubs scored just under six runs a game. The Angels had three 20-game winners and threw 20 shutouts in total. The Orioles had three 20-game winners and threw 12 shutouts; the Bears had two great pitchers in Joe Beggs, at 21–4, and Atley Donald, at 19–2, and pitched 15 shutouts. But neither the Bears nor the Orioles had a hitter who approached Demaree's 45 home runs.

As the years have gone by, these three clubs have developed a legend of their own; each has its proponents. The PCL was isolated from the rest of the nation in the days before World War II, and not many Eastern writers or fans had the opportunity to watch PCL games. For this reason, the Angels might not have received the recognition they deserved. They won more games than any club in history while playing in a top flight minor league. It is difficult to imagine how any other team could have been any better.

12

The Streak Is Broken and the Stars Leave Town

All good things come to an end, and the Angels' dominance of the PCL ran its course in 1935. After winning two pennants in a row, Los Angeles was unable to capture a third when the club was defeated by San Francisco in a post-season playoff. The Angels had won the first half of a split season, but finished a poor fourth to the improved Seals during the second half of what was to be the last split season in the PCL while the Angels were part of the league. In 1936 the Coast League adopted the Shaughnessy playoff system, which had been so successful in sustaining fan interest in the International League and American Association since 1933.

Although there was great respect throughout baseball for the fine performance of the Angels in 1934, in reality the team proved harmful to the financial well-being of the PCL. League attendance had fallen by 230,000 from the previous season, and five of the clubs failed to draw 100,000 spectators. Angels attendance was down by 92,000, with the club attracting a mere 129,672 paying customers to its games, the lowest total since 1918. Fans would not come out when there was no real pennant race.

Clubs could simply not survive without cutting expenses, given the abysmal revenues of the past three years, and at the January meetings the league reduced the team rosters from 20 veteran players to 16. Of equal importance was the development of working agreements with major league clubs. These were not the formal agreements of today, but instead personal agreements between the owners of the clubs, and they usually centered around the acquisition of a specific player. For instance, when Brooklyn purchased the contract of Frenchy Bordagaray from Sacramento, the Dodgers entered into a limited agreement with the Senators to provide several players for the 1935 season. Similar agreements took place between the Yankees and Oakland, the Boston Braves and Seattle, and the Detroit Tigers and Portland. In seasons past the Angels were the only PCL club that could consistently depend upon help from a major league club, but that would no longer be true. The era of major league farm systems had begun in earnest after the great success of the St. Louis Cardinals during the previous ten years.

Another important change at the meetings was the abandonment of the weeklong series that had been traditional in the Coast League. In its place, teams would play two shorter sets each week. More variety in the schedule might bring out more fans, the owners thought.

And the number of scheduled games was reduced to 174, the fewest number in the league since the wartime season of 1918.

The Angels had most of their 1934 team returning when the team assembled at Santa Monica for spring training, with Frank Demaree and Gilly Campbell the only missing regulars. There was an abundance of young players on hand for the first time in many years. During the 1933 and 1934 seasons, the club had begun to sign local players fresh from high school and the sandlots, and entered into a working agreement with Ponca City of the Class C Western Association as a farm team to develop the talent. Now in 1935, several of these youngsters were attending their first Angels camp — infielders Kenny Richardson, Glen "Rip" Russell, Scott Drysdale and Steve Mesner, outfielders Lynn South and Joe Mene, and pitchers Ed Carnett, Ralph Buxton and Newt Kimball. Of this group, Mesner was by far the most impressive. A native of Los Angeles and a graduate of Jacob Riis High School, the stocky infielder was only 17 years old but was extremely strong. Despite his youth, Mesner showed that he was ready to face PCL pitching. The only question was where to play him. He was not particularly fast, and his best position was third base, where Gene Lillard was firmly entrenched. In spite of that uncertainty, Mesner easily made the club that spring along with Buxton and Kimball, and the others were sent out for more seasoning.

The Angels appeared to have a satisfactory replacement for Demaree in Cleo Carlyle, a former member of the Hollywood Sheiks, who was purchased from Newark during the winter. Catching was a bit unsettled, as Art Veltman arrived from Pittsburgh to take over the duties so ably performed by Campbell in 1934. He had played briefly with the Pirates in 1934 after a stellar season in Oakland in 1933, and was expected to be a capable replacement. But Veltman began to complain of mysterious knee problems towards the end of spring training, and by the second week of the season he could not catch at all. The problem was later diagnosed as severe arthritis. Veltman went on the disabled list and appeared in only five games all season. The Cubs rushed Walt Goebel to Los Angeles, but he, too, was afflicted by various injuries, leaving only rookie Glyn Gibson to handle the catching duties. When Goebel returned to action, he was not nearly as good catching every day as he had been as a substitute the prior year. The catching problem plagued the Angels all year and was a major contributor to their demise as champions.

The pitching staff did not appear as strong as in 1934, with Fay Thomas, Roy Henshaw and Dick Ward now wearing major league uniforms, but both Ralph Buxton and Newt Kimball appeared ready to take up some of the slack. The arm problems that had limited Emmett Nelson's work in 1934 were a thing of the past, and he joined returnees Mike Meola, Lou Garland and Whitey Campbell as the starters in Lelivelt's rotation

For the first time a PCL season opened on a Saturday. With Nelson on the mound, and 18,000 fans in attendance, the Angels defeated the Sheiks, 10–8. The club began 1935 very auspiciously with eight straight wins, but then slumped during a two-week home-and-home series with the Seals and Missions. The Angels record was a mediocre 16–13 on May 7, the day that Carl Dittmar severely sprained his ankle. The injury opened the door for Steve Mesner, who replaced him in the lineup. For the next four weeks, the Angels terrorized the league, winning 25 of the 30 games played, including a winning streak of 11 straight, and Mesner seemed to be the catalyst. He won several games with timely hitting and also turned in many sparkling plays in the field. The Angels took the lead on May 31 and improved their record to 41–18 on June 2. At this point the league directors decided to split the season once again, fearing a repeat of the Angels runaway of 1934.

Gene Lillard had not enjoyed a good season in 1934 because of a growth on his hand that inhibited his swing. But surgery in the off-season cured the problem, and the youngster started the new season with a furious rush. He hit eight home runs in six consecutive games beginning on April 19, including three in a doubleheader against Hollywood. Several of his homers were rated among the longest ever hit at Wrigley Field, sailing well over the houses across the street from the park. Lillard batted .428 for the month of April and hit his 20th home run on May 14, one of the earliest dates in league history for the reaching of such a milestone. Jim Oglesby was also enjoying a hot spring, and together they gave the Angels an imposing attack.

Emmett Nelson became the ace of the pitching staff during the first half, supplemented by a fine performance by Glen Gabler, who was enjoying his best season in the PCL. Gabler had been signed by the Angels in 1928 as a hard-throwing right-hander. But he injured his arm the next season and drifted to several PCL teams over the next few years before being released by Oakland at the end of 1934. The Angels signed him for use in relief, where he was very effective, winning four straight decisions. That earned him a starting assignment against Sacramento in the second game of the Memorial Day double header, and Gabler was brilliant, shutting out the Senators, 1–0. For the rest of the season he was used both in relief roles and as an occasional starter, and was effective in both duties. Nelson won three games during the first week of the season and was the most dependable pitcher before his contract was sold to Cincinnati on June 19.

The Angels finished the first half of the season with a five-game lead over San Francisco at 46–25. But the team had played most of its games at home, where Los Angeles enjoyed a 32–12 record. And Lillard and Oglesby were far more effective in Wrigley Field than they were on the road. The beginning of the second half saw the club embark on a 21-game road trip, including its first journey to the Pacific Northwest, where Angels teams traditionally did not play well. Los Angeles managed a 12–9 mark during this period, but the club suddenly appeared to be mortal. Then the Missions won five of seven at Wrigley, and the defending champions had become a .500 club. They would not move far beyond that mark for the rest of the year.

The Angels made several false starts through late July and early August, but could never move above third place. Both San Francisco and the Missions were playing much better during the second half, and each of these clubs had the better of it when they played Los Angeles. If the Angels were to jump back into the pennant race, they would have to do it when they met the Missions in a nine-game series beginning September 5. The Angels won the first four games of the series to go over .500, but then lost four of the remaining five and fell to fifth place. The club limped through the last two weeks of the season, as the Seals pulled away to finish 10½ games ahead of the Angels, who were only two games ahead of the fifth-place Oakland Oaks.

Angels pitching was unreliable during the second half of the season. The loss of Nelson put a real burden on the other starters, and although Mike Meola and Lou Garland enjoyed outstanding years, the rest of the staff was erratic. The club received Keith Frazier from Cincinnati as partial payment for Nelson, but his performance was not up to PCL standards. In 20 games his record was 1–7 with a horrendous 6.08 ERA, and he was frequently knocked out of the box early, throwing an additional burden onto the relievers. Newt Kimball received many starts, most of which he lost as his record fell to 1–9, before he won seven of his last eight decisions over the last six weeks. Campbell enjoyed a fine first half, but was only 6–9 during the last half and was hardly used in September. Gabler tried to pick up where the others had faltered, but he tired badly and won only one game after August 15. Meola and

Garland were steady performers throughout the season, and both enjoyed fine years. Meola finished 18–8 and led the PCL with a 3.00 ERA, while Garland was officially 19–11 in spite of missing almost three weeks with arm trouble. In actuality, he may have been a 20-game winner, for research indicates that a 7–5 victory over San Francisco should have been credited to Garland instead of Ralph Buxton, who was given the win.

The Angels were not in the same class as the Seals by season's end, and they demonstrated it by losing the post-season playoff series, four games to two. The series opened at Seals Stadium where Sam Gibson, the best pitcher in the PCL that year, blanked the Angels, 5–0, in the first game, and a Joe DiMaggio home run beat Gabler, 7–5, in the second contest. The Angels salvaged Game Three, 4–3, behind Garland, and returned home to Wrigley Field with hopes of taking three straight. They won a slugfest, 10–7, to even the series, but in a final doubleheader, the Seals were victorious behind the pitching of ex–Angels Win Ballou and Roy Joiner, beating Meola, 6–3, and Garland, 8–3.

The weakness in the Angels catching department and a deficiency in the infield defense brought Los Angeles back to the rest of the league. The loss of Carl Dittmar at shortstop hindered the team greatly. Although he was definitely past his prime at age 34, he still covered much more ground than Steve Mesner, who was not a natural shortstop. But Lelivelt could not keep his bat out of the lineup. Mesner hit .331 with 99 runs batted in and saw some service at third base, where he was a much better fielder. Reese was also a step slower than he had been during the pennant winning years.

Oglesby and Lillard were the Angels heroes in 1935, each enjoying his finest year in Los Angeles. Lillard established the all-time Angels home run record with 56 four-baggers. This was the third year in a row that a new club standard had been set; Lillard's 43 in 1933 was eclipsed by Demaree's 45 in 1934. The new record is destined to remain for all time, although it is shared with Steve Bilko, who hit 56 in the last year of the club's existence. Lillard hit .361 to go along with this extreme power, and he reduced the number of his strikeouts considerably. He was sold to the Cubs in September.

Oglesby hit .350 with 24 home runs, all but one of which was hit at Wrigley Field. He and Lillard hit 71 of the 101 Angels home runs at Wrigley Field, including games when Hollywood was the home team. A fine fielder, Oglesby was the leading first baseman in the PCL that year and was drafted by the Athletics for the 1936 season. Sadly, a spring training injury that developed into a case of blood poisoning ruined his chances with Philadelphia, and he never received another opportunity to play in the major leagues.

Although the 1935 season was disappointing for Angels fans, there was a strong nucleus of young players on the horizon to provide hope for a new Angels dynasty. Yet, there were many spots that would need to be filled on this veteran team before it could again be a serious contender. The next two years would be a transition period for Los Angeles, one in which the club would not be a major factor in the pennant race.

There were many changes to the Angels and the PCL during the winter of 1935-36. For the first time since 1908, the club had the city of Los Angeles to itself. On February 1, 1936, Bill Lane announced that he was moving the Hollywood franchise to San Diego for the 1936 season, giving that city its first representation in the PCL. The Sheiks had fallen on difficult days during their last two years in Los Angeles, both on the field and at the gate, and relations with the Angels, which were never more than cool, deteriorated badly. When Dave Fleming presented Hollywood with a proposed rent increase to $10,000 for 1936, it represented the last straw for Lane. He began searching for another city for his club — Long Beach was considered a strong possibility, but nothing ever came of it — until finally the city of San Diego presented him with an enticing offer. City officials promised a ballpark to be ready by the opening of the season, with a nominal rent and total control of the concessions. Lane jumped at the chance to move to a place where he would have the entire market to himself, and a profitable move it would be.

As usual, the Angels were very active in the player markets during the off-season. Fay Thomas, who had not enjoyed a successful year with the Browns in 1935, was anxious to return to Los Angeles. The Angels were eager to have him back as well, and they sent Mike Meola to St. Louis in exchange for his contract. The other 19-game winner from 1935, Lou Garland, was sold to Toledo of the American Association for cash. There were many who expressed bewilderment over this deal, but the Angels got rid of him just in time, it seems. Garland had a very poor season in Ohio in 1936, winning but four games, and never again had the success he enjoyed in Los Angeles.

So now, the Angels had only Thomas and Whitey Campbell left from the dominant staff of 1934. They would be starters along with Hugh Casey, a young pitcher up from Ponca City, and Ralph Buxton and Newt Kimball, who had looked good in September. Glen Gabler was back as a spot starter who would also handle the bulk of the relief duties. But this was not enough pitching for a contender, and manager Jack Lelivelt knew it. It was hoped that the Cubs would send additional talent before the season began.

The promotion of Jim Oglesby to the major leagues left a major hole at first base, so the Angels acquired Don Hurst from Columbus of the American Association to replace him. Hurst had spent seven years as the Philadelphia Phillies' first baseman and had enjoyed some fine years, hitting well over .300 and leading the National League in runs batted in during the season of 1932. But he was helped immensely by playing his home games in Baker Bowl, a notorious hitting paradise, and was not really as good a hitter as his numbers indicated him to be. He was unhappy to be back in the minor leagues and tended not to hustle when he went into a batting slump. This caused much friction with Lelivelt throughout the year. Although Hurst hit 19 home runs to lead the Angels, he was not really an asset, and Lelivelt frequently gave rookie Glen "Rip" Russell playing time at first base.

The rest of the infield seemed better defensively than in 1935. Steve Mesner was moved to third base to replace Lillard, and this proved to be a wise move. Mesner was more effective at third, and the position change also gave 20-year-old Bobby Mattick the opportunity to play shortstop. He possessed a fine throwing arm, covered a lot of ground and worked well with Jimmy Reese, who returned at second. Carl Dittmar was still around, relegated to a utility role once again.

The only new addition to the outfield was veteran Wes Schulmerich, who was purchased from Toronto in the International League, where he had played after major league service with the Braves and Phillies. He began the season as the regular right fielder, with Jigger Statz in center field as usual, and Cleo Carlyle moving to left, forcing Marv Gudat to the bench. But Schul-

\Marv Gudat — A key member of the championship teams of 1933–34, he never hit less than .302 during his six years in Los Angeles (courtesy Dick Dobbins).

Carl Dittmar (left) and Truck Hannah, spring training, 1936 (courtesy Helen Hannah Campbell).

merich was now 35 and well past his prime years. Eventually, Carlyle moved back to right field, and Gudat shared time with Schulmerich in left.

The catching situation seemed improved with the purchase of John Bottarini from Sacramento. He had been with Seattle previously and had been in the league since 1933. Although Bottarini was a good hitter, his work behind the plate was average at best. Art Veltman was back in good health and was expected to share the catching duties.

In spite of several obvious question marks, the Angels were selected as the pre-season favorite to win the championship. In retrospect, they appear to have been chosen on reputation more than anything else. Los Angeles was now an old team; Statz was 38, and Reese was 35, and the only regulars under 30 were Mattick and Mesner. The team speed that was so prominent in 1933–34 was a thing of the past, with the exception of Statz, who would lead the PCL in stolen bases for the second straight year. The Angels were never really in pennant contention, finishing fifth in one of the tightest races in PCL history. Although the club was never more than two games over .500, it finished only 8½ games behind the champion Portland Beavers, who finished 1½ games ahead of Oakland and San Diego.

The Angels began the season with a plethora of injuries. Thomas was the opening day pitcher, and although he received credit for a 7–5 win over San Diego, he was hit in his pitching hand by a line drive and was forced out of action for six weeks. Three days later Hugh Casey suffered an injury to his shoulder, and his promising career with the Angels came to a halt. These injuries placed a heavy burden on the pitchers who remained healthy. Catcher Art Veltman then developed a sore arm that rendered him useless behind the plate and led to his subsequent release. The back problems that plagued Jimmie Reese in 1935 were still with him, causing him to miss a number of games and slowing him down while he was able to play. And Bobby Mattick suffered a concussion when he was hit by a foul ball while waiting his turn at bat, an injury that sidelined him until July.

The combination of these injuries led to the worst Angels start since 1927. By April 21, Los Angeles was in last place with a 7–15 mark, and the club remained there for a month. The pitching was completely inadequate after the injury to Thomas. Ralph Buxton, Whitey Campbell and Ed Carnett each suffered losses in their first three starts, and Newt Kimball won only one game in April. The club looked everywhere for reinforcements. Young Bob Joyce was acquired on option from the Yankees, left-hander Ray Prim was purchased from Albany of the International League, and Dutch Lieber was acquired from the Athletics. The Angels traded Mesner to the Chicago White Sox for 1937 delivery, and in exchange received Jack Salveson on option. Buxton, Carnett and Kimball were sent out for more experience, Whitey Campbell was released to San Francisco, Joe Berry was brought up from Ponca City and the club had an entirely new pitching staff.

The moves turned the club around. By the middle of June, Los Angeles was only six games out of first place, although still deep in the second division. The Angels reached the .500 mark on July 5, and there was serious talk among the veterans that they could actually win. Salveson became the ace of the staff. After losing his first two decisions, he began winning with regularity and prevented the club from suffering lengthy losing streaks. Prim won his first five games, as did Thomas after he returned from his injury.

When the club was playing so badly, there were rumors that the relationship between Lelivelt and president Dave Fleming was deteriorating. Finally, during the first week of June, Fleming temporarily relieved the manager of his duties and sent him to the East to obtain player help. "I promised the city of Los Angeles a contender this year, and Jack is going East to get what we need to turn this club into a winning combination," Fleming

Bobby Mattick—He was the most promising shortstop in the league at the time he was hit in the head by a foul ball in June 1936. The injury caused him to have double vision at times; this bothered him for the rest of his life (courtesy Helen Hannah Campbell).

said. Coach Truck Hannah was placed in charge while Lelivelt was away. The Angels played their best ball of the year during Lelivelt's absence, and although he resumed control upon his return, relations with Fleming were obviously strained for the remainder of the year.

The Angels remained at or near the .500 level for the balance of July and August, but were never able to move above fourth place. It seemed that each time the club was ready to make its move it would stumble. The closest the Angels came to the lead was five games on August 30 when they were one game over .500, but the Angels lost six of nine games in Portland the following week to end their pennant aspirations. Two games behind the Missions when the last week of the season began, the Angels managed to tie the Reds for fifth place on the last day of the year.

As usual, the Angels were an offensive force, leading the PCL with a .292 average, but they did not possess the power that was so much in evidence during the championship years. They hit only 78 home runs, 56 of them in friendly Wrigley Field. Carlyle led in average at .339, in his last really good season in the PCL. Mesner was spectacular, hitting .326 with 132 RBIs, and Statz hit .322 while leading the league in runs scored and stolen bases. Hurst had 19 homers to lead in that department, all but three of them at home.

Jack Salveson was without a doubt the Most Valuable Angel in 1936. He earned a return to the major leagues after he posted a 21–7 record with a 2.76 ERA. It was generally conceded that George Caster of the champion Beavers was the best pitcher in the PCL that year, but Salveson was a close second. Included in his victories was a 12-game personal winning streak that kept the club afloat in July and August. Without Salveson the Angels would have been a sorry lot, indeed.

Thomas and Prim enjoyed fine seasons, and Dutch Lieber pitched well during the middle of the season to give the Angels a good starting staff. Joe Berry showed promise after being recalled from Ponca City. He finished 7–7 with several well pitched games. Bob Joyce was effective early, but lost 12 of his last 13 decisions and was returned to the Yankees at the end of the season.

One of the more startling events of the season was the decline in attendance suffered by the Angels. It was expected that with the city to themselves the Angels would attract the fans who had previously attended Hollywood games. But that did not happen. The Angels saw their crowds decline from 153,101 in 1935 to 128,565. This was a smaller number than had attended Sheiks games the previous year! The poor beginning of the season doomed Angels attendance, but the club was not especially interesting either. An aging club that is not winning finds it difficult to attract fans.

At the close of the season, Jack Lelivelt submitted his resignation. He was very discreet in his comments, praising the Angels management and remembering the fond years he spent in Los Angeles. He said he simply needed a change. But everyone knew that there was more to his decision than he would admit. Lelivelt was the most successful manager that the Angels ever had. He posted a record of 801–599, for a .572 winning percentage, and never had a losing season while winning two pennants in 7½ years as the boss. He scouted during the 1937 season but would then resurface in the PCL at Seattle, winning pennants in 1939 and 1940 before his untimely death in January 1941.

13

Truck Hannah Takes the Helm

Dave Fleming did not wait very long before naming a successor to Jack Lelivelt, and his choice was an obvious one. Long time Angels catcher and coach, J. Harrison "Truck" Hannah, was appointed within a day of Lelivelt's resignation. Hannah had been one of the greatest catchers in PCL history and had spent 20 years in the league before assuming the manager's position. He had worn an Angels uniform since 1926 and was dearly beloved by fans and players alike. A big man who conveyed a gruff demeanor, Hannah had acquired a reputation as a good teacher of young players and had shown good managerial abilities when he filled in for Lelivelt during Jack's enforced absence in 1936.

Lelivelt and Fleming had frequently clashed over player personnel issues, but Fleming promised such disputes would not be the case with Hannah. Truck was to be given a free hand in player matters, both in the acquisition of talent and in deciding who would play. In his first press conference, he expressed a need for more power in the lineup and hoped to remedy that deficiency at the winter meetings.

Hannah seemed as good as his word. The Angels purchased outfielder Murray "Red" Howell from Tulsa and infielder Bill McWilliams from St. Paul and received catcher Bob Collins from the Cubs in exchange for pitcher Newt Kimball. Of the three additions, Collins would have the most long term value. The Angels had not had a good catcher since Gilly Campbell in 1934, and Collins put an end to that problem for the next several years. But Howell and McWilliams did not last, in spite of their good credentials. They both earned starting positions during the spring, and McWilliams, especially, emerged as a hot hitter during April and May. But both players slumped badly and were released to the Southern Association in June. Howell would have good years again, most notably with Baltimore of the International League in 1939-40, but none of those seasons would be in Los Angeles.

Other player activity during the off-season saw Wes Schulmerich depart for Portland in exchange for utility player Goldy Holt, pitchers Red Evans and Earl Overman arriving from the White Sox and Birmingham, respectively, and second baseman Jimmie Reese being traded to San Diego for pitcher Archie Campbell. That latter trade was a disaster. Reese was now 35 years old, was no longer the agile fielder that he had been, and the Angels thought it was time for him to move on. Campbell had enjoyed some good years at Hollywood, but he was utterly ineffective in Los Angeles, winning but one game all year and was seldom used after July. Meanwhile, Reese still had two more good years left, and the Angels had a huge hole to fill at second base. No less than six players were tried, and most were found to be less than satisfactory. The club started the season with Dick Atwell, a former player for the House of David, but he lasted only a week before it became obvious that he could not do the job. Carl Dittmar stepped in and later, Goldy Holt, Bill McWilliams, Kenny Richardson and Rip Russell were all used with varying degrees of success. The club played better when Dittmar played at second, but Carl was nearing the end of his career and suffered from chronic back problems that limited his appearances.

But with the change in managers and the presence of all of the new players, along with important changes in the front office, the season of 1937 was almost identical to 1936 as far as win-loss results were concerned. Once again Los Angeles finished in fifth place, this time 12 games behind the Sacramento Solons, who were now operating under the umbrella of the St. Louis Cardinals and would remain a very formidable team over the next several years. The Angels were the sole occupant of fifth place and won two more games than they had in 1936.

There was another close pennant race in 1937, but the Angels were not a part of it. Sacramento, San Francisco and San Diego battled for first place before the Solons took a firm hold in July and then led for the rest of the season, finishing four games ahead of the Seals. Los Angeles was never higher than third place, and that occurred for only a matter of days. The Angels alternated between fourth and fifth place for most of the year and finally fell out of the first division on the last day of the season, finishing one game behind Portland. After May 15, the Angels were never closer than eight games from first place.

Once again, pitching was a question when the season began. Truck Hannah could count on Fay Thomas and Ray Prim to head the rotation, but beyond those two, there was much uncertainty. Earl Overman and Red Evans were given starting assignments, along with Newt Kimball, who had been returned by Chicago. Joe Berry and Dutch Lieber were available for spot starting duty, while Campbell was expected to absorb the bulk of the relief work. Don Hurst was back at first base with Bobby Mattick at shortstop. The outfield saw Jigger Statz, who was now a player-coach, flanked by Howell and Marv Gudat.

The pitching lacked depth from the beginning in 1937, and along with the unsettled situation at second base, was the major cause of the Angels failure to contend for the pennant. Thomas and Prim were brilliant during the entire season, with Thomas winning 23 games and Prim 21. The rest of the staff was suspect. Overman pitched several fine games in April and May, but he injured his shoulder and did not win a game after May 19. Evans was hit hard and taken out of the rotation after several ineffective starts. Not until August, when he won five decisions in a row, was he of any real use to the club. The Cubs provided some help in May when they purchased Jack Salveson on waivers from Washington and sent him to Los Angeles after recalling Newt Kimball. But after winning three of his first four starts, Salveson, too, was afflicted with serious arm trouble and was out of action for two months. When he returned to active duty, it was clear that he would never be the same pitcher he had once been. A hard thrower in the past who was primarily a fast ball pitcher and chalked up many strikeouts, Salveson was forced to rely on curves and change-ups. There would be a transition period before he again became an effective pitcher, and what was expected to be a long successful major league career never materialized. The injuries to Salveson and Overman opened the door for Joe Berry to take a spot in the rotation, and he responded well, winning 13 games with a sparkling 2.77 ERA. But no other Angels player won as many as he lost.

The rest of the club was in a state of transition through much of the year. Don Hurst was no better at first base than he had been at the end of 1936, and finally, Truck Hannah benched the slumping veteran on June 16, giving the job to Rip Russell. He was a much better player at first base than he had been while trying to fill Reese's shoes at second, and his hitting improved after he made the move. Hurst stayed on the bench for a month before the club sold him to New Orleans. The ex–Philly refused to report and went on the voluntarily retired list. By the end of July, he was working at Paramount Studios and playing on the company team.

Steve Mesner was unable to hit major league pitching in his brief trial with the White Sox, and after a month he was returned to Los Angeles, a fortunate event for the Angels. He was restored to third base and proceeded to have another fine year, hitting .329 with 91 RBIs. On June 5, Mesner had a day that he never forgot, when he hit three home runs in a game against Oakland at Wrigley Field. In the remaining eight years of his PCL career, he had only two seasons in which he actually hit more home runs than in that one game! Bobby Mattick

Don Hurst — After a fine season as the Angels first baseman in 1936, during which he hit .303 with 119 RBIs, he was relegated to part-time duty in 1937 before quitting the team in mid–July (courtesy Mark Macrae).

hit a solid .280 and was brilliant in the field. When Kenny Richardson was inserted into the lineup for the last three months of the season, the Angels had a "kiddy" infield with no member over 22 years of age. But Mattick and Mesner were sold to the Cubs in August for 1938 delivery.

During the 1937 season, Oscar Reichow, the long-time business manager of the Angels, was gradually removed from the important operations of the club. In February he was relieved of his radio broadcasting duties and replaced by Art Gleason. Then Howard Lorenz was assigned all office duties and Truck Hannah given responsibility for all player matters, including those at the Angels farm clubs in Tulsa of the Texas League and Ponca City of the Western

Association. Reichow's sole activity was now public relations. At the end of the season, he severed all connections with the club, ending an association that had begun in 1923. In 1938, Reichow assumed the position of general manager with the new Hollywood franchise.

Dave Fleming now had his own people in place to run the Angels. Although he was disappointed in the club's performance in 1937, he thought that Truck Hannah had done a respectable job in his first year as manager, given the material that was available. The Angels were undergoing a period of change from old to young. The overhaul of the Angels that had begun halfway through the 1937 season continued through the next spring. Of the regular players at the end of the year, only Russell, Statz and Collins were back when spring training began in 1938. Although Dave Fleming was very optimistic about the coming year, it did not seem likely that a club that experienced such turnover in personnel as the Angels had would be a pennant contender. Yet, at the end of the season, there they were in first place, 3½ games ahead of second-place Seattle.

Although there were many situations that the Angels needed to fix that spring, none was more glaring than the infield. The second base position had not been properly filled after the ill-advised trade of Jimmie Reese to San Diego, and there were major gaps on the left side of the infield after Bobby Mattick and Steve Mesner were promoted to Chicago. During the winter meetings, the Angels thought they had filled the holes in the middle of the infield when they acquired second baseman Jack Sanford and shortstop Eddie Cihocki from Birmingham, which was now a Cub farm team in the Southern Association. Both of these men had excellent seasons for Birmingham in 1937. Cihocki was no kid, almost 31 when the training period opened, and had seen considerable service with Syracuse in the International League in previous years. Although he had not hit well during his career, he was a fine, steady gloveman, and the club did not miss Mattick. Sanford was less experienced, but he played well during the exhibition season and won the opening day job with ease. Mesner's spot at third was nicely filled when Charlie English was sent to Los Angeles by Cincinnati. He was a fine minor league hitter who had brief trials with the White Sox, Giants and Reds, but never quite made the grade in the major leagues. In 1937 he had hit .325 with Kansas City in the American Association.

The outfield had to be reconstructed as well, and the Angels picked up several new candidates. The Angels sent Cleo Carlyle, Red Evans and Earl Overman to New Orleans for Milt Galatzer and pitcher Sig Jakucki, purchased Johnny Moore from the Phillies at the winter meetings, and sent Kenny Richardson to Jersey City for Paul Carpenter. Galatzer was expected to replace the aging Marv Gudat in left field, while Moore was back in right field after several fine years in the National League. Carpenter was a young prospect who would spell Jigger Statz in center field from time to time. During the spring the Angels picked up Jack Rothrock, a major league veteran who had been an important part of the "Gas House Gang" Cardinals in 1934 and had played with the Philadelphia Athletics in 1937.

The pitching staff had a good nucleus in returning starters Ray Prim and Fay Thomas, along with the promising Joe Berry, and was improved when the Cubs shipped Gene Lillard to Los Angeles after a year of pitching in San Francisco for manager Lefty O'Doul. Lillard had been converted to pitching after the 1936 season, and the change apparently worked, for he won 14 games with the Seals in 1937 by featuring a good variety of pitches. Jack Salveson appeared to be over the arm ailments that had limited his activity during the previous year. And Dutch Lieber was back as both a spot starter and the number one man out of the bullpen.

Left: Gene Lillard—He is shown as a pitcher with San Francisco in this photograph. Years later Lillard confided to the author that "becoming a pitcher was the biggest mistake I ever made in baseball" (courtesy Dick Dobbins). *Right:* Fay Thomas—One of the greatest Angels pitchers ever. This photograph was taken during spring training in 1938 at Ontario, California (courtesy Dick Dobbins).

The Angels began the new season very slowly, and it was clear that not all of the problems had been solved. Neither Jack Sanford nor Milt Galatzer performed as well as expected. Although Sanford was a satisfactory fielder at second base, he was unable to hit PCL pitching with any consistency. Galatzer was a major disappointment in left field and was released after hitting a paltry .162 in 28 games, with Marv Gudat then restored to the left field position. Unfortunately, he broke a toe after only four games and was out for a month. When he returned to action, he was not as mobile in the outfield and was soon benched in favor of Jack Rothrock.

The pitching was also unsettled during the first two months of the season. Neither Prim nor Thomas was as effective as he had been in 1937, and Salveson was not the pitcher that he was before his arm problems. Only Lillard pitched consistently well during April, but he slumped along with the rest of the staff during May. Truck Hannah gave several starts to young pitchers Ed Carnett, Clyde Lahti and Sig Jakucki, but none of them showed the consistent ability to get hitters out on a regular basis. Jakucki was one of the more unusual characters to ever appear in an Angels uniform. He had played ball while in the Army for several years and had appeared in a few games as an outfielder with Oakland in 1936.

"Jack" did not last long in Los Angeles, winning but one game, as his personal habits caught up with him. He was a man who "liked his glass," as they said in the 1930s, and would fight at the drop of a hat. Jakucki later surfaced as a key member of the 1944 American League champion St. Louis Browns. While an Angels player, he somehow managed to find time to write game reports for the *Times* during an early series in San Diego. These articles made for entertaining reading.

By the end of May the Angels had dropped to seventh place and were struggling. In spite of their woes, they remained within striking distance of the top of the league. The PCL was experiencing a very tight pennant race, with only Oakland hopelessly out of contention; at their worst the Angels were only six games out of first place. Los Angeles then made the most important move of the year by purchasing infielder Eddie Mayo from the Boston Bees (formerly the Braves). Mayo was 25 and had briefly played with the Giants and Bees. He could play any infield position but had not yet shown much as a hitter. He quickly put aside any doubts about his hitting ability after joining the Angels on June 1, and within a week he was over .300, never dropping below that figure for the balance of the year. For the next four years, Mayo was a key member of the Angels infield and contributed mightily to two pennants. He finally returned to the major leagues in 1943, this time with the Athletics, and became the star player of the 1945 World Champion Detroit Tigers. Mayo was considered by many to be the most valuable player in the American League that year.

After initially resisting the trade to Los Angeles, Mayo joined the club in San Francisco on June 2 and was immediately installed at second base, with Sanford having been given his outright release. After stumbling through the remainder of the series and falling five games below .500, the Angels began a streak that saw them win 24 of the next 30 games to move into second place on July 4. They defeated first-place Sacramento seven times in a nine-game series in Los Angeles, and then two weeks later pounded the Solons six out of seven in Sacramento. On July 17 the Angels moved into first place and were never headed after that.

The spotty pitching solidified during this hot streak with Lillard winning seven of eight decisions, Dutch Lieber turning in four well pitched games in a row, veteran Guy Bush pitching well in relief, and Prim and Thomas returning to form. The city of Los Angeles, which had been indifferent to the team since the great season of 1934, became excited about this Angels club, and a large crowd turned out to greet the players when they returned from a successful road trip on July 24. At that point the Angels were one game in front with 60 games to play, with only ten of them away from Wrigley Field.

But the pennant race was not over by any means. The Seattle club, now known as the Rainiers under the new ownership of Emil Sick, was improving rapidly under old friend Jack Lelivelt, and the Angels pitching staff began to turn sour. Thomas suffered a recurrence of a leg injury and missed two weeks; then Lillard, who had been the most reliable pitcher all year, broke his ankle while running the bases and was sidelined for the rest of the season. At that point he had won 16 games and seemed certain to win 20. Joe Berry filled the gap with a number of fine performances, and the Angels picked up Dwight Van Fleet from Oakland in a trade for Marv Gudat. He pitched several good games in August when Thomas was sidelined. After playing a little better than .500 through most of August, the Angels won 11 of their next 15 games and clinched the pennant at Oakland on September 16, three days before the end of the season. It was vital that they finished strong, for Seattle won 28 of its last 31 games, including 14 straight. The Rainiers would remain a mighty force in the PCL during the next three years.

The Angels won the 1938 pennant by completely dominating Sacramento, winning 21 of the 27 games in the season series, and 13 of the 17 games played at Wrigley Field. The Solons, who were defending champions and were probably the best team in the league on paper, finished third because of their inability to handle the Angels and, as a result, were matched against them in the first round of the Shaughnessy playoffs. It was the first appearance by Los Angeles in post-season play since the playoff system was adopted, and the Angels were confident that their regular season superiority would continue. But Sacramento surprised the champions by winning the series, four games to two. The Solons took two of the first three games, which were played at Wrigley Field, and outslugged Los Angeles, eight homers to one. Sacramento then dispatched San Francisco to win the Governor's Cup, awarded to the playoff winner, although the Angels were recognized as the champions of the league.

Although the playoff experience was disappointing, the Angels enjoyed a fine year. The team batted .283 with 116 home runs, most of which were hit at Wrigley Field, and had five regulars over .300. Rip Russell found his natural position at first base and improved dramatically over 1937. He led the league with 216 hits and 338 total bases, hit 21 home runs to tie for the club lead with Johnny Moore, and finished with 114 RBIs. In July he had 11 straight hits during a series at Portland. His fielding was vastly improved, and by season's end Russell was recognized as the best first baseman in the league. Unfortunately for the Angels, he was purchased by the Cubs for the 1939 season.

The remainder of the infield — Eddie Mayo, Eddie Cihocki and Charlie English- provided a much improved defense from the previous year. Mayo was the best second baseman in the PCL, and he teamed with Cihocki as if they had played together for years. English was more than adequate at third base, and both he and Mayo were potent offensive forces. Mayo hit .332 to finish well up in the batting race, while English had a career high 143 RBIs to go along with a .303 average. Mayo's contribution to the Angels pennant was recognized when he was selected as the club's most valuable player. The outfield emerged as a force once Rothrock was installed in left field. He hit a solid .287 while both Statz and Moore finished over .300. Rookie Paul Carpenter hit .324 in the role of a substitute.

The pitching staff was good but not great. After their early difficulties, both Thomas and Prim finished well and enjoyed fine seasons. Thomas finished with 18 wins while Prim was right behind at 17. From June 25 to the end of the season, their records were 10-3 and 12-5, respectively. Lillard and Berry finished with identical 16-10 records, and Berry spun a seven-inning no-hitter at Oakland to pad his totals. Dutch Lieber enjoyed his best year in Los Angeles at 10-7 and was an important factor during the Angels rush to the top during June and July. Salveson improved to 12-10 after his injury plagued 1937 season, but a high ERA of 4.08 indicated that he had not returned to the level where he was two years earlier.

One game in 1938 deserves particular attention. On August 30 at San Diego, former Angels pitcher Dick Ward defeated his former team, 1-0, in a 16-inning complete game. Ward pitched 12 and ⅔ innings of hitless ball before Eddie Mayo registered the first Angels hit. This became the longest hitless stretch in PCL history.

Although the Angels team was very popular with the fans and there was much civic support for the club, the attendance figures did not reflect the heightened interest. A total of 188,808 fans appeared at Angels games in 1938, a decline of almost 8,000 admissions from the previous year. Part of this unhappy development could be attributed to the new tenant at Wrigley Field. The Mission franchise was shifted from San Francisco to Los Angeles after the 1937 season, to be reborn as the Hollywood Stars. President Dave Fleming was not pleased with the presence of another team in greater Los Angeles, but recognized that the transfer would be beneficial to the PCL as a whole. The move was made with the understanding that the new Stars would not play at Wrigley Field, but would have their own facility within the confines of the Hollywood district in west Los Angeles. That scenario would not be possible in 1938, however. Fleming then compromised by agreeing to the Hollywood presence at Wrigley Field for the 1938 season, but with the proviso that the team would play in its own park in 1939. A weak Hollywood aggregation drew 103,008 to Wrigley Field; many of those fans would probably have attended Angels games.

The Angels of 1938 were probably the most unexpected champions of all of the Angels pennant winners. They were a mixture of old and young, with several players having the best seasons of their careers. The team was not in the class of the 1933 and 1934 champions, but it was highly entertaining and survived a number of key injuries to hold off the competition from Seattle and Sacramento. Much of the credit for the latest pennant needed to go to Truck Hannah. He kept his club hustling even when it was not playing well, coaxed the most out of a pitching staff that had a number of soft spots, and played an important role in the development of Rip Russell and Eddie Mayo. Unfortunately, it would be the only pennant the Angels would win under his leadership. Jack Lelivelt was building a team in Seattle that was on the verge of dominating the PCL.

14

Hannah Is Out and Statz Is In

The Angels seemed to be well equipped to defend their championship in 1939. They did, however, have two major holes to fill in the infield. First baseman Rip Russell was now a member of the Chicago Cubs and third baseman Charlie English had been recalled by Cincinnati. Everywhere else the club looked solid. The pitching staff seemed a bit stronger, even with the loss of Gene Lillard, who had been recalled by the Cubs. Julio Bonetti had been purchased from the St. Louis Browns, and he appeared capable of being a fine replacement for Lillard. Bonetti possessed an excellent sinker ball, a more than satisfactory curve, and was blessed with pinpoint control. He and Lee Stine, who had been purchased from Newark over the winter, would join the starting rotation, along with holdovers Ray Prim and Fay Thomas. Stine had been in the PCL as far back as 1932, even though he was only 26. He had received several big league trials, with Cincinnati, the White Sox and the Yankees, but a freak injury suffered during an on-field brawl at Cincinnati in 1936 robbed him of his great fastball and prevented him from enjoying a successful major league career. But he was still very capable and was also one of the finest hitting pitchers of his era.

Each spring the Angels seemed to bring up a promising new pitcher, and in 1939 it was right-hander Jess Flores. He had been on option to Bisbee in the Arizona-Texas League the year before and had won 24 games. Joe Berry and Dutch Lieber were still around, and the spring training roster that year featured such youngsters as Jack Hallett and Art Mangini. Jack Salveson was still an Angels player at the start of spring training, but when Flores earned a spot on the staff with his impressive work, Salveson was dealt to Oakland. This trade was a costly mistake. The arm miseries that had plagued Salveson during the previous two years began to disappear at mid-season, and he won 12 games with the seventh-place Oaks. Salveson followed that up with a 19–13 record in 1940 and remained in the PCL until 1953, winning 167 games during that span, a goodly number of which came at the expense of Los Angeles.

One long time Angels player was missing that spring. Carl Dittmar was now the manager at Bisbee after spending 1938 as an Angels coach. Dittmar had been with the club since 1928, playing as the regular shortstop for most of those years. The soft-spoken Maryland native was a bulwark of the Angels defense, along with Jigger Statz, and was the PCL's all-star shortstop in 1934. In spite of a lifetime batting average of .283, Dittmar acquired the label of good-field, no-hit somewhere along the way, and he never earned a chance to play in the major leagues

Nineteen thirty-nine was a transition year for the PCL. During the previous year, the

The 1939 Angels. *Front row (left to right):* Batboy Russell Guiver, mascot John Fleming. *Seated row:* Johnny Moore, Ed Cihocki, Charlie English, Bob Collins, Lou Novikoff, president Dave Fleming, Lou Stringer, Paul Carpenter, Jigger Statz, Rip Collins, Hal Sueme. *Back row:* Trainer Lou Toro, Jack Rothrock, Jess Flores, Eddie Mayo, Truck Lloyd, Fay Thomas, Ray Prim, manager Truck Hannah, Harry Kimberlin, unknown, unknown, Julio Bonetti, unknown, trainer Frankie Jacobs (courtesy Mark Macrae).

Seattle franchise had been purchased by Emil Sick, the owner of the successful Rainier Brewery in Seattle. He provided immediate financial strength for this once moribund club, built a new ballpark that rivaled Wrigley Field and Seals Stadium in appearance, and began to acquire better players. The most important move he made was the installation of former Angels manager Jack Lelivelt as the new boss of the Rainiers, and almost overnight Seattle became a pennant contender, for the first time in 15 years. The Rainiers gave an indication of what was to come when they finished strongly at the end of 1938, and they were now picked to win the PCL in 1939.

    The Hollywood franchise was also given new life when it was purchased in October 1938, by a group headed by Bob Cobb, president of the famous Brown Derby restaurant organization. He immediately announced plans for a new park, and arrangements were made to construct a baseball facility adjacent to Gilmore Stadium, located near the site of what is now the headquarters of CBS Television, at Beverly Boulevard and Fairfax Avenue. Gilmore Field opened on May 2, 1939, immediately giving the Hollywood Stars their own identity. No longer would they be the poor relations of the Angels who shared the same facility, but they would compete for the loyalty of the Los Angeles baseball fan. The Stars further improved their image by hiring Oscar Reichow as business manager. Reichow had been eased out of the Angels picture in early 1938, and there was no love lost between him and Dave Fleming. But he had a reputation as a good baseball man during his time in Los Angeles, and his presence added to the respectability of the Stars.

The continued growth of major league farm systems had virtually forced each independent PCL club to enter into a working agreement with a big league club, as well as developing its own talent. The Angels had been very successful in signing young talent from the Southern California area, and they had established a good working relationship with Ponca City in the Western Association. Los Angeles would send its youngsters out for seasoning, later selling them to the Cubs at a nice profit. But direct competition from the major league clubs made this more difficult to do, and the Angels had become more dependent on talent obtained from Chicago. Then in 1939, the Cubs announced that they had entered into a limited working agreement with the Milwaukee Brewers of the American Association. They would provide that club with player help in exchange for their first choice of Brewer talent. No longer would the Angels have the first right of refusal on the Cub surplus. Over the next several years, there would be players assigned to Milwaukee that a few years earlier would have gone directly to the Angels. During 1939, the Brewers had in their lineup at one time or another former Angels Bobby Mattick, Steve Mesner, Newt Kimball and Ed Carnett, all of whom Los Angeles could have used.

Spring training began on a sour note that year when promising young outfielder Paul Carpenter was beaned during the first intersquad game. Although he was conscious when he left the field and predicted he would be back in a day or two, the injury proved to be very serious. Fluid had to be drained from his spine, and at one point the doctors were uncertain that Carpenter would ever play again. He was not allowed to return to the team until April 11 and did not see action until April 23. The great promise that he had shown completely disappeared. Although he managed to play in 108 games, he hit a weak .229, a drop of almost one hundred points from his fine rookie season with the club.

Additional problems were caused by prolonged holdouts involving Johnny Moore and Eddie Mayo, the latter perhaps using the leverage of his great 1938 season to force a trade to a club near his home in the East. Both players came to terms during the last week of training, and Mayo's holdout turned out to be a blessing in disguise. Truck Hannah was forced to play rookie Lou Stringer, who had a great season at Ponca City in 1938, and the youngster played so well that he earned the opening day nod at second base. He proved to be a better fielder than Mayo and had more power, at least at Wrigley Field, where he hit most of his home runs. Mayo was not in shape when the season started, but Stringer played so well that he could not be taken out of the lineup anyway, so Mayo spent most of the year in a utility role. He hit .263, a huge decline from his great 1938 season.

Just before they broke camp, the Angels finally filled the open infield spots as the Cubs purchased Charlie English from the Reds and sent him to Los Angeles along with veteran first baseman Jim "Rip" Collins. English had been in contention for the open third base job at Cincinnati, but when the Reds acquired Bill Werber from the Athletics, there was no place for him on the team; Chicago claimed him on waivers. It was the last opportunity that English had to establish himself in the major leagues, and he may have lost some of his enthusiasm when he returned to Los Angeles. He hit well for the first six weeks of the season, but then went into a decline, both at bat and in the field. The big RBI man for the 1938 club, English drove in nearly 60 runs fewer in 1939 and was sent to Milwaukee in 1940.

Collins had been a star first baseman with the Cardinals and had led the National League in home runs in 1934 as a member of the Gas House Gang champions. He had been traded to the Cubs in 1937 and appeared to be in decline after two middling seasons in Chicago. But Collins thought he still had major league ability even though he was almost 35, and was determined to show it in Los Angeles.

The Angels roared out of the starting gate that spring. After losing their first two games, they defeated Hollywood, 7–2, behind Ray Prim in his first start. Los Angeles swept Sacramento and Portland, then took four straight from San Diego before finally losing 12–6 on April 22. The Angels had won 19 games in a row, tying a record that had been established by Seattle in 1903. They were eight games in front, and it looked as if the pennant race was over.

Rip Collins and Stringer were the big hitters during the streak, with each providing several game winning hits. Collins hit .400 during April with nine home runs and 40 RBIs. The pitching was excellent; Prim, Thomas and Bonetti each won four games, as did Stine, and Dwight Van Fleet chipped in with two wins. English, Bob Collins and Jack Rothrock also contributed heavily to the Angels rampage.

But the bubble blew up rather quickly, and the club went into reverse, losing 11 of the next 15 games As invincible as the starting pitchers had been during April, they found it difficult to get anyone out in early May. Injuries became a problem, too. Eddie Cihocki, who had played brilliantly in the field, was injured and was out for two weeks, while Lee Stine was beaned on April 30 and seemed to lose his effectiveness after that. Mayo showed that he was not a true shortstop during Cihocki's absence, and by the middle of May the club had lost all of its large lead.

Truck Hannah rallied his forces after the May slump, and by Memorial Day the Angels were back in first place, three games ahead of Seattle. They battled with the Rainiers for the lead over the course of the next six weeks, with the Angels maintaining a slight lead through the middle of July. Then a series of injuries weakened the club, and the Angels gradually fell behind as Seattle surged by them. When Los Angeles lost a doubleheader to Sacramento on July 21 while Seattle was winning two of its own, the Angels fell out of the lead for good.

It was about this time that rumors concerning Hannah's status began to surface. All was not well between him and Dave Fleming, it seemed. The Angels president was very demanding of his managers. He was impatient as well, and nothing less than a pennant would do. But as injuries began to mount and the young players provided by the Cubs fell short of PCL caliber, Hannah was left in an uncomfortable position. There was great pressure on him to develop the young players on his roster — pitchers Emil Kush and Al Epperly, and outfielder Paul Carpenter. However, Carpenter was not the player he had been, nor would he ever be again, and the two young pitchers who were used in relief roles were very inconsistent. When the Angels released Dutch Lieber, the club's most dependable relief pitcher, it was said that the move was made at the direction of the Cubs but over strenuous objections by Hannah. With this turmoil going on, the Angels continued to fall further behind the surging Rainiers. By the end of July, Los Angeles was 4½ games behind, this after suffering shutouts in both ends of a doubleheader at San Francisco.

The Angels remained in the doldrums through much of August, falling nine games out on August 17, and virtually all hope for a pennant disappeared. At this point, they exercised their option to recall outfielder Lou Novikoff from Tulsa, where he had been the leading hitter in the Texas League. He immediately made his presence felt, hitting three home runs in a series with Seattle during the last week of August, and for a time the Angels rallied. But when Jigger Statz broke a bone in his thumb on September 1 and Johnny Moore broke his ankle on Labor Day, the Angels cause was doomed. Los Angeles closed the deficit to six games with one week left in the season, and a sweep of the last series at Seattle would have won the championship. But that outcome was beyond the capability of this club, and

Seattle clinched the pennant by winning the first game of the series. Furthermore, San Francisco overtook the Angels on the last day of the season, and Los Angeles finished in third place, five games behind Seattle.

The Angels opened the Governor's Cup playoff series against the Rainiers and gave their fans much hope when they took the series, winning four of the six games, including the last three at Wrigley Field. However, for the second year in a row, Los Angeles was unable to handle Sacramento in the post-season and lost the Cup to the Solons, who won the series by the same margin. The series was even after four games, but the Angels bats went silent during the next two, the team losing by scores of 3–1 and 8–0 at Sacramento.

Upon their return to Los Angeles, the Angels were surprised to learn that Truck Hannah had been fired as manager. He had officially been notified of his fate on the last day of the season, but public announcement had been held up until the playoffs were over. Dave Fleming said the decision was made because Hannah was not developing young players fast enough and was instead playing the veterans too much. This argument seems false, in retrospect. During his tenure, Hannah sent Rip Russell, Steve Mesner and Bobby Mattick to the majors; Lou Stringer would soon follow. Eddie Mayo would eventually become a major league regular, and Jess Flores would graduate from the PCL to become a dependable major league pitcher. Several of the young players that Hannah had supposedly failed to nurture were never developed by anyone else either. They simply did not have major league ability.

Fleming was a demanding boss who was not satisfied with anything less than a pennant. The Angels managerial position had been stable under the leadership of Joe Patrick, with Marty Krug and Jack Lelivelt enjoying long tenure, but Fleming changed managers every three years. Truck Hannah had done a very creditable job as Angels manager, given the talent he had to work with and the conflicting demands of Fleming to win and develop young players at the same time. The capable Hannah signed a contract to manage Memphis in the Southern Association in 1940.

Although several of the Angels suffered off years in 1939, Eddie Cihocki and Bob Collins had better seasons than the previous year. Cihocki hit .280, his high mark with the club, and led PCL shortstops in fielding. Collins hit .306 and earned a promotion to the Cubs in 1940. Rip Collins had a fine year, too. He hit .334 and led the league with 26 home runs, but this performance did not lead to a return to the major leagues. Collins would return to Los Angeles in 1940.

Bonetti was outstanding in his first year in Los Angeles. His 20–5 record was the league's best, and he probably would have improved on that mark were it not for a series of minor injuries that caused him to miss at least six starts. His control was superb, with only 21 walks in 226 innings, and he enjoyed a stretch in late August when he went 64 innings without walking anyone. Fay Thomas was 17–13 after a sub-par early season, while Prim was a workhorse, but basically a .500 pitcher after his early success, finishing at 20–17. Jess Flores split 18 decisions, working mostly in relief until mid-season.

Angels attendance increased to 224,645 in 1939, the highest figure since 1931. Part of the surge occurred late in the year as fans flocked to the park to see Lou Novikoff, who offered promise for the future. In 36 games he hit .452 with eight home runs in only 135 times at bat. One of the blasts appeared to go over 450 feet at Gilmore Field, by far the longest home run during that park's first year. This was just a prelude to the great year he was to have in 1940.

To the surprise of no one, Jigger Statz was appointed the successor to Truck Hannah as Angels manager. What was somewhat peculiar was that it took Dave Fleming almost a month to make the decision. Statz seemed to be the obvious choice, but he did not sign a contract until the end of October. Was Fleming searching for someone else, and did he settle for Statz when he could find no reasonable alternative? The answers remain unknown. Nevertheless, Jigger was given a two-year contract as the new manager. He indicated that he would rely on the running game more than the Hannah teams had done, a style more fitting to Statz's personal way of playing. Jigger would continue as the club's regular centerfielder, but he hoped to play in fewer games in 1940 than he normally did. He expressed hope that Paul Carpenter would rebound from his poor season in 1939 and return to the high level of play of his rookie year.

The team that Statz inherited was composed mostly of veteran players, virtually all of whom would return in 1940. The most notable absentee was catcher Bob Collins, sold to the Cubs during the off-season, but the Angels took steps to fill that vacancy by sending Charlie English to Milwaukee for Chico Hernandez, a young Venezuelan catcher, and purchasing Billy Holm from the Yankee farm club at Newark in the International League. Eddie

The 1940 Angels. *Front row (left to right):* Trainer Frankie Jacobs, Jimmie Reese, Paul Carpenter, Johnny Moore, Joe Berry, Bob Windisch, assistant trainer Lou Toro. *Middle row:* Ray Prim, Chico Hernandez, Rip Collins, president Dave Fleming, manager Jigger Statz, Lou Novikoff, Bill Holm, Peanuts Lowery, Jesse Flores, Ed Cihocki. *Back row:* Lee Stine, Jack Fallon, Fay Thomas, Bob Weiland, Lou Stringer, Eddie Mayo, Julio Bonetti, Charles Strada (courtesy Mark Macrae).

Mayo would move to third base to replace English, and after making noises that he might retire, Eddie Cihocki agreed to return to Los Angeles for another year at shortstop. Lou Stringer was unchallenged as the second baseman and Rip Collins was back at first. Johnny Moore and Lou Novikoff would flank Statz in the outfield, with fans and writers excited about the Russian's potential. He hit everything thrown to him during spring training, and was beginning to improve in the field as well. Statz worked hard with Novikoff, who gradually became an adequate outfielder. He had a strong arm but was not very mobile, and at times a fly ball would turn into an adventure for him. In terms of pitching, Ray Prim and Fay Thomas were beginning to show their age, and Hannah was fearful that Lee Stine would not be able to overcome the effects of the beaning he had suffered the previous year. These three, along with Jack Fallon, a tall right-hander acquired from Oakland, were scheduled to be the starters, with Jess Flores and Joe Berry available for relief work and occasional starts. During the last week of training, the Cardinals optioned Gene Lillard back to Los Angeles to provide some additional pitching strength. But the staff was not deep enough to withstand the long season ahead.

The Angels played poorly during the first month of the season, and the concerns about the pitching seemed justified. After winning his first start, Thomas pitched badly in several outings and had to be removed from the rotation. Lillard was not particularly effective; although he won four games during April, that was primarily because of the run support he was given. He was also expressing a desire to return to third base where he had been so successful five years earlier. The staff was strengthened when Julio Bonetti was returned by the Cubs at the end of April, but he had not appeared in many games while training with Chicago and did not seem to be in the best of condition. He was hit hard in his early starts, as was Prim. On the other hand, Lee Stine had made a full recovery from his injury and was much improved over 1939.

Novikoff picked up right where he had left off the previous September, and after the first month of the season, he was hitting .412 with 10 home runs. It made absolutely no difference what the pitchers threw to him. With enough strength to hit the outside pitch out of the park, he hit several of his longest home runs on pitches well out of the strike zone. There was no such thing as a "waste" pitch when Novikoff was at bat.

But that was about all Angels fans had to cheer as May progressed. Los Angeles fell into seventh place on May 15, and seemingly out of the pennant race. The next four weeks were no better; meanwhile, Seattle had started well and showed signs of running away with the pennant. Only Oakland, surprisingly improved over previous years, remained close to the leaders. The Angels remained deep in the second division and hit a low point on June 30. On that day Los Angeles was in sixth place, 12½ games behind first-place Seattle.

Suddenly, the Angels turned things around. They proceeded to destroy Hollywood in the next series, winning seven out of the eight games and going over .500 for the first time in two months. The Angels reached third place in the middle of July and moved into second place on August 19. The pitching staff had finally stabilized after the early troubles. The Angels acquired left-hander Bob Weiland from the Cardinals in late May, returning Gene Lillard to St. Louis as part of the transaction. After losing his first two starts, the veteran Weiland, who had been a successful major league pitcher with the Cardinals, White Sox and Red Sox, began to win consistently. Bonetti pitched himself back into shape and was winning as well, and Ray Prim made a complete turnaround. After having all sorts of trouble with his control early in the season, the veteran screwball pitcher was virtually unbeatable from June 9 on, as he improved his dismal 3–6 record. He won 15 of his last 20 decisions, including three shutouts. Many of those wins were at the expense of the Seals; Prim won seven straight decisions from San Francisco in June and July before finally losing on July 28 in the last game of the season between the teams. With the addition of Weiland and Bonetti to the staff, Jack Fallon was relegated to the bullpen, giving the Angels three consistent performers there. Joe Berry was enjoying his finest season as a relief specialist. He appeared in 48 games out of the pen, more than anyone in the league, and posted nine saves. By season's end the Angels pitching, which was suspect early in the year, was probably the best in the league.

Despite the Angels move to second place in August, the club still trailed Seattle by 15 games in what had become a runaway for the Rainiers. Los Angeles managed to cut the lead to 9½ games at the close of the season by winning 22 of their last 29 games, but the Angels were never a legitimate pennant threat. Although they played the best ball in the league after July 1, winning over two-thirds of their games, the Angels were too far behind to make significant inroads on the Seattle lead and were unable to do much whenever they met the Rainiers, losing 13 of the 20 games played head-to-head.

The Angels fared better in the playoffs in 1940 than they usually did. They opened a series against fourth-place San Diego and defeated the Padres, four games to three, when Jess Flores and Bob Weiland threw back-to-back shutouts at San Diego to win Games Six and Seven of the series. This gave the Angels the opportunity to face the Rainiers for the President's Cup, and it was hoped that the pitching success of the last two months would provide the impetus for victory. But Seattle prevailed easily, winning the series in five games. "Kewpie Dick" Barrett, who enjoyed his greatest PCL season that year, won the first two games, and the Rainiers out-slugged the Angels in each of the final two contests at Wrigley Field.

Novikoff had a dream season, leading the league in virtually all important categories. His .363 average was well ahead of the second-place hitter, Edo Vanni of Seattle, and he led in hits, runs scored, total bases, home runs and runs batted in. His season was very comparable to the great year Frank Demaree enjoyed as an Angels player in 1934, a year when hitting tended to be more prevalent than it was six years later. Novikoff's 259 hits and 438 total bases were the most by a player in the PCL since 1935. Not until 1950 would anyone exceed his hit total; Artie Wilson of Oakland had 264 hits in a longer schedule. No one has come close to his total bases and runs batted in since. In spite of this impressive record, Novikoff was not accorded the honor of being chosen the Most Valuable Player of the PCL. It is doubtful that the Angels would have finished in the first division without him, but nevertheless, first baseman George Archie of the champion Rainiers was so designated, a decision that remains puzzling to this day.

Novikoff was enormously popular in Los Angeles, certainly the most popular Angels player up to that time, and as the season wore on, his feats became almost legendary. At the end of the year, his contract was purchased by the Cubs for the then-princely sum of $100,000. The Chicago papers proclaimed him to be the next star of the Cubs, but unfortunately, Lou was a flop in Chicago. He hit .241 in 90 games during the 1941 season and was optioned to Milwaukee in mid-summer. Although he returned to the Cubs in 1942 and hit .300 that year, he never resembled the fearsome hitter that he had been in Los Angeles, and the Cubs returned him to the Angels in 1945. He hit .310 in that wartime season to earn a chance with the Phillies. But after a handful of games, Novikoff was sent to Seattle. He never again played in the major leagues and finished his career in 1950. In none of those years did he have a season that remotely resembled his great year of 1940 with the Angels.

Lou Novikoff — Many observers thought he deserved the Most Valuable Player award for his great season in 1940. Novikoff hit .363 with 41 home runs and 171 RBIs, leading the PCL in all three categories, but George Archie of Seattle was given the MVP honor instead (courtesy Dick Dobbins).

There are several theories as to why Novikoff was not successful in the major leagues. He was a notorious bad ball hitter with a poor knowledge of the strike zone. He was able to prosper in the minor leagues, but when he reached the majors, the pitchers were able to take advantage of his lack of discipline. Few big league hitters have been successful as bad ball hitters — Yogi Berra and Joe Medwick come to mind — and they are both members of the Hall of Fame.

Novikoff was also somewhat of a night person and enjoyed the bar scene. He had a fine singing voice and frequently took to song after a few beers to entertain the customers. But this type of life style can hurt a player's performance, and Novikoff was no exception. Had he worked as hard on his hitting as he did on his singing, he might well have been the superstar that the Cubs once envisioned.

There were other Angels hitters who enjoyed fine seasons. Rip Collins continued to thrive in Wrigley Field, hitting .321 with 118 RBIs. He usually batted fourth, right behind Novikoff, and they made for a fearsome combination through most of the year. Eddie Mayo was determined to return to the majors, and after his poor year of 1939, he came to camp in great shape. With the problems of the previous year's holdout behind him, he became an all-star performer at third base, hitting .322 with 85 RBIs. Third base appeared to be a much better position for him, and the infield defense was considerably better with his change in position. Lou Stringer continued to impress at second base, and although his hitting fell off to .263, his work in the field was exceptional. At the end of the season, he was purchased by the Cubs and was touted as the successor to Billy Herman, the Hall of Fame second baseman who was on his way out of Chicago.

Jigger Statz fell below the .300 mark for one of the few times in his illustrious career, hitting only .289 as advancing years and the additional responsibilities of managing caught up with him. Statz had planned to ease himself out of the center field position given the continued development of Paul Carpenter, and was out of the opening day lineup for the first time since 1929. But the youngster was still showing the effects of his tragic beaning of the spring before and failed to hit once again. So Statz was back in the regular lineup by the end of April and eventually played in 144 games.

Lee Stine and Ray Prim were the leading pitchers with records of 18–10 and 18–11, respectively. It was the best season of Stine's career; he was a steady winner all year long, and during the early weeks he provided some stability to a beleaguered staff. Prim was perhaps the best pitcher in the league during the last two months of the season, as he won virtually every time out. Both pitchers were among the league leaders in ERA as well. Joe Berry enjoyed his finest season as an Angels player, winning seven games in relief and posting a fine 2.39 ERA. Bob Weiland was 12–7 and also pitched many standout games. After being used as a starter early in the year, Jack Fallon found his niche in the bullpen after the arrival of Weiland and Bonetti; he posted seven relief wins as an effective complement to Berry. Fay Thomas showed signs of his age; he was a disappointing 6–11, and his ERA ballooned to 4.97, a far cry from his successful peak with the club.

The pitching uncertainty of the early season cost the Angels any chance of contending for the pennant in 1940. Although the staff was comparable to that of the champion Rainiers by season's end, there was too much ground to make up. Statz showed an intuitive ability to manage a staff once all the pieces came into place, and the team's fine play after June offered encouragement for better things in 1941.

15

As World War II Beckons, the Angels Flounder

Of all the years in their history, the 1941 season was probably the most unsettled for the Angels. The club had played well down the stretch in 1940 and hoped to build on that finish to win another championship; in fact, the Angels were considered the favorite to do just that during the spring training. Instead, Los Angeles suffered a disastrous season, finishing in seventh place. The Angels were never in the race and spent a good portion of the year in the cellar. Only a doubleheader sweep on the last day of the season enabled them to finish .001 percentage points ahead of Portland. The Angels won only 72 games, the lowest total since the war-shortened season of 1918, and failed to win half their games for the first time since 1927.

The roster of the club had changed considerably during the off-season. The fine infield of 1940 was no more, Ed Cihocki having retired and Lou Stringer advancing to the Cubs. This left two big holes in the middle of the defense, and they were never adequately filled. First baseman Rip Collins refused to sign another minor league contract, so the Angels were able to accommodate his wishes by selling him to Pittsburgh at the end of spring training. Collins and Lou Novikoff had provided the bulk of the Angels power in 1940; without their big bats in the lineup, only Johnny Moore posed much of a home run threat.

The training camp of 1941 was full of young players, many of whom had worked their way through the Cub farm system with stops at St. Joseph, Yakima and Tulsa. After two weeks of workouts, manager Statz pronounced the group "the finest crop of rookies ever in an Angels camp." Among the new players were first baseman Wimpy Quinn, infielders Jack Hanson, Lenny Merullo, and Rabbit Mallory, and outfielders Bob Powell, Ralph Samhammer and Gordon Donaldson. Unfortunately, none of them contributed much to the Angels that year, and all were gone by the middle of the season.

Statz again was hopeful of becoming strictly a bench manager, and this year he found his successor in the young infielder, Peanuts Lowrey, who had come up from Tulsa in 1940 and played well in a utility role. Lowrey showed a fine arm with good range in the outfield and seemed to be a much better hitter than he had been previously. Statz elected to open the season with the somewhat more experienced Samhammer in center field, but when he showed an inability to hit Coast League pitching after a month, Lowrey took over for the rest of the year. He was one of the few bright spots in the dismal Angels season, batting third and hitting .311.

The 1941 Angels. *Front row (left to right):* Ray Prim, ball boy Russell Hall, batboy Martin Tryk, Bill Holm, Jimmie Reese, Joe Berry. *Middle row:* Trainer Frankie Jacobs, Johnny Moore, Bill Schuster, Peanuts Lowrey, manager Jigger Statz, president Dave Fleming, Jess Flores, George Coffman, Frank Totaro, John Stamper. *Back row:* Phil Weintraub, Eddie Mayo, Gilly Campbell, Lee Stine, Roy Paton, Bob Weiland, Wally Berger, Harvey Storey, Len Merullo, Fay Thomas, Rabbit Warstler, clubhouse man (unknown) (courtesy Mark Macrae).

Bob Collins was back from Chicago to handle the catching again, along with Billy Holm, and the pitching looked to be satisfactory with Prim, Bonetti, Stine, Weiland and Jess Flores expected to handle most of the starting assignments. Fay Thomas was also available for spot duty in his eighth season with the club. However, Weiland held out for much of the training period, and he apparently needed the work, for he was hit hard in early appearances and was eventually released to Milwaukee after winning only one game.

The Angels opened against Portland with five rookies in the lineup — Wimpy Quinn, Rabbit Mallory and Lenny Merullo in the infield, and Gordon Donaldson, Wally Carroll and Ralph Samhammer in the outfield. The Beavers, behind their ace, Ad Liska, blanked the Angels, 4–0, in a game that seemed to set the pattern for the year. The Angels demonstrated little offense during the first three weeks of the season. None of the rookies was hitting. Within a week, Mallory was sent to Yakima, replaced by Rabbit Warstler, a 36-year-old veteran infielder from the National League, who took over at second base. In the meantime, Johnny Moore returned to his customary right field position. Still, the Angels dropped into last place on April 28 after losing a doubleheader to Hollywood, and they were destined to spend many days in the cellar as the season wore on.

Angels management tried desperately to get some offense into the lineup. Phil Weintraub was purchased from Minneapolis in the American Association to replace the weak-hitting Quinn at first base, and this proved to be a good move. The 34-year-old former Giant hit .302 and tied Moore for the club lead in home runs with 18. Outfielder Wally Berger, a star with the club over a decade ago, was signed as a free agent in May, but he was in the twilight of his career and played infrequently before his release in August.

Gradually, the lineup settled down, with Weintraub, Warstler, Merullo and Mayo in the infield and Moore, Lowrey and Harvey Storey as everyday players in the outfield. Early in June the Angels traded catcher Bob Collins to Seattle for Gilly Campbell, who had caught for the 1934 champions. Campbell strengthened the defense behind the plate, but he did not hit as well as Collins. The pitching, which had been ineffective at the beginning, stabilized behind Julio Bonetti and Fay Thomas, who threw several well-pitched games in a row. By the middle of June, the Angels had advanced to fifth place and were playing at a .500 pace, but still well behind first-place Sacramento, which was showing signs of running away with the pennant

Then the first of several disruptive incidents took place. On July 2 the announcement was made that Bonetti had been permanently banned from baseball by the President of the National Association, Judge W. G. Bramham. Bonetti was accused of having a close association with gamblers. There had been a two-month probe of gambling activities in Los Angeles by Angels management, and at one time or another, all of the Angels players had been under surveillance. It was during this portion of the investigation, specifically on May 7, that Bonetti was seen outside of the Coliseum Hotel receiving a stack of bills from Frenchy Reshaw, a local small time horse owner and alleged bookmaker and gambler. Reshaw then drove off, and Bonetti went into the hotel, where he lived. That night Reshaw went to Wrigley Field, taking bets on Hollywood. Bonetti was the Angels starting pitcher in the game and pitched eight innings without a decision in a game that Los Angeles won, 10–8.

During testimony before Angels president Dave Fleming and PCL president W. C. Tuttle, Bonetti did not deny that he had received money from Reshaw, but his story sounded confused. At first, he said he was cashing large bills for Reshaw; then, later he said that he had just cashed his paycheck with Reshaw and was about to make a deposit in his savings account. He later acknowledged that he may have placed a bet for Reshaw with a bookie in the hotel. Fleming thought the entire account was suspicious and reported accordingly to Judge Bramham, who made his decision. The Judge made it clear that Bonetti was not accused of throwing a ball game. His banishment was a result of the close and inappropriate association that he apparently had with suspected gamblers.

Bonetti vigorously denied that he had done anything wrong and promised to obtain legal advice and appeal the decision. He hired Sidney Chirness, a lawyer who had been an Angels batboy in his youth and had maintained close ties with the Angels players. Chirness made it clear that he was not Bonetti's attorney, but would give him procedural advice and solicit testimony from select Los Angeles businessmen. But all of these efforts were to no avail. At the appeal to the Executive Committee of the National Association, Bramham's decision was upheld, and Bonetti's name remained on the permanently suspended list.

What was Bonetti guilty of? That question remains unanswered to this day, or if it has been, the answer has not been made public. It appears very likely that Bonetti was not betting on baseball games, for no evidence to that effect has ever surfaced. He did spend time at the race track, but that was not an unusual pursuit among ballplayers of that era, despite the known opposition of Commissioner Landis to such activity. There was much concern in Los Angeles about the widespread gambling in the city, and perhaps Bonetti was simply a scapegoat. Both Landis and Bramham acted harshly in their dealings with what they perceived as conduct detrimental to baseball, and frequently, their decisions were quite arbitrary. This case seems to have been one of them.

Bonetti spent much of the remainder of his short life trying to prove his innocence, and finally won reinstatement in 1949. But he was unable to make a comeback after eight years away from the game and sadly died of a heart attack in 1952 at the age of 41. He was the Angels' leading pitcher with a 7–3 record at the time of his suspension, and his absence put an additional strain on a pitching staff that was not doing well. Weiland had been taken out of the rotation because of ineffectiveness, while Lee Stine's work was well below his 1940 performance. Only Ray Prim and Jess Flores were able to give consistently good efforts, although Fay Thomas occasionally showed flashes of his former brilliance.

The Angels moved into fourth place on July 4, and that proved to be the high point of their season. But they strengthened themselves at shortstop for the balance of the season and many years to come when they acquired Bill Schuster from Seattle on waivers and dispatched the light-hitting Merullo to Toronto in the International League. "Broadway Bill" was 29 and had been given brief trials with Pittsburgh and the Boston Bees before surfacing in the PCL in 1940 with the champion Rainiers. He was the regular shortstop in both 1940 and 1941 but the Rainiers wanted the younger Ned Stickle as their regular and opted to trade Schuster in mid-year. Schuster had good range at shortstop and was very steady. He was a fair hitter, but above all else, he was a hustler. His aggressive play on the bases and in the field put him into numerous confrontations with opposing players, but he would be highly popular with the Los Angeles fans for years.

At about the same time, young Johnny Stamper was purchased from Yakima to take over the second base slot, and this move strengthened the Angels' infield further. However, the new infield lasted only until July 16 when third baseman Eddie Mayo was suspended by President Tuttle for one year. His crime occurred on July 13, when he allegedly spit in the face of umpire Ray Snyder during the course of an argument. As in the Bonetti case, events were hazy, but Snyder was convinced that Mayo had spit in his face and filed his report accordingly. An earlier decision by Judge Bramham required that any player who was guilty of this behavior would suffer a year's suspension. Mayo did not accept the verdict and filed an appeal with the Executive Committee to reverse that decision. Coincidentally, the hearing was to be held the same day as Bonetti's. At a preliminary meeting with Bramham, Mayo denied that he spit in Snyder's face. The umpire remained certain that he had. Finally, on September 5, Mayo was exonerated of all charges and allowed to rejoin the Angels. The club was on the road at the time, but when it returned to Los Angeles, Mayo was greeted with a standing ovation by Los Angeles fans.

Mayo was out of action for over eight weeks, and the Angels began their slide to the bottom of the league during his absence. The club was further damaged when Phil Weintraub severely injured his wrist and missed the last six weeks of the season. He was replaced at first base by pitcher Lee Stine, who was a fine hitter but without the power of Weintraub. By the end of August, the Angels had fallen to seventh place and then slipped into last after losing seven straight in Seattle. Only a sweep of the Sunday doubleheader on the season's final day kept Los Angeles from finishing in the cellar.

Johnny Moore and Peanuts Lowrey shared the Angels Most Valuable Player award for 1941. The ageless Moore was the PCL batting champion with a .331 average and led the Angels in runs batted in while tying Weintraub for the home run lead, although he missed 38 games with various injuries. In addition to his excellent work in center field, Lowrey filled in very nicely for Mayo while he was out of action.

In November 1941, the entire Wrigley organization underwent a major change that was to have profound impact on the Los Angeles baseball club. The Angels had operated as a division of the Santa Catalina Island Company, a holding company for the real estate interests of the William Wrigley estate. Included in the company as separate divisions were Catalina Island real estate and Wrigley Field, as well as the ball club itself. The stockholders of the holding company voted to liquidate the Angels club and sell the franchise rights to the Chicago National League club. In effect, the transaction sold one Wrigley property to another. Wrigley Field remained part of the holding company and was rented to the Angels.

For years the Angels had been viewed as a farm club of the Chicago Cubs, but that was not really the case. The stockholders of the two companies were different. Before the concept of the major league farm system became dominant, an independent club such as the Angels could sign its own players and sell them to the major leagues. But in recent years, the Angels and other independent clubs were finding it more difficult to compete with the major leagues for young talent, and eventually, there would be a decline in the quality of play. The Angels had experienced some of those problems in 1941, when they were unable to acquire Glen Russell from the Cubs; he had already been assigned to the Cub farm club at Tulsa in the Texas League. Now Los Angeles would receive first choice of the best Chicago talent available.

With the change in the organizational structure, the era of Dave Fleming was at an end. He had served as Angels president for eight years, and during his stewardship the club had won two pennants as well as a split title in 1935. His successor was Clarence "Pants" Rowland, who had a long association with the Wrigley family. In recent years he had served as president of the Milwaukee club once the Cub relationship with the Brewers had been established. Although he had a much better baseball background than Fleming, Rowland's primary loyalties were with the Cubs. During his tenure Chicago interests would be served first. This pattern would eventually weaken the Angels franchise and dilute the fan loyalty that had developed over many years.

The 1941 season was very nearly the last one for the Angels in Los Angeles. Don Barnes, the owner of the St. Louis Browns of the American League, had been quietly working on a transaction with P.K. Wrigley, whereby he would purchase the Angels franchise and Wrigley Field for one million dollars and move the Browns to Los Angeles for the 1942 season. The Angels would move their operations to Long Beach as a Brownie farm club. Barnes had all of the necessary votes from other American League owners for the transfer, and he would sell Sportsman's Park and his territorial rights to St. Louis to the rival Cardinals, who would provide much of the money to buy the Angels. The scheduling and transportation details had all been worked

Los Angeles Railway Tickets — Los Angeles had a thriving street railway system during the heyday of the Angels, and fans were encouraged to use that method of transportation to get to Wrigley Field. The weekly passes frequently featured Angel players (courtesy Dick Dobbins).

out, and the issue of the transfer was scheduled to be the first item of business at the annual winter meeting of the American League. Unfortunately for Barnes and the Browns, the winter meetings were scheduled to begin on Monday, December 8, and the Japanese had attacked Pearl Harbor only one day before to bring the United States into World War II. No one knew whether there would be any baseball at all in 1942, and the motion to relocate the Browns was quickly tabled. Los Angeles would have to wait another 16 years before major league baseball would arrive in the city.

16

Disaster in Sacramento

The interest and excitement over the complete reorganization of the Angels front office in November 1941, was soon displaced by concern over the Japanese attack at Pearl Harbor on December 7. The coastal regions of the United States immediately came under the jurisdiction of the armed forces command, and throughout December and January a Japanese attack on the mainland was considered to be a distinct possibility. There was serious doubt that baseball would be played in 1942, given those conditions, but in early January, in a reply to an inquiry from Commissioner Landis regarding the status of the game, President Roosevelt gave his approval for baseball to continue. He felt that the game would be important to the morale of the nation, although it would, like all institutions in America, be subject to the demands of waging a war.

The Coast League considered itself to be especially vulnerable to government restrictions, and the league directors were uncertain what to do as the new year opened. Yet, as the danger of attack receded, it was decided that spring training should proceed as scheduled, pending an approval of the 4th Army Command. General John L. Dewitt, the commanding officer, gave his permission for Pacific Coast League baseball in 1942, with the clubs permitted to play night games, as usual. However, attendance at those games could be no greater than the average crowd of the previous year, which meant that the Angels could allow an attendance of no more than 2,900. The Army subsequently withdrew its permission for night games that originated within 15 miles of the coast, meaning that only Sacramento could continue after-dark play. The edict would take effect on August 20, forcing the PCL clubs to reschedule games to late afternoon or twilight hours, neither of which proved to be successful. The Angels decided to revert to an all daytime schedule with games beginning from two to three o'clock; they played their last night game on August 7. The ban on night baseball continued through the 1943 season.

With the uncertainty of operation removed, the PCL went about its business as usual, albeit with some minor changes. The roster limit, which had been increased to 25 the previous November, was reduced back to 20 players, and there was no distinction made between veteran and rookie players. Although a significant number of players enlisted in the service after war had broken out, there were few draft calls during that first wartime year. The first Angels player called to the colors was young pitcher Frank Totaro, who joined the Navy in late December. Eventually, all clubs were heavily impacted by the draft, and by 1945 the Angels had 62 players under contract who were in one branch or another of the Armed Forces. But in 1942 players were readily available.

The Angels had undergone a major overhaul after the dismal season of 1941. Of the pitchers who ended the season, only Ray Prim was returning, while Mayo, Schuster, Moore, Campbell and manager Statz were the regular players on hand. Much movement occurred within the Cub system itself; the Angels sent Joe Berry and Fay Thomas to Tulsa, while Jess Flores and Peanuts Lowrey were promoted to Chicago. From Tulsa the Angels received first baseman Eddie Waitkus and outfielder Barney Olsen, both of whom would play important roles in Los Angeles in 1942. At the winter meetings held just after the Pearl Harbor attack, the Angels acquired second baseman Roy Hughes from Montreal and pitcher Red Lynn from Jersey City, purchased pitcher Paul Gehrman from Birmingham, and traded Phil Weintraub to St Paul for outfielder Fern Bell. Angels fans had not seen such off-season activity for many years.

Waitkus was one of the prime prospects in the Cub system. He was 22 years old, a fine fielding first baseman, and a line drive hitter without a lot of power. In his only year in Los Angeles, Waitkus hit .336 and was selected as the team's Most Valuable Player. He was considered the best prospect in the Cub system and would certainly have been in the major leagues in 1943 had not the military intervened. Hughes had made his major league debut with the Indians in 1935 and later saw service with the Browns and Dodgers before returning to the minors. He, too, was a good fielder with excellent range, and he worked well with Schuster in turning the double play. With Eddie Mayo back at his familiar third base spot, the infield was solid, perhaps the best in Angels history. As a group, the infielders missed only 25 games combined, and no one hit less than .298. The constant movement of players in and out of the lineup that was such a part of the 1941 season was a thing of the past.

Bell and Olsen were installed in left and center field, respectively, with Johnny Moore in right field. The veteran Bell had first appeared in Los Angeles in 1934 with the original Hollywood club and had made the rounds of the minor leagues. He had enjoyed a fine season in the American Association in 1941, but he struggled badly with the Angels, hitting only .228 before his release in late June, when the Cubs returned Peanuts Lowrey to Los Angeles.

Olsen had played in Tulsa with Waitkus the year before and hit better than expected. He started well with the Angels and was the league's leading hitter through the end of May before slumping late in the year to finish at .302. He led the PCL with 33 stolen bases that year and was adequate in center field, although not outstanding; Lowrey replaced Bell in left field upon his return, but he was a better outfielder than Olsen, and the two switched positions in August. Olsen was then sold to the Philadelphia Athletics on a trial basis in September, but his call into the military early in 1943 nullified that deal.

During the spring the Cubs filled out the Angels pitching staff by sending left-hander Ken Raffensberger to Los Angeles, along with Roy "Peaches" Davis, Jess Dobernic, Pete Mallory and Red Adams, who was later to become the Dodger pitching coach for many years. Big Ed Heusser was purchased from Atlanta after a 20-win season there, and he joined the rotation at the beginning of the year. Al Todd, a veteran of many National League seasons, was acquired from Milwaukee to do the bulk of the catching, with Gilly Campbell still around as his backup. It was a formidable team that Pants Rowland had assembled, and the Angels were expected to be a strong contender for the pennant. They started slowly, but a successful week at home when they took six of seven games from the Solons propelled them into second place. Los Angeles took the lead for the first time on May 12 and moved 2½ games ahead on May 17 after splitting a Sunday doubleheader with the defending champion Seattle Rainiers. A crowd of 15,905 showed up for that one, the largest attendance for a game at Wrigley Field since 1933.

16. Disaster in Sacramento

The pitching had been suspect during that first month of the season, but it was immensely strengthened when the Cubs returned Jess Flores on May 10. He joined Ray Prim, Red Lynn and Mallory as regular starters, with Raffensberger and Gehrman used as occasional starters while handling most of the relief work. The Angels fell back out of the lead in late May, falling as low as third during the middle of June, but rebounded with the return of Lowrey and regained the lead on July 16 during the course of a 14-game winning streak. Their main competition was not Seattle, as expected, but rather Sacramento, led by manager Pepper Martin, which was close behind. In head-to-head action, the Angels seemed to be the better team, but they could not pull away from the Solons. At the end of July, the Angels lead was 4½ games, but it was never to be any greater.

The two teams remained close through August, and Sacramento cut the gap to two games when September began. With three weeks to go in the season, the clubs would play each other in the final series of the year at Sacramento. The Angels lead was reduced by a game during the first week, and then the Solons caught Los Angeles on September 12 by winning two straight doubleheaders at Seattle. The next day, however, the Angels appeared to have dealt a major blow to Sacramento when they beat Hollywood twice while the Solons ran afoul of the Rainier aces, Dick Barrett and Hal Turpin, to drop their doubleheader. That restored the Angels lead to two games with a magic number of five to win the pennant; any combination of Angels wins and Solon losses that equaled that number would do the trick. Los Angeles journeyed to Sacramento to begin the critical series, needing three wins for the pennant. But no one expected it to be easy. In their previous series at Cardinal Field, the Angels had lost five of the seven games played, and had not been an especially good road team in 1942.

Both managers opened the series with their best pitchers, Ray Prim against Tony Freitas, and the Angels enjoyed the better of it, winning 5–0 with Prim getting the win, helped by three sparkling innings of relief from Paul Gehrman. The next day saw Los Angeles win again, 5–2, behind a well-pitched game by Red Lynn and a timely home run by Bill Schuster. The Solons used four pitchers in that one as former Angels pitcher Gene Lillard took the loss in relief. That gave the Angels a four-game lead with only five to play. They seemed to have matters well under control the next day behind Jess Flores, who was the Angels' hottest pitcher at that stage of the season. He went into the last half of the eighth inning, leading, 4–1. But then, Buster Adams and Ray Mueller hit back-to-back home runs to tie the game. The Solons threatened to take the lead against Gehrman before Ray Prim came in to stop the rally in his only relief appearance of the season. Then in the ninth, two hits and a throwing error by Roy Hughes allowed the winning run to score.

Sacramento brought back Tony Freitas in game four after only two days rest, and Jigger Statz countered with Ken Raffensberger, who had been a workhorse all year long but had been ineffective for about a month. He failed to retire a single hitter as the Solons scored five runs in the first inning, and Freitas breezed to a 10–2 victory to reduce the lead to two games. The Saturday game was probably the most exciting game of the series. The Angels started Gehrman against Kemp Wicker, and neither was particularly effective, with the game turned over early to Jess Flores, back in action for the second day in a row, and Bill Schmidt. The game went into extra innings, tied at 4–4, when Flores drove in the leading run with a double in the eleventh inning. It seemed like a certain Angels victory with their best reliever on the mound, but when Flores opened the bottom half of the inning with a walk to Adams, Statz decided to bring in Red Lynn. After Mueller sacrificed Adams to second, Gene Lillard was brought in to pinch-hit for pitcher Bill Schmidt. Lillard had spent most of 1942 with Rochester in the International League and appeared in only 29 Sacramento games. But he more than earned his pay on this occasion when he belted Lynn's second pitch over the left field wall to give the Solons a 6–5 victory. Years later, Lillard remembered that game as his greatest thrill in baseball. The Angels lead was now down to one game.

Los Angeles was reeling now, and everyone sensed it. Sacramento could win the flag by sweeping the Sunday doubleheader, and an overflow crowd of 11,600 showed up for the twin bill. The Angels started Prim against Blix Donnelly, each with only two days rest, and neither was around for very long. Los Angeles took the early lead and seemed comfortably ahead until the seventh inning. Then a home run by Mel Serafini reduced the lead to 5–3, and in the eighth, the Solons scored four runs to win, 7–5. Incredibly, Buster Adams and Ray Mueller hit back-to-back home runs in that inning, just as they had in Wednesday's game. Adams' blow off Peaches Davis tied the score, and Mueller's clout off Flores won it. Sacramento brought in Tony Freitas in the ninth to set the Angels down in order. The teams were now tied for first place.

The second game saw Red Lynn back in action against Freitas, with this game decided early. Lynn seemed exhausted and gave up five runs in the first three innings before Jess Dobernic came in to shut out the Solons for the balance of the game. But Freitas allowed only four hits in winning his 24th game of the season, and the Angels were beaten, 5–1. The victory gave Sacramento its first championship in PCL history.

The playoffs seemed anti-climactic after the bitter series in Sacramento. The Angels managed to defeat the fourth-place Padres in seven games in the opening series, but they were not able to handle Seattle in the final set, losing four games to two. All of the games were played at Wrigley Field because of travel restrictions, and the Angels were usually dominant in their own park, but they managed only one home run during the series.

The day after the playoffs ended, Jigger Statz submitted his resignation as manager of the Angels. He issued a statement that indicated his decision was voluntary and was made for the good of the club. The Los Angeles' press corps did not accept this explanation, however, and writers Al Wolf and Paul Zimmerman were emphatic in their refusal to believe it. Jigger was unquestionably under pressure to improve the club in 1942 after its poor showing in 1941. There was some controversy over his handling of the pitching staff; he was thought to have overworked his starters by using them extensively in relief. This may have been a legitimate criticism in the case of Ken Raffensberger, who appeared in 51 games, split almost equally between starts and relief appearances, and seemed worn down in August and September when he lost seven of his last nine decisions. But Jigger was forced to go with what he had, and he was left shorthanded when the dependable Peaches Davis went down with a rib injury for almost two months. Perhaps the real agenda was that Pants Rowland and the Cubs wanted their own man in charge. When the Angels failed to win the pennant, Jigger's time was at an end.

So ended one of the more remarkable careers in American sports. Jigger Statz played in 3,473 professional baseball games, an all-time record until it was broken by Hank Aaron in 1976. He stroked 4,093 hits, behind only Ty Cobb and Pete Rose, and owned a lifetime batting average of .309. His 18 years of service with the Angels remain the most years with one club in minor league annals. He became a legend among Los Angeles fans who were privileged to see him play. Those who played with and against him considered him without a peer as a defensive outfielder. Of those men spoken to in compiling this history, each said that, without a doubt, Statz was the best centerfielder he had ever seen, either in the majors and in the minors. He tended to play a shallow centerfield, but had an uncanny ability to go back on a ball, and few went over his head. Simply put, the spectacular catch was routine for Statz. For years after he had retired, the cry, "Jigger would have had it," was heard after one of his less talented successors failed to make the play.

Statz had very large hands, and he curiously always cut a hole in the center of his glove, the better to feel the ball, he said. The gloves were not very large during his playing days, and when Dr. Statz finished his operation, there was little left indeed. For many years Statz used Carl Dittmar's discarded gloves to perform his magic in the outfield.

Although the Angels of 1942 featured young players Waitkus, Lowrey and Olsen, and young pitchers Gehrman and Raffensberger, the veteran players were perhaps the most valuable. Prim finished with a 21–10 mark and a sparkling 2.47 ERA in his seventh year with the club. He was a workhorse as usual, with 277 innings pitched and not a single missed start. Always blessed with remarkable control, he pitched his finest this year; he walked only 39 batters, roughly one a game. In right field the venerable Johnny Moore hit .347 to pace the hitters, and he finished second to Ted Norbert in the league batting race. Moore's power was off in 1942, but he still drove in 85 runs, a fine performance for a 40-year-old. Eddie Mayo was the premier third baseman of the league in his last year in Los Angeles, hitting .307 and leading the club with 110 RBIs.

Quite likely, the Angels could have won the 1942 pennant with a little luck. Another win here or there, and the last series would have been only so much exercise. The club might have worn out in late July, for it basically played at the .500 level during August and September and was unable to take advantage of games against the weak Portland and Oakland clubs. The Angels could have used a bit more strength in the bullpen, a weakness that became apparent during the fatal series at Sacramento. Nevertheless, this Angels team was a fine group of players who played entertaining ball that was greatly appreciated by the Los Angeles fans who came out in earnest that year. Attendance increased from 162,881 to 271,169, the highest figure since 1930. It was unfortunate that those fans could not have been rewarded with a championship.

17

Wartime Baseball and Two Pennants

Who would replace Jigger Statz? That question was answered in November 1942, when the Angels hired Bill Sweeney as their new manager. Sweeney was a popular figure in Los Angeles, having managed the Stars in 1940–41 and still a resident in the area. He had served as a coach under Statz in 1942 and was a good choice for the job. Although his time with Hollywood was not particularly successful, he did lead Portland to the PCL pennant as a playing manager in 1936.

For a short time there was concern that there might not be a 1943 season for the PCL. Relatively few players had been called into service through much of 1942, but as the year wore on, the number of draft calls began to increase considerably. Transportation restrictions became greater as well; at the winter meeting of 1942, the major leagues elected to forgo spring training in sunnier climes and remained north of the Mason-Dixon line. For the first time in over two decades, there would be no major league team training in California in the spring. With fewer players available many of the minor leagues decided to suspend operations for the duration of the war. At the close of the 1942 season, there were 26 active minor leagues. That number shrank to nine by the opening of spring training.

At the league meeting in January, the Coast League determined that operations would proceed for the new season but at a reduced level. The season would open on April 17, the latest date in league history, and it would be limited to 22 weeks with only 154 games to be played. Night baseball would not be played in 1943, a continuation of the military policy established in August 1942.

Although most PCL clubs experienced a heavy loss of personnel to the military by the opening of the 1943 season, the Angels were not as greatly affected. They lost Jess Dobernic and Eddie Waitkus to the armed forces and would lose rookie catcher Harry Land and infielder Rabbit Mallory during the season, but that was the extent of it. Meanwhile, the Texas League and South Atlantic League were among those who would not operate in 1943, and the Cubs had farm clubs in both of them. The Angels had the pick of all of the available talent from those rosters, as did the Milwaukee club, which still had a connection with Chicago. From Macon the Angels acquired outfielders Johnny Ostrowski and Andy Pafko, and they retrieved catcher Billy Holm from Tulsa. They would be important additions to what was beginning to develop into a very formidable club.

A number of familiar faces had been promoted to the major leagues after the 1942 season. Eddie Mayo and Jess Flores were now with the Athletics, while Ray Prim was finally getting an opportunity with the Cubs after his many successful seasons in Los Angeles. But

The 1943 Angels. *Front row (left to right):* Elmer Mallory, Andy Pafko, Roy Hughes, Bill Schuster, Harry Land, clubhouse boys. *Middle row:* Cecil Garriott, Bill Holm, Paul Gehrman, John Ostrowski, Wimpy Quinn, Red Lynn, Charlie English, batboy Grover Coleman. *Back row:* Trainer Lou Toro, Bob Latshaw, Oren Baker, Ken Raffensberger, Jodie Phipps, manager Bill Sweeney, Pete Mallory, Don Osborn, Ed Fernandes, Johnny Moore (courtesy Mark Macrae).

good replacements for these players were quickly found. Charlie English was purchased from Nashville after winning the 1942 Southern Association batting championship and would take over third base in his second tour of duty with Los Angeles. Prim's spot in the pitching rotation would be filled by right-hander Jodie Phipps, obtained from Utica of the inactive Canadian-American league. He had won 20 games there and was thought to be a good prospect, although Bill Sweeney was not impressed with him in his early outings. Pitchers Don Osborn and Oren Baker joined the Angels in spring training as bullpen help. Roy Hughes and Bill Schuster were back from the great 1942 infield, and the Cubs sent Wimpy Quinn to the Angels as a replacement for Eddie Waitkus at first base.

The Angels opened at Wrigley Field before 12,000 fans, one of the larger opening day crowds in recent years, and they defeated Oakland en route to winning six of their first eight games. Then after losing the opener of the Hollywood series, the club proceeded to make a shambles of the pennant race. They took the next five games from the Stars before closing the series with a 1–1 tie in the second game of a Sunday doubleheader, prior to their first road trip to the Pacific Northwest. The Angels swept six games at Portland, allowing the Beavers a total of only 15 runs, then took seven straight at Seattle, including two shutouts by Red Lynn and a concluding doubleheader shutout by Jodie Phipps and Pete Mallory on

Sunday. That gave Los Angeles an 18-game winning streak as the club returned to Wrigley Field to entertain Hollywood.

The longest winning streak in PCL history was 19 by the 1903 Seattle Siwashes and the 1939 Angels. That record was tied on May 19 when Paul Gehrman defeated the Stars, 10–4, in the first game of a Wednesday doubleheader, and was broken in the nightcap behind Lynn's 4–1 victory. Finally, the streak came to an end on the next day when ex–Angels player Roy "Pappy" Joiner defeated his former club, 4–2. The Angels record was now 26–4, putting them 8½ games ahead. A crowd of 19,016 turned out on Sunday to show its appreciation for what appeared to be an exceptionally fine team.

During this early surge, Lynn won his first eight decisions to establish himself as one of the best pitchers in the league, while Phipps and Gehrman had only one loss between them. Phipps began the season in the bullpen before being given a start in a seven-inning game against Oakland, which he won, 2–1. After he had picked up two wins in relief, Bill Sweeney put him in the rotation, and Phipps responded with three fine efforts during the streak.

In 1939 the Angels had gone into a tailspin after a long winning streak to fall out of the lead, and they never were able to recover from that slump. The 1943 club played at a .500 pace before winning seven straight and improving its record to 47–17 on June 20, 7½ games ahead of second-place San Francisco, the one real competitor in the league. The Seals were scheduled to make their only visit of the year to Wrigley Field at that point, and the Angels were ready for the clash. They took the first six games from San Francisco before losing the second game of the Sunday doubleheader, ending the pennant race for all intents and purposes. Another impressive crowd of 19,132 was present for that match.

During the first two months of the season, Andy Pafko was the talk of the league. He had signed with the Cubs in 1940 and was promoted to Los Angeles after hitting .300 at Macon in 1942. Only 22 years old, Pafko hit better than .400 through June and was the early leader in home runs and runs batted in. He began the season in center field, but when the veteran Johnny Moore was injured in early May, the Angels acquired Cecil Garriott from Milwaukee to play center field, with Pafko moving to right field. Later in the season, when Garriott was injured, Pafko moved back to center field, which appeared to be his natural position. Pafko waged a fierce battle all season long with Johnny Dickshot of Hollywood for the batting title and edged him out by four points, hitting .356 with 118 RBIs, also a league leading figure. At the close of the season Pafko was recalled by Chicago, where he hit .379 in 18 late-season Cub games. That marked the beginning of his distinguished 16-year National League career.

Pafko was not the only Angels player who enjoyed an outstanding year. Although hitting was down generally throughout the PCL, Roy Hughes and Charlie English each posted a .323 average, and the Angels as a team hit .286, far ahead of everyone else. Johnny Ostrowski led the PCL with 21 home runs while hitting .282, but he also led the league in strikeouts with 109. The Angels received fine work from their bench as well. When Hughes was out for an extended period in June, young Rabbit Mallory filled in admirably for him and hit .346, including a 21-game hitting streak, before leaving for the service in August. Rip Russell had been sent from the Cubs during spring training, but he refused to report and stayed on his farm for the early part of the season. But he changed his mind in July and reported to the Angels, where he hit .320 in part-time duty in the outfield.

The Angels drive to the pennant was relentless, and their record peaked at 100–35 on August 28. The championship was clinched on September 1 with the club 21 games ahead.

The Angels spent the last two weeks of the season on the road before beginning the playoffs, where it was expected that Los Angeles would dominate as it had during the regular season. But in a rude shock, the Seattle Rainiers eliminated the Angels in four straight games. The Angels stopped hitting during the last week, and that slump continued into post season play.

In contrast, the Angels pitching staff was outstanding all year long. The overall team ERA of 2.59 was rivaled only by the 1934 champions, and the staff turned in 23 shutouts in a short schedule. Lynn had the best record at 21–8 with five shutouts, but Paul Gehrman and Ken Raffensberger were not far behind. Raffensberger started slowly, losing five of his first eight decisions, but then won nine in a row, finishing with a 19–11 record and a league-leading 2.14 ERA. On September 1 he and Russell were sold to the Philadelphia Phillies for the 1944 season. Raffensberger became an immediate success in the National League, winning 13 games with a bad ball club, and he also emerged as the winning pitcher in the 1944 All-Star game. Years later, he remembered his years with the Angels in 1942–43 and thought the Phillies were not as good as the PCL champions. In the meantime, Paul Gehrman finished at 20–7, while Jodie Phipps posted a 17–5 mark. The staff was exceptionally durable; the pitchers turned in 103 complete games, a number that has not been equaled in the PCL since then.

On the final day of the season, Bill Schuster was selected as the most valuable Angel. He had an outstanding season in 1943, hitting .275 while delivering repeatedly in the clutch. His excellent fielding and fiery play led most observers, Seals manager Lefty O'Doul among them, to declare that Schuster was better than most major league shortstops that year. For the second successive year, Schuster did not miss a game, and that durability certainly helped to solidify an already capable infield. Schuster's fine play earned him a spot on the Cub roster for the 1944 season.

Despite the absence of night baseball in 1943, the Angels attracted 236,642 fans to their games, a very satisfactory figure. This was less than the 1942 total, but the schedule had been reduced by two weeks in length. The league as a whole saw attendance down by 400,000 fans, with the greatest losses suffered at Sacramento and Seattle. Transportation difficulties resulted in an inordinate number of doubleheaders, which reduced the number of dates that a club had at home. Many teams offered twilight games to substitute for the lack of night baseball, but attendance at these games was generally not good. The Angels struggled with different starting times early in the year and finally adopted a policy of no games on Tuesday and doubleheaders starting at 12:30 on Wednesday. This was praised by military defense officials; the early starting time allowed the swing shift to see the first game before reporting for work.

How good was this Angels ball club? Wartime baseball is usually considered inferior to the prewar variety because many of the best players had been called into service and those who remained were thought to have been of lesser quality. While there is much truth to that notion, the 1943 Angels were considerably above average and likely could have held their own against most PCL winners of the past. The infield was on a par with more publicized versions. Roy Hughes and Bill Schuster were very good middle infielders who worked well together, Charlie English was a good fielder and an excellent hitter as well, and Sweeney thought Wimpy Quinn was the best fielding first baseman he had ever seen. Cecil Garriott and Andy Pafko were fine outfielders while John Ostrowski was merely average. Billy Holm behind the plate did not hit much, but he handled pitchers well and was a very good defensive catcher. Overall Raffensberger and Red Lynn would have been solid starting pitchers in any era, and Paul Gehrman was exceptional at times. But probably none would have enjoyed the success he experienced in 1943. There was some question about the quality of the baseballs used late in the year, after all of the 1942 stock had been used. Certainly, a lesser quality of baseball benefited the pitchers.

Bill Sweeney was an unqualified success during his first year as manager of the Angels and enjoyed that season more than any other in his long career. He would manage nine more years in the PCL until his untimely death in early 1956, but he never guided a better ballclub than the champion Angels of 1943.

The stability that the Angels enjoyed in 1942 and 1943 had disappeared by the time the club opened spring training in March 1944. The manpower demands of the war were accelerating rapidly, and all of Organized Baseball was now seriously affected. Players were receiving draft calls almost daily, while replacements were sought out virtually everywhere. Men whose careers had ended years before returned to action even though they were long past prime baseball age. The PCL saw two 48-year-old pitchers in action in 1944 — Sam Gibson of San Francisco and Byron Speece of Portland. Furthermore, youngsters barely out of high school were filling roster spots. The Angels had two 17-year-olds on their opening roster, Dick Kemper and Bill Sarni, who were both catchers. The 1944 season promised to be both interesting and hectic.

Once again the Angels experienced a major change in the front office. On November 15, 1943, Coast League President W. C. Tuttle resigned his position, and two months later Pants Rowland was elected to succeed him. This was a significant move for the PCL. Rowland was among those who strongly believed that the league should be considered for major league status; his new position would provide the forum to expound those views. For the next ten years, until Rowland left office in 1954, the topic would remain the highest priority on his desk.

The new Angels president was Don Stewart, a long-time official for many clubs who most recently had been the business manager at Tulsa. When the Texas League went dormant in 1943, Stewart assumed another position of responsibility in the Cub organization. His selection met with approval around the rest of the PCL.

Few observers thought the Angels would be able to defend their title when spring training opened. The fine 1943 team had been scattered to the winds with only three regular players back — Bill Sarni, who had signed while still a student at Los Angeles High School the previous July, outfielders Johnny Moore and Cecil Garriott, and the only returning pitchers, Don Osborn and Pete Mallory. But Mallory had already received his draft notice and would depart in May. It became difficult to assemble two full teams for intra-squad games during the first week of training. Gradually, players arrived from all destinations, but there would be many holes to fill.

The Angels opened with a very inexperienced lineup, featuring catcher Eddie Fernandes in right field, and a totally rebuilt infield — Glen Russell, returned by the Phillies, at first base; George Ogorek, a rookie from Portsmouth in the class B Piedmont League, at second; Roy Smalley, just out of high school, at shortstop; and Guy Miller at third. Charlie English had been expected back, but he assumed a civilian job with Western Pipe and Supply in Long Beach and was reluctant to leave it. Only Moore and Garriott in the outfield and Ray Prim, back from a brief stay with the Cubs, offered some semblance of order. In addition to Prim, Pete Mallory, Pancho Comellas (a rookie from Cuba), and Dick Conger, obtained from the Phillies as part of the Raffensberger deal, were the starting pitchers as the season opened.

The 1944 Angels. *Front row (left to right):* Bill Sarni, John Ostrowski, Cecil Garriott, Red Adams, Stan Gray, Tony York, Guy Miller, Claude Horton. *Middle row:* mascot Mickey Stein, ball boy Dick Ritchie, Don Grigg, Ray Prim, Don Osborn, Bill Sweeney, Don Stewart, Johnny Moore, Reggie Otero, Hugh Willingham, clubhouse boy Jack Tutt. *Back row:* Trainer Lou Toro, Eddie Fernandes, Ed Sauer, John Rager, Glen Russell, Jodie Phipps, Roy Smalley, Jorge Comellas, Irvin Stein, Ted Norbert (courtesy Stan Gray).

The Angels played well in winning the first two series of the year and were in first place after two weeks, but then a weak batting attack and the inexperience of the infielders began to show. Los Angeles fell below .500 in plunging to sixth place. Fortunately, none of the opposition appeared to be much better, and what looked to be one of the tightest pennant races in history began to develop; only 2½ games separated the first six clubs. Portland was the early leader with San Francisco and Oakland closely behind.

Bill Sweeney changed his lineup regularly as he attempted to find a winning combination. The Angels acquired slugger Ted Norbert from Milwaukee after he refused to report to the Brewers, and he was inserted in left field to replace Moore, who was now 42 and could not play on a regular basis any longer. When Sarni appeared unable to hit Coast League pitching, Fernandes went back behind the plate and newcomer Manny Salvatierra was given an opportunity in right field. Salvatierra was said to be the "Mexican Babe Ruth," but he did not show it during his brief stint as a regular, hitting only one home run. In another change, Charlie English finally came to terms, reporting to the Angels during the first week of May. Guy Miller was moved to shortstop where Roy Smalley was not hitting and would soon be called to the service.

In June the Angels were strengthened when the Cubs sent outfielders Johnny Ostrowski and Ed Sauer to Los Angeles, and first baseman Reggie Otero reported after sitting out most of the first two months. Otero had been purchased from Utica after the 1942 season but did not play in 1943. A native of Havana, Cuba, Otero was the third in a line of fine fielding first basemen to hold down the position for the Angels. He was much flashier than either Eddie Waitkus or Wimpy Quinn had been and was equally as reliable at the bag. When he came to terms, Sweeney moved Rip Russell to second base, and the infield was finally settled.

It was not in the same class as the infields of the previous two years, but it would be satisfactory.

The Angels gradually worked themselves up to the .500 mark by June 25, although they remained in the second division for most of the month. It was clear that the 1944 pennant would go to the first team that could go on a prolonged winning streak, and the Angels proceeded to do just that. They took six of eight games from Hollywood during the first week in July, then won the next two series from Sacramento and San Diego with ease and went into first place on July 21 after an absence of two months. By August 1 the Angels had increased their lead to three games and were beginning to pull away.

Angels pitching took a sharp turn for the better in July. The rotation now consisted of Prim, Dick Conger, Pancho Comellas and Don Osborn, with Red Adams used in occasional starts. Both Comellas and Osborn had started slowly but began to win with regularity in July. And Sweeney made several lineup changes that bolstered the attack. He moved Garriott to the leadoff position, one of the best moves he ever made. Garriott was just a fair hitter and frequently struck out. But he was a switch hitter who had a marvelous eye at the plate, perhaps the best in Angels history, drawing almost a walk a game as the leadoff hitter. He drew 124 bases on balls in 1944, and no one in the league came even close to that number. Garriott also packed surprising power for someone of his small stature, hitting 13 home runs. His important role in the success of the Angels that year was properly recognized at season's end, when he was selected as the club's Most Valuable Player. John Ostrowski was brought in from right field to replace English at third base, where the peppery little veteran was not hitting and was not playing as well in the field as he had in the past. English was sold to Oakland in early August. Sauer took over in right field, and for the rest of the season the lineup hardly changed. Five games over .500 when the changes were made, the Angels went 46–22 from that point on. Their lead of three games on August 1 grew to six games two weeks later. The Angels won 23 games during August, and by the end of the month the pennant was virtually won. They clinched the championship on September 10 with eight games to play The Angels team that ended the year was far different from the crew that had opened the season and was comparable in quality to the lineup of 1943.

Once again, the Angels did not do well after winning a pennant. They defeated Portland in six games and then faced San Francisco in what was a very lively series. The Angels scored one run in the first three games at San Francisco, losing to the Seals' 20-game winners, Bob Joyce, Tom Seats and Ray Harrell, but then won three consecutive one-run games at Wrigley Field that were all decided in the late innings. The final game saw the Angels ahead early, 2–1, but they proceeded to lose the lead and the series when the Seals scored three runs in the fifth inning on a bizarre play. With runners on first

Jorge "Pancho" Comellas — A winner of 18 games in 1944, the Cuban right-hander made only a token appearance of seven games in the major leagues (courtesy Mark Macrae).

and second, Pancho Comellas attempted to retire the lead runner at third on a bunt, but his throw sailed well over rookie Stan Gray's head, rolling all the way to the outfield wall to allow all runners to score.

As they had in 1943, the Angels led the PCL in average and home runs, but the numbers were smaller —.270 with 73 home runs, both low figures for a league leader. Once the lineup was settled, there was much consistency from top to bottom. Rip Russell led the way, hitting .315 with 17 home runs, while only Guy Miller of all the regulars hit below .282. The pitching staff was not quite as good as the 1943 version, but it had its moments, especially during the last six weeks of the year.

Ray Prim had his finest season in an Angels uniform. He won 22 games, the fourth time he had been a 20-game winner in the PCL, and he posted an ERA of 1.70, the all-time low for the Angels. Unfortunately, that impressive mark did not lead the league in 1944; Clem Dreisewerd of Sacramento was slightly better at 1.61. Prim walked only 40 batters, and opponents hit a weak .226 against him. This fine showing gave Prim another opportunity with the Cubs for 1945, even though he would be 39 years old, and he made the most of it, winning 13 games and starting one game in the 1945 World Series. He remained in Chicago for one more year before returning to Los Angeles in 1947 to finish his career. Prim won 150 games in an Angels uniform, second only to Doc Crandall. A smart pitcher who knew the hitters' weaknesses, he was durable, with seven straight seasons of over 230 innings pitched and also had remarkable control. He did not have a particularly good fastball, a deficiency that kept him from a long and successful major league career.

The biggest surprise on the staff was Pancho Comellas. Although he had enjoyed a fine year in the Piedmont League in 1943, he was not expected to be anything more than a mop up man with the Angels. But Sweeney gave

Ray Prim — He won 150 games as an Angels player. Only Doc Crandall won more (courtesy Dick Dobbins).

him a chance as a starter, and he pitched well early, although he lost several close games. He won his first game on May 7 by pitching a seven inning no-hitter at San Francisco, and that earned him a regular spot in the rotation. Comellas proved to be a workhorse, pitching 276 innings and winning 18 games. He and Don Osborn were most effective down the stretch; from July on, Comellas was 11–5 while Osborn went 10–3.

In his first two years as Angels manager, Bill Sweeney had won two pennants, a feat that no other Los Angeles manager would duplicate. It was not easy to create a winning combination during the wartime years of 1943–44, with players coming and going and the level of talent somewhat questionable at best, but "Irish Bill" did it both years. It was a remarkable accomplishment, one that has never been given the attention that it deserved.

The champions of 1944 had little time to rest on their laurels. During the off-season, the fine team that ended the season running away with the PCL pennant was almost completely dismantled, with only Guy Miller, Rip Russell and Don Osborn returning in 1945. There would be a parade of new faces during the coming season and very little continuity from one game to the next. In spite of Bill Sweeney's best efforts, the Angels found it impossible to contend in 1945 and suffered through one of the dreariest seasons in club history. They finished in seventh place, only three games ahead of the last-place Hollywood Stars. It was the only year in PCL history that the two Los Angeles teams resided at the bottom of the league.

The demands of the war reached their peak during the winter of 1945, even though the conflict was nearing successful conclusion. But the last gasp effort of Nazi Germany during the Battle of the Bulge in December 1944, and the severe casualties inflicted on American armies resulted in greater demands upon baseball from the War Department. Men who had formerly been deferred because of their dependents or disqualified by various ailments were suddenly reclassified as 1-A and ordered to report for induction. Draft calls for ballplayers had increased somewhat in 1944, but they were much greater in 1945, with virtually all men under the age of 40 ordered to take their pre-induction physicals. Every club had to scramble for players, and all season long at virtually every level of Organized Baseball, lineups would include many athletes who would not have played professional baseball during normal times.

The Cubs made heavy demands on the Angels after the 1944 season, purchasing Pancho Comellas, Red Adams, Ray Prim and Reggie Otero from Los Angeles. Cecil Garriott and Ed Sauer had been drafted, while Johnny Ostrowski had been recalled by Chicago. It was expect that he would soon be called to the armed forces as well.

By 1945 the Cubs had some semblance of a farm system, and they were able to send the Angels prospects from Nashville in the Southern Association to fill in the gaps that had resulted. Third baseman Pete Elko and first baseman Mel Hicks were part of this group, and they quickly earned starting positions. Ray Viers, a product of Hamilton High in Los Angeles who was purchased from Atlanta in the same league, was installed as the second baseman, with Guy Miller back at shortstop. Hicks showed that he was a very solid player, and when the Cubs returned Otero in April, Hicks was moved to the outfield where he proved more than adequate. When the Cubs recalled Otero in September, Hicks moved back to first.

The most prominent new face in 1945 was Lou Novikoff. Although he had hit .300 for the Cubs in 1942, he never really performed to the satisfaction of Cub management and was the subject of much ridicule in Chicago newspapers for his fielding efforts. The Cubs finally gave up on him after a mediocre season in 1944 and sent him outright to Los Angeles in February 1945. It was a blow to the Mad Russian's ego, and he announced that he would not report. But a month later, he reported to spring training as if nothing had happened. He was installed in left field, alongside of minor league veteran Jim Tyack, who was purchased from Toronto in the International League. Tyack had seen brief action with the Angels in 1932 and had made the rounds since then, including service with the Philadelphia Athletics in 1943. He proved to be very dependable in the field and hit a solid .326. With Rip Russell in right field for most of the year, the Angels outfield was the strongest part of the club.

But the pitching staff was another story. The Cubs sent a number of young pitchers to Los Angeles to fill in for the losses of Comellas, Adams and Prim, but virtually none of them could compete, even at the reduced level of skill in this wartime year. With the exception of Don Osborn and Charlie Cuellar, another product of the Nashville connection, the Angels were forced to go with completely inexperienced players during April — Joe Slotter, 16-year-old Richie Colombo, Ken Hicks, and Hank Glor were all part of the starting rotation, and the results were not good. After winning five of their first seven games, the Angels lost eight to fall into seventh place. That was to be their ultimate resting place, even though the club played better than expected for the first two months of the season and rose as high as fifth place.

The Cubs offered some help when they returned Adams and Comellas to Los Angeles to strengthen the pitching staff. But the Angels really could have used John Ostrowski, who had been declared 4-F after his physical. For reasons that aren't apparent today, he was sent to the Yankees farm club in Kansas City. This may have been a prelude to the deal for Hank Borowy in July, a trade that enabled the Cubs to win the National League pennant. Lou Novikoff was the major source of power for the Angels, and when he was drafted in mid-July, the Angels had little else. They could have employed Ostrowski's big bat in Wrigley Field, where he always hit well. In total, the club hit 63 home runs that year, the fewest since the Angels had occupied Wrigley Field in 1925.

The club had been playing poorly when Novikoff received his marching orders, losing 13 of 15 games to fall permanently into seventh place, and the subsequent loss a few days later of slick fielding shortstop Guy Miller to the military doomed the club to a low finish. From July 15 on, Los Angeles played at a .364 pace and avoided the cellar only because Hollywood played even worse. The Stars managed to play well when they faced the Angels, however, winning the season series between the clubs for the first time since 1941.

But the Angels managed to stay ahead of Hollywood and gave themselves some breathing room by defeating San Francisco in a doubleheader on the last day of the season to finish three games ahead of the Stars. The lineups that day were much different from those that opened the season, with returning servicemen Russ Peterson at second base, Leroy Paton in left field, and rookie Frank Jelincich in right field.

The Angels of 1945 had two very good pitchers in Don Osborn and Red Adams. Adams won 21 games to earn another trial with Chicago in 1946, and provided an extra bat when he was in the lineup, hitting .349 with two home runs. Osborn finished 18–14 after a slow start, winning eight of his last ten decisions. Charlie Cuellar was effective early, but appeared to lose stamina late in the year, a puzzling development until it was learned that he was suffering from diabetes. The club expected a repeat of 1944 from Comellas after he returned from Chicago, but a glandular disorder sapped his strength and ruined his season. After pitching well for a month, he lost his last 11 decisions to finish at 6–16.

Rip Russell was the best player for the 1945 Angels. He enjoyed his finest year in the PCL, hitting .342 with 14 home runs, and earned another major league chance when his contract was sold to the Boston Red Sox for the 1946 season. Reggie Otero hit .344 after returning from Chicago, but he was strictly a singles hitter who led off the batting order most of the time, collecting only nine extra base hits among his 114 safeties. He had one memorable game in Seattle on August 16 when he rapped out six hits, all of them singles. In addition, Johnny Moore wound down his long Angels career with a flourish. Although 43 years old, Moore was still a fine hitter even though his legs would not allow him to play the outfield for more than a few innings at a time. Bill Sweeney used him almost exclusively as a pinch-hitter, and the veteran delivered time after time, hitting .340 with four homers and 26 runs batted in. This record so impressed the Cubs that they purchased him in September to help in their drive for the National League pennant.

It could be assumed that this weak Angels team drew poorly, but such was not the case. The number of fans that showed up on opening day was 8,889, and the next day, a Sunday, saw 12,188 in attendance. Crowds were satisfactory all year despite the team's woeful showing, and a total of 349,917 paid to see Angels baseball, the third best figure since the opening of Wrigley Field. After the deprivations of the war, people were hungry for entertainment, and baseball was at the top of their list. The Angels would set attendance records for themselves during the next few years when the game returned to normal conditions.

18

A Third Major League? Meanwhile, the Angels Win Another Pennant

The boys were back. In the spring of 1946, with the war finally over and the country converting back to a peace time economy, the Angels did not lack for manpower in spring training as they had in 1945. Sixty-five players reported to the Angels training camp in Fullerton, the largest number ever, and many of them were returning after years of military service. There was a large contingent of players who had performed at lower classifications before the war, but they would be gone when the parent Cubs reduced their surplus as the training period wore on. Other service veterans would be mustered out after the season had begun. 1946 would be another season in transition, just as the previous year had been, but now the talent level would be appreciably better.

The Angels welcomed back outfielders Barney Olsen and Harvey Storey, pitchers Oren Baker and Dick Conger, and infielder Rabbit Mallory from the armed forces, and later would receive infielders Bill Schuster and Reggie Otero, outfielder Ed Sauer and pitcher Red Lynn from the Cubs. This group of experienced players provided a good nucleus from which to build. Loyd Christopher, who had seen limited outfield duty in 1945 because of a badly injured knee, underwent surgery during the winter and looked fit when training opened. Don Osborn was the only returning pitcher from 1945, although the Angels were hopeful that Red Adams would be returned by the Cubs. Just as the season was about to begin, Chicago sent catchers Joe Stephenson and Dewey Williams to Los Angeles along with infielder Cy Block. Bill Sweeney now had many choices when he prepared his opening day lineup.

During the winter meetings of 1945, PCL President Pants Rowland presented the first of what would be several proposals to the Major League Executive Committee to recognize the Coast League as a major league. Under his plan, the league would be given major league status, effective with the 1946 season. It would no longer be subject to the major league draft and would be entitled to option players to the other Class-AA minor leagues, the International League and the American Association. (All three were to be reclassified as AAA, beginning with the 1946 season. The Texas League and Southern Association were promoted to AA). Eventually, the PCL would become a participant in the World Series with the timing to be determined at a later date.

The committee agreed to review Rowland's petition, but at a hearing on March 18, 1946, the proposal was denied. There were several reasons cited, but the primary one was the lack of adequate ballparks in the PCL. The proposal would again be reviewed at the minor league meetings of that year, which coincidentally were to be held in Los Angeles in December. At those meetings, the Executive Committee reaffirmed its original decision, although it did agree to increase the indemnity to any league and any club should its territory be taken as a result of a transfer of an existing major league club.

PCL fans and writers were intrigued by the possibility of major league baseball on the Pacific Coast, and throughout the summer of 1946 there was much conjecture as to what could be done to achieve that objective. The most commonly voiced solution, and one which Rowland outlined in several of his many press releases on the subject, was to convert the existing Coast League to a major league entity, with certain park and financial requirements, and under new ownership where necessary. Financial responsibility was most important, for a large sum of money would be required to bring the existing parks up to major league standards, or in some cases, to build a replacement facility. The league would operate independently from the existing major leagues for a period of five years, during which time the clubs would develop their own talent, establish farm systems as appropriate, and hire their own scouting staffs. After that period, the Coast League would become a full-fledged partner of the American and National leagues.

The idea made for interesting reading, but it was a few years ahead of its time. There was simply no way that the owners of the existing major league clubs would willingly share their monopoly with the PCL owners. They were not concerned that major league baseball stopped at the banks of the Mississippi River in St. Louis. But that was before the tremendous surge in attendance during the 1946 Coast League season. 1945 had been a good year for the PCL; the league had set an attendance record with the clubs drawing 2,918,966 fans. But that record was short-lived; in 1946, a total of 3,709,716 spectators paid to watch PCL games. San Francisco drew 670,563 to its games, a minor league record that was to stand for 37 years. Oakland was not far behind, and the Angels and Hollywood each drew over 500,000 that year. Those numbers served notice on the major leagues that there were large profits to be made in the West, and it quickened their interest in participating in those opportunities. Exactly how that would be done was subject to much discussion during the next several years.

Meanwhile, the Angels were constructing a capable ball club for 1946. The early season lineup was a mixture of youth and experience; first baseman Jack Richards and third baseman Maury Donovan were the rookies. Neither was ready for PCL competition, and they were sent to the Cub farm team at Tulsa in the Texas League after a month-long trial. Veteran Bill Schuster was back at his familiar shortstop position alongside of second baseman Rabbit Mallory; the outfield consisted of Barney Olsen, Loyd Christopher and Ed Sauer. Dewey Williams and Joe Stephenson shared the catching duties, with a starting staff of Don Osborn, Red Lynn, Dick Conger and rookie Cliff Chambers. The latter was a tall left-hander out of Washington State College; he had pitched half a season with Tulsa in 1942 before going into the service for the next three years. Chambers had an exceptional fastball and would compile many strikeouts against Coast Leaguers who were seeing him for the first time.

After three weeks, the Angels were in second place behind the very strong Seals, on the strength of a 10-game winning streak, but that would be their high mark for the season. Several problem positions developed early. Olsen, who had started well, suffered a shoulder injury while sliding into third base in mid–May and was forced out of action for several games. When he returned, it was apparent that his hitting was seriously affected by the injury, and he was in and out of the lineup for the balance of the season, never to realize the great potential he had shown in 1942. Mallory was not the hitter he had been before his military duty and was little better than average in the field. Richards had demonstrated no power in his trial at first base, and he departed the Angels when Wimpy Quinn was mustered out of the military during the first week in May. But Quinn was unable to hit and was replaced by Reggie Otero, an early holdout before he finally agreed to report. Quinn later split some of the first base duty, but the lack of power at the position was a year-long problem.

The Angels solved their concerns at third base when George Archie was purchased from the St. Louis Browns. He had enjoyed several good years with Seattle and was the Most Valuable Player in the PCL in 1940. His hitting in 1946 was not at his prewar level, however, although he was adequate in the field. But Bill Sweeney may have overlooked a solution on hand when he released Harvey Storey after only two brief appearances. Storey signed with Portland, where he played the remainder of the season at third base and became the PCL batting champion, hitting .325. This was an offensive presence that the light-hitting Angels could have used. The second base question was not answered until the Cubs sent Albie Glossop to Los Angeles in May. He had spent several seasons in the National League and saw most of the action after Mallory, veteran Stu Martin, and rookie Hank Schenz had all been tried and found wanting.

George Archie—He won the Most Valuable Player award as a first baseman with Seattle in 1940 but played mostly third base upon joining the Angels after the war (courtesy Mark Macrae).

The constant shifting of infielders did not bode well for the Angels, who fell out of contention by the end of May. 1946 belonged to Oakland and San Francisco. The two Bay Area clubs battled for the pennant all year, with the Angels well in back of them. They dropped to 15½ games behind after losing back-to-back series with San Francisco and Hollywood and spent the balance of the year attempting to fend off the improving Stars, who saw their play improve after Jimmy Dykes replaced Buck Fausett as manager in early August. The Angels managed to stay ahead of the Stars through August, but Los Angeles played poorly during a two-week trip to Portland and Seattle in early September. Hollywood moved into third place with a week to play. The Angels were not able to catch up and finished one game behind the Stars, in fourth place and only 1½ games in front of Sacramento and 21 games behind the champion Seals.

The Angels of 1946 did not have much offense. What little power they had came from the bats of Loyd Christopher and Ed Sauer, who together hit 46 of the club's 72 home runs that year. Christopher had an outstanding first half of the season and led the league in batting and home runs through much of July, but he suffered a series of minor injuries and slumped to .304 by season's end, though he was able to maintain his lead in home runs with 26. Sauer hit .273 with 20 home runs and demonstrated one of the most powerful throwing arms in the league in right field. Other respectable averages were compiled by center fielder Leon Treadway, a singles hitter with no power who was purchased from Newark in May, and shortstop Bill Schuster, with both hitting .286. The Angels team batting average of .253 was the lowest for a Los Angeles team since the dead ball year of 1910. The PCL, in total, saw less offense than usual that year, and it was determined that the baseballs used were manufactured from inferior wartime materials, a situation that league officials promised to correct in 1947.

Angels pitching was brilliant at times, but as a whole was very unpredictable. Red Lynn began the year in dominant fashion, winning his first five decisions, which included two shutouts, and by the end of June had already compiled 12 wins. But after that, his record was only 5–10; on the few occasions he pitched well, the Angels bats were silent. Lynn was the victim of five shutouts over the last two months of the year and finished 17–16. Yank Terry, acquired from Boston in the deal for Rip Russell, almost matched Lynn in the first half of the season, but won only one game after July 28 to finish at 12–15. The Angels would have fallen out of the first division had the Cubs not sent Red Adams and Bill Fleming in July, and they were the most dependable pitchers on the staff by season's end, each winning nine games. Cliff Chambers led the club with 18 wins and was the league strikeout leader during much of the season before tiring in the last month. His contract was purchased by the Cubs for 1947 delivery. Oren Baker and Jess Dobernic provided outstanding relief work for most of the year, although they both slumped during the last weeks of the season.

The fans were not disturbed by the mediocre Angels play of the last two months as they turned out in droves to set a new club attendance record of 501,259. The Angels surpassed their 1945 attendance by mid–July in achieving the new record, which would last only a year. For one of the few times in their history, the Stars outdrew the Angels, with 513,056 paying to see baseball at Gilmore Field.

Once again Los Angeles did not play well in the playoffs for the Governor's Cup. They faced the second-place Oaks, a team they had problems with all season, and were defeated in the series, four games to three. After losing two of three games in Wrigley Field, the Angels seized the lead in the series by defeating Oakland in a doubleheader. They had Cliff

Chambers going against Ralph Buxton, an Angels player ten years earlier, in what could have been a clinching sixth game. But the left-hander lost a heartbreaker, 2–1, to tie the series, and in the final game the Angels lost, 6–5, when Max Marshall's double scored Ray Hamrick from first base in the bottom of the ninth inning.

The most valuable player in 1946 was Bill Schuster, and few questioned that choice. He provided the only stability in the infield, skillfully used the hit-and-run while batting in the second position most of the time, and was an excellent base runner, stealing home twice during the season. Although he had spent the 1944–45 seasons with the Cubs, Schuster had played in every game since he first joined the Angels, a total of 489 in a row before missing the game of June 19. His exuberant play in the field and on the bases won him the most popular Angel award as well.

Throughout the season, there were rumors that manager Bill Sweeney would not be back at the helm in 1947. The Cubs wanted one of their own men as the Angels manager, or so the rumors went. Stan Hack, the long-time Cubs third baseman who had expressed a desire to manage, was said to be the leading candidate for the job. By September it was generally thought that Sweeney was out and Hack was in; yet, when the season ended and the playoffs were underway, nothing had been done. Finally, Sweeney submitted his resignation, stating that he had received an offer from Detroit to serve as a Tiger coach in 1947. He accepted the offer and spent the next two years in the American League before returning to the PCL as manager of the Portland Beavers in 1949. After three years there, he spent two years as the Seattle manager before returning to Los Angeles in 1954 for a second managerial term. One of the most beloved of Angels managers, Sweeney posted a record of two pennants and one fourth-place finish under the trying circumstances of the wartime era, an admirable achievement. The Angels would miss him.

On January 2, 1947, the club announced that Bill Kelly was the new manager, and his hiring was curious, to say the least. Kelly was no stranger to Organized Baseball, having begun his career in 1920 when he received a tryout with the Philadelphia Athletics. Although he had a short major league career, Kelly earned a reputation as a feared hitter with Buffalo in the International League during the 1920s and ended his career with a lifetime .307 average. He served as an umpire in several leagues in the 1930s, including the season of 1935 in the PCL. But his managerial experience was very limited. 1947 would mark only his third year in that role, and he had never risen above the level of Class B, where he had managed Davenport in the Three-I league in 1946. The choice of Kelly was dictated by Cubs general manager Jim Gallagher, another indication of how closely the Angels fortunes were now tied to Chicago.

The Angels of 1946 had three major soft spots at first base, second base and behind the plate, and during the winter the club took important steps to strengthen those positions. Catcher Eddie Malone was acquired from Columbus in a trade for outfielder Barney Olsen, who had not lived up to his pre-war promise. Malone, a local boy from Washington High School, had been a durable catcher since his debut in 1939. He caught 101 games at Columbus in 1946 and increased that number to 142 with the Angels. Malone had a great arm, was a good handler of pitchers, and was a respectable hitter. His 80 assists tied Ed Fitzgerald for the PCL lead in 1947 and were the most for an Angels catcher since the days of Bob Collins in the 1930s.

The uncertainty at second base finally ended when the Cubs sent Lou Stringer to Los Angeles. The great promise that he had shown as an Angels second baseman in 1939–40 had not materialized in Chicago, and the Cubs gave up on him after his play in 1946 seemed to indicate that he was no longer of major league caliber. But he was exactly what the Angels needed to fill their pressing needs in the infield. Stringer was an outstanding fielder who teamed up with shortstop Bill Schuster to form the best double play combination in the league. Stringer was exceptionally reliable in the field and forged a span of 64 errorless games during the middle of the season. With the addition of center fielder Cecil Garriott, released to Los Angeles by the Cubs after his military duty, the Angels had remarkable defensive strength down the middle.

First base was the last piece in the puzzle, one which would not be completed until after the season had begun. The Angels opened with Reggie Otero, but his fine fielding was not enough to overcome his glaring lack of power, and he did not hit consistently in spring training. The club then signed minor league veteran Larry Barton, who had been released by Oakland, and sent Otero to Portsmouth. Barton was 34 and had begun his career in 1932 in the Cardinal organization. By 1947

Top: Bill Kelly — He had limited managerial experience before joining the Angels in 1947, but he won a pennant in his first year at the helm (courtesy Mark Macrae). *Bottom:* 1947 Angels. *Front row (left to right):* Batboy Ralph Hack, Elmer Mallory, Lou Stringer, Don Osborn, John Ostrowski, Jess Dobernic, Bob McCall, Reggie Otero, batboy Jack Roberts. *Second row:* Bo Palica, Bill Schuster, Eddie Malone, coach Jack Warner, manager Bill Kelly, Red Lynn, Bill Sarni, Tuck Stainback, Cecil Garriott, Red Adams, Larry Barton. *Back row:* Trainer Joe Liscio, Clarence Maddern, Bill Fleming, Ed Sauer, Cliff Chambers, Russ Bauers, Loyd Christopher, Al Glossop, Paul Gillespie, Oren Baker, Ray Prim, assistant trainer Dave Flores (courtesy Dick Dobbins).

he had made the rounds of the top minor leagues and had already spent over seven years in the PCL, but he would never play in the major leagues. Barton was a good fielder, perhaps not as good as Otero but certainly comparable, and a consistent but not exceptional hitter. Wrigley Field was an ideal park for him, and he would enjoy a solid season in 1947 with 18 home runs, most of them in Los Angeles.

The Cubs had supplied the Angels with other talent as well. John Ostrowski returned to take over the third base position, George Archie having been sent to San Antonio in the Texas League. Ostrowski would never become an established major league player, but he enjoyed several fine years in Los Angeles, and 1947 would be one of them. Promising young outfielder Clarence Maddern was brought up from Tulsa as a replacement in left field for Loyd Christopher, who had been drafted by the White Sox; the Angels also signed free agent Tuck Stainback as a spare outfielder. Stainback was nearing the end of a long career that had begun so auspiciously in Los Angeles in 1932, but he was still a very useful player who filled in quite well when slumps and injuries affected the other outfielders. In 87 games he hit .279. Ed Sauer was back in right field, and the White Sox later returned Christopher to Los Angeles after they could not agree on contract terms.

The pitching staff, however, was becoming a matter of concern. Bill Fleming and Russ Bauers, a veteran of the National League who had been obtained from the Cubs, were afflicted with arm problems during spring training, leaving a staff dangerously thin in starters. Red Lynn was given the opening day assignment, and he was joined in the starting rotation by Cliff Chambers and Red Adams, who were returned to Los Angeles by the Cubs just as the season began. A rookie left-hander, Bob "Dutch" McCall, showed some promise, and manager Bill Kelly also experimented with Oren Baker as a starter.

The Angels opened at home against Portland and won the first game, 8–6, on a three-run pinch-hit home run by rookie catcher Ted Pawelek. The next two games featured a lot of offense, and the Angels won those by scores of 5–4 and 11–7. No Angels pitcher went the distance in those three games, and that would remain a common event during the year. Kelly did not hesitate to replace a faltering pitcher, often as early as the third inning, and would use what we now call a "closer" to finish up the game. As the season wore on, he began to rely more and more on Jess Dobernic in this role. Dobernic had been successful as a relief pitcher in the last half of 1946 and thrived under Kelly.

PCL executives had promised a livelier baseball in 1947, and they made good on their word. Balls were flying out of all the parks at a furious pace during the first month of the season as the Coast League was becoming a hitter's paradise. Distances to the fences at Oakland, San Diego and San Francisco had been reduced significantly during the previous two years, and with the better balls being used, the number of home runs increased dramatically. The league as a whole saw the number of home runs increase by 73 percent over the 1946 season, more than doubling the number hit at Seattle, San Diego and San Francisco. This was the greatest increase from one year to the next in PCL history.

The Angels came out slugging with all the other teams. They hit 15 home runs during the first two-week home stand, and although that pace slackened a bit as the season wore on, they hit 151 home runs to lead the league, the highest total since 1929. They surpassed their 1946 total before the season was even half over, and many of the blows came in the late innings to win ball games. The new style of play was very entertaining to the Los Angeles fans, who were coming out in droves. The attendance record set in 1946 was destined to last less than a year.

There were no great teams in the PCL in 1947, but there were several very good ones, and the weaker clubs were not far below the top. The Seals were not as good as the year before, having lost Larry Jansen and Ferris Fain to the major leagues, and the Angels were definitely a contender. The two clubs stayed in first or second place through the first two months of the season, with Oakland not far behind. Only one game separated the three clubs at the end of May, with Portland a close fourth. The Angels showed signs of breaking from the pack, but suffered a number of minor injuries that forced Stringer, Ostrowski and Maddern out of the lineup for brief periods. They finally appeared to take charge of the race after sweeping a series at home from San Diego in mid–June, which allowed them to move into first place. They maintained the lead through all of July and were four games ahead at the end of the month. By August 14 the lead had increased to 7½ games, and it appeared that the pennant race had been decided.

The pitching staff had finally stabilized in June, and Cliff Chambers was its ace. He won his first eight decisions and did not taste defeat until May 23 at Sacramento. Despite facing more potent offenses in 1947, Chambers was not giving up many more runs than he did in 1946. The difference this year was that the Angels were scoring more and turning many of the close losses into victories. Chambers had San Francisco's number, winning six in a row from the Seals through early July. Adams and Lynn were consistent winners, and Russ Bauers came back from his early arm troubles to post eight wins in June and July. Bill Fleming was able to contribute as well, and with the relief efforts of Dobernic, Oren Baker and Don Osborn, the pitching problems of the early spring seemed to be solved.

Then the Angels season began to go sour. The club lost two straight series in Oakland and Portland and lost four games of its lead over the Seals while letting these clubs back in the race. Angels pitching was hammered in the two series. Bauers suddenly could not win; he lost his last five decisions, while Dutch McCall lost his last seven. The seemingly insurmountable lead was all but erased by the end of August, when only one game separated the top four clubs.

Chambers won his 20th game on September 1 in the first half of a doubleheader sweep at Portland to temporarily stop the slide, and when the Angels swept San Diego the following Sunday, the lead was back to 3½ games. But the Seals were now playing at their best and surged past the Angels on September 14, as Los Angeles played poorly at Sacramento. Although the Angels were able to handle San Diego during the next series and swept a doubleheader on September 21, the Seals held a two-game lead going into the last week of the season.

It did not seem likely that the Angels could overcome the San Francisco lead. They were facing Sacramento, a team that had been troublesome for them all year, while the Seals were traveling to San Diego for a set against the last-place Padres. But the Angels hitters overpowered the Solons early in the series, rookie Don Carlsen pitching a fine game to give the tired bullpen some rest. The club caught the Seals on Friday, September 26. Both clubs won on Saturday, Chambers pitching his 23rd win, and Adams followed with a gem in Sunday's first game, 6–1, to keep pace with the Seals. All hopes were dimmed when a brilliant effort by Lynn in the second game was wasted, Sacramento winning its only game of the series, 1–0, behind Rex Cecil. The Seals' game was not over yet, and they could win the pennant if they could break a 3–3 tie. But a three-run homer in the last of the ninth inning by Max West won the game for the Padres, leaving San Francisco and Los Angeles in a tie for the lead at the end of regular season play.

A one-game playoff was scheduled as a tie-breaker, and it would be played in Los Angeles on Monday, September 29. The game was the most memorable in the history of

Angels baseball. The largest crowd for a single game in Wrigley Field was on hand — 22,996 announced and hundreds turned away. Neither of the starting pitchers was well rested. Chambers started for the Angels, even though he had pitched on Saturday. He was opposed by right-hander Jack Brewer, a graduate of the University of Southern California, who had a 16–14 record and had pitched a complete game victory on Saturday. The logical choice for the Seals in this game would have been their ace, Bob Chesnes, who had won 22 games. But manager Lefty O'Doul had elected to use him in relief during Sunday's first game and doubted that he could come back in a starting role.

The pitchers were at their best in this classic game. Going into the last of the eighth inning, there was no score, and then after one out....

Years later, Bill Schuster remembered it well.

Bill Schuster — A fan favorite, Schuster was probably the best shortstop of his era. He is a member of the Pacific Coast League Hall of Fame (courtesy Dick Dobbins).

"Garriott walked. After one pitch I put the hit and run on and just managed to hit a ground ball to the right of second. (Hugh) Luby dived for it, but he couldn't get it and Cece went to third. Brewer looked a little shaky while pitching to Ed Sauer. I turned to their first baseman, (Bill) Matheson, and said something like, 'If he doesn't watch out, he's gonna hit him.' Sure enough, he did, and the bases were loaded. Now Maddy was up. He got one and pulled it down the line. I remember yelling, 'Cece, tag up,' because I didn't think it would go out. The ball kept going and going and just barely cleared the wall."

A grand slam! Maddern's 15th home run of the season gave the Angels the lead, and Larry Barton followed with a drive into the right field bleachers to make the score, 5–0. Maddern and Barton were each mobbed by their teammates when they crossed home plate. Then, Chambers easily retired the Seals in the ninth inning to finish a five-hit shutout. It was his seventh win of the season over San Francisco.

The playoffs for the Governor's Cup represented somewhat of an anti-climax after the excitement of the pennant race, but for the first time in their history, the Angels were winners of a post-season championship. They defeated third-place Portland in five games, with Dobernic starring in relief by winning twice and saving the final game. The final series with Oakland also went to the Angels in five games, with Dutch McCall finally ending his losing ways with two victories and Dobernic once again performing well in relief. Larry Barton hit the clinching blow in the final game, a tremendous home run into the centerfield bleachers at Emeryville. For their efforts, the winning Angels earned a sum of $15,000, a fine payout for that era.

The Angels won the 1947 pennant with defense and home run power. They led the PCL in fielding, with the best infield and centerfielder in the league. Both Lou Stringer and Bill Schuster were All-Stars at their positions and Cecil Garriott played center field better than any Angels player since Statz was at his peak. The pitchers did not seem to be of championship quality beyond Chambers and Dobernic, but were helped immensely by the defense behind them, and Angels pitchers allowed the fewest runs in the league.

Clarence Maddern — His grand slam in the 1947 playoff game with San Francisco gave the Angels the pennant.

Angels power was spread throughout the lineup, with Schuster the only regular failing to reach double figures in home runs. Maddern was the only .300 hitter, finishing at .332 with a 21-game hitting streak in September, but Stringer and Ostrowski were close at .293 and .292, respectively. Garriott had his best year as an Angels player with 22 home runs and 131 walks. There were no superstar players in this lineup, but there were no easy outs, and the club boasted a fine bench that performed well when the regulars were forced from

Left: Cecil Garriott — One of the best lead-off men in Angels history, Garriott led the league in walks on three occasions while playing a fine center field. *Right:* Cliff Chambers — The ace of the 1947 pitching staff, he spent the next six years in the National League (courtesy Mark Macrae).

the lineup. Albie Glossop could play any infield position and was a dangerous pinch-hitter as well. Paul Gillespie provided the Angels with an excellent back-up catcher.

Cliff Chambers, the best pitcher in the PCL in 1947, was poised for a successful major league career. His 24 victories were the most for an Angels pitcher since Fay Thomas won 28 games in 1934. Chambers struck out 175 batters, somewhat below his 1946 record, but that figure was sufficient to lead the PCL; he also set a Los Angeles single-game strikeout record when he fanned 15 Padres on September 17. He joined the Cubs in 1948 to begin a seven-year major league career with several National League clubs.

Dobernic appeared in 55 games, all in relief, and had 23 saves, a statistic that was not kept officially at the time. Bill Kelly did not hesitate to use him when the game was at risk, and he gave plenty of work to Don Osborn and Oren Baker as well. No other manager in the league used his relief pitchers as extensively as Kelly did, and he may have been ahead of his time in his careful use of relievers. Russ Bauers was very effective for a six-week period in the middle of the season and pitched as well as anyone on the staff during the time when the Angels were surging into the lead. His arm miseries of the spring seemed to have returned later in the year, when he pitched just well enough to lose. Adams and Lynn were dependable starters, but neither could get much beyond the .500 mark.

The exciting pennant race in 1947 led to a new PCL attendance record of 4,068,422, almost 10 percent greater than the previous record set in 1946. Los Angeles set a club record of 622,485, and combined with Hollywood, over 1,100,000 fans attended PCL games in the Los Angeles metropolitan area that year. It gave added credence to Clarence Rowland's effort to win major league recognition for the PCL in yet another attempt by the league to earn such stature. The proposal was presented to the major league executive committee in July and was promptly tabled until December. Meanwhile, other issues developed. Paul Zimmerman, the sports editor of the *Los Angeles Times*, advanced the thought that Los Angeles fans would prefer to have an existing major league club transferred to Southern California and offered a survey of fans that would endorse that view. It was suggested that the Los Angeles Coliseum would be an appropriate site for the new club, and artist's renderings were prepared to show how that could be done. In August a group of major league officials, which included Commissioner Happy Chandler, and Will Harridge and Ford Frick (presidents of the American and National leagues, respectively), agreed to visit Southern California to pass judgment on the suitability of the area for major league baseball. They visited San Diego and the greater Los Angeles area, and were impressed by what they saw, but once again concluded that the area needed better facilities before it could be considered as a possible major league site, either for an existing major league team, or as an afterthought, the PCL itself. The position of Rowland and the Coast League was not helped by this visit.

At the National Association meetings in December, the PCL changed its approach slightly. The league was now looking for a special status, not immediate recognition as a third major league. The Coast League wanted to increase the time period for a player to become eligible for the draft from four years to six, and establish the draft price at $25,000, well above the existing figure of $7,500. The league also proposed that only one player per team per year, either by sale or the draft, could be sold to the major leagues. But Rowland was not able to sell this plan to the other Triple-A minor leagues and could not gain the necessary three-fourths vote from the other leagues to support it. The majors rejected it as well. It would be several years before the PCL would win any concession from the rest of Organized Baseball regarding its status.

The 1947 season was to be the high point of Bill Kelly's tenure as manager of the Angels, and in fact, he would win no other championships during the remainder of his managerial career. He had duplicated Bill Sweeney's success by winning a pennant in his first year on the job, but the resemblance would end abruptly. The Angels were about to begin the darkest period of their history.

19

Decline and Fall

The Angels success of 1947 was to be short lived. The key players in the championship year were promoted to the major leagues after the season. The Cubs recalled Cliff Chambers and Clarence Maddern, Lou Stringer was sold to the Giants and Johnny Ostrowski was drafted by the Red Sox. Although the Angels were able to find satisfactory replacements, the club that assembled for spring training in 1948 was not as strong as the one that concluded the 1947 season. They waged a game fight to defend their championship and were in first place as late as July 25, but the club faltered over the last six weeks of the season to finish in third place, 12 games behind the Oakland Oaks, winners of their first pennant since 1927. In actuality, the Angels record of 102–86 was only four games off their 1947 record.

This would be the last Angels club that would find itself in pennant contention for quite a while. Not until 1955 would Los Angeles be a factor in the race, and by that time the club had lost much of its loyal fan base that had developed over the years. Concurrent with the decline in Angels fortunes, the arch-rival Hollywood Stars would begin their greatest years of prosperity. They would win three pennants, lose a fourth in a one-game playoff in 1954, and finish no lower than third place over the next seven years. Their exciting play captured the fan interest in Los Angeles, where the Stars received most of the press coverage. The Angels became "nobodies," with only a hard core of devoted fans interested in their play. Attendance, which had peaked in 1947 at 622,485, declined to less than half of that number by 1955.

What caused this rapid deterioration of what had once been the finest minor league franchise in America? There were many reasons, but probably the greatest single factor was the increasing importance of the major league farm system. By 1948 the day of the independent minor league operator was nearing its end. The major leagues controlled the majority of the playing talent, leaving the minor leagues almost completely dependent on them for players. No longer did Coast League clubs sign and develop their own players. Major league scouts took the best of the players, and the local clubs were forced to enter into working agreements in order to guarantee that they would have competitive teams. It became very difficult to acquire good players on the open market.

The Angels would seem to have had an advantage as a result of their affiliation with the Chicago Cubs, but at this time what had been a premier franchise in the National League was being transformed into a chronic second-division club through inept management and poor player development practices. The talent signed by the Cubs in the postwar period was inferior to most teams, and unfortunately, much of it found its way to Los

Angeles. After 1948 the Angels were almost wholly dependent on Chicago for their players, most of whom were not as good as those available to other Coast League teams. As a result, the Angels were barely competitive during this gloomiest of all periods in Angels history.

To replace the important player losses to the major leagues, the Angels drafted pitcher Dewey Adkins from Atlanta, purchased outfielder Dom Dallessandro from the Cubs, traded outfielder Loyd Christopher to Oakland for infielder Mickey Burnett, and purchased third baseman Jim Tabor from the Boston Red Sox. These new players filled most of the vacancies resulting from the off-season transactions. One important cog in the 1947 machine that remained irreplaceable was relief pitcher Jess Dobernic, who had been promoted to the Cubs after his fine season. The Angels picked up pitcher Walt Lanfranconi from the Braves shortly before the season began in hopes that he would absorb some of the load in the bullpen. Other new pitchers were funneled through the Cub farm system — Hal Kleine, Don Carlsen and Lee Anthony, all up from Tulsa. They would join holdovers Red Lynn, Russ Bauers, Bill Fleming and Red Adams. Although not a bad pitching staff, the only left-hander available to the Angels was Kleine, leaving them very vulnerable to strong left-handed hitting teams such as Oakland and San Francisco.

The Angels opened the 1948 season on the road for one of the few times in their history, winning at San Diego, 7–4, and they played reasonably well during the first six weeks of the season, firmly entrenching themselves in third place. Los Angeles opened with holdovers Larry Barton and Bill Schuster in the infield along with second baseman Burnett and Albie Glossop at third base, filling in for the injured Tabor. Dallessandro joined holdovers Cecil Garriott and Ed Sauer in the outfield, and Eddie Malone was counted on to do most of the catching, with promising youngster Rube Novotney as his backup. Bill Kelly's tendency was to use many pitchers, and he looked at several youngsters during April. Herb Chmiel, Howard Auman and Lee Anthony were given opportunities, but only Anthony appeared ready for the PCL. Kelly used him out of the bullpen, where he was impressive, posting two wins, and then promoted him to a starting role, joining Adams, Lynn and Fred Schmidt in the rotation. Adkins did not join the club immediately, because of the death of his young daughter, but posted his first win in late April in relief. He soon moved into a starting role, replacing Schmidt, and that foursome would start most of the games for Los Angeles.

Dom Dallessandro — "Dim Dom Dal," as he was called, was a solid performer in 1948. It was his first year back in the PCL after leading the league with a .368 average at San Diego in 1939.

Angels hitting seemed to be as strong as it was during the previous year, and the club looked to improve on its league-leading home run totals. Dallessandro was an early home run leader and Ed Sauer was on the verge of his finest year in Los Angeles. When Tabor returned to action, he added power to a lineup that was strong from top to bottom. First base was becoming a problem, however, with Larry Barton unable to duplicate his success of the previous year after suffering a sprained ankle. On May 15, the major league cut-down date, the Angels made several lineup changes. They released Barton after acquiring first baseman Jack Sanford from Jersey City, sent Tabor to Sacramento, and received Johnny Ostrowski back from the Red Sox, where he was unable to make the club. The Cubs sent outfielder Cliff Aberson, shortstop Lenny Merullo, infielder Don Johnson and pitcher Doyle Lade. The Angels were now a very different team from the one that opened the season.

The new players did not improve matters, so Los Angeles dropped to fourth place, eight games behind first-place San Francisco, this after losing the first three games of the series with the Seals. But the club then took the next four games, including a sweep of the Memorial Day doubleheader, to cut the deficit in half. The doubleheader was costly, however. Ed Sauer suffered a broken bone in his knee when hit by a Tommy Fine fastball and was forced out of action for a month. It was the first of many injuries the Angels suffered during June, many of them minor but enough to force some of the veteran players out of the lineup. Still, the Angels were fortunate to have a good bench. Aberson received his opportunity when Sauer was forced out of the lineup, and he delivered a number of home runs. Eddie Lukon filled in, both at first base and in left field, when Dallessandro began having back problems. And Albie Glossop played everywhere in the infield, first when Mickey Burnett went down after a beaning by Seattle's Steve Peek, then later when Johnson and Ostrowski suffered injuries.

Aberson proved to be a very valuable acquisition. A former football player for the Green Bay Packers, he had played part of the 1947 season with the Cubs after tearing up the Western League with Des Moines. He was not a particularly good outfielder, and his arm was merely average, but he had tremendous power. During his first six weeks in the lineup, Aberson hit 17

Cliff Aberson — The former Green Bay Packer showed great potential as a power hitter, but he spent only a part of one season in the major leagues.

home runs, including several shots that cleared the center field wall. About the only weakness he showed at the plate was a high tendency to strike out; Aberson fanned 99 times in only 116 games.

The Angels played well during much of June and July and finally caught the Seals on July 25, when they moved into first place by half a game after winning the first game of a doubleheader from San Diego, 7–6. The pitching had been excellent; the Angels had gone through a stretch when the starters completed 17 out of 19 games. Lynn was having an outstanding season at 14–4, and Bill Kelly had received several nice games from rookie Don Carlsen. The Angels were 16 games over .500 and seemed ready to make a determined run at the pennant. Sauer was back, and most of the other veterans were healthy.

But it was not to be. The second game of that doubleheader was one of the more significant games of the 1948 season, and in retrospect, it marked the real beginning of the Angels decline. Red Adams started that second game, and after two scoreless innings faced Padre slugger Jack Graham. A veteran of many minor league seasons, Graham was enjoying his greatest year. He had hit 46 home runs to that point of the season and seemed certain to exceed the PCL record of 60, set by Tony Lazzeri of Salt Lake City in 1925. Graham had already hit six home runs in Wrigley Field that year, including one in the opener. He had grounded out against Adams in his first time at bat, and this time an inside fast ball caught Graham just above his ear. The big slugger fell as if he had been pole-axed and had to be carried off the field on a stretcher. He would be out for six weeks and hit only two more home runs for the rest of the season. The incident caused some controversy since the Padres thought Adams may have deliberately thrown at Graham, but later the slugger admitted that he had lost the ball in the late afternoon shadows. A shaken Adams was touched up for four runs and lost, 4–0, as the Angels fell out of first place. They would not be as high in the standings again so late in the season for eight years.

The impact of the Graham beaning may have been felt by the Angels, who played listlessly through most of the next series with San Francisco, losing five of the seven games to fall 3½ games behind on August 1, and dropping further behind after another rash of injuries struck the club. Dallessandro missed a number of games with leg problems, Anthony passed up several starts because of a nagging back injury, and iron man Bill Schuster had to miss several games because of his daughter's illness. The Angels dropped to 7½ games behind before closing the gap to five games by the end of the month. But a home series against Seattle proved fatal to Angels chances. The Rainiers took six of seven games from Los Angeles before the Angels put a stop to the slide by sweeping the Labor Day doubleheader. But by that time, the Angels were 9½ games behind the surging Oaks and hopelessly out of the race. The last two weeks were merely for exercise, and entertainment with the Angels firmly entrenched in third place.

The Angels were matched with Oakland in the first round of the playoffs, and they gave a good account of themselves, although they lost the series in six games. The first three games were played at Oakland, with the Angels winning the opener, 10–9, and coming back to win the second game, 9–7, on late-inning home runs by Aberson and Dallessandro. But those were the only games Los Angeles would win in the series. Oakland won the third game, 10–9 in 11 innings, when Dewey Adkins walked in the winning run, and then swept a doubleheader at Wrigley Field to go into the lead. The Oaks rallied in the late innings of each game to win, 6–3 and 23–15. The second game was especially outrageous. The Angels had a 14–6 lead after six innings, only to see Oakland score 17 runs in the last three innings. Seven home runs were hit in the game, including two grand slams by Johnny Ostrowski, and the six Angels pitchers allowed 27 Oakland hits. The final game saw the Angels blow another comfortable lead, this time, 9–2, before a grand slam homer by Les Scarsella brought Oakland close. The Oaks then scored two runs in the tenth inning to win.

The 1948 Angels suffered from insufficient pitching, erratic defense and inconsistent hitting. In spite of all that power, the Angels finished seventh in team batting at .267, were outscored by three other clubs, and led in strike outs. The 178 home runs were notable, the highest total in the PCL since 1930, but many of them came in games that the Angels led comfortably. The pitching was also thin after the four starters. Lynn was once again the workhorse of the staff with 244 innings pitched and a 19–10 record. Dewey Adkins was right behind him at 17–10, with Anthony at 16–11 and Adams at 14–11 enjoying good years. But no other Angels moundsman won in double figures. Kelly could never get his bullpen together; Walt Lanfranconi and Tom Hafey had their moments, but they were both undependable at times. The Angels also made a mistake when they sent Bill Fleming to Portland early in the year. He was 6–2, coming out of the Beaver bullpen in 50 games. He might have been an adequate replacement for Jess Dobernic, who was enjoying a fine year at Chicago in 1948.

Ed Sauer was the Most Valuable Angel in 1948. His .305 average and a team-leading 121 RBIs would result in his return to the major leagues in 1949. Cliff Aberson supplied most of the power for the club with 34 home runs and boasted a .329 average to boot. Dom Dallessandro was the club's other .300 hitter at .307, and produced 21 home runs. Injuries slowed him considerably after the first two months. The infield suffered from inconsistent

Ed Sauer — One of the stalwarts of the 1947 champions, Sauer enjoyed two fine seasons in Los Angeles before moving up to the Boston Braves in 1949 (courtesy Mark Macrae).

play and injuries as well. Mickey Burnett was enjoying a fine year, hitting .321 after the first 50 games and sparkling in the field, but the beaning he suffered against Seattle ruined his season. He was out of action for three weeks and was never able to reclaim his position for any length of time. In a positive development, Albie Glossop was indispensable to the team. Playing in 150 games, he filled in at both second and third base for long stretches, and hit .283 with 17 home runs, three of which were of the pinch-hit variety.

Attendance at Wrigley Field dropped to 576, 372 in 1948 from the record high of the previous year. Part of this loss could be attributed to a new element in American society—

Left: Albie Glossop — A superb utility player who could play all of the infield spots and hit with some power as well. *Right:* Red Lynn — Won 141 games in the PCL over a ten-year career, mostly with the Angels.

television. The first Angels home game was telecast in 1947, and by the middle of the 1948 season the club was televising all of its weekend home games. The number of games on TV would increase again in 1949, with another decline in attendance. No one really knew how to handle the issue of television in the PCL in 1948, and television policy varied from city to city. But it would be a force to be dealt with in the years to come and would have a major impact on the fortunes of the league.

The drive to attain major league status was beginning to lose some of its intensity in 1948. Although President Rowland presented another proposal to the major leagues at the All-Star break in mid–July, it was really no different than the one that failed at the previous winter meetings. Again, the PCL was requesting an increase in the price for a drafted player to $25,000 and asking to increase the service time from four to six years before eligibility. Once again, the request was tabled for further study. In Southern California more emphasis was placed on the possible movement of an existing major league team to Los Angeles. The St. Louis Browns had indicated some interest in moving, and this possibility was given considerable mention during the summer. A rumored expansion of the major leagues to ten teams each, which would include annexing Oakland, San Francisco, Los Angeles and Hollywood, also received some press coverage. This rumored plan was opposed by Rowland in no uncertain terms.

The Cubs did not harvest many prospects from the 1948 Angels, with only Cliff Aberson and Dewey Adkins promoted to Chicago. Ed Sauer was drafted by the Cardinals, but the rest of the team remained relatively intact over the winter. Unfortunately, this veteran team was aging badly, with most of the players well past their prime. Glossop, Schuster, Dallessandro, Johnson and Hafey were all past 35; Lynn, Garriott, Sanford and Bauers were past 30. The future for these men was limited, as the Angels were about to find out in 1949.

20

The Angels Fall to the Bottom

Absolute bottom. No Angels fan expected that to be the result in 1949, although admittedly, no one anticipated that Los Angeles would be much of a pennant contender either. There were too many question marks on the team, especially on the pitching staff. But despite a reasonable performance during the first month of the season, the Angels soon found their way into the second division, and by June 14 they were in the cellar. They were to remain there for the balance of the year, finishing 35 games out of first place and ten games behind the seventh-place Seals. This was the first time that Los Angeles had finished in eighth place since 1927, and the club's winning percentage of .396 was the lowest since 1911.

All of the pitching problems that were of concern to manager Bill Kelly during spring training came to fruition, and the Angels put up their worst staff in history. They finished utterly last in the league, giving up 5.75 runs per game, almost a run a game worse than any other club. Not a single pitcher had an ERA of less than 4.00, no Angels pitcher won as many as ten games, and only Don Carlsen and Alan Ihde won more than they lost. Kelly used 19 different pitchers at one time or another in an effort to stem the opposition bats. Although the Angels still showed some power with 150 home runs, they finished only sixth in team batting and struck out far too often, leading the league in that dubious department. Many an Angels rally was quashed by a strikeout coming at a critical point in the game.

It did not appear that the club would be quite so bad during the training session. The infield appeared capable enough with Butch Moran, a Hollywood mainstay for several years, at first base; rookie Wayne Terwilliger, a fine young prospect that the Cubs had signed the previous year, at second base; and veterans Bill Schuster and Johnny Ostrowski holding down shortstop and third base. Another great looking prospect from the Cubs, Ransom Jackson, saw some early action at third base before he was sent out for further seasoning in the Texas League. Returning to the outfield were veterans Dom Dallessandro and Cecil Garriott, along with another young Cub prospect, Carmen Mauro. Eddie Malone was back to handle most of the catching duties, and he had a very capable backup in Nelson Burbrink, a long time minor leaguer who was seeing his first action at the Triple-A level. Although the lineup had a bit of age to it, most observers thought that it would be competitive.

Pitching was another story. Kelly had three experienced hurlers to build around in Red Lynn, Red Adams and Lee Anthony, but beyond that there was a great deal of uncertainty. Bob Kelly was a rookie, up from Des Moines in the Class A Western League, who looked impressive during the spring, as did Alan Ihde, who had pitched at Macon in the Sally League in 1948. He was counted on to do the bulk of the relief work, with Anthony becoming

The 1949 Angels. *Front row (left to right):* Batboy, Bob Kelly, Don Watkins, Booker McDaniels, Don Carlsen, Gordon Van Dyke, Don Alfano, Cecil Garriott. *Middle row:* Coach Jack Warner, Bob Sturgeon, Gordon Goldsberry, Clarence Maddern, Cliff Aberson, Carmen Mauro, Butch Moran, Bob Rhawn, Albie Glassop, batboy. *Back row:* Trainer Joe Liscio, manager Bill Kelly, Ken Gables, Cal McLish, Bryan Stephens, Lee Anthony, Alan Ihde, Nels Burbrink, Frank Gustine, Rube Novotney, assistant trainer Dave Flores (courtesy Dick Dobbins).

a full-time starting pitcher. Other pitchers on hand were Pete Mazar from Houston in the Texas League; Hank Wyse, a National League veteran who had experienced arm trouble the previous two years; Don Watkins, another youngster from Class-A; and returnee Walt Lanfranconi. Just as the season began, the Cubs returned Don Carlsen to Los Angeles, and he moved right into a starting assignment.

Opening day was a disappointment for the Angels, and it set the tone for what would be a dismal year. Hank Wyse started and pitched well against Seattle for five innings while the hitters built a comfortable lead of 7–1. But he was hit hard in the sixth inning, Angels relief pitchers were unable to contain the Seattle offense, and Los Angeles fell, 9–7, with Anthony suffering the loss. That would become a familiar scenario as the year wore on. Nevertheless, the Angels played reasonably well through April and were at the .500 mark at the end of the month. Wayne Terwilliger and Carmen Mauro were hot hitters during this period, along with Eddie Malone and John Ostrowski, who were major contributors. But the pitching was worse than expected. Red Lynn pitched a shutout in his first start, but that was to be his only win for over a month. Red Adams was so unimpressive in his first four starts that the Angels gave up on him and sent him to San Diego for third baseman Lee Handley. Lee Anthony was hit hard in his starts and was moved back to the bullpen where he was no more effective. Bob Kelly and Don Carlsen had fine outings, and Alan

Ihde picked up three wins in relief during the first two weeks of the season. But the rest of the staff was unimpressive at best.

The pitching weakness finally began to take its toll, and the club sagged to seventh place on May 22, well out of contention. About this time, the roster began to resemble a revolving door. The Cubs returned Cliff Aberson, Rube Novotney and Clarence Maddern to Los Angeles at the major league cut-down date of May 15, along with pitcher Cal McLish. Of this group, Maddern and McLish were the most useful. Aberson had experienced a dreadful spring with the Cubs and was subject to so much criticism from manager Charlie Grimm and the Chicago press that his confidence was shattered; he bore only faint resemblance to the player he was in 1948. Although he managed 17 home runs, his average dropped almost one hundred points, to .230, and he struck out nearly one-fourth of the time. Never would he realize the fine potential he had shown the previous year.

The club continued its poor play and finally fell into last place on June 14 after a 4–3 loss at Portland. New players were arriving almost daily but with little impact. Among them was outfielder Pat Seerey, acquired on option from the White Sox. He had made a name for himself in 1948, when he hit four home runs in a game at Philadelphia; he was one of the few men in major league history to do so. But Seerey lasted only 13 games in Los Angeles before moving on. He showed some of his power on Memorial Day when he slammed two enormous home runs across 41st Place, but he also struck out frequently and suffered through a record-setting game on June 2 when he committed four errors in left field. That performance no doubt hastened his departure.

The Cubs sent catcher Forrest "Smokey" Burgess to Los Angeles, and he showed a great ability to come off the bench, hitting two pinch home runs in his limited duty. But Bill Kelly did not think much

Butch Moran — Led the league in doubles with 56 in 1945 (courtesy Dick Dobbins).

of his catching ability and used him in left field for several games after Seerey left, before eventually sending him to Nashville.

Bill Schuster was running out of time in Los Angeles. He had not begun the season well, hitting below .200 in the first weeks of the season and appearing a bit slower in the field. In frustration as much as anything, Schuster began to confront umpires in virtually every game and was frequently ejected, a behavior pattern that did not please Kelly. He began to keep Schuster out of the lineup, using young infielders Joe Damato and Don Alfano in his place at shortstop. Finally, on July 10 the Angels traded Schuster to Seattle for shortstop Bob Sturgeon, a resident of Long Beach who had seen major league duty with the Cubs and Braves. He was a fine fielder who had never hit a great deal, but was eight years younger than Schuster. The press and fans did not like this deal — "A fish for a foul" was how one newspaper described the trade. Although it was unpopular, the trade was probably a good one, for at that stage of their careers, Sturgeon was much faster and would cover more ground than "Broadway Bill," who was nearing the end of the line.

Eddie Malone was one of the few Angels who was playing better in 1949 than he did in 1948. He enjoyed a fast start with the bat and was among the league leaders with a .341 mark through June. In July he was sold to the White Sox in a straight cash deal, and three weeks later, the Angels sent their other big hitter, John Ostrowski, to the Sox for cash and

Left: John Ostrowski — He had a career high of 32 home runs in 1949. That led to his purchase by the Chicago White Sox, but he never quite made the major league grade (courtesy Dick Dobbins). *Right:* Eddie Malone — A solid backstop for several Coast League teams, he had his best year in 1949 with the Angels, hitting .341 before he was purchased by the White Sox in July (courtesy Dick Dobbins).

infielder Bobby Rhawn. Wayne Terwilliger, who had been a solid performer at second base, was promoted to the Cubs at the end of July, in exchange for Frank Gustine, a long time Pittsburgh Pirate who had been a major disappointment in his first year with Chicago. The combination of these three moves just about finished the Angels for the year. Although they were in last place, they had been respectable at times, but that would no longer be the case. The club lost two-thirds of its games over the last two months of the season, including a 12-game losing streak, beginning on August 27, as part of a stretch where the Angels lost 18 out of 20 games.

Making matters worse for the 1949 Angels was the emergence of the Hollywood Stars as the premier team in the PCL. The Stars had been a second-division team since relocating to Los Angeles in 1938 from San Francisco, but prior to the 1949 season, owner Bob Cobb negotiated a working agreement with the Brooklyn Dodgers, and that arrangement solidified the franchise. The excess Brooklyn talent that came to Hollywood, combined with a strong nucleus already on hand, was molded by new manager Fred Haney into a championship team. The Stars would win the 1949 pennant and would be a strong contender for the next several years. They became the team of choice in Los Angeles, while the Angels were forgotten as they lay buried in the cellar.

The dismal play of the Angels was costly at the box office, with only 402,089 fans attending games in 1949. That was a drop of over 170,000 from the previous year, putting them next to last in the league. Only Portland drew less, and the Stars outdrew the Angels by 100,000; during the last month of the season, weekday crowds at Wrigley Field were frequently below 2,000. Although the club's poor performance caused a good deal of the decline, television was a major contributor. In 1949 the Angels and Stars both adopted a policy of televising all home game, and the fans of both clubs were finding it more convenient to stay at home and watch games.

Wrigley Field was receiving its share of criticism as well. Fans were especially concerned about the lack of parking facilities at the ballpark. There was only one lot available with limited capacity, and on big attendance days, fans had to park on private property for which they were charged what were generally considered exorbitant amounts. Public transportation in Los Angeles was not as good as it had been, causing more and more fans to drive their own cars, with massive traffic jams resulting around the park. This was a chronic condition, even on days when the crowds were small, and it would never improve. As a result, there was some question that Wrigley Field would ever be adequate for a major league team.

There were a few bright spots in the generally dismal situation in Los Angeles, but not many. The club saw promise in young pitchers Bob Kelly, Cal McLish and Don Carlsen, each of whom turned in several nice games. Kelly was more effective early in the year, winning only twice after July 4, while Carlsen suffered an elbow injury in late July that sidelined him for the balance of the season. McLish was probably the most effective pitcher during the miserable months of August and September. Don Watkins also picked up some slack after Carlsen was injured, but he was unable to win consistently. Offensively, John Ostrowski had his best year as an Angels player and was voted the club's Most Valuable Player. But president Don Stewart vetoed that selection, commenting that a club like this had no MVP.

An important event in Angels history took place in early June, when the club purchased the contract of pitcher Booker McDaniels from the Kansas City Monarchs of the Negro American League. McDaniels was the first African American to wear an Angels uniform. He was not a pitcher that the club could build around, since McDaniels was at least 37 years old when he joined the club, but he was still an effective pitcher. He debuted at

Portland on June 15, winning, 8–3, and followed that up with a shutout at home, 17–0, against the Rainiers, a game in which he fanned 12. This was the largest shutout margin in Angels history. McDaniels, who was called "Cannonball," won his first four decisions before subsiding to a final record of 8–9.

Once again in 1949, the PCL presented its proposal to eliminate the draft to the major league executive committee, but this time there seemed to be less enthusiasm for the action than previously. More emphasis was being placed on securing a good working agreement with a major league club; even Paul Fagan, the owner of the Seals who had always been adamant about relying completely on their own resources, admitted that San Francisco was actively seeking a strong affiliation with a major league team for the 1950 season. Sentiment in Los Angeles now seemed in favor of moving an existing major league team to Southern California. That summer there was continuing speculation that the St. Louis Browns would be moving west in 1950.

The Chicago Cubs suffered through their second consecutive last-place finish in the National League to match Angels futility. The gloom was thick around Wrigley Field when the 1949 season finally ended, and there was little optimism that 1950 would be any better.

Not many of the players who contributed to the last-place finish of 1949 would be around to greet the new season. Don Stewart was given total discretion to improve the club, and he proceeded to completely change the roster. By the time the winter meetings started in early December, there were only eight holdovers from the team that ended the season. The Cubs recalled the most promising of the younger Angels to Chicago — Carmen Mauro, Don Carlsen. and Bob Kelly — and Stewart flushed out the rest. The disappointing Cliff Aberson and Lee Anthony were sent to Hollywood along with pitcher Ben Wade as part of a trade between the Dodgers and Cubs, whereby Chicago gained pitcher Paul Minner and first baseman Preston Ward, neither of whom would find his way to Los Angeles. The Angels acquired pitchers Ralph Hamner and Emil Kush and outfielder Les Layton, who had spent 1949 in Memphis, to fill some of the gaps. They expected more moves at the winter meetings.

However, the Angels received stunning news at the meetings when it was announced that the Cubs had purchased the Newark franchise in the International League and would move that club to Springfield, Massachusetts, where it would operate as a Cub farm club, at the same level as the Angels. The acquisition would not be finalized for another 30 days, but the announcement did not bode well for Los Angeles. Springfield would receive the most promising young players in the Cub system, and the Angels would be forced to rely on veteran players whose best years were behind them. As an indication of what would happen, the Cubs sent veteran pitcher Bob Muncrief to Los Angeles while transferring Alan Ihde to Springfield for further development. The objective at Los Angeles was to win games, not develop players for the big leagues. The 1950 Angels team would be constructed with that philosophy in mind. Unfortunately, the new philosophy did not result in many victories as the Angels finished in seventh place.

The PCL had seen an increase in attendance in 1949, but now the league was about to begin a downturn that would last for more than a decade. Despite a longer schedule in 1950 — the number of games was increased to 200 — league attendance declined by 579,000. The tremendous growth in minor league attendance in the post-war period had reached an end, and a general retrenchment of leagues was in process. Not for over 20 years would this trend be reversed. There was also much less discussion of the PCL becoming a third major

The 1950 Los Angeles Angels (courtesy Mark Macrae).

league, and in reality, the quality of play had begun to decline. A revision of the draft rules was now the major concern of the executives.

There were many reasons for the reduced attendance, with the major culprit thought to be television. Once again, Hollywood and Los Angeles chose to televise all of their home games, and both clubs were subject to much criticism from the rest of the league for this decision. Although the Angels felt that television would create new fans who would eventually attend the games, they paid a heavy short-term price for their decision. Attendance was down by 80,000 from the 1949 debacle, despite the longer schedule, and during the last two weeks of the season, crowds seldom numbered even 1,000 for the weekday games. A new factor in 1950 was the spread of radio broadcasting of major league games into Coast League cities. The Mutual Broadcasting System was transmitting a *Game of the Day* from coast to coast, an event that had the effect of making fans in minor league cities more conscious of the major leagues and less interested in their local teams. Certainly, this new activity had a great impact on the PCL.

On the field, Bill Kelly was back for what would be his final year as Angels manager. Although he thought the club would be improved, he was not overly optimistic. The Angels had lacked their customary punch in 1949, and they attempted to remedy that by bringing in former major leaguers Elbie Fletcher and Stan Spence. Fletcher was a fine fielding first baseman who was signed after his release by the Boston Braves, and he proved to be a valuable acquisition. The same could not be said about Spence. The 35-year-old outfield veteran who had enjoyed several good years with Washington was purchased from the St. Louis Browns. The Angels needed a strong left-handed hitter in their lineup, and when Spence rejected his initial contract, the club quickly met his demands. Although he slugged 22 home runs, Spence was a major disappointment, hitting below .200 through May. He was taken out of the regular lineup when the Cubs returned Clarence Maddern to Los Angeles at the major league cutdown date.

Second baseman Johnny Lucadello was another pickup from the Browns, but the most important addition to the club took place just before spring training broke up, when the Cubs sent outfielder Frank Baumholtz to Los Angeles. Baumholtz was 31 and had experienced a poor season for Chicago in 1949, hitting only .229 in 85 games. It was thought that he, too, was at the end of the line, like so many of the Angels veterans, but Baumholtz was anything but that. He broke into the lineup with several hits and then, after missing several games, began to hit with amazing frequency. He moved to the top of the league, hitting .458 during the first month and remaining over .400 until June. Baumholtz began the season as the leadoff hitter, but was such a consistent hitter that Kelly dropped him to third, where he was much more valuable. The veteran responded with 89 RBIs and 15 home runs, both personal highs.

The Angels played surprisingly well during April and were one game over .500 as the month closed. Kelly had assembled a satisfactory pitching staff with a rotation of Ralph Hamner, Bob Muncrief, Cal McLish and Herm Besse, obtained from Seattle during the winter and the only left-hander on the staff. Other early starters were Pete Mallory, a wartime Angels player who had a big year at Nashville in 1949; Dewey Adkins, back from Chicago after an unimpressive year; and Charlie "Red" Barrett, down from the Braves.

The outfield looked decent with Spence, Garriott and Frank Baumholtz, but the infield was suspect. Frank Whitman, up from Grand Rapids in the Central League, opened at shortstop, and played reasonably well before suffering an allergic reaction to penicillin; he was never the same player. He was replaced by Bob Sturgeon, while Johnny Lucadello played second base. Rookie Lloyd Lowe started at third base and hit well during the first week of the season. The jump from the Three I League to the PCL was a bit more than he could handle, however, and he was replaced by Albie Glossop. But Glossop was not a natural third baseman and was nearing the end of his career. Sturgeon did not hit and Johnny Lucadello appeared slow in the field at second. The club purchased Lou Klein from Cincinnati in May, benched Glossop and moved Lucadello to third. Klein was 33 and had jumped to the Mexican League from the Cardinals in 1946. He lost three years of his career as a result of this decision, but was still a very useful player. In spite of a number of injuries, Klein enjoyed a fine year in Los Angeles and became one of the club's most productive hitters.

Los Angeles continued to surprise through May and even reached third place before dropping back into the second division in early June. The Angels were especially effective against Hollywood, winning two straight series from the Stars, with Bob Muncrief winning four of the games. Baumholtz enjoyed a 33-game hitting streak and was leading the league, in hitting with Fletcher right behind him. Cal McLish had started to realize some of his great potential by winning seven of his first eight decisions. But the club began to slide during consecutive series with Seattle and Portland, and was then overpowered by Oakland in a Wrigley Field series that dropped the Angels ten games below .500 and into seventh place. They would not rise from that position for the balance of the year.

The lack of team speed was most apparent in the infield, where the Angels took steps to remedy the problem by acquiring shortstop Gene Baker and third baseman Leon Brinkopf from the Cub farm at Des Moines. Baker had been purchased by the Cubs from the Kansas City Monarchs of the Negro American League and had played a few games at Des Moines in 1949. He was hitting .321 and was the best shortstop in the Western League when he was brought up to Los Angeles on July 1. The third African American to wear an Angels uniform that season — UCLA football great Kenny Washington had been given a brief look in May — the 25-year-old Baker was a tall, slender man who experienced an adjustment period before he began to hit. Kelly moved him to the leadoff position in late July, where he remained for the balance of the year, and he improved to finish at .280. In the field he was much quicker than either Whitman or Sturgeon and had a good but not outstanding arm. He would occupy the shortstop position for the next three years and would progress greatly before finally earning a promotion to the Cubs in 1954.

Leon Brinkopf was installed at third base and played the position for the balance of the year. He was hitting .336 at Des Moines and showed good power potential, but this did not materialize in the PCL right away. Brinkopf hit .267 with only four home runs in 88 Angels games, but more importantly, he added some speed and stability to an infield that had lacked both. The Angels defense was greatly improved after Baker and Brinkopf joined the club and vastly better than the shambles that existed in 1949.

By the end of July, the Angels were solidly entrenched in seventh place, ahead of Sacramento and just behind Portland. The pitching, which had been very impressive earlier, had become less reliable. Only Cal McLish was a steady winner; Ralph Hamner and Herm Besse suffered through losing streaks and Muncrief seemed to follow every good outing with a bad one. Kelly tried Pete Mallory and Dewey Adkins as spot starters, but they were both ineffective. Adkins was not the pitcher he had been in 1948, and in July it was learned that he was suffering from a hernia, which explained part of the problem. He was sidelined for virtually the remainder of the season. Frank Marino was given an opportunity in late July after several good relief appearances, and he responded well, winning a spot in the rotation in August and September. The relief pitching was weak; Ken Gables had enjoyed a good season in 1949 but had become very undependable this year, and the club lost a number of games when he and Emil Kush were unable to hold the lead. The Angels attempted to shore up the bullpen in early August, when they traded Lucadello and Gables to Sacramento for Jess Dobernic, their ace reliever in 1947. But Dobernic was not as effective as he had been, and in his first two outings gave up game-winning home runs to Max West at San Diego and Earl Rapp at Oakland.

The Angels made a run for sixth place in late August and put themselves within one-half game behind Portland on Labor Day. But that was as high as they would go. They lost 12 of the next 14 games, including a losing streak of eight, and then later played a bizarre series at Portland that featured five doubleheaders, with the Angels losing four of them. The season ended amidst a gloomy atmosphere once again, with the Angels playing out the last week in virtual privacy. Only 194 fans paid to see a Thursday night game and a mere 277 showed up the next night for a doubleheader. With Oakland having clinched the pennant two weeks previously and no playoffs in store, interest in the PCL was virtually non-existent in Los Angeles and elsewhere as well. The decision to increase the schedule to 200 games had not been wise; in 1951 the number of games would be reduced to 168 games, with the season ending three weeks earlier.

Although the Angels were in no way a pennant contender in 1950, they did have a significant impact on the race. The Hollywood Stars were attempting to defend their 1949 championship against a very strong Oakland club, and the Angels made this task most difficult by winning three of the four series between the clubs, and taking the season's series by a margin of 18 games to ten. McLish was 4–0 against the Stars, including two shutouts, while Muncrief, who had worn a Hollywood uniform ten years before, won seven of nine decisions. Los Angeles proved especially difficult for the Stars during the two series in late August, winning ten of 14 games, including a doubleheader sweep on September 3, at a time when the Stars still had a chance of winning the pennant.

In contrast, the Angels were an easy mark for Oakland. The Oaks won all four series between the clubs, winning 22 of the 31 games played, including a 12–5 record in Wrigley Field. Some of the scores were embarrassing: 18–2, 23–7, a doubleheader loss at home on July 4 by scores of 17–2 and 9–1, and 11–1. The Oaks hit 24 home runs at Wrigley Field; Earl Rapp posed the greatest menace with five. Muncrief was 1–5 against Oakland and a frequent victim of home runs. Certainly, the Angels' play against the two contenders played a major role in the Oakland pennant that year, the last that would be won by that club.

Frank Baumholtz was the PCL batting champion in 1950, and his performance was one of the greatest in Angels history. Baumholtz hit .379, just four points below the club record set by Frank Demaree in 1934, and he finished with 254 hits. No PCL hitter has come close to that number since. In addition to his 33-game hitting streak during April and May, Baumholtz also enjoyed an 18-game streak in September. At the end of the season, he was recalled to Chicago, where he showed that his performance in Los Angeles was not a fluke. Baumholtz hit .284 in 1951 and finished second in the batting race to Stan Musial of the Cardinals in 1952, when he hit .325.

The Angels might have had a second contender for the batting crown that year had Elbie Fletcher not been afflicted with the mumps in July. He was hitting .341 when he went out of action for two weeks, and when he returned to duty, he was still so weak that he immediately went into a slump that saw his average drop by 60 points. Fletcher rallied to finish at .289 and played well in the field. A surprising contributor was outfielder Les Layton, who was pressed into action in April when Spence was unable to hit. Layton saw duty in all three outfield positions and found Wrigley Field much to his liking, hitting 27 home runs to lead the Angels in that department. Cal McLish was the ace of the pitching staff, and his 20–11 record earned him a trip to Chicago for the 1951 season. Bob Muncrief's record of 15–17 was not as impressive, but his performance resulted in the Yankees taking him in the post-season draft.

At the end of the season, manager Bill Kelly said goodbye to Los Angeles. The Angels' skipper was exchanging places with Springfield manager Stan Hack. This move was concurrent with yet another change in Cub operating policy. Los Angeles would once again become a developer of young talent for the Cubs, but an effort would be made to put a winning team on the field as well. The slow, veteran teams of 1949 and 1950 would be no longer, and the Angels of the future would be comprised mostly of young players, the cream of the Cub farm system. It was felt that Hack might be better suited to this kind of team than Kelly. His Springfield team had finished in fifth place in the International League and for a time was in contention for the pennant.

There were other factors, too. Kelly's home was in the East, and he had deep roots in the International League as well. The managerial move was a popular one, for Hack was a native of Sacramento and was well known on the Coast. Kelly's managerial skills were also subject to much criticism in Los Angeles, and he was the major target for the boo-birds who were more evident in Wrigley Field in recent years. But, in fairness, the talent level was at an all-time low in 1949 and 1950, and it is doubtful that anyone else could have had better results.

21

Smilin' Stan in Charge

Of all of the Angels managers, Stan Hack was probably the best known when he assumed the job. After hitting .352 at Sacramento in 1931, he was purchased by the Cubs and became their regular third baseman in 1934. A perennial All-Star, Hack was a consistent .300 hitter as the Cub leadoff hitter through 1947, played in three World Series, and was perhaps the finest fielding third baseman of his time. When he retired as an active player, Hack was given the opportunity to manage in the Cub farm system. He was an immediate success, leading Des Moines to the Western League pennant in 1948. After another good year there, he was promoted to the new Cub farm team at Springfield in 1950. That club surprised the rest of the International League, finishing in fifth place after briefly leading the league in late June. For this, Hack was given much of the credit. He was considered to be an excellent handler of young players, and with the change in philosophy within the Chicago organization, he was considered a natural choice for the Angels post.

In his first appearance in Los Angeles that winter, Hack indicated that he wanted to emphasize speed and youth with the Angels, and within days after his arrival the club began a thorough house cleaning. Veterans Elbie Fletcher and Albie Glossop were let go, as were Stan Spence and Emil Kush. Before spring training began, only Les Layton, Gene Baker, Leon Brinkopf and pitchers Herm Besse and Ralph Hamner remained from the regulars of 1950. Cecil Garriott was still on hand as a part-time player, but he was released in June so that he could sign with Visalia in the California League to act as their manager. The young players who had performed well at Springfield came west with Hack — pitchers Bob Spicer and Bill Moisan, second baseman Jack Hollis, and outfielder Bob Talbot. Early in the season, the Angels sent Nelson Burbrink to Springfield in exchange for catcher Les Peden, and the Cubs optioned pitcher Warren Hacker, another Springfield alumnus, to Los Angeles.

The Angels did not plan to rely exclusively on youth, so they filled out their roster with the acquisition of several established players. Slugging outfielder Max West came from San Diego in a trade for Clarence Maddern; catcher Billy Raimondi, a veteran of 18 PCL seasons with Oakland and Sacramento, was signed as a free agent; and outfielder Tom Neill was purchased from Nashville after hitting .346 for the 1950 Vols.

The Cubs, as usual, were in a state of organizational turmoil. Wid Mathews, the director of Cub playing personnel, had expanded his duties during the winter of 1950-51 and was now director of the farm system as well. He had worked for Branch Rickey in Brooklyn for a number of years and attempted to fill the vacancies in the Cub system by purchasing Dodger surplus. Most of the transactions turned out badly for Chicago, but one that looked promising involved the purchase of two first basemen — Chuck Connors and Dee Fondy. Neither had received much of an opportunity to make the Dodger roster, what with Gil Hodges fully entrenched at first base, but each had enjoyed good years in the Brooklyn system and were both better than anything the Cubs had at the time. The two waged a strong battle for the position during spring training, and when the Cubs went east to open the season, they left Connors in Los Angeles, with Fondy opening in Chicago. That was about the extent of the help that the Cubs were able to supply the Angels that year. But the addition of Connors and West gave the Angels two fine left-handed hitters who would remedy the lack of power that was so evident the previous year.

After the 1950 season ended, PCL officials, recognizing that the 200-game schedule was not a success, adopted a 168-game schedule for 1951, with a split week schedule for the first time since the 1930s. The playoffs, which had been abandoned in 1950, were reinstated, and the season would end on September 13, well before the close of the major league season and before the usual interest in football began to take its toll. The reasons for these major changes were primarily economic. More frequent visits by the teams would stimulate attendance somewhat, and competition for the playoff positions would sustain interest longer in those cities where the team was out of the pennant race. The results of these changes would be mixed. Although some teams improved their attendance from the previous year, others suffered major declines, and the PCL as a whole lost 890,000 spectators. There was a great deal of belt-tightening in all cities, further dampening the enthusiasm to create a third major league. The construction of new ballparks in Portland and San Diego was postponed indefinitely.

The Angels opened the season at Wrigley Field with a flurry of home runs. Although they lost the opening series to Seattle, they swept a four-game set from San Francisco, with Connors and West each hitting three home runs in a game — only Cleo Carlyle, Steve Mesner, Jack Fournier and Loyd Christopher had ever performed that feat in an Angels uniform. Connors had five home runs in the first five games of the season and was among the league leaders through May. The slugging of Connors and West kept the Angels competitive, but they were not able to move much past .500.

Pitching, while seemingly improved over 1950, remained a problem, and many of the early games were slugfests The early starters were Bill Moisan, Herm Besse, Bob Spicer and left-hander Fred Baczewski, a hard throwing rookie up from Des Moines, with Frank Marino, Vern Fear and Ralph Hamner earning opportunities as well. Baczewski and Besse were the early leaders. Fear and Marino were sent to Springfield at the end of April, with Hamner relegated to relief duty along with Dewey Adkins, another veteran who was bothered by arm trouble through much of the early season. When Warren Hacker arrived from Chicago during the first week of May, he was inserted into the starting rotation in place of Besse, who went on the shelf with serious arm trouble after winning his first five decisions. Later in the month, the Cubs sent Doyle Lade and Ed Chandler to Los Angeles. With all of these comings and goings, the Angels gradually developed an effective pitching corps.

The pennant race in 1951 was very close, with Seattle and Hollywood the early leaders and four other teams not far behind. The Angels remained at the .500 level through the middle of June, when they went into a tailspin that saw them lose 12 of 15 games. By the end of June the club was in sixth place and seemed to be well on the road to another second-division finish. The hitting had fallen off considerably, with Les Layton, West and Connors in deep slumps. Then on July 2 the Cubs dealt the Angels a severe blow when they recalled Connors to Chicago. Angels fans, who had begun to return to Wrigley Field after the drought years of 1949–50, were outraged at this move. Connors was the club's most popular player, both on the field and off. An accomplished after-dinner speaker, Connors was quite a comedian as well, and he would eventually put these talents to work in the entertainment world after his baseball career ended. The fans were very disappointed with the personnel change, and a season that was once filled with great promise now seemed doomed to another dismal finish.

But sometimes things are not always what they seem. The replacement for Connors was Dee Fondy, who had started the 1951 season as the regular Cub first baseman. He had done reasonably well through the first two months of the season, but had slumped during the last two weeks of June and was hitting .271 when the Cubs decided to send him to Los Angeles. Chicago was in desperate need of power, but Fondy had hit only three home runs; Connors had 22 home runs at Los Angeles and seemed likely to continue at that level in the National League. Fondy joined the Angels on July 4, had pinch-hits in his first two appearances in Los Angeles, and then had three hits in his first Angels start.

In his first two weeks in the lineup, Fondy hit .510. On July 15 he collected six hits in an 8–7 win over Sacramento, in a game that included three home runs, one each over the left, center and right field walls. Fondy was a line drive hitter who was more agile around first base than Connors and was also a better base runner. In 70 games with the Angels, he hit .376 and was on his way back to the majors. Clearly, the Angels were a much better team with Fondy in the lineup. With a record of 47–52 upon his arrival, the Angels then went ten games over .500 for the balance of the season. By the end of July, they were back in third place, and although the club was never able to threaten the Rainiers and Stars, Los Angeles proved to be the best of the rest.

Fondy was not the entire reason for the improvement of the Angels. The Angels pitching had settled down considerably. Bill Moisan had been ineffective through June, but won seven of eight decisions after July 1. Bob Spicer pitched consistently well and was the club's big winner while Doyle Lade and Hacker, after miserable starts, pitched well over the last two months of the season. Ralph Hamner had not been effective as a starter, but confined to the bullpen, he turned in several nice efforts. Dewey Adkins came back after mid-season arm miseries to pitch well in relief. During the last month of the season, the Angels staff was as good as any in the league.

The Angels stayed in third place through much of August, but they did not clinch the position until the last week of the season, winning seven of their last nine games to finish five games over .500. The club had an excellent starting lineup but had little reserve strength. When a series of injuries in late August reduced the number of available outfielders, Stan Hack was forced to use catcher Les Peden in right field, bringing in rookie Bob Dant from Springfield to catch. The Angels became iron men in 1951. The opening day infield remained intact for the first two months of the season, and of the regulars, only catcher Peden played in fewer than 135 games. This was a far cry from the previous two years, when the Angels lineup changed nightly.

The Angels led the league in home runs and defense in 1951. They hit 167 home runs, with Max West leading the way. His 35 home runs were second only to Joe Gordon of Sacramento, and his 110 runs batted ranked fourth in that department. The friendly dimensions of Wrigley Field were ideal for West, a strong pull hitter. Les Layton also had a fine year, hitting .305 with 23 home runs. Leon Brinkopf hit 25 home runs to go along with his .279 average and also played a fine third base. The Angels infield was their best in years. The club turned 166 double plays with Gene Baker and Hollis involved in most of them.

Angels fans especially liked the red headed second baseman. Although Hollis was slightly below major league standards in ability, he played hard every day and made the most of his talent. Talbot was the best center fielder that Angels fans had seen since Cecil Garriott was in his prime.

Bob Spicer was the big winner for the Angels with a record of 17–13. He did not throw especially hard, but had a fine slider that was difficult to pick up during night games. Fred Baczewski was the early leader of the staff, but he was bothered by wildness all year and won only one game after July, finishing at 12–10. He led the league in walks allowed with 121. Baczewski had one especially horrible game, on May 17, when he walked 11 Seals, an all-time Angels record. Warren Hacker was the most spectacular Angels pitcher. He lost several close games early and had a 3–12 record on July 22, but he improved dramatically after that and finished at 8–15 with five shutouts. Included among his wins was a no-hitter at Seattle on September 7, on a night in which he permitted only one base runner. Hacker overcame an early propensity to throw home run balls, which cost him several victories. Joe Gordon of Sacramento beat him twice with late-inning homers, and Joe Brovia of Portland victimized him as well. But the blond ex–Marine developed a devastating knuckle ball that was almost impossible to hit, and he used this pitch to good effect along with a fine fast ball and curve. In 1952, Hacker would win 15 games at Chicago and went on to enjoy a ten-year major league career with several teams.

In the dugout, Hack's style of managing was considerably different from that of Bill Kelly. He preferred to use a set lineup and run with the hot hand on the mound. The Angels fans took to this 1951 team and began to return to Wrigley Field. The attendance of 328,294 was an improvement on the 1950 season, even though fewer games were played. The fans enjoyed a competitive team that played as well as it could given the limited resources on hand.

Meanwhile, the PCL had finally lost patience with the major league executive committee. In August 1951, the directors met once again to prepare yet another proposal to free the league from the major league draft, and this time there was more urgency to it. Led by owners Brick Laws of Oakland and Paul Fagan of San Francisco, there was an implicit threat of bolting the National Association should the request be denied. This proposal was simpler than those that had gone on previously. The PCL wanted complete freedom from the major league draft, a recognition from the major leagues of the league's territorial rights, and a favored status that would allow the league to contract directly with the majors on administrative and procedural issues. The proposal was unanimously approved by all clubs on October 25 and would be presented at the winter meetings.

But events had caught up with the PCL. In September 1951, Congressman Emanuel Cellar began a series of hearings that would address the favored anti-trust exemption that baseball enjoyed. The baseball establishment was fearful of the outcome, and as an early response to Congress, the major leagues created an Open Classification status in October. Any league that met the established criteria could become a superior minor league. The league needed to have an aggregate population of 10,000,000, an average annual attendance of 2,250,000 over the preceding five years, and park capacity of 120,000. Any league meeting those qualifications could apply, provided six clubs approved the decision. The benefits of Open Classification would be a higher price for drafted players—$15,000. Players would be allowed the right to exempt themselves from the draft; the league would have the right of first refusal on all drafted players returned to the minor leagues; and the league would have representation on a major-minor league governing council and the right to draft before any other minor leagues.

At the time, no minor league other than the PCL could meet those requirements. Accordingly, the Coast League applied for the new favored status, which was granted in December. That made the league's proposal moot and eliminated the threat of a possible withdrawal from the National Association. There was an immediate increase in interest among PCL cities, and many felt that Open Classification would be the first step towards ultimate recognition as a third major league. To emphasize that this was the goal of the PCL, the directors agreed in January 1952, that no club would accept players on option from the majors, beginning with the 1953 season. The 1952 schedule was increased to 180 games with an indication that this would become the standard for the future.

The Angels retained many of their players from 1951 and were listed as a preseason favorite for the pennant. Dee Fondy was recalled by Chicago, but the Cubs returned Chuck Connors to Los Angeles after he had failed to hit National League pitching with any consistency over the last half of 1951. All other infield regulars excepting Brinkopf would be back, as would outfielders Max West, Bob Talbot and Les Layton. Catcher Les Peden was also on hand, giving the Angels a degree of stability that they had not enjoyed since the 1930s.

The pitching staff was virtually intact as well. Warren Hacker was the only significant absentee in spring training, so Stan Hack molded a starting rotation of Eddie Chandler, Doyle Lade, Bill Moisan and Bob Spicer. Ralph Hamner and young pitchers Don Watkins

The 1952 Angels. *Front row (left to right):* Batboy Harold Crecy, Don Watkins, Bill Raimondi, Bob Zick, Elvin Tappe, Bob Talbot, batboy Bill Hollis. *Second row:* Bob Usher, Doyle Lade, coach Jack Warner, manager Stan Hack, Ron Northey, Chuck Connors, Fred Baczewski. *Third row:* Bob Ramirez, Eddie Chandler, Les Peden, Gene Baker, Tod Davis, Max West, Bob Spicer, Dave Flores. *Back row:* Jack "Red" Hollis, Leon Brinkopf, Bill Moisan, Cal McLish, Ralph Hamner, Les Layton, Walt Dubiel (courtesy Mark Macrae).

and Bob Zick would handle the relief duty, with additional help expected when the Cubs made their final roster cuts.

Los Angeles had one of its best starts in history, winning ten of the first 11 games, with Chandler and Moisan each winning his first three decisions. Chandler was especially effective, opening the season with a 1–0 victory at Sacramento, then following with another shutout and an 8–1 victory over Hollywood. But on April 12 after the club had out-slugged the Stars, 10–7, Connors suffered what was in effect a career-ending injury when he slipped in the shower after the game and tore muscles in his shoulder. He was unable to return to regular action until May 17, and when he came back, he had lost much of his power. His average was buried below .220 until early June, and he never regained the fine batting stroke that he had demonstrated so well in 1951. In July, Connors injured his shoulder again in a collision while running the bases and was forced out for another month. He hit only six home runs all year, and at the end of the season elected to retire in favor of what was to be a brilliant career in motion pictures and television. Meanwhile, the Angels were devastated by the loss of Connors.

The Angels dropped a doubleheader to the Stars the day after Connors' initial injury and began a slump that saw them lose 19 of the next 28 games, as they fell below .500 into fourth place. West replaced Connors at first base, and the club would not have been hurt too badly had Layton been able to deliver as he had in the past. But the veteran outfielder suffered from various ailments, was in and out of the lineup, and was not particularly effective when he was able to play. Hack tried both Grant Dunlap, a rookie from Shreveport in the Texas League, and Ed Lavigne from Springfield, in right field, but neither hit consistently, and they were soon gone. The Cubs sent Ron Northey, a left-handed power hitter who had missed the entire 1951 season with a back injury, but he was slow afield and did not hit much when he was away from Wrigley Field.

After the promising start, the pitching declined as well. The first major disappointment was Bob Spicer, who had been so dependable the previous year. He failed to impress in his first two starts and was assigned to the bullpen where he was no more effective. Eventually, it was determined that he had arm trouble, which put him on the shelf for a month. He was no better when he returned and saw limited action over the balance of the year. Fred Baczewski was returned by the Cubs along with Cal McLish in early April, but neither was an adequate replacement. Baczewski was bothered by control problems and won only one game before he was sent to Shreveport in July. McLish was burdened with arm trouble that limited his effectiveness early, although he improved later in the season. Doyle Lade began the season with three straight wins before running into a stretch where he had difficulty getting anyone out. Only Bill Moisan was consistently effective, winning nine of his first 11 decisions.

At the major league cutdown date of May 15, the Cubs sent pitcher Walt Dubiel, outfielder Bob Usher and third baseman Leon Brinkopf to Los Angeles, and for a time the club rallied. Usher took over in left field, with Layton moving back to his usual right field position, and Brinkopf improved the infield defense, although he did not hit. Dubiel was a steady worker who threw several nice games.

The club played at or near .500 through the middle of July to remain in fourth place. The pennant race was a two-team affair, between Hollywood and Oakland, with the Angels not far behind. The Angels received additional pitching help from the Cubs, who sent veterans Joe Hatten and Willard Ramsdell to Los Angeles, with Dubiel going to Springfield. Hatten had once been a hard-throwing left-hander with Brooklyn, but an arm injury in

Angels Old-Timers at Wrigley Field, 1952. *Front row (left to right):* Clyde Barfoot, Ernie Johnson, Jack Fournier, Elmer Phillips, Carl Sawyer, Cedric Durst. *Second row:* Jigger Statz, Jess Orndorff, Walter Boles, Charlie Root, Wally Hood, Clyde Beck, Clarence Twombly, Marty Krug. *Third row:* Clarence Brooks, Nick Dumovich, Walter Golvin, Walter Nagle, Emil Meusel, Charlie Deal, Henry Mangerina. ***Back row:*** Harry Williams, Dave Fleming, writer Matt Gallagher, Boots Weber, Wade Killefer, Dr. Corbis Bernard, John Grody (courtesy Mark Macrae).

1950 had forced him to rely more on breaking pitches. He pitched a shutout at Portland in his Angels debut. Ramsdell had been an important member of the 1949 Hollywood champions and had spent the two previous years with Cincinnati. He had a fine knuckleball that could still baffle Coast League hitters.

A bad trip to the Northwest saw the Angels fall to sixth place by the end of July, but they took measure of the Oaks when they returned to Wrigley Field and were ten games back when they began what would be the key series of the year with Hollywood on August 4. Back-to-back 1–0 shutouts by Bill Moisan and Doyle Lade and a 3–2 win by Eddie Chandler cut the deficit to seven games, and the Angels thought they had a chance. The fans thought so, as well. A crowd of 23,497 swarmed into Wrigley Field on Thursday, only to see Ramsdell drop a 6–5 decision in a hard fought game that the Angels could have easily won. That completely burst the Angels bubble. The Stars proceeded to take the remaining four games of the series, leaving the Angels 12 games behind and effectively out of the race. The doubleheader sweep of August 10 left the Angels fans in a riotous mood, with umpire

Ed Runge assaulted by an irate spectator, and two other Angels partisans jailed for their over-zealous activities.

The Angels continued their losing ways at Oakland and extended their losing streak to nine before subduing the Oaks, 15–10, on the following Saturday. By this time the club was solidly entrenched in sixth place and stayed there for the last month of the season. The Angels won their last five games to make a run at-fifth place San Diego but finished one game behind the Padres and five games out of the first division.

Hitting was down in 1952, and there was some suspicion that the baseball had been modified, although the directors professed ignorance of any such attempt. Whatever the reason, there were only three qualifiers for the batting championship who hit better than .300, and home runs were down 25 percent from the 1951 total, despite a slightly longer schedule. The Angels finished third in team batting at .256 and again led the PCL in home runs with 145. With 35 home runs, Max West finished with a rush to win the home run crown for the third time in his illustrious career. Leon Brinkopf hit 27 after a very slow start, but hit only .238 and struck out 84 times to lead the club in that dubious department. Les Peden hit 18 home runs in an iron man role behind the plate, catching 148 games, and was selected as the club's Most Valuable Player. Les Layton was the biggest disappointment in the power category, hitting only five home runs after exceeding 20 in each of the two preceding seasons. For much of the season, opposing pitchers could pitch around West, knowing there was no real power source behind him; West walked 101 times.

For the first time since 1911, the Angels had no regular who hit over .300. Bob Usher was the leader at .293, with Peden and Bob Talbot each hitting .279. Talbot hit over .300 for most of the season before he wore down in the last three weeks and continued to draw much praise for his fine work in center field. Gene Baker sparkled at shortstop and set an Angels record for most consecutive games played, appearing in 420 straight games through August 31.

The pitching was improved over 1951 in spite of the frequent changes during the year. For most of the year Bill Moisan was the staff leader. He won 16 games, led in innings pitched with 238, and might have won 20 had the offense not deserted him in September. In five consecutive starts, all of which he lost, he received a total of eight runs of support. Eddie Chandler also won 16 to tie Moisan for the club lead. No other starter won more than he lost. Joe Hatten was spectacular during his two months with the club. His record of 8–8 included five shutouts with a stretch of 30 consecutive scoreless innings, and an ERA of 2.25. Cal McLish was not the same pitcher he had been in 1950, as he went 10–15, and Lade slumped to 8–12 after his impressive start. On the whole, the staff threw 14 shutouts, the most since 1946.

Angels paid attendance increased to 359,161, and an additional 90,000 ladies were on hand as well. But Los Angeles was the bright spot in the PCL that year. In spite of the longer schedule, league attendance was down by 118,000 fans, with big losses at Seattle and Sacramento. This was the third straight year that attendance had declined in the league, with some of the same factors still present. Television coverage was somewhat lessened, except for Los Angeles where the Angels televised all of their home games in 1952. There were fewer radio broadcasts of major league games, but the damage had been done to minor league teams. And the exciting National League playoff of 1951, which was televised nationwide, had the effect of making Coast League fans even more interested in the major leagues. The first year of Open Classification baseball did not appear to open the doors of prosperity for the PCL.

Although the sixth-place finish in 1952 was disappointing, there was general agreement that Stan Hack had done a creditable job in his second year as manager. Injuries severely limited his team. Specifically, the club never recovered from the early injury to Chuck Connors and the arm problems of Spicer, the Angels' best pitcher in 1951.

In the second year of Open Classification baseball, the Angels reversed their numbers of 1952 and finished in third place with a win-loss record of 93–87.

But in reality, 1953 was not that much different from 1952. Each year Los Angeles started fast and led the league during much of the first month, only to fade from contention. The injuries that wrecked the 1952 season were not as prevalent in 1953, and as a result, the Angels were able to remain in the first division. They were ten games above .500 at the end of April, in a tie for first place with Seattle, and although they faded a bit in May and June, were still only eight games out of first place at the end of June. A hot streak by the defending champion Hollywood Stars, combined with mediocre play by the Angels, effectively eliminated Los Angeles from contention during July. On the bright side, the club never dropped out of third place, despite a rush by Portland in August, and eventually finished a game ahead of the Beavers, 13 games behind Hollywood.

Nineteen fifty-three was a very difficult year for the Pacific Coast League. The league decision to refuse optioned players from the major leagues was now in force, and the concern of all was centered on where to find players. The consensus was that the clubs would have to expand their own scouting staffs to sign and develop their own talent, but this would mean an immediate decline in the quality of play. Those players obtained from the majors outright would undoubtedly be those who were no longer prospects or were now on the downside of their careers. The Angels were in an especially difficult position. They had begun to rely heavily on players optioned to Los Angeles by the Cubs, and now this source of talent would no longer be available. During the winter meetings, the Angels purchased

The 1953 Angels. *Front row (left to right):* Batboy Bill Holman, Bob Talbot, Eddie Chandler, Bob Spicer, Bud Hardin, Spec Padget, Frank DiPrima, Gene Baker, batboy Art Chocek. *Middle row:* Bill Raimondi, Joe Ostrowski, Les Peden, Dixie Upright, Fred Richards, coach Jack Warner, manager Stan Hack, Tod Davis, Max West, Willard Ramsdell. *Back row:* Clubhouse man Bob Ramirez, Bob Usher, Dick Smith, Bill Moisan, Alan Ihde, Randy Gumpert, Al Evans, Joe Hatten, Cal McLish, trainer Dave Flores (courtesy Mark Macrae).

veteran pitchers Joe Ostrowski and Randy Gumpert, from the Yankees and Senators, respectively, and acquired pitchers Bill Padget, Herm Besse and Alan Ihde from Springfield in exchange for Ron Northey. The only help they would receive from Chicago would be on outright assignment to Los Angeles.

The PCL also implemented two other decisions that would cause problems during the year. The size of the playing roster was reduced to 21, the lowest it had been in years. And the schedule of 180 games, which was originally supposed to be balanced, was anything but that. Each club would play more games against its so-called core rivals than the other teams in the league. The Angels would play 91 games with Hollywood, San Francisco and Oakland, and only 89 games against the other four clubs. This arrangement actually benefited the Angels, for they had more home games with Hollywood, their best drawing opponent. But the image of the PCL as a potential third major league was not helped by these shortsighted policies.

Nineteen fifty-three was also a very eventful year in baseball history. The face of the game was changing for the first time in years. In March, the Boston Braves transferred to Milwaukee, the first relocation of a major league franchise since 1903. The Braves were dying in Boston, and the move to Wisconsin proved successful beyond anyone's projections. In Milwaukee, the team had a new stadium, which the Braves filled almost every day, drawing 1,826,397 fans in their first year, a National League record at the time. These events demonstrated clearly what could happen when major league baseball moved into new territory. The St. Louis Browns had been making overtures to Milwaukee before the Braves made their decision to move, but Bill Veeck was thwarted by his fellow owners, and the Browns were forced to stay in St. Louis for the 1953 season. They were now a lame duck franchise, one which was certain to move in 1954. Where would the Browns go? During much of the season, there was tremendous speculation as to the ultimate destination of such a forlorn club. Naturally, Los Angeles and San Francisco were considered prime candidates. The attention given to the possible movement of the Browns and the Philadelphia Athletics to California took some of the focus off the PCL that summer. As Hollywood began to run away with the pennant in August, all of the clubs suffered at the gate.

The Angels had several openings to fill when spring training began. First base was expected to be a problem, but Los Angeles acquired Fred Richards from the Cubs on an outright basis, and he was just what the club needed. Richards had been in the Cub farm system since 1946 and had played for Hack at Des Moines in 1949. He made brief appearances in Chicago during the previous two years but was no longer considered a prospect. A catching vacancy occurred when Les Peden was drafted by Washington, and once again the Cubs provided help, releasing American League veteran Al Evans to Los Angeles. Later, Chicago would send pitcher Joe Hatten back to the Angels.

The rest of the club looked about the same as 1952. Gene Baker, Jack Hollis and Tod Davis rounded out the infield, but Frank DiPrima, a seasoned minor league veteran who had been drafted from Macon in the South Atlantic League, had a very impressive spring and made the club. When Hollis was forced out of the lineup with minor injuries, DiPrima played so well that the incumbent could not get his job back. Hollis appeared in only 23 games before being sent to Springfield at the end of May.

The outfield of 1952 was intact, with the exception of Les Layton, who was sent to Shreveport, and a new addition in rookie Dick Smith, who was drafted from Great Falls in the Pioneer League. All of the pitchers were veterans. Hack opened with a starting staff of Eddie Chandler, Cal McLish, Willard Ramsdell and Bob Spicer with Bill Moisan, Bill

Padget and Alan Ihde expected to handle most of the relief duties. The club started with a rush, winning its first three series and moving into first place. Chandler and Ramsdell had several good starts between them, Chandler winning his first three decisions as he had in 1952. Padget was impressive both in relief and as a spot starter. Max West hit two home runs in the first week, but an ailing knee forced him out of action, allowing Smith to receive some playing time. The rookie helped win several games with home runs, but he generally appeared in over his head in the PCL.

Max West submitted to knee surgery on May 2, and the prognosis for an early return was not good. The Angels purchased outfielder Dixie Upright from the Browns as a replacement. He hit a pinch home run in his first time at bat as an Angels player to give the club a 3–2 win over Sacramento. Upright moved into left field, with Bob Usher taking over West's position in right. This remained the lineup for most of the remainder of the season.

When Les Peden was returned by Washington on May 15, the Angels' lineup was set for the rest of the year. But third base became somewhat of a problem when Tod Davis went out of action with a serious back injury. He had enjoyed a terrific month of April, hitting .486 and fielding spectacularly. Bud Hardin, an infielder who had joined the club in August of the previous year, took over the position, but he was a natural shortstop and neither hit nor fielded as well after the move. Although Davis returned to the lineup later in the month, his injury was serious and limited him to 59 games in the field. In August, the Angels signed Murray Franklin after his release by San Diego, and he handled the position for most of the last month of the year.

As the season wore on, the pitching staff became less dependable, so Stan Hack was forced to make many changes. Chandler lost his effectiveness after his fine beginning, and failed to complete any of his next 15 starts. Ramsdell was relegated to spot duty after several failures and was eventually released. Padget and Moisan took their places and did well. Padget won his first five decisions and finished 11–7, while Moisan was the club's best pitcher through early August, before losing his last five decisions to finish at 10–11. McLish started slowly as did Hatten, but they both finished well and were among the best pitchers in the league by season's end. McLish went 16–11, and Hatten 17–11, including a stretch of seven straight wins beginning on August 19. He also threw four shutouts, including a seven-inning no-hitter at San Diego on June 7. The arm miseries that Bob Spicer had suffered during 1952 seemed to disappear as the season wore on, and he, too, finished strongly at 12–10. But the overall inconsistency of the staff prevented the Angels from becoming a legitimate pennant threat.

Offensively, the club improved over 1952, as did the league as a whole. The Angels led the PCL in hitting at .276 and hit 153 home runs. Bob Usher was the club leader at .304, while Dixie Upright hit .306 in 80 games. Fred Richards had the best year of his career, hitting over .300 for most of the year and finishing at .296 with 27 home runs. Included in his fine performance was a 20-game hitting streak in July. Richards had 92 RBIs and probably would have had more if he hit lower in the batting order. Stan Hack used him in the second position in every game. Bob Talbot had another fine year in center field and showed he was ready for the major leagues. Batting lead-off, he started slowly but finished at .287 and scored 113 runs, second in the league. Gene Baker also had an outstanding year, hitting .284 with 20 home runs. He led the club with 99 RBIs and was selected as the Most Valuable Angel.

With the reduced playing rosters, most PCL clubs were limited in their bench strength, but Hack had a secret weapon in his pitching staff. It was the most effective group of pinch-hitters in the league. Moisan was the best of the lot. In 50 attempts he had three home runs while hitting over .300. McLish and Padget also delivered pinch home runs. Overall, the Angels pitching staff hit 12 home runs, while Alan Ihde hit .387, Spicer .358, and Moisan .284.

Perhaps the most remembered event of the 1953 season was the famous riot of August 2 at Gilmore Field. The Stars and Angels mixed it up in a fight of enormous proportions, one which received nationwide attention. In the first game of the doubleheader that day, Frank Kelleher, the veteran Hollywood slugger, was hit by a pitch thrown by Joe Hatten. Kelleher had been a true tormentor of the Angels lefty and was in the midst of a streak of six straight hits against him. He charged the mound, and the two scuffled on the ground before the umpires could finally break up the fight. Kelleher was ejected as the instigator, and that should have ended the matter. But that was merely the preliminary bout. Pinch-runner Ted Beard, running for Kelleher, raced to third base on an extra-base hit and slid, spikes high, into third baseman Murray Franklin, who was appearing in his first Angels game. Franklin was wounded by Beard's efforts, leapt onto the Hollywood runner, and the fight was on. Both benches emptied, with the hostility between the old rivals rising in earnest that day. Many players received bumps and bruises, catcher Eddie Malone of the Stars was spiked during the fray, and Angels infielder Bud Hardin was nursing a black eye. In one famous photograph, Angels catcher Al Evans was caught in the act of throwing a punch that, had it successfully connected, would have leveled umpire Joe Iacovetti. A further complication developed when a squad of uniformed policemen appeared on the scene. Los Angeles Chief of

Gene Baker—He was the first African American position player with the Angels. Along with Ernie Banks, he also broke the color line with the Chicago Cubs (courtesy Dick Dobbins).

Police William Parker, watching the game on television at his home, became so concerned that he ordered police reinforcements to restore order.

When the umpires regained control, Franklin and Beard were ejected along with Gene Handley of the Stars and Fred Richards of the Angels. All of these participants were fined for their display of temper, along with Kelleher. Umpire Cece Carlucci then ordered the reserves from both clubs to adjourn to the clubhouse, where they remained for the balance of the doubleheader. "I had no choice," Carlucci recalled many years later. "The crowd was angry and restless. Another incident could have caused a lot of problems. The security forces might not have been able to keep the fans in the stands." Carlucci was probably right. A similar incident the previous year at Wrigley Field resulted in a fan attack of the umpires on the field.

In 1953, Los Angeles led the PCL in attendance for the last time in the history of the franchise. The paid attendance of 363,818 was slightly higher than the 1952 figure, but the league as a whole saw a decline of 19 percent, the fourth straight year of reduced ticket sales. Miserable spring weather, increased television coverage, and the uncertainty caused by the speculation over the relocation of major league clubs to the West Coast were all responsible for the fall. In June, owner Paul Fagan announced that the Seals were for sale, and when there were no bidders, he turned the franchise back to the league. Owner Brick Laws had suffered major losses in Oakland and was said to be considering the abandonment of his club. Sacramento was in dire financial condition and had offered Edmonds Field to the city, as a way of raising capital. An emergency meeting of the directors was called for September to address some of the problems facing the league. For the foreseeable future, talk of the PCL becoming a third major league would be stilled.

22

Bill Sweeney Is Back in Town

Virtually everyone associated with the Angels assumed it would be a matter of time before Stan Hack was promoted to Chicago as manager of the Cubs, but absolutely no one expected this move to happen in 1954. He had signed a contract for another year at the Angels helm and was hard at work with the club in spring training at Fullerton on March 30, when one of many bizarre incidents involving the Cubs occurred. Chicago owner P. K. Wrigley fired his manager, Phil Cavarretta, marking the first time in major league history that a pilot had been removed during spring training. The reason? A few days earlier, Mr. Wrigley had met with Cavarretta for an assessment of the team's potential for 1954. He received an earful. A long time favorite of Cub fans who had spent 20 years with the club, Cavarretta candidly told Wrigley that his team, as presently constituted, was terrible and would not come close to moving out of the second division, and would finish closer to last place than to first. The Cub owner took these comments under advisement, and on March 30 announced that Cavarretta was guilty of "defeatism" and would be replaced by Hack.

This bit of startling news was disruptive, to say the least. Cavarretta was offered the opportunity to go to Los Angeles as the Angels manager, but he declined and terminated his long relationship with the Cubs. With the opening of the season only a week away, the Angels hastily appointed Bill Sweeney to the position. He had been hired as an Angels coach during the winter after managing Seattle to a second-place finish in 1953. Sweeney was a well-known figure around the sporting scene in Southern California. He had been popular with the fans and sportswriters during his previous tour of duty as Angels manager from 1943 to 1946, and his re-appointment was met with universal approval.

After the disastrous season of 1953, the PCL rescinded the edict that prohibited clubs from receiving players on option from the major leagues, a wise move indeed. The situation in San Francisco was settled in December, when the so-called "Little Corporation" was created, and the franchise was purchased from the league. And the Oakland situation seemed promising as Brick Laws hired Charlie Dressen as manager after he refused to sign a new one-year contract with Brooklyn. Finally, PCL officials again adjusted the length of the schedule, this time to 168 games, and the Governor's Cup playoff series was restored after a two-year absence.

There were more players available to the Angels for 1954 after the Cubs terminated their agreement with Springfield and turned that franchise back to the International League. During the winter months, the Angels acquired catcher John Pramesa, outfielder Herb Adams, pitcher Sheldon Jones and infielder Gene Hooks, and later picked up outfielder

The 1954 Angels. *Front row (left to right):* Batboy Bill Holman, Al Evans, Sheldon Jones, Bob Usher, Jacques Monette, Bob Boring, Chris Kitsos, unknown player, Bubba Church, batboy Art Chocek. *Middle row:* Dixie Upright, Fred Richards, Tommy Brown, Hal Meek, coach Jack Warner, manager Bill Sweeney, Bob Spicer, Bud Hardin, Don Robertson, Bruce Edwards. *Back row:* Clubhouse man Bob Ramirez, Dick Smith, John Pramesa, Joe Hatten, Max West, Randy Gumpert, John Pyecha, Tom Simpson, Bill Moisan, Cal McLish, Trainer Dave Flores (courtesy Mark Macrae).

Tommy Brown and pitcher Tom Simpson when the Springfield players were dispersed. And the Angels could count on having the first claim on players from the Cubs, now that optioned players were allowed. Player traffic in and out of Los Angeles ran very heavy that winter. When spring training began, the club had major holes to fill at shortstop, third base and center field. The right side of the infield was stable, with Fred Richards returning at first base and Gene Mauch, a light-hitting second baseman who had seen major league service with Brooklyn and the Cubs, at second base. In 1953, Mauch had managed the Atlanta Crackers of the Southern Association and was purchased by the Angels at the winter meetings. He would become an important part of the club over the next three years.

Shortstop and third base remained questionable well into the season. Bud Hardin was given the first opportunity to replace Gene Baker, and he proved to be a sure handed fielder with good range but not much of a hitter. His versatility as a fielder allowed Sweeney to plug him in at second and third base when the club was hampered by injuries. Frank DiPrima opened at third base, but that was not a natural position for him, and he was soon sold to Atlanta. Brown filled in for a time, and then the Cubs returned the once-promising Leon Brinkopf to Los Angeles in early May. He had missed all of the 1953 season while recovering from back surgery, and it soon became apparent that he was not the player he had been when he was the Angels' Most Valuable Player in 1951; the Angels optioned him to Des Moines. Later on the Cubs sent Bruce Edwards to Los Angeles as a replacement third baseman. A former catcher with Brooklyn, Edwards no longer had the arm for that position and was barely adequate at third base. But he was a good hitter and played the position for the balance of the year, despite his obvious deficiencies in the field.

Sweeney opened with an outfield of Dixie Upright, Herb Adams and Bob Usher, but very quickly this combination was changed when Adams was sent to Columbus and Upright appeared to be a liability in the field. Usher was shifted to center field, while Tommy Brown took over in left field. The club had hoped to give Max West the majority of the right field work, but he had not fully recovered from his knee surgery of the year before and saw limited duty in the outfield. Jacques Monette, a rookie from Longview in the Big State League, showed some promise but was very inexperienced and was sent to Beaumont in the Texas League after a brief trial. As the year went on, the Cubs sent Don Robertson to Los Angeles, and Vic Marasco was acquired on option from the Dodger farm system. They shared most of the right field duty over the last half of the year.

Al Evans returned to handle the catching duties with Pramesa, and the pitching staff looked to be adequate. Joe Hatten, Cal McLish, Bob Spicer and Sheldon Jones were designated as the early starters, and Lorenzo Hinchman, a rookie up from Macon, was given several early starts.

The club opened the season at San Diego and was shut out by the Padres, 5–0, but played reasonably well during April to reach the .500 mark. But it was very clear that the club had some serious problems. The hitting had fallen off dramatically. Fred Richards, who had enjoyed a fine year in 1953 while batting in the second position in the lineup, was shifted to the cleanup spot, where he seemed utterly helpless. Although he was an early leader in home runs, all but one of his first 12 were hit with the bases empty. When his batting average seemed locked at .180, Bill Sweeney dropped him in the batting order. He continued to hit home runs, but not much else, and did not get above .200 until July. Bob Usher did not seem to be the same defender in center field as he had been in left and right, and his hitting appeared to be affected, too. Dixie Upright was far below his 1953 numbers as well. Only Gene Mauch showed any consistency at the plate.

With the Angels generating little offense besides an occasional solo home run, Sweeney was constantly changing his lineup. Bud Hardin saw some extended service at third base as the club tried two rookies at shortstop, first Chris Kitsos and later Hank Nasternak. Kitsos was a fine fielder, but did not hit at all and was sent to Beaumont to make room for Nasternak, who was called up from Des Moines. He broke in with four hits in his first game and hit .404 in his first two weeks with the club, but he was only an average fielder, and his hitting soon cooled off. The impact of the personnel changes on the infield was most apparent in the club's inability to turn double plays. The Angels finished last in the league in that important department.

The pitching held up surprisingly well during the first six weeks of the season, but the lack of offense and the shoddy defense was too much to overcome. The Angels began a long decline that saw them fall into the cellar on July 4 after losing a doubleheader to San Diego. Joe Hatten and Bob Spicer pitched well as did Cal McLish, but each went into a period where he was unable to win. The Cubs sent additional pitching help on May 15, when the major league roster cuts were made. Bill Moisan, Bubba Church and John Pyecha bolstered the staff somewhat. Church had been a fine pitcher during his first two years at Philadelphia, but he had suffered arm ailments while with Cincinnati and the Cubs; he no longer had a good fast ball. Moisan once more failed to make the grade with Chicago, and this time he did not provide much help to the Angels. Used primarily in relief, he lost his first seven decisions in Los Angeles before winning his only game on July 10.

Los Angeles remained in last place for the month of July, finally managing to climb out of the basement in August, but not by very much. Attendance at Wrigley Field, which had not been impressive to begin with, declined seriously in late July, and with the continuing emphasis on major league expansion to the Pacific Coast, interest in the team was limited. It did not help that Hollywood again appeared to be on its way to a pennant, while the daily televising of Angels home games had its impact on the gate. Weekday crowds seldom reached 2,000, and a doubleheader crowd of 3,617 in July marked the lowest Sunday attendance since 1939. But two weeks later, only 2,607 turned out to see the Angels lose a doubleheader to Portland and fall back into the cellar. The low point of the season had now been reached. The club was now 23 games below .500 and appeared to be the worst Angels team since the miserable 1949 club.

But at that juncture the Angels rallied and played consistent baseball for the remainder of the season. A four-game winning streak against Seattle brought them out of last place a week later, and eventually they moved into sixth place, where they finished the season, two games ahead of last-place Portland and one game in front of Sacramento. Their sixth-place finish was in keeping with the offense, which ranked seventh in batting and sixth in runs scored, averaging less than four runs a game. The Angels suffered 19 shutouts, were last in walks and finished second in strikeouts No Angels player hit .300 though Bruce Edwards came close at .298. The club hit 140 home runs, again leading the league, but somehow most of them seemed to be hit with the bases empty or in one-sided games.

Meanwhile, the pitching improved as the season wore on. Bubba Church was the best pitcher during the last six weeks. He seemed to receive more run support than the others,

An aerial view of south Los Angeles in the early 1950s, looking west with Wrigley Field and the Los Angeles Coliseum as prominent structures. The University of Southern California is to the north of the Coliseum, and the Harbor Freeway can be seen under construction to the east (courtesy Al Parnis).

but he was also brilliant at times. A no-hitter against Portland on August 3 was the highlight of the year; Church managed to go 12⅓ innings over two games before he allowed a hit. He won six games over the last five weeks of the season to finish with a record of 11–9, making him the only starter over .500. John Pyecha was an important contributor during this stretch as well, winning seven games with a 3.24 ERA. Bob Spicer, Joe Hatten and Cal McLish each won 13 games with ERA's below 3.60, but they were also big losers. McLish went for a month without a victory, and Hatten finished on the losing end of seven shutouts. Angels relief pitching was vastly improved during the last half of the season, especially after the Cubs released Turk Lown to Los Angeles. He had not been effective as a starter in Chicago, but he turned his career around in Los Angeles as a relief pitcher. In 30 games, he was 5–3 with a 2.48 ERA and no home runs allowed, an amazing feat for a pitcher in Wrigley Field. He would improve on those numbers in 1955 and find himself back in the major leagues.

Angels attendance was the lowest of the post-war period so far. Only 238,567 fans paid their way into Wrigley Field, and even the Ladies Day games were not well attended that year. The PCL as a whole was slightly better, primarily a result of an improved market in San Francisco and a first-place finish in San Diego for the first time in that city's history. But it seemed apparent that the days of minor league baseball in Los Angeles were numbered. Major league expansion to the Pacific Coast was thought to be only a matter of time, especially in view of the successful moves to Milwaukee and Baltimore the past two seasons.

In December 1954, a third major league franchise shift took place when the Philadelphia Athletics were sold by the Mack family and transferred to Kansas City. There had been some early speculation that the A's might be coming to Los Angeles, and San Francisco was said to have been a bidder as well. Again that year at the winter meetings, there was much discussion over the viability of the PCL as a third major league. Could it qualify at some time in the future? So far, the new Open Classification had not worked well. Or would another major league club decide to pull up stakes and move to the West? These questions remained to be answered.

23

Sgt. Bilko and His Gang

Generally, after the Angels had experienced a disappointing year, they made a large number of roster changes; 1955 was no exception. By the time the club assembled for spring training in Fullerton, there were only eight holdovers from the woeful 1954 aggregation. Spring training in 1955 was unusual in that many of the players who would perform the bulk of the duty when the season started were not actually in the Angels camp. The Cub farm system appeared to be producing young talent for the first time during the Wid Mathews regime. Many of these players were a year or two away from the PCL, but training with the Angels before arriving at their final destination at a lower level of play. The prime prospects were in the Cub camp and would join the Angels later.

Just as the 1954 season had ended, Angels president Don Stewart died suddenly. His replacement was John Holland, the son of a long-time minor league owner. Holland had grown up in the Cub system and served as the general manager at Des Moines before his promotion to the Angels. Los Angeles was very definitely a Cub farm team by this time, and there was very little talent on the Angels roster that did not originate within the organization. There were some exceptions, most notably third baseman Jim "Bus" Clarkson, who had been drafted from Dallas of the Texas League. Clarkson was a veteran player from the Negro Leagues who had spent his best years outside of Organized Baseball before the color line was finally broken. Although he was 41 years old, Clarkson had led the Texas League with 42 home runs in 1954 and was expected to do well in Los Angeles.

The talk of major league expansion to the West Coast filled the newspapers that winter, so much so that Commissioner Ford Frick issued an edict to the major league officials to cease the discussion of moving to the West. Such talk was having a very detrimental effect on the PCL, especially in the Bay Area, where interest in the Seals and Oaks was probably at its lowest ebb in history. The Cubs spent much money on Wrigley Field that winter, replacing 3,400 box seats and repainting the park. Further improvements were planned for 1956, so that Wrigley Field would be raised to major league standards in the event that a major league team should move to Los Angeles.

On March 30, less than a week before the PCL season was to begin, the Cubs made a wholesale roster reduction and sent what would become the nucleus of the 1955 Angels to Los Angeles — pitchers Jim Brosnan, Don Elston, Bob Zick, Bill Tremel and Joe Stanka, catcher Joe Hannah, shortstop Eddie Winceniak, and outfielders Don Robertson and Bob Talbot. All of these players came on option. The most important addition that day, one that dwarfed all others, was the outright assignment of first baseman Steve Bilko to the Angels.

The 1955 Angels. *Front row (left to right):* Batboy, Bob Zick, Joe Hatten, Bob Coats, Don Elston, Solly Drake, Bud Hardin, batboy, batboy Bill Marr. *Middle row:* Steve Bilko, Bus Clarkson, Jim Fanning, Eddie Winceniak, coach Jack Warner, manager Bob Scheffing, Gene Mauch, Elvin Tappe, Bob Usher, Turk Lown. *Back row:* Trainer Joe Liscio, George Piktuzis, Ray "Moe" Bauer, Piper Davis, Jim Brosnan, Hy Cohen, Hal Rice, Gale Wade, Bubba Church, assistant trainer Bill Holmes (courtesy Mark Macrae).

Bilko was a massive right-handed hitter who was 26 years old, standing 6'1" and weighing anywhere from 230 to 265 pounds. He had begun his professional career in the Cardinal system in 1945, finally joining St. Louis as the regular first baseman in 1953. He hit 21 home runs that year, an impressive number for a right-handed hitter in Sportsman's Park, but he struck out 125 times and was not especially mobile around first base. When the Cardinals purchased Tom Alston from San Diego prior to the 1954 season, they sent Bilko to Chicago. There he competed with former Angels player Dee Fondy but was unable to beat him out in 1954, appearing in only 47 Cub games. When Fondy once again appeared to be the better player in the spring of 1955, the Cubs released him to Los Angeles.

Wrigley Field was the perfect ballpark for Steve Bilko. He hit most of his home runs to left field, but some of them went to left-center and right-center field, where the power alleys in Los Angeles were notoriously short. He tended to hit high fly balls, many of which would reach the prevailing wind currents at Wrigley and sail out of the ballpark And he was strong enough to take the outside pitch to right field. Bilko could be pitched to, particularly high and tight inside, but there was little margin for error, and many a PCL pitcher would regret his decision to go inside.

Bilko would spend three fabulous years as an Angels player, leading the league in home runs in each of them, and hitting well over .300. He related extremely well to the fans and was undoubtedly the most popular player to ever wear a Los Angeles Angels uniform. The news of his death, in 1978 at the early age of 49, earned extensive coverage in the sports section of the *Times*, which devoted a long column to Bilko and what he had meant to base-

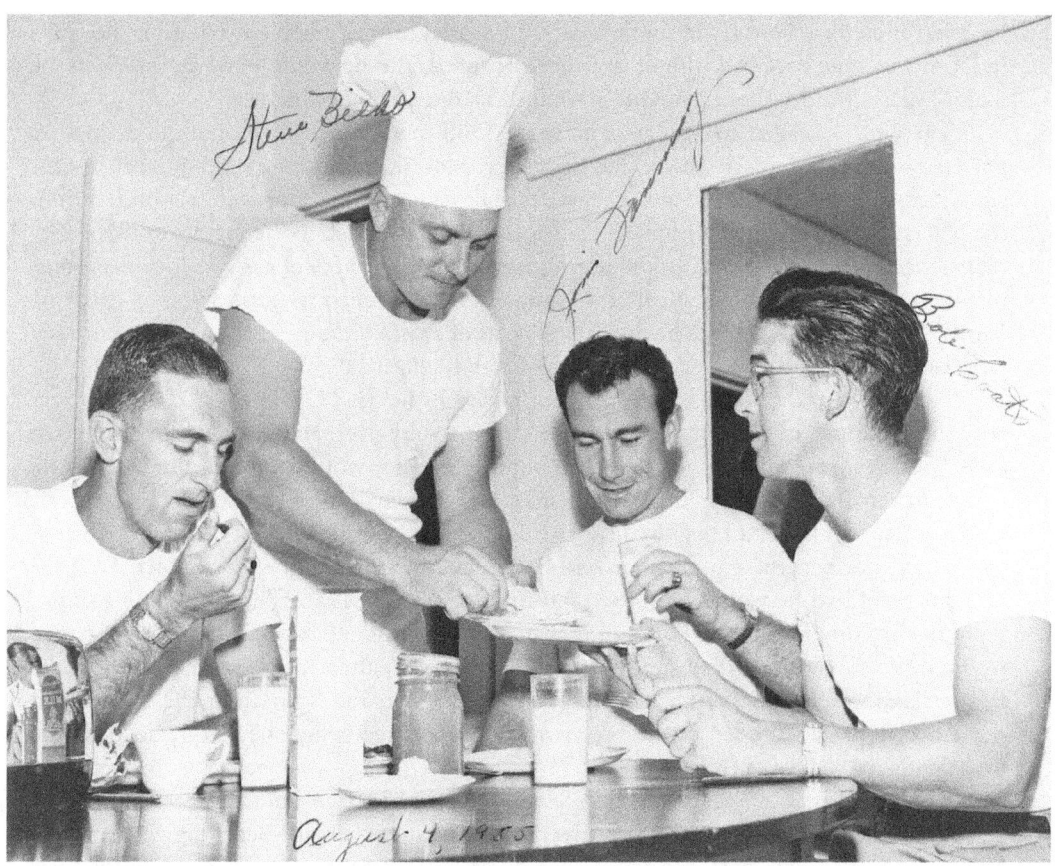

Ray Bauer, Steve Bilko, Jim Fanning and Bob Coats enjoy a lunch prepared by the Angels first baseman, August 4, 1955 (courtesy Hy Cohen).

ball in Los Angeles. In the mid–1950s, Bilko was just what the Angels needed at that point in their history. He reinvigorated interest in the PCL at a time when it was rapidly dying. Once more, the league became an important part of the Southern California sport scene and would remain so through the remaining years of the Angels' existence.

The Angels opened the season with John Pramesa behind the plate, an infield of Gene Mauch, Bud Hardin and Bus Clarkson to go along with Bilko, and an outfield of Don Robertson, Bob Talbot and Bob Usher. The opening rotation would be Joe Hatten, back for his fourth and final year with the club, Cal McLish, Jim Brosnan, and rookie left-hander George Piktuzis, a returning Army veteran, who had not pitched above Class B.

The Angels won the opening day match with Portland, 9–5, featuring home runs by Hatten and reliever Turk Lown, but the lineup was not to remain intact for long. Pramesa had at one time been a very promising young catcher, but after his back surgery in 1953, he was never the same. He had bad knees as well and would be released to Des Moines by July. Hardin was a fine fielder but a light hitter, and after a week, manager Bill Sweeney tried Eddie Winceniak at shortstop to give the offense some more punch. The outfield soon became a shambles. Robertson could not handle PCL pitching and was gone after two weeks, replaced by Bob Coats, who had enjoyed a fine season at Macon in 1954. In center field, Bob Talbot was not the player he had been during his previous stint in Los Angeles.

He had suffered a severe ankle sprain that did not heal properly while playing for the Cubs in 1954. The injury robbed him of considerable speed, and he would never to return to the major leagues. And Usher seemed to have lost his once-fine batting eye.

The club managed to stay at or near the .500 mark through the middle of May as players came and went with increasing frequency. McLish was unimpressive in his first four starts and was sold to San Diego, a major mistake, as it turned out. He rebounded from the poor start to win 16 games for the Padres and would be back in the majors in 1956. Piktuzis started well with two shutouts during April, winning three of his first four decisions, but he struggled with his control and gradually lost his effectiveness. Sweeney used Joe Kuncl, Bill Tremel, John Pyecha and Dwight Stoddard in various pitching roles, but they were soon dispatched to other points in the Cubs system.

In early May the Cubs sent additional help. Outfielder Hal Rice, once a fine player with the Cardinals, catcher Jim Fanning, a promising youngster, and pitchers Bubba Church and Hy Cohen would strengthen the team, but Bill Sweeney would not be around to witness the improvement. He resigned as Angels manager on May 23, on advice from his doctor. The popular Irishman had begun to suffer from various health problems during the spring, and the daily managerial grind had become too much for him. In a press conference, Sweeney said he hoped that he would be able to return to baseball in 1956. That he was able to do, replacing Tommy Holmes as Portland manager in the middle of the season. But his return would be short; Sweeney died suddenly on April 18, 1957, after beginning the season at the Beaver helm. Sweeney was only 52. He had spent 19 years managing four PCL teams and was especially well regarded in the Southern California area, where he had made his home for many years.

The new Angels manager was Bob Scheffing, a Cubs coach under Stan Hack in 1954 and 1955 after an eight-year catching career in the National League. Scheffing was 39 when he took over the Angels post. He had a much different personality than the amiable Sweeney, and there would be an adjustment period for the players. The Angels were 25–25 when Scheffing took over, in fifth place, nine games out of the lead, and had begun a slide that would see the club fall ten games below .500 by the first week in July. The offense had suffered a severe blow on May 1, when Bus Clarkson broke his ankle and missed the next six weeks. Piper Davis was acquired from Oakland to fill in, and he became a valuable addition. The pitching collapsed during this period as Scheffing tried to develop an effective staff. George Piktuzis lost seven straight games while both Hy Cohen and Bubba Church lost their first three decisions before settling down. Scheffing made an important move when he began to use Don Elston as a starter after several impressive relief appearances.

Gradually, the team stabilized. Steve Bilko had started slowly. He struck out ten times during the first week at home without hitting a home run, and was roundly booed when he failed in several crucial situations. He did not hit his first home run at Wrigley Field until April 20, a 400-foot blast off Angels-killer Allen Gettel of Oakland, but by the end of April he was the league leader. His average remained low for the first two months of the season, however, and he did not reach the .300 mark before the end of June. But from that point on, Bilko hit over .360, and the club began to play better. The outfield improved when Scheffing sent the disappointing Bob Talbot to Toledo in exchange for Gale Wade, who was playing there on option from the Cubs. At these respective stages of their careers, Wade was the better player. He had more power than Talbot, had good speed, and was a fine base runner. The outfield regulars were now Hal Rice, Wade and Bob Usher, with Bob Coats seeing plenty of duty. He did not have much power but consistently reached base.

When Usher seemed unable to solve his season long slump, Scheffing benched him in late July, obtaining outfielders Solly Drake from Chicago as a replacement. The veteran saw only pinch-hitting duty for the rest of the season before he was sold to San Diego in September.

Drake was installed as the regular left fielder during the first week of August, and for the balance of the season the Angels might have been the best team in the league. They went over the .500 mark on August 7, and after losing a series at Hollywood in the middle of the month, they came back with gusto to take six of seven from the Stars at home to tie the season series with their arch rivals. The crowds came back to Wrigley Field that week, with 18,007 in the stands on September 1, and 15,217 on hand to watch the Angels sweep a doubleheader two days later. Los Angeles was on a streak that saw the club win seven straight games and climb into third place two days before the season ended. The Angels finished tied for that position with Hollywood, only four games behind champion Seattle.

When the city series ended in a tie, John Holland and Bob Cobb agreed that the two clubs should meet in a playoff to determine the champion. That the two clubs then tied for third place added some more excitement to the best-of-five series. All of the games were played at Wrigley Field, and Hollywood was victorious. The Stars won the first two games, and then it was the Angels' turn, before a barrage of six home runs gave Hollywood the final game, 7–6.

This turned out to be the most exciting season that Angels fans had enjoyed since 1947. Attendance was low at the beginning of the year, but as the club played better, the fans came out in large numbers on the weekends. Attendance finished at 335,491, including women, an increase of almost 70,000 over 1954. Steve Bilko was responsible for much of this increased interest. He was devastating in 1955, hitting .328 with a league-leading 37 home runs and 124 RBIs, just one behind league leader Earl Rapp of San Diego Although most of his homers were hit at Wrigley Field, Bilko was a force around the league ballparks as well. He hit what may have been the longest home run in history at Emeryville on May 4, a drive that was said to carry 552 feet to dead center field. The Angels as a team led the PCL in home runs, as usual, with 143, but placed only sixth in team batting and led the league in strikeouts.

Gene Mauch had another fine year, hitting .296, and was beginning to demonstrate some of those qualities that would lead him to a long major league managerial career. Hal Rice had 25 home runs, second on the club behind Bilko, but he hit only .262 and struck out frequently. Gale Wade hit .310 in 101 games and led the Angels with 23 stolen bases. But the offense was badly hurt when Clarkson went down with his injury in May. He was limited to 100 games while hitting .294 with 13 home runs.

Jim Brosnan and Don Elston led the pitchers with 17 wins each. Elston's 17–6 record was compiled in 53 games, 31 of them in relief. Eventually, he would become one of the National League's premier relief pitchers with the Cubs, as would Brosnan with several teams. The Angels featured the best bullpen in the league with Elston and Turk Lown. Lown turned his career around in Los Angeles that year. He posted a 12–5 record in 59 appearances and allowed only 4 home runs, a remarkable record for a pitcher who worked in Wrigley Field. Lown also had ten saves, five of them in games where Brosnan received the win. Although Brosnan was a durable pitcher, he had a tendency to develop blisters on his pitching hand in the late innings, and Lown was often called upon to finish the game for him. After his slow start, Bubba Church posted an 11–8 mark and Joe Hatten matched his 11 victories. Hy Cohen and George Piktuzis pitched well in spots, but Piktuzis was limited by arm problems, and Cohen received the worst offensive support on the staff. In four of his nine losses, the Angels were held to one run or less. Piktuzis finished at 7–13, a disappointment after his fine start. On July 21, he pitched a no-hitter at San Francisco, a spectacular performance that was witnessed by only 780 fans; it was his last win of the year.

In spite of the proclamation by Commissioner Ford Frick, there was continued speculation throughout Los Angeles in 1955 about the possibility of a major league team playing in the city. The idea of an expansion team was frequently discussed, but for the first time, the association of the Brooklyn Dodgers with Los Angeles began to develop. On August 18, Dodgers team president Walter O'Malley announced that his team would not play in Ebbets Field beyond the 1958 season. Shortly thereafter, the Los Angeles city council authorized Mayor Norris Paulson, councilman Ed Roybal and councilwoman Rosalind Wyman to schedule a visit to Brooklyn in September in hopes of discussing the possibility of moving the Dodgers to Los Angeles. Although Mr. O'Malley refused to meet with the group at this time, the first contacts had been made.

In the meantime, a long pennant drought was about to end. After eight years of generally mediocre and often poor play, the Angels were on the verge of a championship. As it had done during the winter of 1954-55, the club again divested itself of many veterans who had made up the roster of the third-place team of 1955. Before spring training had begun, pitchers Bubba Church and Joe Hatten, outfielder Hal Rice and infielder Bus Clarkson had been sent away. Advancing to Chicago were pitchers Don Elston, Jim Brosnan and Turk Lown, along with outfielder Gale Wade. The 1956 Angels would have an entirely new look. But the results went far beyond what anyone could have expected, and the new season would be one of the most satisfying in the history of the franchise.

The nucleus of 1955 was still in place. Steve Bilko and Gene Mauch were back and were poised for their greatest seasons. New infield additions included third baseman George Freese, who had been drafted from New Orleans, and shortstop Casey Wise, a youngster who had worked his way up through the Cub farm system and was about to enjoy a breakthrough season. He had seen limited action in Los Angeles in 1955 before being sent out to Beaumont in the Texas League. This new combination would form one of the finest infields in Angels history.

In contrast, the outfield situation was uncertain. The Cubs had sent Jim Bolger to Los Angeles during the winter, and he opened the season in center field, flanked by returnee Bob Coats and newcomer Eddie Haas, up from Des Moines. The opening day catcher would be Joe Hannah, another rookie. It was not a strong group of outfielders and catchers, but the Angels expected that the Cubs would provide some additional help.

The pitchers that spring were young, mostly under the age of 23. The most impressive of the group were two 20 year olds, Bob Anderson and Dick Drott. Drott was from Cincinnati and was only two years removed from an American Legion championship team. He had spent the 1955 season at Burlington in the Class-B Three I league and was attempting to make the big jump to Open Classification baseball. Drott had a wonderful fastball and a wide sweeping curve that froze the hitters, leading to many strikeouts. He was wild at times, but his marvelous curve ball helped him out of many tight situations, and he earned a spot in the starting rotation. Anderson was also a hard thrower, but he did not have a good breaking pitch to complement his speed. He tended to overpower hitters with his great fastball, so Bob Scheffing decided to use him in the bullpen as the season began.

Other pitchers were more experienced. The Cubs sent left-hander Harry Perkowski, a veteran of several National League seasons with Cincinnati and Chicago, and Dave Hill-

The 1956 Angels. *Front row (left to right):* Batboy Ralph Coats, batboy Bob Scheffing, Jr., Bob Thorpe, Richie Myers, Jim Bolger, Bob Coats, batboy Bill Meyer. *Second row:* Gene Fodge, Red Adams, Casey Wise, manager Bob Scheffing, coach Jack Warner, Chick Pieretti, Gene Mauch. ***Third row:*** Trainer Joe Liscio, Harry Perkowski, Ray Bauer, Bob Anderson, Bob Speake, Piper Davis, John Pyecha, Dave Hillman, assistant trainer Bill Holmes. *Back row:* Johnny Briggs, Dick Drott, Steve Bilko, George Freese, Gale Wade, Elvin Tappe, Joe Hannah (courtesy Dick Dobbins).

man, a right-hander who was 16–11 with Beaumont in 1955 after a brief trial with the Cubs. Other pitchers on the opening day roster were George Piktuzis, Hy Cohen and John Andre, all of whom were questionable; Piktuzis had not fully recovered from his arm ailments of the previous year. Thankfully, the Cubs promised additional pitching help once the season had begun.

Steve Bilko enjoyed a fine training camp even though the club did not, losing 16 of the 21 exhibition games. He felt that the reason for his slow start in 1955 was his virtual inactivity in Chicago the previous year. He predicted that would not be a factor this year. His goals were to hit .360 with 40 to 50 home runs in 1956. Up the middle, Mauch and Casey Wise worked well together, and it appeared that the defense would be considerably better.

The PCL schedule for 1956 was reduced to 168 games, and would be completely balanced for the first time in over 20 years, with each team playing 24 games against all other clubs, 12 at home and 12 away. For the first time since 1938, a franchise had changed cities. The Oakland club, an original PCL franchise, was shifted to Vancouver, to be called the Mounties. This resulted after a series of losing years made it impossible for Brick Laws to continue operations in the East Bay. In addition, the Seals franchise was in better hands. It had been sold to the Boston Red Sox and would now have first call on the best Red Sox prospects. On the whole, these changes improved the financial picture for the league, with most clubs in their best fiscal condition of the 1950s. All teams except Sacramento were now affiliated with a major league team, and the quality of play throughout the league would be improved as a result.

The Angels opened the season in San Diego, all decked out in new uniforms designed by Max West, who was now in the sporting goods business. Steve Bilko hit a home run to highlight the opener, won by Harry Perkowski, 9–3. The club played at a .500 pace during the first two weeks in a series of games that featured a great deal of hitting but not much pitching. The early starters were Perkowski, who won three quick decisions during this period, along with Cohen, Drott and Gene Fodge, up from Des Moines. Bilko had six home runs while hitting .434, and he appeared on the way to a titanic year. One of his early homers cleared the right-field bleachers at Seals Stadium and was estimated at 500 feet.

The Angels needed all of his power, and then some, simply to stay close in games, because of the unsettled pitching. Rookies Tom LeGros, John Andre and John Hricinak were given opportunities, but none was effective. The club acquired right-hander Chick Pieretti from Sacramento after a week's play; he had won 19 games for the Solons in 1955 and was immediately placed in the starting rotation. Bob Anderson and Ray "Moe" Bauer were kept busy, used in relief almost every other day.

Early help was received from the Cubs when they sent outfielder Bob Speake to Los Angeles on April 14. Speake had been a National League sensation during the early weeks of 1955, when he won several games with his clutch hitting. But the pitchers soon discovered that he was vulnerable to high fastballs, and he faded to a .218 average for the season with only one home run after June. He was still a fine prospect, however, and the Cubs thought that playing every day in Los Angeles might eliminate his

Steve Bilko — He was the most popular Angel of all time. The television series *Sergeant Bilko and His Gang* was named after him (courtesy Dick Dobbins).

hitting flaw. Speake was installed in left field upon his arrival; he played there virtually every day for the balance of the season. He provided good left-handed balance between Bilko and George Freese in the lineup, as Coats was relegated to part-time duty.

On April 24, the Angels took over first place with a win at Sacramento and followed that up with a four-game sweep at Hollywood. In his second start, Dick Drott amazed the crowd with ten strikeouts. He followed that up with nine more strikeouts in a 9–0 win at Vancouver, marking his third straight win. Clearly, he was a star in the making. But the rest of the pitching staff was suspect. Dave Hillman and John Pyecha had been sent to Los Angeles in late April, but they were of little immediate help because of arm problems. Pyecha proved to be useless to the Angels, as did sore-armed George Piktuzis. Neither won a game for the club and soon both left the scene. Hillman was ineffective in three early starts before winning his first game on May 10. Nevertheless, the Angels remained in first place for most of the month of May, with Seattle and Sacramento close behind.

The Angels were putting on a tremendous offensive display. They were simply outslugging the opposition on the many days that the pitching was subpar. Bilko was on pace to have one of the greatest seasons in PCL history. After 19 games, his average stood at .500, and he showed no signs of slumping. Mauch was hitting well above .400 for the first month of the season, and Jim Bolger delivered time and time again in a clutch role. He had a reputation as a fine fielder, but his hitting was a great surprise. He emerged as the early RBI leader despite hitting in the seventh spot in the lineup most of the time.

Most of the early damage was done at Wrigley Field where the Angels won 22 of their first 27 games. Part of the reason for the increased hitting at home may have been the club's decision to play its weekday games in the daytime. After years of night baseball, except on the weekend, the Angels reverted to an almost all daytime schedule. Night games were played on Fridays only. Coincidentally, the club's TV policy was modified so that only the Friday home games would not be televised. It remains uncertain why the change to day baseball was made. But Wrigley Field in Chicago had no lights at that time, and P. K. Wrigley was known to have a philosophical opposition to night baseball. There was less competition from daytime television, and Angels management might have thought that crowds would improve during the day. But that did not happen; the Angels rarely drew over 1,000 paid spectators for weekday games.

At the major league cutdown date of May 15, the Angels lineup received its final modifications when the Cubs returned Gale Wade and Elvin Tappe to Los Angeles, along with pitchers Bob Thorpe and Johnny Briggs, and infielder Richie Myers. Eddie Haas was sent to Des Moines, with Bolger shifting to right field and Wade back in center field. To make room for these additions, the Angels sent Bus Clarkson and Hy Cohen to Tulsa. The decision to release Cohen was puzzling, to say the least. He had started five games, won them all, and was the staff leader at that point. But he had received great run support and had an ERA of 5.70 for those five games, and, Cub management apparently looked at that number in deciding to send him away. Cohen ended up at New Orleans, where he finished 11–7 and was among the best pitchers in the Southern Association.

The Angels were four games ahead of Seattle after the Memorial Day doubleheader, but then went through a stretch where they played .500 ball, and the Rainiers caught them in mid–June. The pitching miseries continued during this period, and the offense fell off slightly. The falloff did not include Steve Bilko, however, as he hit his 23rd home run on June 5 and enjoyed a 24-game hitting streak that finally ended on June 17. Mauch continued his fine hitting as well, and the two Angels remained at the top of the batting leaders.

The pitching remained erratic. Dick Drott had lost some of his early magic and was unable to finish his starts, while Gene Fodge and Chick Pieretti were inconsistent in their outings. Only Dave Hillman seemed able to give a consistently good effort, placing a heavy burden on the bullpen. The Angels dropped to two games behind Seattle at the end of June where they remained through July 4. On that date, Bilko hit his 36th home run to put him well ahead of Tony Lazzeri's pace in 1925, when he established the PCL record of 60. Lazzeri did not hit his 36th home run until July 19 of that year.

For the first ten days of July, the Angels and Seattle remained close, with Los Angeles finally taking over first place for good with a 19–4 rout of Portland in a game where the club scored 12 runs in the first inning. The day before, Fodge had won his first game since June 13. He was beginning a period during which he would win nine straight decisions to take some of the pitching burden off the shoulders of Dave Hillman. For the next five weeks, the combined record of these two pitchers was 14–1 as the Angels began to run away with the pennant.

The critical day of the 1956 season was July 15, when the Angels entertained Seattle in a doubleheader at Wrigley Field. The Angels had been routed, 15–3, the day before to cut their margin over the Rainiers to one game. A good crowd of 11,174 showed up to watch Los Angeles sweep the doubleheader, 10–4 behind Hillman in the first game, with Bilko, Wade and Bolger hitting home runs, and 6–2 behind Fodge in the seven-inning nightcap. That gave the Angels a three-game lead, which they widened to five games by early August and then to 11½ by August 16. The club went 23–6 during this span, as Seattle began to play itself out of the race amidst rumors of player discontent with manager Luke Sewell, who was fired before the season was over. The pennant race had effectively been decided.

The Angels continued their fine play through the month of August and extended their lead to 16 games. By now, all attention was focused on Steve Bilko, who was making a determined effort to set a new PCL home run record. He hit his 47th on August 12, and with 40 games to go, it appeared that he had a good chance to do so. He hit his 50th on August 26, with 24 games remaining. But 15 games were to be played in Portland, Seattle and Vancouver, where Bilko had not done particularly well. He managed to hit three on the trip, his 53rd coming on September 3 in the first game of a doubleheader at Seattle. But he did not hit another until September 9, connecting against Hollywood when the club returned home, and he hit his last home run on the next to last day of the season eight days later.

Bilko's 1956 season was one of the best in PCL and Angels history, as he won his second consecutive Most Valuable Player award. His performance resembled the seasons that Frank Demaree had in 1934 and Lou Novikoff enjoyed in 1940. Each of the three led the league in hitting, home runs and runs batted in. A comparison of the three follows:

	AB	R	H	2B	3B	HR	RBI	TB	AVG.
Demaree	702	190	269	51	4	45	173	463	.383
Novikoff	714	147	259	44	6	41	171	438	.363
Bilko	597	163	215	18	6	55	164	410	.360

It is difficult to make a fair comparison between the men because the playing conditions were somewhat different in each of these years. Suffice it to say, they all had great seasons, but Bilko played in fewer games than the others. Had he appeared in another 10 to 15 games, it seems reasonable to expect that he would have topped the 60-home run plateau and would have approached some of the numbers that Demaree and Novikoff had posted.

Although Bilko was clearly the dominant force on the Angels of 1956, he had a fine supporting cast. Gene Mauch finished second to the hulking first baseman in the batting race as he enjoyed the finest season of his career, hitting .348 with 20 home runs. Batting second in the lineup behind Casey Wise, Mauch was especially proficient at the hit-and-run. He earned another opportunity to return to the major leagues and was sold to the Boston Red Sox in September. Jim Bolger was another player who had his best season. His .326 average was impressive, and he finished second behind Bilko in RBIs with 147. That was a remarkable performance, considering that he batted in the seventh position virtually all year, just ahead of the light-hitting catcher, Elvin Tappe. George Freese and Bob Speake both drove in over 100 runs with 113 and 111, respectively. Freese tied a club record set in 1924 by Bill Whaley when he drove in eight runs in the 19–4 rout at Portland in July. Each of the outfield regulars hit 20 or more home runs; Bolger had 28, Speake hit 25 and Gale Wade, never considered a power hitter, had 20 home runs in 101 games. Freese also contributed 22 homers.

Offensively, the Angels were the best team of the post-war era. The club scored exactly 1,000 runs, an average of six per game. No PCL club had scored that many since the 1931 Angels. As a team, the Angels stayed above the .300 mark virtually all year long before the bats cooled in September, and the club closed at .297. That mark had not been exceeded since the 1935 Seals batted .305. The Angels had a good opportunity to set a new PCL home run record, but like Bilko, the club just missed the mark. Los Angeles hit 202 home runs, just behind the 204 hit by Salt Lake City in 1923 in a much longer schedule. The Angels were utterly devastating at home, hitting 136 home runs at Wrigley Field and posting a won-loss record of 61–23.

Unfortunately, the pitching staff was not of the same caliber as the offense. Although Dick Drott was an exciting young pitcher and led the PCL with 184 strikeouts, his inexperience and wildness resulted in a 13–10 record and an unimpressive 4.39 ERA. Of the starters, only Dave Hillman had an ERA below four. He was the big winner with 21 victories, the first Angels 20-game winner since Cal McLish in 1950 and the last pitcher in franchise history to win that many. Gene Fodge won 19 games after a very slow start. He saw considerable relief duty early and was not consistent in a starting role until July. But during his nine-game winning streak that stretched into late August, he may have been the club's best starting pitcher.

The other starters were not particularly noteworthy. Bob Thorpe was probably not ready for Open Classification ball at that point in his career. He showed great stuff at times and turned in several well-pitched games, but his high fastball resulted in many home runs at Wrigley Field. Johnny Briggs was troubled all year with elbow problems and finished with a 5–5 record in limited activity. He pitched three fine games in a row during the last two weeks in July, when the Angels were beginning their pennant drive in earnest. Harry Perkowski was a great disappointment after winning three early games; he was sent to Tulsa after winning only one more game.

The best pitcher on the 1956 Angels club was Bob Anderson, who along with Moe Bauer formed the heart of the best bullpen in Angels history. Anderson appeared in 70 games to establish a new league record, erasing the former mark of 69 that had been set by Milo Candini of Oakland in 1952. Relief pitchers were used differently in 1956 than in the present era. Managers would not restrict their so-called "closers" to one inning of activity, but would often put them in when the game was still on the line. They would accumulate more wins and losses than present-day relief specialists, but would also have fewer saves. The save was actually not an official statistic in 1956; it did not become recognized until the early 1960s. Anderson had 25 saves to go along with his record of 12–4 and a fine 2.65 ERA. He had the best fastball on the staff, even better than Drott's. And Bauer appeared in 49 games with a record of 6–1 and four saves. He was more of a finesse pitcher and provided a great contrast to the power pitching of Anderson.

Bob Scheffing was voted the manager of the year in the PCL for 1956. A fine choice, he built the club around Bilko and Mauch, worked in the young players, and developed a club that ranks among the best in PCL history. He extracted the most out of a very questionable pitching staff, and his decision to use Anderson as a full-time reliever despite his youth was brilliant. Scheffing was a no-nonsense type of manager, a contrast to his two easygoing predecessors, Bill Sweeney and Stan Hack. His fine work did not go unnoticed in Chicago. The Cubs stumbled to their worst season up to that time in 1956, and a major housecleaning took place after the season. Stan Hack was fired as Cub manager, and Scheffing was named to replace him. Many of the 1956 Angels would follow him to the 1957 Cubs.

About the only discouraging aspect of the 1956 season was attendance. The club lagged well behind the 1955 figures until the middle of the season, when it became apparent that a championship club was developing. Even then, only the weekend crowds were respectable. The experiment with day baseball had not been successful. With the early spring in Los Angeles was colder than normal, crowds were held down, but even during the summer months there were frequent days when paid attendance was less than 1,000. Los Angeles fans had been accustomed to night baseball every night during the week since 1930 and did not respond to daytime baseball. The paid attendance of 271, 982 was almost 20,000 below the 1955 figure.

In the years that have passed since the 1956 Angels dominated the PCL, there has been a kind of mystique surrounding this team that does not seem to exist for other clubs of the era. Certainly, it was a great offensive team and likely the best team of the post-war period. The pitching staff was subpar, and as a result, the 1956 Angels were probably a level below the greatest teams of PCL history. But it was a very entertaining club with several colorful players, and its lineup from top to bottom could be matched by very few. Another strong pitcher or two, and it would have ranked with the 1934 Angels.

24

Dodger Blue

The final bell began to toll for the Angels franchise during the winter of 1956-57.

By the middle of the 1950s, the aspirations of the PCL to become a third major league had virtually ended. The financial problems of the league, the development of television as an entertainment rival, and the encroachment of the major leagues on PCL territory through major league radio and television broadcasts all served to take away interest from what was now perceived as nothing more than a top-flight minor league. The consensus was that major league baseball would eventually arrive in California, either through the transfer of an existing franchise or by adding additional teams to the American or National leagues. Throughout 1956, there was consensus that expansion was the most likely avenue, but that it would not occur for several more years.

Los Angeles politicians had attempted to make a presentation to Walter O'Malley of the Brooklyn Dodgers in 1955, but nothing tangible appeared to have developed. In 1956, the city made a proposal to owner Calvin Griffith of the Washington Senators. There was some interest on Griffith's part, but late in that season the board of directors of the club determined that the Senators would remain in the nation's capital indefinitely.

The situation in Brooklyn was becoming complicated as the 1956 season drew to a close. As far back as 1952, Walter O'Malley had expressed concern over the viability of Ebbets Field; he suggested that the Brooklyn portion of the World Series that fall be played in Yankee Stadium to take advantage of the greater seating capacity. As the years went on, it became apparent that O'Malley would at some point move the Dodgers from Ebbets Field. The park had opened in 1913 with a seating capacity that was adequate then, but would never exceed 32,000. It was located near Prospect Park in Brooklyn, where it was the epitome of a neighborhood ballpark. But as the years went by, the demographics of Brooklyn changed. The Dodger fans began to move farther out on Long Island to the suburbs, where they were more dependent on the automobile for transportation. But there was limited parking at Ebbets Field, with only enough space for approximately 700 cars. The long-term prospects for expanding the size of Ebbets Field or increasing its parking were very doubtful.

O'Malley wanted to remain in Brooklyn and made several proposals to the reigning park authority of New York City. Essentially, what he wanted to do was to build his own ballpark on land that would be made available to him through condemnation of property in downtown Brooklyn under the right of eminent domain. The location that O'Malley preferred was in an area of approximately 100 city blocks in the vicinity of Flatbush and

Atlantic Avenues, located in the heart of Brooklyn, near a major terminal of the Long Island Railroad. The ballpark would be part of what would have been a major urban renewal project that would solve many of the problems that currently existed with Ebbets Field. There would be ample parking as well as satisfactory public transportation, and the entire area would be transformed. The Dodgers would obtain funds for the new ballpark from the sale of Ebbets Field.

It is beyond the scope of this book to analyze the situation in Brooklyn and the many political issues that surfaced over the years. But it is useful to point out that O'Malley was dealing with perhaps the most powerful man in New York City government at the time, Robert Moses, who headed the city's parks, highways and urban development projects. The vision that Moses had for New York did not include a new ballpark in Brooklyn that would be subsidized in part by the taxpayers. His position created an impossible obstacle for O'Malley to overcome.

O'Malley had already put the city on notice as far back as August 1955, when he announced that the Dodgers would not play in Ebbets Field beyond the 1958 season. In December he made arrangements for the club to play seven 1956 games at Roosevelt Stadium in Jersey City. A park that formerly housed the minor league Jersey City Giants of the International League, Roosevelt Stadium seated only 25,000 fans, but was seen as an option for the Dodgers should they be unsuccessful in negotiating a solution to the Ebbets Field situation. The games at Jersey City were not overwhelmingly successful, but average attendance for the seven games exceeded the normal weekday attendance in Brooklyn, and O'Malley renewed the agreement for the 1957 season.

In October 1956, Ebbets Field was sold to realtor Marvin Kratter, who signed a three-year lease with the Dodgers through the 1959 season. It is unclear why an additional year was added, given O'Malley's stated intention to leave after 1958, but it indicated that perhaps O'Malley remained hopeful that the Flatbush-Atlantic proposal would be approved within the next year. The estimated proceeds from the sale were said to be $3,000,000. Brooklyn had also realized another million through the earlier sale of Delormier Stadium in Montreal. That would provide enough capital for O'Malley to build his new park. The overriding question involved where it would be located.

O'Malley had been subject to much persuasion from Mayor Norris Poulson of Los Angeles and had visited the city on at least two occasions. Yet, there was no real indication that he was interested in Los Angeles as a final destination for the Dodgers until county supervisor Kenneth Hahn visited with the Dodger president during the 1956 World Series. There was some speculation concerning what may have been discussed, but it quickly passed until the middle of February 1957, when an important hurdle to a possible move to Los Angeles was removed. On February 21, the Dodgers announced that they had purchased the Angels franchise and Wrigley Field from the Cubs for an estimated price of $3,250,000, which included the rights to the Dodger farm club at Fort Worth in the Texas League. This transaction had to be approved in writing by the board of directors of the Santa Catalina Island Company, which remained the holder of all of the Angels' Class-A stock. This approval did not take place until October 1957, and it was not generally believed to be necessary at the time the transaction took place. But now the Dodgers would have a park to play in should they decide to move to Los Angeles, once the approval had been given. In addition, they would pay no indemnity to the local teams; the Angels had exclusive rights to the territory and permitted the Hollywood club to operate within the area at their pleasure.

At the time, O'Malley denied that he had any intention of moving to Los Angeles, but events would soon suggest otherwise. The other PCL directors were alarmed over the Dodger purchase, and there were indications that the transaction would not be approved by the league. Much of the resistance came from the northern club owners, who feared the demise of the PCL. Emil Sick of Seattle threatened to cease operations should the deal be approved. But after some assurances from the Dodgers that they intended to maintain the Angels in Los Angeles as their primary farm club, PCL directors approved the sale on March 2.

There had been considerable activity within the Angels organization following the successful 1956 season. In addition to the promotion of Bob Scheffing to Chicago, Angels president John Holland was hired as the new general manager of the Cubs. He would be replaced in Los Angeles, at least on an interim basis, by former PCL president Clarence Rowland, who had maintained his Cubs connection after he left the league office in 1954. Most of the regular players were advanced to the 40-man roster for the 1957 season, the most notable exception being Steve Bilko. He had waived his rights to be exposed to the major league draft in his original Angels contract and could not be purchased by the Cubs until he had gone through that process. The big slugger would play another season in Los Angeles. It was rumored that several clubs had inquired about his availability, but the Angels' asking price was too high.

The sale of the Angels to Brooklyn resulted in a complete overhaul of the Los Angeles roster. Chicago agreed to leave 12 players with the Angels; the group included Bilko, Piper Davis, Elvin Tappe, Chick Pieretti and Bob Coats from the 1956 club, and still others whom the Cubs had sent during the off-season — outfielders Monte Irvin, Don Robertson and Bob Borkowski, infielders Jack Caro and Wally Lammers, and pitcher Jim Hughes. The original choice of the Cubs to manage the Angels, Gene Handley, exchanged places with Fort Worth manager Clay Bryant. He was a long-time Brooklyn organization man who had successfully managed several Dodger farm clubs. Bryant was optimistic that the Dodgers would see that the Angels were well stocked with talent, and he reaffirmed that Brooklyn intended to make Los Angeles the top farm club in the system.

But Los Angeles politicians did not see matters that way, and Mayor Poulson announced that it was his goal to convince the Dodgers to move to Los Angeles. Various engineering studies had been completed within the city, examining several sites, and these were reactivated. The Chavez Ravine area, just north of downtown Los Angeles, was seen as the most favorable location. Shortly after the beginning of spring training, Poulson and Kenneth Hahn flew to the Dodger camp in Vero Beach, Florida, to confer with O'Malley. At the conclusion of the meeting, both parties announced that nothing had been agreed upon, but it seemed clear that the general outline of the arrangement between the city of Los Angeles and O'Malley had been prepared. Nothing official was presented to the Dodgers until September 16; by that time the National League had given permission to both the Brooklyn club and the New York Giants to move, should they wish to do so. The Giants accepted a proposal from the city of San Francisco and announced their intention to move there for the 1958 season on August 19.

The Los Angeles proposition called for the transfer of the Chavez Ravine area to the Dodgers for $4,400,000. The city would also grade the site, and Los Angeles County would spend $2,700,000 for connecting roads and freeways. The city would also buy Wrigley Field from the Dodgers for $2,500,000. The proposal was approved by the Los Angeles city council and the county board of supervisors; the issue would have to appear on the ballot, as well, but was expected to be approved by the voters. The Dodgers could not claim the

Los Angeles territory until October 1, and a last minute effort by New York governor Nelson Rockefeller to keep the Dodgers in Brooklyn went for naught. On October 8, 1957, the Brooklyn club directors voted unanimously to move to Los Angeles. Major league baseball would be played in Los Angeles in 1958.

Meanwhile, the Angels were put together for what would be their last season in Southern California. New players from the Dodger system included second baseman George Anderson and third baseman Jim Baxes. They both had strong Los Angeles connections. Anderson, who would later become famously known as "Sparky," had starred at Dorsey High School and had been a batboy for the Hollywood Stars in 1949. Baxes was an important member of that club but had never quite lived up to his early promise. Others who would play an important role in 1957 were infielder Roy Hartsfield, outfielder Tom Saffell and pitchers Bob Darnell, Dick Hanlon and Bill George.

The season opened with an infield of Bilko, Anderson, Baxes and shortstop Jack Caro, and an outfield of Irvin, Saffell and Borkowski. Of that latter trio, only Saffell was able to contribute anything substantial. After homering in the opening day victory, 4–2 over Vancouver, Irvin suffered a career-ending back injury in the season's fourth game. Irvin's injury was a harbinger of things to come. The Angels were beset by one injury after another, and after a surprisingly fast start through the middle of May, the club stumbled into sixth place during the first week of June and remained there for the rest of the year. They were never a pennant threat after Memorial Day.

Pitching was the major problem for the Angels in 1957. Only Ralph Mauriello won more than nine games, and his 11–5 record was blemished somewhat by a 4.21 ERA. Vito Valentinetti, who came over from St. Paul in May, was probably the club's best pitcher. He posted a 9–5 record in slightly more than two months of play before being sold to Cleveland in early August. Rookie Dick Hanlon showed early promise, winning five of his first six decisions, before he was victimized by arm trouble, and did not win a game after May. Nor did Bob Darnell, expected to be a major contributor, after a fine start. He lost his last eight decisions and was 4–11 when he was sent to Montreal for Connie Grob on August 1. Tom Lasorda, acquired from Denver at the end of May, won his first three starts in impressive style, but finished 7–10, as a frequent victim of enemy home runs. John Jancse turned in several nice games late in the year, but his 9–12 mark reflected several close losses in which he received limited run support. Jim Hughes, Glen Mickens and Bill George provided good bullpen strength for the Angels, but all too frequently, they served in a mop-up role after the starters had failed.

With the constant turnover of the roster and the anticipation of the Dodger arrival in 1958, interest in the Angels was very low in 1957. The only real excitement centered on Steve Bilko's second straight attempt to break the league home run record. He started slowly, beset by many minor injuries, and saw his average drop to .264 in early June. There was no power in the lineup to support him, and he was striking out at a record pace.

But then the big slugger went on a tear. He hit 11 home runs in 13 games during the last two weeks in June and raised his average to .311 by the second week in July. After a torrid week against Vancouver in which he hit five homers in 27 times at bat, he had 32 home runs, only four behind his pace of the previous year. That might have been enough for one season, but once again the streaky slugger went on a hitting tear, blasting 19 home runs during the month of August. He hit his 48th and 49th at Gilmore Field on August 25 in the last Angels-Stars game ever played; he hit his 50th the next day at home against Vancouver and his 51st on August 28. There were 23 games left on the schedule, plenty of time to reach 60. He reached 54 on September 5 at Portland, with 13 games to go, all of them at Wrigley Field. On September 9, he belted number 56 to tie Gene Lillard's club record, with eight games to go. Sadly, that proved to be the last homer Bilko hit in a PCL Angels uniform. Despite being moved to the leadoff position to garner more times at bat, Bilko hit no home runs during the remainder of the season.

The final Angels games were played at Wrigley Field on Sunday, September 15, under bizarre conditions. During the first game of the doubleheader, a telephone caller announced that a bomb had been planted in the clubhouse. Both dugouts were cleared for the second game, which started after a short delay, and the players from both clubs spent the game on benches a short distance away. Los Angeles lost both games to San Diego, 9–4 and 5–1, with 18 Angels going down on strikes. Tom Saffell hit the last Angels home run, while Jim Fridley singled in the last inning of the nightcap for the last Angels hit. Ralph Mauriello and Chuck Page took the losses, with Glen Mickens pitching the final Angels inning. Only 6,712 paid to see the final games, bringing the paid attendance for the year to a disappointing 220,547, the lowest total since the end of the war.

Once the Dodger move was officially announced, the Angels franchise was finished in Los Angeles. The map of the Pacific Coast League would be altered dramatically prior to the 1958 season. At the winter meetings the PCL directors approved the transfer of the Los Angeles franchise to Spokane and the Hollywood club to Salt Lake City. The San Francisco Seals were moved to Phoenix. There were no Angels, Stars or Seals in their new locations. All three took new nicknames, leaving the old names as pleasant memories for their fans. The PCL dropped from Open Classification to Triple A, where it has since remained.

It was assumed that the Dodgers would play their games at Wrigley Field in 1958, but Walter O'Malley had other ideas. The park was too small to accommodate all those who would want to attend Dodger games in their first season in Southern California, and the parking situation bore too strong a resemblance to the one O'Malley left behind at Ebbets Field. The Dodgers soon made arrangements to play their games at the Los Angeles Coliseum until such time as their new park would be completed in Chavez Ravine. When the 1958 season began amidst the teeming throngs that filled the huge Coliseum, cozy Wrigley Field became a park of ghosts, with only memories of the great Angels teams of the past.

Epilogue

Wrigley Field is gone, of course. When the Dodgers chose to play their games at the Coliseum in 1958, pending construction of the yet unnamed Dodger Stadium, the ballpark that was once the pride of Los Angeles was doomed. The city found itself with an unwanted property after the Chavez Ravine transaction had been approved by the voters. There were limited uses for the facility. Some high school baseball games were played there in 1958 and 1959, and late that year a television production called *Home Run Derby* was filmed there. It featured a series of major league sluggers competing for prize money and consisted of 26 episodes of home run hitting exhibitions.

Then in 1961 came the final season for the park. The American League elected to expand to ten teams for the season and granted one of its new franchises to Los Angeles. That new team—what else could it be called but the Angels?—was allowed to play in Los Angeles only by virtue of Walter O'Malley's willingness to share the territory. But he was not willing to share ballparks immediately. The new Angels were directed to play in Wrigley Field, and as part of the agreement, they would be required to play in the new Dodger Stadium when it opened in 1962, as a tenant of the Dodgers.

Thus, Wrigley Field finally became a major league park, if only for one season. A disappointing total attendance of 603,510 paid to watch the debut of American League baseball on the Pacific Coast; that was barely a third of what the Dodgers drew at the Coliseum that year. What they saw mostly were home runs. Major league hitters made the most of their only look at the hitter-friendly dimensions of Wrigley Field, hitting 248 homers, by far the most in the major leagues that year, and a record that stood for 35 years. Five Angels hit 20 or more home runs in 1961, and this group included long-time favorite Steve Bilko, who was nearing the end of his career. After the 1957 season, Bilko had been sold to Cincinnati and then came back to Los Angeles in a mid-season trade to the Dodgers. He played poorly in a part-time role and was released to Spokane in 1959. Back in the PCL where he had enjoyed his greatest years, Bilko hit .305 and was then purchased by Detroit at the end of the season. The Tigers made him available in the expansion draft, and the Angels grabbed him. Bilko hit .279 with 20 home runs while sharing first base duties with several other players. Fittingly, in a pinch-hitting role on the last day of the season, Big Steve hit the last home run ever at the fine old ballpark.

After the Angels moved to Dodger Stadium in 1962, Wrigley Field was allowed to age in a graceful manner until it was razed in March, 1969. This author last saw the park in 1965. The famous Wrigley Tower looked as majestic as ever. The big scoreboard had a few gaps in it, but it looked ready for the next day's game, with "Visitors" and "Angels" perfectly visible from the street below.

A number of baseball movies were filmed in Wrigley Field over the life of the park, and the last major film produced there was *Damn Yankees* in the late 1950s. That film was shot in color, and the red brick walls are very visible.

Today, the Gilbert W. Lindsay Community Center stands on the site of Wrigley Field, along with several soccer fields. There is also a Little League facility that was built in 1999, appropriately reflecting the Wrigley Field name. It is hoped that with the rebirth of baseball on that spot, the memory of the Angels of the past will once more come to life.

The number of former Angels who are still living is dwindling by the day, but one of them remained active in the game in 2010. Wayne Terwilliger, the second baseman on the 1949 club, had a long playing and coaching career, and for the past several years has been an important part of the Fort Worth Cats of the independent American Association. He was still in uniform as a coach for the club in 2010.

The Angels franchise remained in Spokane as a Dodgers farm club, then moved to Albuquerque in 1972, where it remained through 2000. It was then moved to Oregon and was reborn as another version of the Portland Beavers. The club was a San Diego Padres affiliate through the 2010 season. In 2011 it moved to Tucson, where it became the Tucson Padres.

The PCL has gone through many configurations since 1957 and has added more teams. Today it is a 16-team league that stretches from Nashville, Tennessee, to Sacramento, the only remaining member city of the original Coast League.

Appendix A: All-Time Los Angeles Angels Roster

This listing includes all Angels players who appeared in at least one regular season game, and the first, and in some cases the only, year in which he played.

During the early years of the league, the first names of players were not always included in the guides for those who played in fewer than 10 games, and consequently, there are several players for whom only a last name is available. The list is as complete as my research could make it, but there may be some omissions and errors, for which I apologize.

Abbott, Pete 1911
Abernathy, Chuck 1949
Aberson, Cliff 1948
Abstein, Bill 1914
Accardo, Tom 1945
Adams, Herb 1954
Adams, Jim 1906
Adams, Red 1942
Adkins, Dewey 1948
Agnew, Jim 1911
Akin, Roy 1911
Aldridge, Vic 1919
Alfano, Don 1949
Anderson, Andy 1952
Anderson, Bob 1956
Anderson, George 1957
Andre, John 1956
Andrews, Red 1920
Anheier, Clyde 1921
Anthony, Lee 1946
Arbogast, Carl 1913
Archie, George 1946
Atchley, Jim 1950
Atwell, Dick 1937
Atz, John 1905
Augustus, Ray 1918
Auman, Howard 1948
Baczewski, Fred 1951

Baecht, Ed 1929
Baker, Gene 1950
Baker, Loris 1931
Baker, Oren 1943
Baldwin, Earl 1921
Ballou, Win 1930
Balser, Ernie 1945
Barfoot, Clyde 1928
Barrett, Red 1950
Bartholemy, Al 1920
Barton, Carroll 1914
Barton, Larry 1947
Barton, Vince 1931
Bassler, Johnny 1916
Bates, Ray 1919
Battey, Earl 1957
Bauer, Ray 1955
Baum, Spider 1903
Baumholtz, Frank 1950
Baxes, Jim 1957
Beall, Johnny 1909
Beck, Clyde 1922
Beck, John 1932
Beer, Sam 1919
Bell, Fern 1942
Berger, Joel 1912
Berger, Walter 1927
Bergmann, Fred 1906

Bernard, Curt 1904
Berry, Joe 1936
Besse, Herm 1950
Betts, Harry 1905
Bigbee, Carson 1928
Bigbee, Lyle 1924
Bilko, Steve 1955
Billings, John 1924
Birrer, Werner 1957
Blackburn, Byron 1932
Blair, Clarence 1932
Bliss, Jack 1906
Block, Cy 1946
Boehler, George 1929
Boles, Walter 1912
Bolger, Jim 1956
Bonetti, Julio 1939
Borkowski, Bob 1957
Bottarini, John 1936
Bowman, Frank 1904
Brandt, Dutch 1930
Brant, Grover 1915
Brashear, Kitty 1914
Brashear, Roy 1914
Brazill, Frank 1926
Brenner, Bill 1945
Brent 1925
Brewster, Charlie 1945

Appendix A: All-Time Los Angeles Angels Roster

Briggs, John 1956
Brinkopf, Leon 1950
Briseno, Midget 1903
Briswalter, Andy 1908
Broadbent, Al 1905
Brock, Ken 1934
Brooks, Clarence 1911
Brosnan, Jim 1955
Brown, Curly 1917
Brown, Mace 1941
Brown, Tommy 1954
Browne, Harvey 1949
Browne, Pidge 1956
Buchanan, George 1933
Buckley, Walter 1906
Buemiller, Al 1916
Burbrink, Nels 1949
Burgess, Smokey 1946
Burke, Speck 1920
Burkett, Howard 1928
Burnett, Mickey 1948
Burns, Bill 1906
Burns, George 1931
Burns, Leo 1929
Bush, Guy 1938
Butler, John 1915
Buxton, Ralph 1935
Byler, Butch 1923
Byrnes, Jim 1913
Byrnes, Milt 1950
Caffey, Ira 1922
Caldera, Leon 1919
Caldwell 1918
Calvo, Jack 1914
Campbell, Archie 1937
Campbell, Gilly 1931
Campbell, Whitey 1934
Candini, Milo 1952
Carlisle, Walter 1906
Carlsen, Don 1947
Carlyle, Cleo 1935
Carnes, Fred 1907
Carnett, Ed 1936
Caro, Jack 1957
Carpenter, Paul 1938
Carroll, Dixie 1921
Carroll, Wally 1939
Carson, Clarence 1905
Casey, Hugh 1935
Casey, Tom 1921
Cash, Ray 1950
Caster, George 1932
Castleton, Roy 1910
Catton, Bob 1957
Chambers, Cliff 1942

Chance, Frank 1904
Chandler, Ed 1951
Chase, Hal 1904
Chech, Charlie 1912
Chesley, Harry 1928
Chess 1909
Chition 1910
Chmiel, Herb 1948
Chozen, Myer 1933
Christopher, Loyd 1945
Church, Bubba 1954
Church, Ed 1931
Cihocki, Eddie 1938
Clarkson, Bus 1955
Coats, Bob 1955
Coffman, Slick 1941
Cohen, Hy 1954
Coleman, George 1911
Coleman, Ralph 1923
Collins, Bob 1937
Collins, Jim "Rip" 1939
Colmar, John 1937
Colombo, Richie 1945
Comellas, Jorge 1944
Conger, Dick 1944
Connors, Chuck 1951
Conrad, Otto 1905
Cooper, Claude 1918
Corbett, Joe 1903
Core, John 1912
Couchman, Bob 1911
Cox, Dick 1927
Crabb, Roy 1913
Cracchiolo, Frank 1945
Crandall, "Doc" 1916
Crandall, Al 1924
Crandall, Karl 1919
Crandall, Rufus 1906
Crane, Bob 1952
Cravath, Gavvy 1903
Crawford, Ivan 1933
Crawford, Sam 1919
Criger, Elmer 1910
Cronin, Bill 1932
Cruise, Walton 1924
Cuellar, Charlie 1945
Cunningham, Bruce 1927
Cunningham, Dave 1953
Curtis, Dan 1932
Cutting, Ed 1922
Daley, Pete 1909
Dallessandro, Dom 1948
Daly, Tom 1922
Damato, Joe 1949
Daniels, Bill 1915

Danning, Ike 1933
Dant, Bob 1951
Darnell, Bob 1957
Davelia 1934
Davenport, Charles 1934
Davis, Bill 1911
Davis, Bob 1916
Davis, Peaches 1942
Davis, Piper 1955
Davis, Tod 1951
Day, Clyde 1926
De Cuir, Eddie 1931
Deakins 1910
Deal, Charlie 1922
Deal 1911
Delaney, Art 1930
Delhi, Flame 1909
Delmas, Bert 1906
Demaree, Frank 1934
DeViveiros, Bernie 1932
Dillon, Cap 1903
DiPrima, Frank 1953
Dittmar, Carl 1928
Dobernic, Jess 1941
Doerr, Hal 1935
Dolan, Bob 1957
Donaldson, Gordon 1940
Donovan, Elmer 1933
Donovan, Maury 1946
Dotson, Lew 1927
Douglas, Hal 1945
Douglas, Ken 1921
Downs, Jerry 1918
Drake, Solly 1955
Drinkwater, Vianello 1903
Driscoll, Babe 1911
Driscoll, Paddy 1919
Drott, Dick 1956
Dubiel, Walt 1952
Dulin, Cliff 1911
Dumovich, Nick 1920
Dunlap, Grant 1952
Durst, Cedric 1924
Dwyer, Ray 1926
Dye, Otto 1906
Eager, Bob 1903
Easterly, Ted 1907
Easterwood, Roy 1945
Edwards, Bruce 1954
Ehmke, Howard 1914
Elko, Pete 1944
Ellis, Rube 1905
Elston, Don 1955
Emmerich, Bill 1949
Emory 1934

Encoe, Chief 1908
English, Charlie 1938
Ennis, Russ 1925
Epperly, Al 1939
Errickson, Dick 1946
Evans, Al 1953
Evans, Russ 1937
Fabrique, Bunny 1919
Fahey, Howard 1913
Fallon, Jack 1940
Fanning, Jim 1955
Farrell, "Doc" 1931
Fear, Vern 1948
Felderman, Marv 1947
Ferguson, Les 1925
Fernandes, Ed 1943
Ferree, Elmer 1935
Fisher, Bob 1916
Fittery, Paul 1918
Fitzhenry 1911
Fitzke, Bob 1932
Flater, Jack 1912
Flaugher, Will 1941
Fleming, Bill 1946
Fletcher, Elbie 1950
Flood, Tim 1904
Flores, Jess 1939
Flowers, Ben 1957
Flowers, Wes 1937
Fodge, Gene 1956
Fondy, Dee 1951
Foulke, Leon 1944
Fournier, Jack 1917
Franklin, Murray 1953
Frazier, Keith 1935
Freese, George 1956
Fridley, Jim 1957
Friene, Charley 1911
Fritsch, Ted 1944
Gabler, Glen 1927
Gables, Ken 1949
Galatzer, Milt 1938
Galloway, Jim 1916
Gamble, Bill 1907
Gandil, Chick 1906
Gantenbein, Joe 1946
Gardner, Earle 1917
Gardner, Hal 1927
Garland, Lou 1934
Garner, Tom 1915
Garriott, Cecil 1943
Garrity, Rabbit 1916
Gazella, Mike 1933
Gedeon, Joe 1914
Gehrman, Paul 1942

George, Bill 1957
George, Ron 1952
Gibson, Glyn 1935
Gill, Roy 1910
Gill, Warren 1913
Gillespie, Paul 1947
Glazner, Whitey 1925
Glor, Henry 1945
Glossop, Albie 1946
Gober, E.E. 1912
Gochnaur, John 1906
Goebel, Walter 1934
Goldsberry, Gordon ... 1949
Goldstein, Izzy 1931
Golvin, Walter 1923
Goodwin, Bunny 1905
Goodwin, Pep 1913
Goryl, John 1956
Gray, Dolly 1903
Gray, Stan 1944
Green, Cecil 1931
Green, Len "Doc" ... 1945
Gregory, Howard 1913
Gregory, Nick 1943
Grigg, Don 1944
Griggs, Art 1920
Grimes, Ray 1924
Grindle, Pinkie 1909
Grob, Connie 1957
Groebling, Frank 1917
Gudat, Marv 1933
Gumpert, Randy ... 1953
Gunther, Fred 1924
Gustine, Frank 1949
Haas, Eddie 1956
Haas, Ernie 1922
Hackharth 1907
Hafey, Tom 1936
Hall, Charley 1916
Hall, Herb 1922
Hall, Rusty 1903
Halla, John 1911
Hallett, Jack 1939
Hallman, Eddie ... 1910
Hamilton, Earl ... 1926
Hamner, Ralph ... 1950
Hamric, Bert 1957
Handley, Lee 1949
Haney, Fred 1919
Hanlon, Dick 1957
Hanna, Roy 1923
Hannah, Joe 1956
Hannah, Truck ... 1926
Hanson, Jack 1940
Hardin, Bud 1952

Hargrave, Bob 1937
Harkins, Pat 1914
Harper, George 1930
Harper, Harry 1914
Harris, Herb 1935
Hartsfield, Roy 1957
Hatch, Sid 1909
Hatten, Joe 1952
Hausmann, Clem 1946
Haynes 1925
Head, Claire 1903
Heitmuller, Heinie 1911
Hemingway, Ed 1926
Henshaw, Roy 1934
Hernandez, Chico 1940
Herrmann, Leroy 1931
Hess, Bert 1907
Heusser, Ed 1942
Hicks, Ken 1945
Hicks, Mel 1945
Hillman, Dave 1955
Hinchman, Lorenzo ... 1954
Hitt, Roy 1904
Hoag, Oliver 1906
Hodges, Red 1919
Hoffman, Dutch 1912
Hoffmeister, Paul 1955
Hogan, Happy 1907
Hogg, Brad 1916
Holling, Carl 1929
Hollingsworth, H. ... 1903
Hollis, Jack 1952
Holm, Billy 1940
Holmes, Les 1926
Holt, Goldy 1937
Hood, Wally 1923
Hooks, Gene 1954
Hopkins, John ... 1906
Horan, Joe 1925
Horne, Berlyn ... 1930
Horton, Claude ... 1947
Hosp, Franz 1907
Howard, Ivan ... 1908
Howard, Robert ... 1909
Howell, Murray ... 1937
Hoy, Dummy 1903
Hricinak, John ... 1956
Hughes, Jim 1957
Hughes, Roy 1942
Hughes, Thomas J. 1914
Hughes, Thomas L. 1919
Hurlburt, Ed 1903
Hurst, Don 1936
Ihde, Alan 1949
Intlekofer, John ... 1933

Irvin, Monte 1957	Kumulae, Clarence 1933	Marasco, Vic 1954
Isekite, Floyd 1940	Kuncl, Joe 1955	Marino, Frank 1950
Jackson, Charley 1913	Kush, Emil 1939	Marks, Fred 1912
Jackson, Ransom 1949	Lade, Doyle 1948	Marsden, John 1936
Jacobs, Elmer 1925	Lafayette, George 1928	Marshall, Max 1947
Jacobs, Jack 1928	Lahti, Clyde 1933	Marshall, Ralph 1945
Jacobs, Willie 1903	Laird, Bill 1912	Martin, Stu 1946
Jahn, Art 1926	Lammers, Paul 1945	Martinke, Felix 1911
Jakucki, Sig 1938	Lammers, Wally 1957	Mason, Del 1904
James 1924	Land, Harry 1943	Mattick, Bob 1934
Jancse, John 1957	Lanfranconi, Walt 1948	Mattos, Ernie 1927
Jasper, Hi 1917	Lapan, Pete 1917	Mauch, Gene 1954
Jelincich, Frank 1945	Larner, Bud 1908	Mauriello, Ralph 1945
Jenkins, Bob 1957	Larsen, Spike 1915	Mauro, Carmen 1949
Jenkins, Joe 1924	Lary, Al 1955	Mayo, Eddie 1938
Jensen, Woody 1927	Lasorda, Tom 1957	Mazar, Pete 1949
Johnson, Clayton 1950	Latshaw, Bob 1943	McAuley, Jim 1920
Johnson, Don 1948	Lauters, Don 1956	McCabe, Bill 1921
Johnson, Ernie 1913	Lavigne, Ed 1952	McCafferty, Chas. 1912
Johnson, Everett 1950	Lawler, Jack 1903	McCall, Dutch 1947
Joiner, Roy 1935	Layton, Les 1950	McClelland, Lou 1927
Jones, Bob 1928	Leathers, Hal 1918	McClelland, Walter 1906
Jones, Oscar 1903	LeBrand, Deke 1905	McCoy, Paul 1927
Jones, Percy 1923	LeGros, Tom 1952	McDade, Eddie 1954
Jones, Sheldon 1954	Leguin 1906	McDaniels, Booker 1949
Joyce, Bob 1936	Lelivelt, Jack 1931	McDonald, Tex 1920
Judd, Oscar 1934	Leonhardt, Elmo 1907	McDonnell, Speed 1915
Kahler, George 1916	Leverenz, Walter 1911	McDougal, Art 1934
Kahn, Jack 1927	Lieber, Dutch 1936	McGinnity, Bugs 1917
Kane, John 1916	Lightfoot, Charlie 1933	McKenry, Pete 1913
Keane, Jack 1931	Lillard, Gene 1932	McLarry, Polly 1916
Keating, Ray 1920	Lindimore, Howard 1921	McLish, Cal 1949
Kelly, Bob 1949	Lloyd, Truck 1939	McMinn, Glenn 1957
Kemper, Dick 1944	Loane, Bob 1934	McMullen, Hugh 1933
Kennedy, John 1910	Lober, Ty 1911	McMullin, Fred 1915
Kenworthy, Duke 1917	Love, Slim 1914	McQuaid, Herb 1922
Kerrigan, George 1927	Lowe, Lloyd 1950	McWilliams, Bill 1937
Kies, Joe 1933	Lown, Turk 1954	Meek, Dad 1914
Killefer, Wade 1918	Lowrey, Peanuts 1940	Meek, Hal 1954
Kimball, Newt 1935	Lucadello, John 1950	Mene, Joe 1936
Kimberlin, Harry 1939	Lukon, Eddie 1948	Menking, Paul 1951
Kitsos, Chris 1954	Lynn, Red 1942	Meola, Emile 1934
Klein, Eddie 1910	Lyons, George 1921	Merkle, Warren 1945
Klein, Lou 1950	Maddern, Clarence 1941	Merullo, Len 1941
Kleine, Hal 1946	Maggert, Harl 1913	Mesner, Steve 1934
Knapp 1921	Malis, Cy 1936	Metzger, George 1911
Koerner, Phil 1915	Mallory, Pete 1941	Meusel, Irish 1913
Koestner, Bob 1908	Mallory, Rabbit 1940	Mickens, Glenn 1957
Korndor, Hans 1933	Malone, Eddie 1947	Middledorf, Bert 1932
Kowalski, Ed 1949	Maltzberger, Gordon 1932	Middleton, Charlie 1905
Kraus, Jack 1950	Mangerina, Henry 1905	Miller, Abe 1932
Kreevich, Mike 1932	Mangini, Art 1939	Miller, Guy 1944
Kreitner, Al 1945	Mann 1926	Miller, O. 1909
Krug, Marty 1923	Manning, Ed 1911	Miller, Oscar 1933
Kruger, Art 1913	Manville, Dick 1950	Miller, Russ 1929

Milstead, George 1925
Mitchell, John 1926
Mohler, Orv 1933
Moisan, Bill 1948
Moncrief, Charlie 1930
Monette, Jacques 1954
Montgomery, Alvin 1929
Moore, Charlie 1906
Moore, Dee 1934
Mooty, Jake 1943
Moran, Butch 1949
Morgan, Vern 1955
Morley, Jim 1905
Mosolf, Jim 1928
Moss, Malcolm 1931
Moss, Ray 1927
Muncrief, Bob 1950
Murphy, Herb 1916
Murray, Bob 1929
Musser, Paul 1912
Myer, Myron 1937
Myers, Elmer 1924
Nagle, Walter 1905
Nast, Gene 1910
Nasternak, Hank 1954
Negray, Ron 1957
Neill, Tom 1951
Nelson, Emmett 1933
Nelson, Lynn 1931
Newlin, Otto 1909
Newsom, Buck 1933
Newton, Doc.......... 1903
Niehoff, Bert 1919
Niles, John 1927
Norbert, Ted 1944
Norgren, Swede 1927
Novakovich, John 1941
Novikoff, Lou 1939
Novotney, Ralph 1947
O'Neal, Oran 1924
Oakes, Rebel 1908
Oglesby, Jim 1932
Ogorek, George 1944
Ograin, Cliff 1933
Olsen, Barney 1942
Olson, Bill 1957
Olson, Herb 1957
Orndorff, Jess 1908
Osborn, Bob 1927
Osborn, Don 1944
Ostrowski, Joe 1953
Ostrowski, John 1943
Otero, Reggie 1944
Overman, Earl 1937
Padget, Spec 1953

Pafko, Andy 1943
Page, Bill 1912
Page, Chuck 1957
Palica, Ambrose 1947
Palmer, George 1911
Parker, Art 1929
Passarella, Al 1930
Paton, Leroy 1941
Pawelek, Ted 1947
Payne, George 1924
Paynich, Rudy 1957
Peckham, Frank 1925
Peden, Les 1951
Pepe, Joe 1918
Perkowski, Harry 1956
Perritt, Pol 1912
Pertica, Bill 1918
Peters, Will 1927
Peterson, Russ 1940
Petty, Jess 1931
Phillips, Elmer 1925
Phillips, Pat 1908
Phipps, Jodie 1943
Piercy, Bill 1927
Pieretti, Chick 1956
Piktuzis, George 1955
Pillette, Ted 1934
Pittenger, Clarke 1925
Pitts 1909
Plitt, Norman 1928
Ponder, Elmer 1922
Pontarelli, Mike 1943
Powell, Bob 1940
Powell, Larry 1947
Pramesa, John 1954
Prim, Ray 1936
Prince, Bill 1934
Prout, Len 1932
Pyecha, John 1954
Quinn, Wimpy 1941
Raffensberger, Ken 1942
Rager, John 1944
Raimondi, Bill 1951
Ramsdell, Willie 1952
Ramsey, Buck 1924
Randolph, Red 1906
Rawlings, John 1930
Raymond, Tealy 1903
Read, Bert 1926
Reams, Babe 1912
Reeder, Bill 1952
Reese, Jimmie 1920
Rego, Tony 1920
Reinhart, Art 1921
Reppy, Gaylord 1919

Reyes 1920
Reynolds, Carl 1940
Rhabe, Nick 1945
Rhawn, Bob 1949
Rice, Hal 1955
Richards, Fred 1953
Richardson, Kenny 1934
Rieger, Elmer 1906
Roberts, Red 1929
Robertson, Don 1954
Robertson, Larry 1923
Rogers, Brown 1913
Root, Charlie 1924
Ross, Art 1903
Rossbach, Henry 1912
Rossomondo, Joe 1945
Roth, Bill 1910
Rothrock, Jack 1938
Rowe, Ralph 1949
Ruby, Harry 1940
Ruether, Dutch 1913
Russell, Glen 1936
Ryan, Jack 1913
Saffell, Tom 1957
Salvatierra, Manny 1944
Salveson, Jack 1936
Samhammer, Ralph 1940
Sandberg, Gus 1925
Sandel, Warren 1949
Sanders, Herb 1925
Sanford, George 1938
Sanford, Jack 1948
Sarni, Bill 1943
Sauer, Ed 1944
Sawyer, Carl 1913
Schaefer, George 1911
Scheel, Karl 1945
Schenz, Hank 1946
Scherf, Charlie 1927
Schick, Maurice........ 1919
Schlafly, Larry 1905
Schmidt, Frank 1947
Schmidt, Fred 1948
Schmidt, Harry 1906
Schoor, Ed 1916
Schulmerich, Wes 1927
Schulte, John 1931
Schultz, Dick 1929
Schultz, Joe 1916
Schultz, Toots 1919
Schuster, Bill 1941
Scoggins, Jim 1916
Seaton, Tom 1917
Seerey, Pat 1949
Shealy, Al 1931

Sheely, Earl 1932	Stroud, Ralph 1926	Vusich, John 1930
Sherry, Larry 1957	Struss, Clarence 1936	Wade, Ben 1949
Shoap, Art 1933	Sturgeon, Bob 1949	Wade, Gale 1955
Sigafoos, Frank 1930	Sueme, Hal 1938	Waitkus, Eddie 1942
Simpson, Tom 1954	Sullivan, Jack 1912	Wakeham, Fred 1938
Skaff, Mike 1944	Sullivan, John 1922	Walby 1927
Skiff, Bill 1930	Summa, Homer 1931	Wallace, Bob 1920
Slagle, Walt 1912	Swanson, Don 1956	Walsh, Augie 1929
Slotter, Joe 1945	Sweeney, Bill 1942	Walters, John 1923
Smalley, Roy 1943	Sweetland, Les 1932	Ward, Dick 1932
Smith, Al 1927	Tabor, Jim 1948	Ware, Andy 1915
Smith, Bart 1928	Taitt, Doug 1925	Waring, Ted 1910
Smith, Dick 1953	Talamante, Richard 1935	Warren, Dallas 1928
Smith, Elmer 1928	Talbot, Bob 1951	Warren, Henry 1933
Smith, Jud 1903	Tappe. Elvin 1952	Warstler, Rabbit 1941
Smith, K 1909	Tatum, Tom 1941	Washington, Kenny 1950
Smith, Red 1923	Teck, Eddie 1911	Waterbury, Frank 1904
Smith, Walter 1908	Teed, Dick 1957	Watkins, Don 1949
Snodgrass, Fred 1905	Tepler, Boyd 1944	Weathersby, Tex 1926
Sorey, Ray 1923	Terry, Yank 1946	Webb, Earl 1929
Soria, Lefty 1921	Terry, Zeb 1914	Weiland, Bob 1940
Sousa, Henry 1928	Terwilliger, Wayne 1949	Weinert, Phil 1924
South, Lynn 1934	Thomas, Claude 1920	Weintraub, Phil 1941
Spasoff, Pete 1956	Thomas, Fay 1933	Weis, Art 1926
Speake, Bob 1956	Thompson, Howard 1909	West, Hi 1915
Spence, Stan 1950	Thompson, Lefty 1916	West, Max 1951
Spencer, Ed 1924	Thornton 1923	Wetzel, Buzz 1931
Spicer, Bob 1951	Thorpe, Bob 1956	Whaley, Bill C. 1924
Spies, Heinie 1903	Thorsen, Bull 1908	Whaley, Bill F. 1941
Spindel, Hal 1946	Tierney, Martin 1928	Whaling, Bob 1906
Spores 1927	Tindall, Dick 1955	Wheat, Mack 1922
Stabelfeld, Elvin 1950	Tobey, Dan 1926	Wheeler, George 1903
Stadille, Art 1911	Todd, Al 1942	Whitman, Frank 1950
Stainback, Tuck 1932	Tolson, Charlie 1928	Williams, Dewey 1946
Staley, Gale 1926	Toman, Jim 1903	Williams, John 1915
Stamper, John 1941	Toren, Roy 1905	Willingham, Hugh 1944
Stanage, Oscar 1921	Totaro, Frank 1941	Wilson, Dick 1949
Standridge, Pete 1916	Tozer, Bill 1905	Wilson, Harry 1933
Stanka, Joe 1953	Trabous, Manuel 1955	Wilson, Jake 1911
Starr, Fay 1941	Treadway, Leon 1946	Winceniak, Eddie 1955
Statz, Jigger 1920	Treager, Del 1907	Windish, Bob 1940
Stefani, Lou 1939	Tremel, Bill 1955	Winsell, George 1932
Stein, Irv 1944	Twombly, Clarence 1922	Winslow, Bob 1940
Steiner, Jim 1935	Tyack, Jim 1945	Wise, Casey 1955
Steitz, Chris 1906	Upright, Dixie 1953	Wolfe 1909
Stephens, Bryan 1949	Usher, Bob 1952	Wolter, Harry 1914
Stephenson, Joe 1946	Valencia, Ralph 1918	Woodend, George 1945
Stephenson, Walt 1936	Valentinetti, Vito 1957	Wotell, Mike 1913
Sterger, Ted 1951	Van Dyke, Gordon 1949	Wright, Bill 1946
Stewart, Gabby 1942	Van Fleet, Dwight 1938	Wright, Gene 1905
Stine, Lee 1939	Vann 1932	Wright, Wayne 1925
Stitzel, Hal 1931	Vaughn, Bob 1917	Wyse, Hank 1949
Stoddard, Dwight 1955	Veltman, Art 1935	Yarrison, Rube 1926
Storey, Harvey 1941	Vernon, Harry 1912	Yates, Bob 1911
Stringer, Lou 1939	Viers, Ray 1945	Yerkes, Carroll 1930

York, Tony 1944
Zabel, Zip 1916
Zaby, Charlie 1933
Zanic, John 1924
Zeider, Rollie 1920
Zick, Bob 1952
Zoeterman, George 1949
Zuber, Bob 1950

Angels by the Numbers

Uniform numbers were not worn in the PCL until the early 1930s, but by the end of the season of 1933, all clubs wore them. The Angels adopted the practice during the early part of that year. The following is a list of numbers and some of the players who wore them. Frequently, a player would change his number from year to year, and on occasion, several times during the same season. Because of this practice, the number shown may not be the same number that one remembers.

1   Jack Lelivelt, Truck Hannah, Bob Rhawn, Wally Berger.
2   Bill Sweeney, Bill Schuster, Dave Hillman, Bob Talbot, Bob Sturgeon
3   Jim Oglesby, George Anderson, Tuck Stainback, Wimpy Quinn, Eddie Waitkus
4   Cecil Garriott, Roy Hughes, Gene Mauch, Jimmie Reese
5   Carl Dittmar, Gale Wade, Bud Hardin, Carmen Mauro, Bill Schuster, Len Merullo
6   Gene Lillard, Eddie Mayo, Casey Wise, Charlie English, Larry Barton, Butch Moran, Leon Treadway
7   Marv Gudat, Rube Novotney, Barney Olsen, Andy Pafko, Bob Coats, Bert Hamric, Don Elston
8   Jigger Statz
9   Johnny Moore, Reggie Otero, Cleo Carlyle
10 Gilly Campbell, Glen Russell, Eddie Malone, Tom Saffell, Eddie Winceniak, Gordon Goldsberry
11 Mike Meola, Peanuts Lowrey, Fern Bell, Bill Sarni, Jack Warner
12 Fay Thomas, Al Todd, Ed Sauer, Elvin Tappe, Bob Kelly
13 (Never worn)
14 Bob Collins, Cal McLish, Ray Bauer, Bill Holm, Red Lynn
15 Piper Davis, John Ostrowski, Gene Fodge, Rabbit Mallory
16 Lee Stine, Peaches Davis, Bus Clarkson, Jim Bolger, Ken Raffensberger
17 Ray Prim, Bubba Church, Don Osborn, Joe Hannah, Nels Burbrink
18 Joe Berry, Cliff Aberson, Clarence Maddern, George Freese, Jim Fanning, Red Lynn
19 Julio Bonetti, Joe Hatten, Jess Dobernic, Chick Pieretti, Clarence Maddern, Pete Mallory
20 Bob Mattick, Phil Weintraub, John Briggs, Cecil Garriott
21 Bob Usher, Whitey Campbell, Jodie Phipps
22 Albie Glossop, Bob Speake, Ralph Mauriello, Eddie Fernandes, Harvey Storey
23 John Pramesa, George Piktuzis
24 Dick Drott, Paul Gehrman, Dutch McCall
25 Red Adams, Glen Stewart, Steve Mesner, Lee Anthony, Bob Coats
26 Loyd Christopher, Tom Lasorda, Don Carlsen, John Ostrowski
27 Bob Anderson, Alan Ihde
28 John Ostrowski, Harry Perkowski
29 Bob Thorpe
30 Steve Bilko, Booker McDaniels, Jess Flores
31 Lou Stringer
33 Clay Bryant
34 Paul Gillespie
36 Ray Prim
41 Cliff Chambers
42 Bill Kelly, Steve Bilko
45 Hy Cohen
46 Bob Scheffing
47 Bob Zick
48 George Piktuzis
49 Jim Brosnan

Opening Day Lineups

1919
Wade Killefer 2B
Claude Cooper CF
Bill Kenworthy 3B
Jack Fournier 1B
Sam Crawford RF
Rube Ellis LF
Paddy Driscoll SS
Walter Boles C
Curly Brown P

1920
Wade Killefer CF
Fred Haney SS
Tex Mcdonald LF
Art Griggs 1B
Sam Crawford RF
Johnny Bassler C
Karl Crandall 2B
Bert Niehoff 3B
Claude Thomas P

1921
Wade Killefer CF
Jimmy Mcauley SS
Dixie Carroll LF
Art Griggs 1B
Sam Crawford RF
Howard Lindimore 2B
Bert Niehoff 3B
Oscar Stanage C
Doc Crandall P

1922
Dixie Carroll CF
Jimmy Mcauley SS
Clarence Twombly RF
Art Griggs 1B
Bill Mccabe 2B
Howard Lindimore 2B
Wade Killefer LF
Tom Daly C
Doc Crandall P

1923
Clarence Twombly RF
Dixie Carroll CF
Charlie Deal 3B
Art Griggs 1B
Wally Hood LF
Marty Krug 2B
Jimmy Mcauley SS
Red Baldwin C
George Lyons P

1924
Babe Twombly RF
Jimmy Mcauley SS
Bill Whaley CF
Wally Hood LF
Ray Jacobs 3B
Walter Golvin 1B
Marty Krug 2B
Butch Byler C
Doc Crandall P

1925
Babe Twombly CF
Clarke Pittenger SS
Bill Whaley 3B
Shags Horan RF
Ray Grimes 1B
Wally Hood LF
Gus Sandberg C
Clyde Beck 2B
Charley Root P

1926
Jigger Statz CF
Johnny Mitchell SS
Ray Jacobs 1B
Frank Brazill 3B
Art Weis RF
Wally Hood LF
Gale Staley 2B
Truck Hannah C
Elmer Jacobs P

1927
Ray Jacobs 2B
Dick Cox CF
Frank Brazill 3B
Art Jahn LF
Art Weis RF
Wally Hood 1B
Johnny Mitchell SS
Truck Hannah C
Wayne Wright P

1928
Wes Schulmerich CF
Carl Dittmar SS
Wally Hood RF
Chuck Tolson 1B
Walt Berger LF
Bobby Jones 3B
Howard Burkett 2B
Truck Hannah C
Clyde Barfoot P

1929
Wes Schulmerich CF
Bobby Jones 3B
Earl Webb RF
Charlie Tolson 1B
Walt Berger LF
Ray Jacobs 2B
Johnny Butler SS
Dallas Warren C
Clyde Barfoot P

1930
Fred Haney 3B
Johnny Moore LF
Frank Sigafoos 2B
George Harper RF
Ray Jacobs 1B
Jigger Statz CF
Carl Dittmar SS
Dallas Warren C
Clyde Barfoot P

1931
Jigger Statz CF
Loris Baker 2B
Doc Farrell 3B
Vince Barton RF
Ray Jacobs 1B
Carl Dittmar SS
Homer Summa LF
John Schulte C
Jess Petty P

1932
Fred Haney 3B
Homer Summa LF
Jigger Statz CF
Earl Sheely 1B
Clarence Blair 2B
Mike Kreevich RF
Carl Dittmar SS
Gilly Campbell C
Leroy Herrmann P

1933
Jigger Statz CF
Jimmie Reese 2B
Marv Gudat LF
Tuck Stainback RF
Jim Oglesby 1B
Gene Lillard 3B
Carl Dittmar SS
Bill Cronin C
Fay Thomas P

1934
Jigger Statz CF
Jimmie Reese 2B
Marv Gudat LF
Frank Demaree RF
Jim Oglesby 1B
Gene Lillard 3B
Carl Dittmar SS
Gilly Campbell C
Fay Thomas P

1935
Jigger Statz CF
Jimmie Reese 2B
Marv Gudat LF
Art Veltman C
Jim Oglesby 1B
Gene Lillard 3B
Cleo Carlyle RF
Carl Dittmar SS
Lou Garland P

1936
Jigger Statz CF
Marv Gudat LF
Steve Mesner 3B
Don Hurst 1B
Wes Schulmerich RF
Jimmie Reese 2B
Bob Mattick SS
Art Veltman C
Fay Thomas P

1937
Cleo Carlyle RF
Jigger Statz CF
Bill Mcwilliams 3B
Don Hurst 1B
Murray Howell LF
Dick Atwell 2B
Bob Mattick SS
Bob Collins C
Ray Prim P

1938
Jack Sanford 2B
Jigger Statz CF
Marv Gudat LF
Johnny Moore RF
Glen Russell 1B
Eddie Cihocki SS
Charlie English 3B
Bob Collins C
Jack Salveson P

1939
Jigger Statz CF
Eddie Mayo 2B
Charlie English 3B
Johnny Moore RF
Rip Collins 1B
Jack Rothrock LF
Eddie Cihocki SS
Bob Collins C
Fay Thomas P

1940
Paul Carpenter CF
Eddie Mayo 3B
Lou Stringer 2B
Rip Collins 1B
Lou Novikoff LF
Gordon Donaldson RF
Eddie Cihocki SS
Billy Holm C
Gene Lillard P

1941
Ralph Samhammer CF
Len Merullo SS
Eddie Mayo 3B
Wally Carroll RF
Wimpy Quinn 1B
Gordon Donaldson LF
Bob Collins C
Elmer Mallory 2B
Ray Prim P

1942
Barney Olsen CF
Eddie Waitkus 1B
Roy Hughes 2B
Johnny Moore RF
Fern Bell LF
Eddie Mayo 3B
Bill Schuster SS
Gilly Campbell C
Ray Prim P

1943
Bill Schuster SS
Roy Hughes 2B
Andy Pafko CF
Johnny Moore LF
Charlie English 3B
Bob Latshaw 1B
Wimpy Quinn RF
Billy Holm C
Ken Raffensberger P

1944
George Ogorek 2B
Eddie Fernandes RF
Cecil Garriott CF
Glen Russell 1B
Johnny Moore LF
Roy Smalley SS
Guy Miller 3B
Bill Sarni C
Ray Prim P

1945
Hal Douglas CF
Ray Viers 2B
Glen Russell 3B
Lou Novikoff LF
Mel Hicks 1B
Jim Tyack RF
Roy Easterwood C
Guy Miller SS
Don Osborn P

1946
Rabbit Mallory 2B
Bill Schuster SS
Ed Sauer RF
Barney Olsen CF
Leroy Paton LF
Jack Richards 1B
Maury Donovan 3B
Dewey Williams C
Don Osborn P

1947
Cecil Garriott CF
Bill Schuster SS
Ed Sauer RF
Clarence Maddern LF
John Ostrowski 3B
Lou Stringer 2B
Reggie Otero 1B
Eddie Malone C
Red Lynn P

1948
Cecil Garriott CF
Bill Schuster SS
Dom Dallessandro LF
Ed Sauer RF
Larry Barton 1B
Albie Glossop 3B
Mickey Burnett 2B
Eddie Malone C
Red Lynn P

1949
Cecil Garriott CF
Bill Schuster SS
Butch Moran 1B
Dom Dallessandro LF
John Ostrowski 3B
Ralph Rowe RF
Wayne Terwilliger 2B
Eddie Malone C
Hank Wyse P

1950
Frank Whitman SS
Cecil Garriott CF
Frank Baumholtz RF
Stan Spence LF
Elbie Fletcher 1B
John Lucadello 2B
Lloyd Lowe 3B
Rube Novotney C
Bob Muncrief P

1951
Jack Hollis 2B
Gene Baker SS
Chuck Connors 1B
Max West RF
Tom Neill LF
Leon Brinkopf 3B
Bill Raimondi C
Bob Talbot CF
Ralph Hamner P

1952
Gene Baker SS
Jack Hollis 2B
Chuck Connors 1B
Max West RF
Les Layton LF
Tod Davis 3B
Les Peden C
Bob Talbot CF
Ed Chandler P

1953
Bob Talbot CF
Fred Richards 1B
Bob Usher LF
Max West RF
Gene Baker SS
Tod Davis 3B
Jack Hollis 2B
Elvin Tappe C
Ed Chandler P

1954
Herb Adams CF
Gene Mauch 2B
Bob Usher RF
Fred Richards 1B
Dixie Upright LF
Frank Diprima 3B
Al Evans C
Bud Hardin SS
Cal Mclish P

1955
Bob Talbot CF
Gene Mauch 2B
Bob Usher RF
Bus Clarkson 3B
Steve Bilko 1B
Don Robertson LF
John Pramesa C
Bud Hardin SS
Joe Hatten P

1956
Bob Coats LF
Gene Mauch 2B
Eddie Haas RF
Steve Bilko 1B
George Freese 3B
Joe Hannah C
Jim Bolger CF
Casey Wise SS
Harry Perkowski P

1957
George Anderson 2B
Gale Wade CF
Bob Borkowski RF
Steve Bilko 1B
Monte Irvin LF
Jim Baxes 3B
Elvin Tappe C
Jack Caro SS
Bob Darnell P

Appendix B: Team Batting, Fielding and Pitching

Year	Batting Average	Home Runs Total	Home Runs at Home	Fielding Average	ERA	Shutouts Pitched
1903	.269*	25	**	**	2.75	26
1904	.257	24	**	.942	2.63	21
1905	.238	27	**	.953	2.25	33*
1906	.243	13	**	**	2.57	21
1907	.248	37	**	**	2.29	32*
1908	.254*	21	**	**	2.54	20
1909	.235	34	**	**	2.48	25
1910	.225	22	**	**	2.68	23
1911	.255	28	**	.955*	3.59	6
1912	.275	42	**	.962*	3.20	18
1913	.254	46	**	.955	2.96	19
1914	.274	29	**	.961	2.48	24
1915	.267	42	**	.961	2.74	19
1916	.260	36	**	.962	2.75	23
1917	.267	23	**	.965*	2.86	17
1918	.274	8	**	**	2.00*	19
1919	.271	48	18	.969*	2.86	11
1920	.262	29	4	.965	2.33	8
1921	.280	42	11	.962	2.97	11
1922	.277	35	19	.963	3.02	15
1923	.288	74	24	.964	3.82	7
1924	.289	87	23	.961	4.05	8
1925	.274	82	36	.964	3.60	8
1926	.289	82	36	.971*	2.93*	20
1927	.295	115	67	.956	3.59	2
1928	.281	111	66	.964	4.46	12
1929	.303	180	107	.969	4.78	6
1930	.304	139	74	.974*	4.05	12
1931	.299	112	74	.965	4.72	5
1932	.289	76	59	.965	4.44	8
1933	.300	147*	100	.966	3.66*	10
1934	.299*	127*	91	.970*	2.63*	20
1935	.298	117*	79	.968	4.11	7
1936	.292*	78	56	.966	4.07	7

Year	Batting Average	Home Runs Total	Home Runs at Home	Fielding Average	ERA	Shutouts Pitched
1937	.281	95	78	.966	3.71	6
1938	.284	118	81	.972	3.72	10
1939	.286	117*	86	.975*	3.49	17
1940	.281	115*	80	.973	3.42	14
1941	.270	76	57	.960	3.96	11
1942	.280	70	47	.973*	3.05*	12
1943	.281*	97*	71	.978*	2.59*	22
1944	.270*	73*	48	.964	2.74*	20
1945	.281	63*	38	.964	3.79	10
1946	.253	71	43	.969	3.15	19
1947	.269	151*	97	.974*	3.53	11
1948	.267	178*	109	.972	3.89	10
1949	.263	150	88	.969	5.22	10
1950	.267	145	107	.975	4.81	10
1951	.274	167*	93	.976*	4.19	11
1952	.256	145*	95	.973	3.62	14
1953	.276*	153*	93	.975	3.80	12
1954	.252	140*	85	.973	3.73	13
1955	.257	143*	92	.976	3.87	14
1956	.297*	202*	136	.973	4.45	7
1957	.253	167*	115	.974	3.81	10

*led league
**records not available for these years

Angels Home Runs by Park

1919

Washington Park (18) Crawford 5, Killefer 5, Fournier 2, Bates, Boles, Driscoll, Ellis, Kenworthy, Lapan; **Oakland (4)** Ellis, K. Crandall, Kenworthy; **Portland (7)** Crawford 5, Fournier 2; **Sacramento (2)** Crawford, Fournier; **Salt Lake City (14)** Fournier 5, Niehoff 4, Crawford 2, Boles, K. Crandall, Kenworthy; **San Francisco (0)**; **Seattle (2)** Bassler, Crawford; **Vernon (1)** Fournier.

Total: Home 18, Road 30

1920

Washington Park (4) Crawford 3, Mcauley; **Oakland (0)**; **Portland (1)** Crawford; **Sacramento (4)** Bassler, Crawford, Mcdonald, Niehoff; **Salt Lake City (14)** Crawford 6, Ellis 2, Mcauley 2, Niehoff 2, Brown, K. Crandall; **San Francisco (0)**; **Seattle (1)** Statz; **Stockton (1)** Griggs; **Vernon (2)** Crawford, Griggs.

Total: Home 4, Road 23

1921

Washington Park (11) Crawford 4, Niehoff 3, Griggs 2, Crandall, Lyons; **Oakland (2)** Griggs, Niehoff; **Portland (10)** Griggs 4, Niehoff 3, Crandall, Crawford, Killefer; **Sacramento (1)** Lindimore; **Salt Lake City (9)** Crandall 2, Crawford 2, Carroll, Griggs, Mccabe, Niehoff, Statz; **San Francisco (6)** Griggs 2, Baldwin, Crawford, Niehoff, Statz; **Seattle (3)** Carroll, Crawford, Niehoff; **Vernon (0)**.

Total: Home 11, Road 31

1922

Washington Park (19) Griggs 10, Deal 5, Carroll, Lindimore, Mccabe, Sullivan; **Oakland (1)** Griggs; **Ogden (1)** Baldwin; **Portland (1)** Carroll; **Sacramento (0)**; **Salt Lake City (9)** Griggs 7, Carroll, Crandall; **San Francisco (2)** Griggs 2; **Seattle (0)**; **Vernon (2)** Deal, Griggs.

Total: Home 19, Road 16

1923

Washington Park (24) Griggs 9, Hood 8, Mccabe 2, Deal, Jacobs, Lyons, Smith, Twombly; **Oakland (3)** Mccabe 2, Griggs; **Portland (9)** Griggs 2, Hood 2, Twombly 2, Deal, Mccabe, Smith; **Sacramento (8)** Hood 3, Griggs 2, Baldwin, Krug, Mcauley; **Salt Lake City (14)** Hood 5, Deal 2, Krug 2, Douglas,

Golvin, Lindimore, Mccabe, Twombly; **San Francisco (11)** Griggs 6, Hood 3, Baldwin, Krug; **Seattle (3)** Carroll, Golvin, Twombly; **Vernon (2)** Griggs, Rego.
Total: Home 24, Road 50

1924
Washington Park (23) Hood 9, Durst 5, Jacobs 2, Jenkins 2, Beck, Crandall, Cruise, Grimes, Mcauley; **Oakland (4)** Durst, Hood, Krug, Twombly; **Portland (12)** Durst 3, Hood 3, Jenkins 2, Beck, Grimes, Spencer, Twombly; **Sacramento (5)** Beck, Hood, Jacobs, Krug, Spencer; **Salt Lake City (22)** Cruise 4, Jacobs 4, Durst 3, Hood 3, Jenkins 2, Mcauley 2, Beck, Grimes, Myers, Whaley; **San Francisco (6)** Beck, Hood, Hughes, Spencer, Walters, Whaley; **Seattle (12)** Durst 5, Hood 4, Golvin 2, Grimes; **Vernon (3)** Jacobs 2, Beck.
Total: Home 23, Road 64

1925
Washington Park (25) Hood 10, Jacobs 6, Beck 5, Grimes, Krug, Root, Spencer; **Oakland (3)** Beck 2, Mcauley; **Portland (14)** Beck 4, Horan 3, Grimes 2, Hood 2, Krug 2, Glazner; **Sacramento (2)** Beck, Hood; **Salt Lake City (6)** Jacobs 3, Hood 2, Sandberg; **San Francisco (10)** Hood 4, Krug 2, Beck, Jacobs, Statz, Wright; **Seattle (7)** Beck 3, Hood 2, Grimes, Twombly; **Vernon (4)** Hood 2, Grimes, Jacobs; **Wrigley Field (11)** Hood 4, Jacobs 2, Beck, Grimes, Krug, Statz, Taitt.
Total: Home 36, Road 46

1926
Hollywood (10) Brazill 2, Hannah 2, Jacobs 2, Statz 2, Hood, Weis; **Mission (4)** Jacobs 3, Krug; **Oakland (2)** Hood 2; **Portland (10)** Brazill 2, Jahn 2, Weis 2, Hannah, Hood, Jacobs, Yarrison; **Sacramento (5)** Hood 2, Brazill, Jacobs, Krug; **San Francisco (7)** Jacobs 2, Brazill, Hood, Jahn, Sandberg, Weis; **Seattle (8)** Brazill 3, Jahn 2, Hood, Jacobs, Statz; **Wrigley Field (36)** Jacobs 12, Brazill 10, Hood 5, Jahn 3, Weis 3, Hannah, Sandberg, Statz.
Total: Home 36, Road 46

1927
Hollywood (4) Brazill 2, Jahn 2; **Mission (10)** Cox 2, Hood 2, Brazill, Cunningham, Hannah, Jacobs, Jahn, Kahn; **Oakland (2)** Cox, Hannah; **Portland (8)** Weis 3, Cox 2, Hood 2, Hannah; **Sacramento (1)** Berger; **San Francisco (17)** Jacobs 5, Jahn 4, Brazill 2, Cox 2, Weis 2, Cunningham, Hemingway; **Seattle (5)** Weis 3, Brazill 2; **Wrigley Field (67)** Brazil 14, Hood 13, Jahn 10, Jacobs 7, Weis 5, Cox 4, Hannah 4, Berger 2, Cunningham 2, Sandberg 2, Kahn, Mitchell, Staley, Wright.
Total: Home 67, Road 47

1928
Hollywood (11) Berger 4, Hood 4, Tolson 3; **Mission (7)** Schulmerich 3, Berger 2, Hood, Tolson; **Oakland (7)** Berger 3, Hood 2, Schulmerich, Tolson; **Portland (5)** Schulmerich 2, Barfoot, Berger, Tolson; **Sacramento (4)** Hood 2, Hannah, Sandberg; **San Francisco (8)** Schulmerich 2, Tolson 2, Hood, Jones, Sandberg, Warren; **Seattle (3)** Mosolf, Peters, Schulmerich; **Wrigley Field (66)** Tolson 20, Berger 10, Hood 10, Schulmerich 10, Barfoot 2, Burkett 2, Cunningham 2, Dittmar 2, Hannah 2, Staley 2, Jensen, Mosolf, Warren, Wright.
Total: Home 66, Road 45

1929
Hollywood (17) Schulmerich 4, Tolson 4, Jacobs 3, Webb 3, Berger 2, Barfoot; **Mission (17)** Webb 5, Tolson 4, Berger 3, Schulmerich 2, Sandberg, Statz, Warren; **Oakland (1)** Parker; **Portland (8)** Berger 4, Schulmerich 2, Webb 2; **Sacramento (6)** Berger 2, Webb 2, Barfoot, Dittmar; **San Francisco (17)** Berger 4, Webb 4, Dittmar 3, Jacobs 2, Haney, Holling, Sandberg, Statz; **Seattle (7)** Berger 3, Tolson 2, Schulmerich, Webb; **Wrigley Field (107)** Berger 22, Webb 20, Tolson 18, Jacobs 15, Schulmerich 10, Sandberg 5, Warren 5, Holling 3, Butler 2, Jones 2, Walsh 2, Dittmar, Hannah, Statz.
Total: Home 107, Road 73

1930
Hollywood (13) Jacobs 4, Dittmar 2, Moore 2, Sigafoos 2, Harper, Schulmerich, Statz; **Mission (18)** Moore 5, Schulmerich 5, Sigafoos 3, Dittmar 2, Harper, Jacobs, Warren; **Oakland (2)** Dittmar, Schulmerich; **Portland (1)** Dittmar; **Sacramento (6)** Schulmerich 4, Jacobs, Statz; **San Francisco (21)** Jacobs 5, Moore 3, Sigafoos 3, Haney 2, Schulmerich 2, Warren 2, Ballou, Dittmar, Hannah, Statz; **Seattle (5)** Harper 3, Schulmerich 2; **Wrigley Field (74)** Moore 16, Schulmerich 13, Sigafoos 11, Jacobs 9, Dittmar 7, Haney 5, Hannah 3, Harper 3, Warren 3, Statz 2, Barfoot, Parker.
Total: Home 74, Road 66

1931
Hollywood (12) Barton 3, Campbell 2, Jacobs 2, Moore 2, Baker, Haney, Schulte; **Mission (1)** Burns; **Oakland (3)** Barton, Jacobs, Moore; **Portland (8)** Dittmar 3, Farrell 2, Barton, Haney, Statz; **Sacramento (4)** Burns 2, Dittmar, Farrell; **San Francisco (2)** Campbell, Haney; **Seattle (8)** Barton 3, Baker,

Burns, Farrell, Jacobs, Moore; **Wrigley Field (74)** Jacobs 14, Barton 9, Campbell 7, Farrell 7, Baker 6, Burns 6, Statz 5, Dittmar 4, Schulte 4, Nelson 3, Summa 3, Moore 2, Shealy 2, Herrmann, Parker.
Total: Home 74, Road 38

1932

Hollywood (6) Baker, Campbell, Haney, Kreevich, Sheely, Stainback; **Mission (0)**; **Oakland (0)**; **Portland (5)** Stainback 2, Lillard, Oglesby, Sheely; **Sacramento (1)** Lillard; **San Francisco (0)**; **Seattle (5)** Stainback 2, Ballou, Dittmar, Statz; **Wrigley Field (59)** Kreevich 14, Campbell 8, Sheely 8, Haney 5, Stainback 5, Statz 5, Oglesby 4, Dittmar 3, Lillard 3, Blair 2, Deviveiros 2.
Total: Home 59, Road 17

1933

Hollywood (11) Lillard 5, Oglesby 3, Gudat, Moore, Stainback; **Mission (0)**; **Oakland (4)** Stainback 2, Lillard, Mohler; **Portland (9)** Lillard 3, Mcmullen 2, Gazella, Oglesby, Ograin, Thomas; **Sacramento (7)** Lillard 2, Stainback 2, Statz 2, Mcmullen; **San Francisco (4)** Lillard 3, Cronin; **Seattle (12)** Stainback 4, Statz 3, Gazella 2, Lillard 2, Chozen; **Wrigley Field (100)** Lillard 27, Oglesby 16, Stainback 10, Gudat 9, Mcmullen 8, Dittmar 5, Mohler 5, Statz 5, Gazella 4, Ograin 4, Reese 4, Cronin, Kies, Ward.
Total: Home 100, Road 47

1934

Hollywood (17) Demaree 6, Lillard 3, Oglesby 3, Statz 2, Campbell, Dittmar, Reese; **Mission (3)** Lillard 3; **Oakland (3)** Lillard 2, Demaree; **Portland (1)** Lillard; **Sacramento (6)** Demaree 4, Lillard, Reese; **San Francisco (4)** Demaree 3, Ward; **Seattle (2)** Statz, Thomas; **Wrigley Field (91)** Demaree 30, Lillard 17, Campbell 16, Oglesby 12, Gudat 4, Statz 3, Dittmar 2, Goebel 2, Gazella. Henshaw, Ograin, Reese, South.
Total: Home 91, Road 36

1935

Hollywood (22) Lillard 13, Oglesby 4, Mesner 3, Carlyle, Goebel; **Mission (3)** Lillard 3; **Oakland (0)**; **Portland (1)** Lillard; **Sacramento (7)** Lillard 2, Mesner 2, Ferree, Oglesby, Statz; **San Francisco (2)** Lillard 2; **Seattle (3)** Carlyle, Mesner, Statz; **Wrigley Field (79)** Lillard 35, Oglesby 18, Carlyle 10, Mesner 7, Goebel 3, Gibson 2, Gudat 2, Garland, Reese.
Total: Home 79, Road 38

1936

Mission (3) Bottarini, Mesner, Schulmerich; **Oakland (2)** Bottarini, Schulmerich; **Portland (3)** Hurst 3; **Sacramento (2)** Mesner, Russell; **San Diego (3)** Carlyle 2, Schulmerich; **San Francisco (4)** Bottarini 3, Mesner; **Seattle (5)** Mesner 3, Dittmar, Bottarini; **Wrigley Field (56)** Hurst 16, Mesner 11, Schulmerich 11, Bottarini 6, Russell 4, Statz 3, Carlyle, Gabler, Gudat, Mattick, Salveson.
Total: Home 56, Road 22

1937

Mission (1) Mcwilliams; **Oakland (1)** Mesner; **Portland (5)** Hurst 2, Richardson 2, Mcwilliams; **Sacramento (2)** Collins, Russell; **San Diego (2)** Collins, Hurst; **San Francisco (0)**; **Seattle (5)** Collins, Holt, Hurst, Richardson, Russell; **Wrigley Field (78)** Russell 11, Collins 10, Mesner 9, Carlyle 7, Mcwilliams 7, Gudat 6, Hurst 6, Holt 5, Howell 5, Richardson 4, Hargrave 3, Mattick 2, Statz 2, Overman.
Total: Home 78, Road 16

1938

Hollywood (12) English 4, Russell 4, Carpenter, Cihocki, Collins, Moore; **Oakland (3)** Lillard, Rothrock, Russell; **Portland (5)** Moore 2, Russell 2, English; **Sacramento (5)** Lillard 2, Collins, Moore, Salveson; **San Diego (2)** Moore, Salveson; **San Francisco (1)** Russell; **Seattle (7)** Russell 2, Cihocki, English, Mayo, Moore, Rothrock; **Wrigley Field (81)** Moore 14, English 13, Russell 11, Cihocki 9, Collins 9, Mayo 8, Lillard 4, Rothrock 4, Carpenter 2, Gudat 2, Sanford 2, Statz 2, Salveson.
Total: Home 81, Road 35

1939

Hollywood (12) Stringer 3, Novikoff 2, Cihocki, J. Collins, R. Collins, Epperly, Moore, Rothrock, Thomas; **Oakland (2)** Moore, Stringer; **Portland (4)** J. Collins, English, Novikoff, Sueme; **Sacramento (5)** J. Collins 2, Novikoff, Rothrock, Stringer; **San Diego (2)** English, Moore; **San Francisco (0)**; **Seattle (3)** J. Collins, Novikoff, Stringer; **Wrigley Field (86)** J. Collins 21, Moore 12, English 11, Stringer 9, R. Collins 7, Mayo 6, Statz 4, Cihocki 3, Novikoff 3, Carpenter 2, Rothrock 2, Stine 2, Carroll, Kush, Flores, Hargrave.
Total: Home 86, Road 28

1940

Hollywood (7) Novikoff 3, Collins 2, Cihocki, Stringer; **Oakland (3)** Mayo, Novikoff, Stringer; **Portland (10)** Mayo 4, Novikoff 3, Moore 2, Collins; **Sacramento (4)** Novikoff 4; **San Diego (7)** Collins 2, Mayo 2, Novikoff 2, Moore; **San Francisco (1)** Cihocki; **Seattle (4)** Stringer 2, Cihocki, Novikoff; **Wrigley Field (80)** Novikoff 26, Collins 13, Stringer 10, Hernandez 6, Mayo 6, Moore 6, Car-

penter 4, Cihocki 3, Donaldson, Lowrey, Samhammer, Statz, Strada, Weiland.
Total: **Home 80, Road 36**

1941
Hollywood (6) Berger 2, Holm, Lowrey, Mayo, Weintraub; **Oakland (0)**; **Portland (1)** Mayo; **Sacramento (0)**; **San Diego (4)** Weintraub 2, Berger, Mayo; **San Francisco (3)** Berger 2, Weintraub; **Seattle (5)** Weintraub 2, Holm, Lowrey, Moore; **Wrigley Field (57)** Moore 17, Weintraub 12, Mayo 10, Lowrey 4, Berger 3, Holm 3, Powell 2, Storey 2, Collins, Merullo, Schuster, Stine.
Total: **Home 57, Road 19**

1942
Hollywood (5) Bell, Mayo, Moore, Olsen, Todd; **Oakland (2)** Schuster, Todd; **Portland (3)** Mayo 2, Bell; **Sacramento (9)** Bell 2, Olsen 2, Schuster 2, Lowrey, Mayo, Todd; **San Diego (3)** Mayo, Olsen, Statz; **San Francisco (1)** Olsen; **Seattle (0)**; **Wrigley Field (47)** Olsen 10, Waitkus 9, Mayo 7, Moore 6, Lowrey 4, Schuster 3, Todd 2, Bell, Campbell, Hughes, Statz, Stewart, Raffensberger.
Total: **Home 47, Road 23**

1943
Hollywood (10) Ostrowski 5, Quinn 2, English, Pafko, Russell; **Oakland (2)** English, Quinn; **Portland (2)** Garriott, Quinn; **Sacramento (7)** English 3, Quinn 2, Ostrowski, Schuster; **San Diego (1)** English; **San Francisco (1)** Schuster; **Seattle (3)** Garriott, Ostrowski, Pafko; **Wrigley Field (71)** Pafko 16, Ostrowski 14, English 10, Garriott 8, Russell 6, Quinn 5, E. Mallory 3, Schuster 3, Holm 2, Latshaw, Moore, Raffensberger, Sarni.
Total: **Home 71, Road 26**

1944
Hollywood (9) Russell 3, Garriott 2, Sauer 2, Norbert, Ostrowski; **Oakland (1)** Ostrowski; **Portland (4)** Garriott 2, English, Norbert; **Sacramento (10)** Russell 6, Fernandes 2, Norbert, Sarni; **San Diego (0)**; **San Francisco (0)**; **Seattle (1)** Ostrowski; **Wrigley Field (48)** Garriott 8, Russell 8, Norbert 7, Ostrowski 7, Sarni 4, Fernandes 3, Moore 3, Sauer 3, English, Horton, Prim, Salvatierra, Smalley.
Total: **Home 48, Road 25**

1945
Hollywood (5) Moore 2, Russell 2, Tyack 1; **Oakland (5)** Elko 2, Novikoff 1, Russell 1, Tyack 1; **Portland (7)** Tyack 2, Elko 1, Greene 1, Moore 1, Novikoff 1, Russell 1; **Sacramento (2)** Greene 1, Tyack 1; **San Diego (3)** Brewster 1, Hicks 1, Russell 1; **San Francisco (0)**; **Seattle (3)** Greene 1, Novikoff 1, Tyack 1; **Wrigley Field (38)** Hicks 9, Russell 9, Novikoff 6, Viers 3, Adams 2, Greene 2, Tyack 2, Brenner 1, Douglas 1, Easterwood 1, Elko 1, Moore 1.
Total: **Home 38, Road 25**

1946
Hollywood (7) Christopher 3, Sauer 2, Archie, Schuster; **Oakland (4)** Christopher 3, Olsen; **Portland (5)** Sauer 3, Christopher, Otero; **Sacramento (3)** Sauer 2, Williams; **San Diego (6)** Christopher 4, Adams, Glossop; **San Francisco (0)**; **Seattle (3)** Sauer 2, Archie; **Wrigley Field (43)** Christopher 15, Sauer 11, Glossop 4, Schuster 3, Stephenson 3, Archie 2, Donovan 2, R. Mallory, Olsen, Quinn.
Total: **Home 43, Road 28**

1947
Hollywood (11) Stringer 3, Schuster 2, Barton, Glossop, Maddern, Malone, Ostrowski, Sauer; **Oakland (8)** Garriott 2, Ostrowski 2, Chambers, Christopher, Glossop, Stringer; **Portland (4)** Barton 2, Garriott, Malone; **Sacramento (11)** Maddern 3, Ostrowski 2, Garriott, Glossop, Malone, Sauer, Schuster, Stringer; **San Diego (14)** Maddern 3, Sauer 3, Ostrowski 2, Stainback 2, Barton, Garriott, Gillespie, Malone; **San Francisco (3)** Garriott, Ostrowski, Stringer; **Seattle (3)** Barton 2, Garriott; **Wrigley Field (97)** Ostrowski 16, Garriott 15, Barton 12, Sauer 12, Maddern 8, Stringer 7, Malone 6, Glossop 5, Christopher 4, Gillespie 4, Schuster 3, Dobernic, Mallory, Marshall, Pawelek, Sarni.
Total: **Home 97, Road 54**

1948
Hollywood (16) Dallessandro 4, Tabor 3, Sauer 2, Schuster 2, Burnett, Garriott, Johnson, Malone, Novotney; **Oakland (11)** Dallessandro 4, Garriott 3, Glossop 2, Johnson, Sauer; **Portland (7)** Aberson 4, Malone 2, Glossop; **Sacramento (3)** Sauer 2, Tabor; **San Diego (18)** Aberson 2, Burnett, 2, Garriott 2, Malone 2, Schuster 2, Anthony, Barton, Dallessandro, Glossop, Lukon, Ostrowski, Sanford, Sauer; **San Francisco (6)** Aberson 2, Glossop 2, Garriott, Lukon; **Seattle (7)** Aberson 3, Glossop, Malone, Novotney, Schuster; **Wrigley Field (109)** Aberson 23, Ostrowski 14, Garriott 12, Dallessandro 11, Glossop 10, Sauer 10, Lukon 9, Schuster 6, Sanford 5, Johnson 3, Malone 3, Novotney 2, Hafey.
Total: **Home 109, Road 68**

1949
Hollywood (7) Terwilliger 3, Ostrowski 2, Handley, Maddern; **Oakland (16)** Aberson 5, Ostrowski 3,

Burbrink, Dallessandro, Garriott, Jackson, Maddern, Mauro, Moran, Terwilliger; **Portland (9)** Maddern 3, Gustine 2, Damato, Garriott, Malone, Ostrowski; **Sacramento (4)** Moran, Aberson, Ostrowski; **San Diego (10)** Garriott 3, Aberson 2, Ostrowski 2, Goldsberry, Gustine, Terwilliger; **San Francisco (8)** Ostrowski 4, Aberson, Burgess, Mauro, Terwilliger; **Seattle (8)** Maddern 3, Ostrowski 2, Aberson, Burbrink, Mclish; **Wrigley Field (88)** Ostrowski 17, Mauro 10, Aberson 7, Dallessandro 5, Maddern 7, Garriott 6, Glossop 5, Moran 5, Malone 5, Schuster 4, Seerey 3, Burbrink 2, Stephens 2, Terwilliger 2, Burgess, Damato, Goldsberry, Gustine, Jackson, Mcdaniels, Novotney, Rhawn.
Total: **Home 88, Road 62**

1950
Hollywood (7) Layton 3, Baker, Cash, Fletcher, Mclish; **Oakland (10)** Spence 3, Baumholtz 2, Klein 2, Cash, Glossop, Layton; **Portland (4)** Baumholtz, Fletcher, Layton, Maddern; **Sacramento (1)** Cash; **San Diego (7)** Layton 3, Maddern 2, Baumholtz, Spence; **San Francisco (5)** Spence 2, Burbrink, Klein, Layton; **Seattle (4)** Layton 2, Brinkpof, Maddern; **Wrigley Field (107)** Layton 16, Spence 16, Baumholtz 11, Klein 11, Garriott 10, Maddern 10, Novotney 8, Fletcher 7, Cash 4, Glossop 4, Brinkpof 3, Lucadello 2, Baker, Handley, E. Johnson, Lowe, Mclish.
Total: **Home 107, Road 38**

1951
Hollywood (10) Baker 2, Brinkpof 2, Fondy 2, Connors, Layton, Peden, Talbot; **Oakland (19)** West 8, Connors 3, Baker 2, Neill 2, Besse, Brinkpof, Fondy, Talbot; **Portland (12)** Davis 3, West 3, Fondy 2, Baker, Connors, Peden, Talbot; **Sacramento (5)** Layton 2, Brinkpof, Hollis, Lade; **San Diego (8)** Layton 2, West 2, Cash, Connors, Neill, Talbot; **San Francisco (11)** Layton 3, Baker 2, Connors 2, Brinkpof, Hollis, Peden, Talbot; **Seattle (9)** Baker 2, West 2, Brinkpof, Hollis, Layton, Peden, Talbot; **Wrigley Field (93)** West 20, Brinkpof 19, Connors 14, Layton 14, Fondy 7, Peden 7, Neill 4, Talbot 3, Baker 2, Cash, Davis, Moisan.
Total: **Home 93, Road 74**

1952
Hollywood (7) Peden 2, West 2, Baker, Brinkpof, Usher; **Oakland (8)** Northey 2, West 2, Baker, Brinkpof, Connors, Lavigne; **Portland (6)** Brinkpof 2, Baker, Hollis, Peden, Talbot; **Sacramento (4)** Connors, Davis, Peden, Talbot; **San Diego (11)** West 5, Connors 2, Layton 2, Brinkpof, Peden; **San Francisco (6)** Peden 3, West 3; **Seattle (8)** Baker 2, Dunlap 2, West 2, Hatten, Hollis; **Wrigley Field (95)** Brinkpof 22, West 21, Baker 10, Peden 10, Northey 9, Usher 9, Talbot 4, Layton 3, Connors 2, Davis, Dunlap, Hollis, Moisan, Mclish.
Total: **Home 95, Road 50**

1953
Hollywood (8) Smith 3, Baker 2, Richards, Talbot, Usher; **Oakland (12)** Richards 5, Usher 3, Baker, Diprima, Moisan, Padget; **Portland (16)** Talbot 3, Davis 2, Peden 2, Smith 2, Usher 2, Baker, Diprima, Mclish, Richards, Upright; **Sacramento (4)** Baker, Davis, Peden, Usher; **San Diego (8)** Davis 4, Usher 2, Baker, Peden; **San Francisco (7)** Richards 3, Franklin, Peden, Smith, Upright; **Seattle (5)** Davis, Peden, Talbot, Upright, West; **Wrigley Field (93)** Richards 16, Baker 14, Talbot 9, Upright 9, Diprima 7, Davis 6, Smith 6, Usher 6, Peden 5, West 4, Moisan 3, Mclish 3, Evans 2, Ihde, Padget, Spicer.
Total: **Home 93, Road 60**

1954
Hollywood (9) Richards 3, Mauch 2, Usher 2, Pramesa, Upright; **Oakland (15)** Mauch 3, Richards 3, West 3, Edwards 2, Robertson 2, Brown, Mclish; **Portland (9)** Richards 2, Upright 2, Brown, Evans, Marasco, Mauch, Nasternak; **Sacramento (10)** Edwards 3, Brown 2, Marasco 2, Pramesa 2, Usher; **San Diego (7)** Richards 2, West 2, Meek, Pramesa, Usher; **San Francisco (2)** Pramesa, West; **Seattle (3)** Monette 2, Edwards; **Wrigley Field (85)** Richards 14, Brown 10, Usher 9, Upright 7, Pramesa 6, West 6, Mauch 5, Robertson 5, Cunningham 4, Evans 4, Edwards 3, Hardin 2, Marasco 2, Mclish 2, Monette 2, Nasternak 2, Brinkpof, Church.
Total: **Home 85, Road 55**

1955
Hollywood (3) Bilko, Clarkson, Usher; **Oakland (10)** Bilko 3, Rice 3, Hannah, Mauch, Wade, Winceniak; **Portland (9)** Rice 4, Bilko, Church, Usher, Wade, Winceniak; **Sacramento (6)** Davis 2, Rice 2, Bilko, Winceniak; **San Diego (13)** Bilko 3, Clarkson 2, Mauch 2, Wade 2, Brown, Pramesa, Rice, Winceniak; **San Francisco (8)** Rice 3, Bilko, Davis, Fanning, Morgan, Wade; **Seattle (2)** Clarkson 2; **Wrigley Field (92)** Bilko 27, Rice 12, Clarkson 8, Usher 8, Winceniak 8, Mauch 5, Fanning 4, Lown 3, Talbot 3, Wade 3, Coats 2, Pramesa 2, Brosnan, Davis, Drake, Hatten, Morgan, Piktuzis, Robertson.
Total: **Home 92, Road 51**

1956

Hollywood (5) Freese 2, Bilko, Mauch, Wade; **Portland (15)** Freese 4, Bilko 2, Bolger 2, Drott 2, Speake 2, Anderson, Hannah, Mauch; **Sacramento (10)** Bilko 3, Bolger 3, Davis 2, Mauch, Wade; **San Diego (10)** Speake 3, Bilko 2, Haas 2, Bolger, Mauch, Tappe; **San Francisco (10)** Bilko 4, Wade 3, Bolger 2, Haas; **Seattle (10)** Bilko 3, Bolger 2, Freese 2, Speake 2, Mauch; **Vancouver (6)** Bilko 3, Davis, Lauters, Speake; **Wrigley Field (136)** Bilko 37, Bolger 18, Speake 17, Mauch 15, Wade 15, Freese 14, Wise 7, Davis 3, Perkowski 2, Tappe 2, Briggs, Fanning, Goryl, Haas, Lauters, Thorpe.

Total: Home 136, Road 66

1957

Hollywood (12) Bilko 4, Hartsfield 2, Lammers 2, Baxes, Jenkins, Marasco, Wade; **Portland (8)** Bilko 3, Battey 2, Anderson, Baxes, Jenkins; **Sacramento (7)** Baxes 2, Bilko 2, Hamric, Jenkins, Olson; **San Diego (13)** Bilko 6, Hamric 4, Battey, Fridley, Hartsfield; **San Francisco (6)** Jenkins 2, Battey, Baxes, Bilko, Hamric; **Seattle (4)** Bilko 2, Hartsfield, Saffell; **Vancouver (2)** Bilko 2; **Wrigley Field (115)** Bilko 36, Hamric 13, Fridley 12, Baxes 11, Jenkins 8, Wade 6, Battey 5, Saffell 5, Olson 4, Dolan 3, Hartsfield 3, Lammers 3, Anderson, Borkowski, Darnell, Irvin, Sherry, Valentinetti.

Total: Home 115, Road 52

Appendix C: Individual Batting and Pitching, by Season and Career

Angels Season Statistics (by year)

1903 — 1st Place (133–78)
Manager, Cap Dillon

		G	AB	AVG	HR	RBI
1B	Cap Dillon	190	752	.364	3	*
2B	George Wheeler	198	757	.226	1	*
3B	Jud Smith	198	790	.290	1	*
SS	Jim Toman	172	594	.224	1	*
OF	Gavvy Cravath	209	804	.274	7	*
OF	Dummy Hoy	212	808	.257	0	*
OF	Art Ross	198	747	.288	2	*
C	Heinie Spies	184	641	.251	1	*

		G	IP	W-L	ERA	SHO
P	Rusty Hall	53	468	32–19	*	7
P	Doc Newton	49	411	34–13	*	5
P	Dolly Gray	51	406	23–20	*	2
P	Joe Corbett	41	347	23–16	*	8
P	Vianello Drinkwater	21	169	10–8	*	2
P	George Wheeler	12	75	8–1	*	2

1904 — 2nd Place (119–97)
Manager, Tim Flood

		G	AB	AVG	HR	RBI
1B	Hal Chase	190	702	.279	2	*
2B	Tim Flood	209	784	.270	2	*
3B	Jud Smith	193	740	.272	0	*
SS	Jim Toman	193	697	.222	0	*
OF	Gavvy Cravath	211	769	.270	13	*
OF	Curt Bernard	195	754	.308	1	*

*Not tabulated in this year
**Record with more than one team

		G	AB	AVG	HR	RBI
OF	Art Ross	196	680	.251	2	*
C	Heinie Spies	175	597	.219	1	*
UTL	Bobby Eager	84	215	.228	0	*

		G	IP	W-L	ERA	SHO
P	Doc Newton	60	478	39-16	*	11
P	Dolly Gray	55	439	24-22	*	3
P	Spider Baum	53	404	25-22	*	4
P	Rusty Hall	46	347	16-23	*	3
P	Oscar Jones	12	93	6-3	*	0

1905 — 1st Place (120–94)
Manager, Cap Dillon

		G	AB	AVG	HR	RBI
1B	Cap Dillon	216	778	.271	2	*
2B	Tim Flood	188	716	.243	5	*
3B	Jud Smith	198	752	.249	3	*
SS	Kitty Brashear	189	653	.303	4	*
OF	Gavvy Cravath	204	703	.259	9	*
OF	Curt Bernard	193	736	.246	2	*
OF	Art Ross	208	725	.241	0	*
C	Heinie Spies	127	395	.190	0	*
C	Bobby Eager	122	381	.194	0	*
UTL	Jim Toman	96	323	.173	0	*

		G	IP	W-L	ERA	SHO
P	Spider Baum	57	445	27-28	*	9
P	Dolly Gray	52	419	27-16	*	9
P	Bill Tozer	39	343	22-16	*	10
P	Rusty Hall	41	330	18-14	*	3
P	Bunny Goodwin	26	167	9-9	*	1
P	Walter Nagle	14	118	11-0	*	1

1906 — 4th Place (93–91)
Manager, Cap Dillon

		G	AB	AVG	HR	RBI
1B	Cap Dillon	156	555	.297	0	*
2B	Jim Toman	162	587	.189	2	*
3B	Walt Mcclelland	127	428	.171	1	*
SS	Bert Delmas	182	661	.233	3	*
OF	Gavvy Cravath	177	633	.270	6	*
OF	Curt Bernard	170	645	.276	0	*
OF	Rube Ellis	145	489	.204	1	*
C	Bobby Eager	116	378	.209	0	*
C	Jack Bliss	107	371	.226	6	*
2B	Kitty Brashear	67	238	.324	2	*

		G	IP	W-L	ERA	SHO
P	Fred Bergmann	53	425	25-22	*	8
P	Bill Burns	35	293	16-16	*	3
P	Red Randolph	39	326	22-14**	*	5**

		G	IP	W-L	ERA	SHO
P	Johnny Hopkins	39	306	13–21**	*	1
P	Walter Nagle	27	214	9–16	*	3
P	Rusty Hall	20	164	5–14**	*	0
P	Bill Tozer	10	82	7–2	*	1
P	Dolly Gray	9	79	7–2	*	0

1907 — 1st Place (115–74)
Manager, Cap Dillon

		G	AB	AVG	HR	RBI
1B	Cap Dillon	181	631	.304	5	*
2B	Kitty Brashear	159	581	.270	0	*
3B	Jud Smith	118	432	,243	0	*
SS	Bert Delmas	175	604	.227	2	*
OF	Gavvy Cravath	182	614	.303	10	*
OF	Walter Carlisle	179	648	.259	14	*
OF	Rube Ellis	171	578	.239	4	*
C	Hap Hogan	117	375	.168	1	*
C	Bobby Eager	97	282	.202	0	*
2B-OF	Curt Bernard	141	539	.271	0	*
UTL	Walter Nagle	69	213	.249	0	*

		G	IP	W-L	ERA	SHO
P	Dolly Gray	51	421	34–14	*	8
P	Bill Burns	45	365	24–17	*	7
P	Fred Carnes	41	329	16–19**	*	5**
P	Red Randolph	41	320	20–17**	*	4**
P	Walter Nagle	34	266	16–13	*	6
P	Franz Hosp	23	191	12–7	*	2
P	Fred Bergmann	13	90	5–5	*	0

1908 — 1st Place (110–78)
Manager, Cap Dillon

		G	AB	AVG	HR	RBI
1B	Cap Dillon	168	629	.271	7	-
2B	Curt Bernard	129	507	.272	1	-
3B	Jud Smith	161	612	.239	0	-
SS	Bert Delmas	177	624	.248	2	-
OF	Rebel Oakes	192	736	.288	0	-
OF	Rube Ellis	184	646	.269	5	-
OF	Kitty Brashear	156	537	.259	2	-
C	Ted Easterly	123	376	.309	3	-
C	Hap Hogan	99	275	.164	0	-
UTL	Walter Nagle	62	184	.179	0	-

		G	IP	W-L	ERA	SHO
P	Dolly Gray	46	386	26–11	*	6
P	Franz Hosp	36	334	22–14	*	4
P	Walter Nagle	37	301	24–10	*	8
P	Bob Koestner	38	283	11–23	*	1
P	Andy Briswalter	18	157	13–5	*	1
P	Bull Thorsen	17	100	6–3	*	0
P	Red Randolph	12	96	5–7	*	0

1909 — 3rd Place (118–97)
Manager, Cap Dillon

		G	AB	AVG	HR	RBI
1B	Cap Dillon	119	416	.243	1	*
2B	Ivan Howard	171	596	.240	5	*
3B	Jud Smith	212	754	.223	3	*
SS	Bert Delmas	215	740	.243	8	*
OF	Bunny Godwin	191	687	.224	0	*
OF	Pete Daley	198	682	.264	2	*
OF	Johnny Beall	181	626	.289	6	*
OF	Art Ross	126	404	.233	0	*
C	Jess Orndorff	156	449	.171	2	*
UTL	George Wheeler	141	428	250	2	*

		G	IP	W-L	ERA	SHO
P	Bill Tozer	45	382	30–12	*	7
P	Bob Koestner	40	317	19–16	*	5
P	Walter Nagle	34	292	20–10	*	5
P	Bull Thorsen	37	275	13–19	*	0
P	Franz Hosp	30	257	16–14	*	4
P	Andy Briswalter	27	196	12–12	*	4

1910 — 5th Place (100–122)
Manager, Cap Dillon

		G	AB	AVG	HR	RBI
1B	Cap Dillon	189	629	.238	2	*
2B	Ivan Howard	206	748	.241	6	*
3B	Bill Roth	124	431	.225	0	*
SS	Bert Delmas	212	663	.226	3	*
OF	Frank Murphy	190	670	.228	1	*
OF	Pete Daley	224	831	.262	2	*
OF	Curt Bernard	187	642	.257	2	*
C	Kid Smith	122	330	.170	1	*
C	Jess Orndorff	95	250	.172	0	*
C	Ted Waring	61	155	.213	0	*
INF	Eddie Hallinan	104	358	.201	0	*
UTL	George Wheeler	91	249	.193	3	*
P-OF	Walter Nagle	55	150	.240	1	*

		G	IP	W-L	ERA	SHO
P	Walter Nagle	51	401	25–16	*	8
P	Bill Tozer	42	363	18–22	*	2
P	Bull Thorsen	43	319	16–20	*	3
P	Elmer Criger	38	291	11–23	*	
P	Roy Castleton	27	201	8–15	*	3
P	Flame Delhi	25	193	10–10	*	2
P	Andy Briswalter	15	109	6–7	*	2

1911 — 6th Place (82–137)
Manager, Cap Dillon

		G	AB	AVG	HR	RBI
1B	Cap Dillon	172	580	.253	3	*
2B	Charlie Moore	143	526	.298	2	*

		G	AB	AVG	HR	RBI
3B	George Metzger	198	735	.253	1	*
SS	Bert Delmas	163	570	.254	1	*
INF	Roy Akin	123	464	.244	0	*
OF	Ivan Howard	168	646	.251	7	*
OF	Pete Daley	194	708	.302	5	*
OF	Heinie Heitmuller	78	300	.343	4	*
OF	Ty Lober	63	316	.171	1	*
OF	Curt Bernard	69	238	.303	0	*
OF-C	Kid Smith	135	424	.212	2	*
C	Pete Abbott	110	307	.215	1	*

		G	IP	W-L	ERA	SHO
P	Flame Delhi	56	446	27–23	*	2
P	Elmer Criger	35	224	8–17	*	7
P	Jim Agnew	33	220	5–20	*	0
P	Walt Leverenz	30	194	10–12	*	0
P	Jack Halla	30	152	11–15	*	2
P	Bill Tozer	13	86	4–5	*	0
P	Bob Couchman	13	73	2–6	*	0
P	Bull Thorson	10	72	2–7	*	0

1912 — 3rd Place (110–930)
Manager, Cap Dillon

		G	AB	AVG	HR	RBI
1B	Cap Dillon	121	368	.293	1	*
2B	Ivan Howard	184	742	.284	11	*
3B	George Metzger	181	612	.240	2	*
SS	Joel Berger	197	722	.278	7	*
INF	Billy Page	102	321	.287	0	*
INF	Charlie Moore	94	317	.290	1	*
OF	Heinie Heitmuller	151	556	.335	15	*
OF	Pete Daley	174	639	.332	2	*
OF	Ty Lober	154	508	.244	1	*
OF	Babe Driscoll	94	302	.235	0	*
OF	John Core	95	265	.283	0	*
C	Clarence Brooks	105	262	.286	0	*
C	Walter Boles	97	299	.231	0	*

		G	IP	W-L	ERA	SHO
P	Charlie Chech	48	360	25–14	*	3
P	Walt Leverenz	52	334	23–13	*	7
P	Bill Tozer	38	262	16–14	*	2
P	Walt Slagle	42	265	16–17	*	3
P	Jack Halla	37	236	10–12	*	2
P	Walter Nagle	22	107	8–6	*	1
P	Jack Flater	14	70	3–2	*	0
P	Pol Perritt	11	70	3–6	*	0

1913 — 5th Place (100–108)
Manager, Cap Dillon

		G	AB	AVG	HR	RBI
1B	Charlie Moore	131	490	.259	2	*
2B	Billy Page	186	716	.254	1	*

		G	AB	AVG	HR	RBI
3B	George Metzger	125	382	.196	0	*
SS	Ernie Johnson	177	602	.266	4	*
INF	Pop Goodwin	104	290	.276	1	*
OF	Harl Maggert	204	715	.316	13	*
OF	Rube Ellis	183	648	.275	8	*
OF	Ivan Howard	204	770	.265	9	*
OF	Art Kruger	154	540	.230**	1	*
OF	Mike Wottell	77	193	.207	1	*
C	Walter Boles	86	268	.231	0	*
C	Carl Arbogast	71	205	.195	2	*
C	Clarence Brooks	50	126	.262	0	*

		G	IP	W-L	ERA	SHO
P	Pol Perritt	51	342	20–19	*	6
P	Jack Ryan	39	307	17–17	*	3
P	Charlie Chech	43	305	18–20	*	2
P	Bill Tozer	38	254	15–16	*	2
P	Walt Slagle	35	227	12–12	*	3
P	Roy Crabbe	41	204	10–10	*	3
P	Howie Gregory	18	92	4–7	*	0

1914 — 2ND PLACE (116–94)
MANAGER — CAP DILLON

		G	AB	AVG	HR	RBI
1B	Bill Abstein	202	769	.308	1	108
2B	Billy Page	148	486	.237	1	52
3B	George Metzger	186	656	.239	0	61
SS	Ernie Johnson	165	581	.289	4	67
INF	Charlie Moore	129	393	.239	0	32
IOF	Harry Wolter	203	802	.328	8	76
IOF	Rube Ellis	208	756	.310	6	120
IOF	Harl Maggert	203	754	.288	3	82
IOF	Harry Harper	70	132	.288	0	21
C	Walter Boles	113	318	.242	1	24
C	Clarence Brooks	107	283	.244	1	31
C	Dad Meek	98	172	.308	2	20

		G	IP	W-L	ERA	SHO
P	Jack Ryan	45	342	24–11	1.84	6
P	Tom Hughes	46	348	24–16	1.91	4
P	Pol Perritt	42	295	17–14	2.26	2
P	Slim Love	37	183	10–9	2.46	2
P	Howard Ehmke	40	232	12–11	2.79	3
P	Charlie Chech	46	297	20–16	2.88	3
P	Paul Musser	35	166	8–12	3.46	4

1915 — 3RD PLACE (110–98)
MANAGER — CAP DILLON

		G	AB	AVG	HR	RBI
1B	Phil Koerner	158	529	.318	8**	*
1B	Bill Abstein	57	219	.192	0	*
2B	Fred Mcmullin	184	681	.279	1	*

		G	AB	AVG	HR	RBI
3B	George Metzger	144	397	.171	1	*
SS	Zeb Terry	191	648	.264	1	*
INF	Al Buemiller	135	381	.228	2	*
IOF	Harry Wolter	150	518	.359	5	*
IOF	Rube Ellis	200	705	.271	5	*
IOF	Harl Maggert	201	736	.307	12	*
IOF	Harry Harper	67	192	.286	2	*
C	Walter Boles	136	425	.289	0	*
C	Clarence Brooks	81	232	.267	0	*

		G	IP	W-L	ERA	SHO
P	Slim Love	59	359	23–15	1.95	4
P	Jack Ryan	60	373	26–21	2.72	5
P	Bill Burns	59	274	14–15	2.79	3**
P	Tom Hughes	45	279	19–16	3.03	1
P	Pol Perritt	38	185	9–12	3.06	2
P	Jim Scoggins	48	244	12–9	3.10	3
P	Charlie Chech	34	228	12–14	3.28	1**

1916 — 1st Place (119–79)
Manager — Frank Chance

		G	AB	AVG	HR	RBI
1B	Phil Koerner	197	720	.276	3	*
2B	Polly Mclarry	168	553	.293	5	*
3B	Jim Galloway	153	544	.244	9	*
SS	Bobby Davis	188	618	.265	3**	*
INF	Johnny Butler	122	380	.184	1**	*
IOF	Harry Wolter	173	615	.296	6	*
IOF	Rube Ellis	197	755	.254	2	*
IOF	Harl Maggert	182	672	.274	6	*
IOF	Charlie Jackson	52	125	.184	0	*
C	Johnny Bassler	124	349	.304	0	*
C	Walter Boles	101	307	.287	2	*

		G	IP	W-L	ERA	SHO
P	Jack Ryan	48	350	29–10	2.19	5
P	Zip Zabel	44	272	17–13	2.38	3
P	Pete Standridge	44	267	20–10	2.53	4
P	Oscar Horstman	44	272	11–14	2.56	4
P	Brad Hogg	42	232	16–9	2.64	3
P	Doc Crandall	17	108	5–5	2.90	1
P	Charlie Hall	22	129	6–6	3.37	2
P	Jim Scoggins	31	144	11–8	3.70	1

1917 — 2nd Place (116–94)
Manager — Frank Chance/Wade Killefer

		G	AB	AVG	HR	RBI
1B	Jack Fournier	144	512	.305	7	*
2B	Duke Kenworthy	142	510	.302	1	*
3B	Bobby Davis	169	511	.213	1	*
SS	Zeb Terry	150	509	.251	0	*
IOF	Irish Meusel	210	811	.311	7	*

		G	AB	AVG	HR	RBI
IOF	Wade Killefer	171	594	.295	0	*
IOF	Rube Ellis	179	616	.273	4**	*
C	Walter Boles	133	428	.266	6	*
C	Johnny Bassler	94	264	.284	0	*

		G	IP	W-L	ERA	SHO
P	Brad Hogg	47	335	27–13	2.23	3
P	Doc Crandall	49	364	26–15	2.77	4
P	Curly Brown	48	309	18–14	2.80	4
P	Tom Seaton	22	129	8–8	2.93	3
P	Jack Ryan	29	129	12–11	2.94	0
P	Charlie Hall	49	313	14–19	3.04	2
P	Pete Standridge	30	196	10–13	3.90	1

1918 — 2ND PLACE (57–47)
MANAGER — WADE KILLEFER

		G	AB	AVG	HR	RBI
1B	Jack Fournier	104	400	.325	4	*
2B	Wade Killefer	99	387	.295	0	*
3B	Joe Pepe	93	316	.237	1	*
SS	Zeb Terry	94	342	.263	0	*
INF	Johnny Butler	37	128	.258	0	*
IOF	Claude Cooper	72	248	.270	1	*
IOF	Rube Ellis	104	366	.270	1	*
IOF	Sam Crawford	96	356	.289	1	*
C	Walter Boles	78	266	.256	0	*
C	Pete Lapan	51	123	.252	0	*

		G	IP	W-L	ERA	SHO
P	Curly Brown	22	173	12–7	1.51	5
P	Doc Crandall	27	222	16–9	1.90	3
P	Ralph Valencia	21	88	1–6	2.15	1
P	Bill Pertica	23	180	12–7	2.30	4
P	Paul Fittery	25	209	11–13	2.63	4
P	Pete Standridge	15	80	5–5	2.94	1
P	Charlie Chech	34	228	12–14	3.28	1

1919 — 2ND PLACE (108–72)
MANAGER — WADE KILLEFER

		G	AB	AVG	HR	RBI
1B	Jack Fournier	169	638	.328	11	*
2B	Bill Kenworthy	119	458	.222	2	*
3B	Bert Niehoff	110	385	.221	2	*
SS	Bunny Fabrique	130	502	.239	0	*
INF	Karl Crandall	28	106	.273	2	*
INF	Fred Haney	43	103	.252	0	*
LF	Rube Ellis	176	616	.258	3	*
CF	Wade Killefer	168	691	.320	5	*
RF	Sam Crawford	173	664	.360	14	*
IOF	Ray Bates	92	301	.279	2	*
IOF	Maurice Schick	29	110	.273	2	*

Appendix C: Individual Batting and Pitching, by Season and Career

		G	AB	AVG	HR	RBI
C	Walter Boles	78	273	.223	2	*
C	Johnny Bassler	78	259	.274	1	*
C	Pete Lapan	41	139	.295	1	*

		G	IP	W-L	ERA	SHO
P	Curly Brown	39	314	25–8	2.03	3
P	Doc Crandall	47	355	28–10	2.41	3
P	Vic Aldridge	31	221	15–10	2.89	1
P	Paul Fittery	47	301	18–20	3.02	2
P	Bill Pertica	50	306	17–20	3.23	2
P	Toots Schultz	29	107	5–4	4.38	0

1920 — 4TH PLACE (101–95)
MANAGER — WADE KILLEFER

		G	AB	AVG	HR	RBI
1B	Art Griggs	94	373	.306	2	*
2B	Karl Crandall	168	572	.250	2	*
3B	Bert Niehoff	154	548	.250	3	*
SS	Jimmy Mcauley	168	572	.255	3	*
INF	Rollie Zeider	102	373	.247	0	*
INF	Tex Mcdonald	48	177	.226	1	*
LF	Rube Ellis	176	619	.249	3	*
CF	Wade Killefer	187	730	.286	0	*
RF	Sam Crawford	187	719	.332	12	*
IOF	Jigger Statz	101	386	.236	0	*
C	Johnny Bassler	147	454	.319	1	*
C	Pete Lapan	90	279	.219	0	*

		G	IP	W-L	ERA	SHO
P	Bill Pertica	46	296	15–13	2.82	2
P	Vic Aldridge	39	296	18–15	2.88	3
P	Doc Crandall	38	277	15–13	2.92	1
P	Claude Thomas	49	304	21–19	3.02	1
P	Ray Keating	37	292	18–14	3.03	0
P	Curly Brown	33	228	7–14	3.35	0
P	Tom Hughes	23	94	7–4	3.63	1

1921 — 1ST PLACE (108–80)
MANAGER — WADE KILLEFER

		G	AB	AVG	HR	RBI
1B	Art Griggs	177	678	.294	10	119
2B	Bert Niehoff	179	646	.293	11	87
3B	Howard Lindimore	132	457	.269	1	21
SS	Jimmy Mcauley	177	665	.299	0	53
INF	Bill Mccabe	85	254	.315	1	19
LF	Dixie Carroll	180	686	.292	3	93
CF	Jigger Statz	153	584	.310	2	34
RF	Sam Crawford	175	626	.318	9	103
IOF	Wade Killefer	103	349	.272	1	28
C	Earl Baldwin	108	339	.242	1	19
C	Oscar Stanage	96	323	.279	0	17

		G	IP	W-L	ERA	SHO
P	Vic Aldridge	33	283	20–10	2.16	1
P	Nick Dumovich	34	148	8–7	2.61	0
P	Tom Hughes	36	241	14–14	2.84	1
P	Art Reinhart	36	233	15–5	3.05	3
P	Doc Crandall	40	328	24–13	3.13	3
P	Claude Thomas	42	225	12–17	3.52	1
P	George Lyons	41	232	14–14	3.92	2

1922 — 3RD PLACE (111–88)
MANAGER — WADE KILLEFER

		G	AB	AVG	HR	RBI
1B	Art Griggs	175	639	.338	20	129
2B	Howard Lindimore	190	672	.271	1	71
3B	Charlie Deal	168	667	.331	6	87
SS	Jimmy Mcauley	181	639	.213	0	34
INF	Clyde Beck	46	136	.279	0	10
LF	Dixie Carroll	186	710	.297	3	63
CF	Bill Mccabe	183	722	.291	7	84
RF	Clarence Twombly	178	671	.300	2	79
IOF	Wade Killefer	53	139	.295	0	10
IOF	Vern Spencer	39	158	.203	0	2
IOF	John Sullivan	38	117	.291	1	12
C	Tom Daley	124	412	.294	0	45
C	Earl Baldwin	91	323	.266	1	35
C	Tony Rego	33	98	.255	0	1

		G	IP	W-L	ERA	SHO
P	Elmer Ponder	16	122	10–2	2.14	4
P	Nick Dumovich	45	294	20–11	2.36	2
P	George Lyons	40	333	17–17	2.70	6
P	Claude Thomas	45	263	18–11	2.98	0
P	Tom Hughes	31	231	17–9	3.08	0
P	Doc Crandall	37	269	17–19	3.65	2
P	Herb Mcquaid	27	88	3–3	3.78	0
P	Bob Wallace	33	159	7–10	4.03	0
P	Ken Douglas	17	52	1–5	4.15	1

1923 — 6TH PLACE (93–109)
MANAGER — WADE KILLEFER/MARTY KRUG 3/21/23

		G	AB	AVG	HR	RBI
1B	Art Griggs	153	495	.329	21	88
2B	Walt Golvin	118	327	.248	2	45
3B	Charlie Deal	94	349	.316	4	49
3B	Red Smith	67	235	.328	3	21
SS	Jimmy Mcauley	179	668	.238	1	47
INF	Howard Lindimore	121	407	.290	4	35
LF	Bill Mccabe	173	674	.286	6	82
CF	Wally Hood	193	745	.340	21	128
RF	Clarence Twombly	195	781	.332	5	74
IOF	Dixie Carroll	79	190	.316	2	17
C	Earl Baldwin	101	307	.293	0	33

Appendix C: Individual Batting and Pitching, by Season and Career

		G	AB	AVG	HR	RBI
C	Butch Byler	77	231	.247	0	26
C	Tony Rego	41	114	.281	1	13

		G	IP	W-L	ERA	SHO
P	Doc Crandall	30	258	17–12	3.10	0
P	George Lyons	37	269	18–16	3.41	3
P	Elmer Ponder	27	172	7–9	3.61	0
P	Percy Jones	44	267	16–17	3.88	1
P	Claude Thomas	50	247	9–15	3.94	2
P	Tom Hughes	36	235	14–16	4.29	1
P	Bob Wallace	46	205	9–18	5.71	0

1924 — 2nd Place (107–92)
Manager — Marty Krug

		G	AB	AVG	HR	RBI
1B	Walt Golvin	100	328	.216	2	29
1B	Ray Grimes	65	247	.320	4	46
2B	Marty Krug	133	456	.265	2	65
3B	Ray Jacobs	147	517	.276	9	76
SS	Clyde Beck	148	482	.268	6	53
INF	Jimmy Mcauley	154	514	.276	3	48
LF	Wally Hood	195	757	.338	22	184
CF	Cedric Durst	185	705	.342	17	130
RF	Clarence Twombly	134	471	.312	2	46
IOF	Bill Whaley	179	704	.328	2	82
IOF	Walton Cruise	67	151	.318	5	23
C	Joe Jenkins	89	278	.263	6	51
C	Ed Spencer	61	217	.281	3	27
C	Butch Byler	50	137	.241	0	13
C	Josh Billings	29	97	.227	0	9

		G	IP	W-L	ERA	SHO
P	Doc Crandall	34	256	19–11	2.71	1
P	George Payne	48	315	21–13	2.83	1
P	Buck Ramsey	45	143	7–3	2.89	0
P	Charlie Root	55	322	21–16	3.69	4
P	Elmer Myers	43	260	15–17	4.61	0
P	Tom Hughes	31	208	12–14	4.67	1
P	Phil Weinert	21	63	2–3	5.28	0
P	Nick Dumovich	40	158	9–12	6.15	1

1925 — 4th Place (105–93)
Manager — Marty Krug

		G	AB	AVG	HR	RBI
1B	Ray Grimes	167	623	.294	6	104
2B	Clyde Beck	188	668	.272	17	104
3B	Marty Krug	141	490	.294	6	59
SS	Ray Jacobs	150	539	.310	13	75
INF	Bill Whaley	155	464	.258	0	56
INF	Jimmy Mcauley	93	331	.205	1	22
LF	Wally Hood	195	758	.327	27	157
CF	Jigger Statz	130	545	.264	2	45

		G	AB	AVG	HR	RBI
RF	Clarence Twombly	182	656	.329	1	75
IOF	Joe Horan	64	214	.262	3	42
IOF	Doug Taitt	63	143	.266	1	18
C	Gus Sandberg	135	471	.231	2	55
C	Russ Ennis	58	181	.238	0	18
C	Ed Spencer	41	109	.273	1	10

		G	IP	W–L	ERA	SHO
P	Elmer Phillips	21	47	1–2	1.91	0
P	Elmer Jacobs	15	121	9–5	2.75	1
P	Charlie Root	52	324	25–13	2.87	5
P	Doc Crandall	39	239	20–7	3.46	0
P	Tom Hughes	23	89	5–4	3.94	0
P	George Payne	54	310	18–19	4.00	1
P	Wayne Wright	37	229	10–16	4.29	0
P	Whitey Glazner	41	259	14–18	4.31	1
P	George Milstead	27	73	2–4	5.62	0

1926 — 1st Place (121–81)
Manager — Marty Krug

		G	AB	AVG	HR	RBI
1B	Ray Jacobs	178	580	.255	22	102
2B	Ed Hemingway	172	628	.278	0	64
3B	Frank Brazill	179	551	.336	19	111
SS	John Mitchell	183	561	.264	0	83
INF	Marty Krug	52	131	.390	2	29
LF	Art Jahn	175	623	.337	8	118
CF	Jigger Statz	199	823	.354	4	59
RF	Art Weis	157	543	.317	7	80
OF/1B	Wally Hood	170	502	.301	13	82
C	Truck Hannah	131	389	.237	4	55
C	Gus Sandberg	79	234	.226	2	18

		G	IP	W–L	ERA	SHO
P	Elmer Phillips	13	62	3–2	1.89	0
P	Elmer Jacobs	40	278	20–12	2.20	3
P	Doc Crandall	33	245	20–8	2.20	4
P	Earl Hamilton	40	279	24–8	2.48	5
P	Wayne Wright	31	222	19–7	3.08	4
P	Clyde Day	41	160	6–11	3.65	1
P	Ralph Stroud	17	79	1–2	3.87	0
P	Whitey Glazner	39	209	11–15	3.88	0
P	Byron Yarrison	32	176	13–8	4.09	3
P	Les Holmes	15	57	1–4	5.69	0

1927 — 8th Place (80–116)
Manager — Marty Krug

		G	AB	AVG	HR	RBI
1B	Ray Jacobs	97	359	.323	13	64
2B	Gale Staley	159	563	.318	1	64
3B	Frank Brazill	148	545	.327	21	76

Appendix C: Individual Batting and Pitching, by Season and Career 219

		G	AB	AVG	HR	RBI
SS	John Mitchell	128	381	.215	0	34
INF	Ed Hemingway	95	322	.295	1	31
INF	Marty Krug	58	173	.266	0	19
INF	Jack Kahn	47	167	.192	2	17
LF	Art Jahn	187	682	.343	17	146
CF	Art Weis	161	527	.317	13	77
RF	Dick Cox	168	618	.345	11	50
OF/1B	Wally Hood	174	600	.298	17	116
IOF	Wes Schulmerich	31	115	.322	0	14
C	Gus Sandberg	124	344	.273	2	60
C	Truck Hannah	114	317	.265	7	37

		G	IP	W-L	ERA	SHO
P	Harry Sanders	18	56	1–3	3.42	0
P	Tex Weathersby	51	293	16–18	4.45	0
P	Wayne Wright	33	227	13–11	4.56	0
P	Bruce Cunningham	42	175	9–10	4.57	0
P	Bill Piercy	45	267	17–20	4.68	0
P	Will Peters	37	212	8–13	4.69	1
P	Hal Gardner	21	71	4–5	5.19	0
P	Earl Hamilton	30	145	7–16	5.46	1
P	Al Smith	31	75	2–4	5.52	0
P	Ray Moss	13	46	1–6	8.64	0

1928 — SPLIT SEASON:
5TH PLACE (48–44), 7TH PLACE (39–60) 87–104
MANAGER — MARTY KRUG

		G	AB	AVG	HR	RBI
1B	Charlie Tolson	149	501	.351	28	108
2B	Gale Staley	157	608	.301	2	51
3B	Bobby Jones	162	594	.296	1	55
SS	Carl Dittmar	180	626	.254	2	63
INF	Howard Burkett	110	357	.260	2	30
INF	Ray Jacobs	36	111	.207	0	11
LF	Wally Berger	138	535	.327	20	94
CF	Wes Schulmerich	192	717	.317	19	56
RF	Wally Hood	167	599	.290	20	106
IOF	Carson Bigbee	92	258	.252	6	16
IOF	Woody Jensen	47	150	.246	1	16
C	Truck Hannah	97	262	.271	3	27
C	Gus Sandberg	82	221	.231	2	29
C	Dallas Warren	43	122	.275	2	13

		G	IP	W-L	ERA	SHO
P	Will Peters	48	246	14–11	3.62	2
P	Clyde Barfoot	44	311	20–19	3.84	2
P	Bruce Cunningham	51	277	17–13	4.23	3
P	Wayne Wright	20	104	5–8	4.32	0
P	Glen Gabler	27	80	1–4	4.84	0
P	Tex Weathersby	43	212	12–18	5.01	2
P	Norm Plitt	41	236	12–19	5.11	1
P	Bob Osborn	26	120	5–9	5.70	0

1929 — SPLIT SEASON:
5TH PLACE (47–52), 3RD PLACE (57–46) 104–98
MANAGER — MARTY KRUG/JACK LELIVELT 7/5/29

		G	AB	AVG	HR	RBI
1B	Charlie Tolson	134	487	.359	28	122
2B	Ray Jacobs	178	591	.332	20	118
3B	Bobby Jones	135	441	.281	2	58
SS	Carl Dittmar	154	505	.303	5	43
INF	Fred Haney	150	586	.292	1	51
INF	Johnny Butler	60	169	.266	2	29
LF	Wally Berger	199	744	.335	40	166
CF	Jigger Statz	195	799	.308	3	75
RF	Earl Webb	188	658	.357	37	164
IOF	Wes Schulmerich	134	360	.328	19	77
C	Gus Sandberg	131	377	.289	7	55
C	Dallas Warren	95	202	.272	6	31
C	Truck Hannah	67	136	.213	1	15

		G	IP	W-L	ERA	SHO
P	Ed Baecht	29	180	14–7	3.44	3
P	Clyde Barfoot	42	236	18–12	4.53	3
P	Norm Plitt	39	200	10–11	4.63	0
P	Augie Walsh	48	294	21–14	4.83	0
P	Will Peters	49	156	7–8	5.07	0
P	Red Roberts	48	225	10–14	5.32	0
P	Berlyn Horne	9	49	5–4	6.06	0
P	Carl Holling	38	163	8–13	6.07	0
P	Harry Chesley	34	98	4–5	6.52	0

1930 — SPLIT SEASON:
1ST PLACE (57–42), 2ND PLACE (56–42) 113–84
MANAGER — JACK LELIVELT

		G	AB	AVG	HR	RBI
1B	Ray Jacobs	196	710	.304	20	130
2B	Frank Sigafoos	165	702	.365	19	103
3B	Fred Haney	180	673	.312	7	80
SS	Carl Dittmar	166	622	.310	14	125
INF	Art Parker	88	204	289	0	26
LF	Wes Schulmerich	189	692	.380	28	130
CF	Jigger Statz	161	558	.360	5	84
RF	George Harper	160	546	.308	8	97
IOF	Johnny Moore	142	546	.342	26	101
C	Truck Hannah	125	329	.267	4	48
C	Dallas Warren	83	205	.224	6	30
C	Bill Skiff	62	149	.215	0	13

		G	IP	W-L	ERA	SHO
P	Ed Baecht	49	364	26–12	3.23	4
P	Win Ballou	44	238	16–7	3.77	3
P	Art Delaney	39	278	13–19	3.91	1
P	Berlyn Horne	31	175	13–7	4.47	0
P	Carroll Yerkes	25	141	12–7	4.66	2

		G	IP	W-L	ERA	SHO
P	Clyde Barfoot	36	186	12–10	5.03	0
P	Will Peters	48	172	12–14	5.07	1
P	Augie Walsh	32	85	6–4	6.99	1

1931 — SPLIT SEASON:
5TH PLACE (43–47), 2ND PLACE (55–42) 98–89
MANAGER — JACK LELIVELT

		G	AB	AVG	HR	RBI
1B	Ray Jacobs	124	386	.298	18	73
1B	George Burns	88	359	.327	11	72
2B	Loris Baker	150	556	.273	8	71
3B	Doc Farrell	185	727	.327	11	127
SS	Carl Dittmar	139	470	.285	8	95
INF	Fred Haney	85	335	.301	3	37
INF	Art Parker	54	129	.271	1	8
LF	Homer Summa	187	754	.341	4	89
CF	Jigger Statz	184	748	.332	6	107
RF	Vince Barton	83	334	.302	17	67
IOF	Johnny Moore	80	317	.366	6	69
C	Gilly Campbell	113	261	.306	10	56
C	John Schulte	101	240	.283	5	33
C	Truck Hannah	71	204	.265	0	28

		G	IP	W-L	ERA	SHO
P	Win Ballou	48	286	24–13	3.71	3
P	Leroy Herrmann	47	251	20–11	4.08	1
P	Jess Petty	41	267	15–16	4.51	0
P	Malcolm Moss	44	243	15–14	4.55	1
P	Lynn Nelson	39	163	5–9	5.85	0
P	Carroll Yerkes	25	87	2–4	5.90	0
P	Will Peters	32	68	2–6	6.09	0
P	Hal Stitzel	16	72	5–4	6.37	0
P	Al Shealy	32	109	4–8	6.60	0

1932 — 5TH PLACE (96–93)
MANAGER — JACK LELIVELT

		G	AB	AVG	HR	RBI
1B	Earl Sheely	117	417	.319	11	102
1B	Jim Oglesby	64	261	.323	5	61
2B	Loris Baker	141	527	.262	1	39
3B	Fred Haney	149	617	.300	6	62
3B	Gene Lillard	40	141	.312	5	28
SS	Carl Dittmar	174	583	.299	4	78
INF	Bernie Deviveiros	72	217	.217	2	24
INF	Footsie Blair	46	138	.232	2	23
LF	Homer Summa	134	543	.297	0	64
CF	Jigger Statz	188	737	.347	6	93
RF	Mike Kreevich	162	561	.294	15	70
IOF	Tuck Stainback	124	433	.356	10	91
C	Gilly Campbell	153	498	.319	9	93
C	Bill Cronin	78	199	.216	0	24

		G	IP	W-L	ERA	SHO
P	Leroy Herrmann	32	211	21–7	3.71	3
P	Win Ballou	55	305	18–21	4.36	2
P	Ed Baecht	44	258	12–14	4.58	0
P	Malcolm Moss	40	148	11–8	4.70	2
P	Hal Stitzel	46	256	13–17	4.72	0
P	Charlie Moncrief	33	160	6–12	4.83	1
P	Dick Ward	9	61	4–3	4.85	0
P	Les Sweetland	28	102	6–8	6.28	0

1933 — 1st Place (114–73)
Manager — Jack Lelivelt

		G	AB	AVG	HR	RBI
1B	Jim Oglesby	186	723	.313	20	137
2B	Jimmie Reese	104	393	.330	5	38
3B	Gene Lillard	183	645	.307	43	149
SS	Carl Dittmar	149	478	.264	5	49
INF	Mike Gazella	83	235	.264	7	47
INF	Orv Mohler	58	188	.303	6	35
LF	Marv Gudat	183	741	.333	10	113
CF	Jigger Statz	182	767	.325	10	73
RF	Tuck Stainback	187	789	.335	19	148
C	Hugh Mcmullen	134	400	.268	11	59
C	Bill Cronin	82	254	.303	2	31

		G	IP	W-L	ERA	SHO
P	Buck Newsom	56	320	30–11	3.17	7
P	Dick Ward	43	285	25–9	3.25	1
P	Win Ballou	50	217	12–19	3.59	1
P	Fay Thomas	42	300	20–14	3.75	0
P	Leroy Herrmann	29	188	16–9	4.59	0
P	Hal Stitzel	30	105	4–3	4.79	0
P	Emmett Nelson	27	96	3–6	4.86	1

1934 — Split Season:
1st Place (66–18), 1st Place (71–32) 137–50
Manager — Jack Lelivelt

		G	AB	AVG	HR	RBI
1B	Jim Oglesby	188	725	.312	15	139
2B	Jimmie Reese	180	733	.311	3	85
3B	Gene Lillard	171	592	.289	27	119
SS	Carl Dittmar	151	517	.294	3	73
INF	Bob Mattick	53	137	.277	0	10
INF	Mike Gazella	51	116	.190	1	13
LF	Marv Gudat	188	758	.319	4	125
CF	Jigger Statz	183	760	.324	6	66
RF	Frank Demaree	186	702	.383	45	173
C	Gilly Campbell	145	459	.305	17	97
C	Walt Goebel	60	148	.297	2	29

		G	IP	W-L	ERA	SHO
P	Emmett Nelson	29	171	14–5	2.53	3
P	Fay Thomas	41	295	28–4	2.59	3

		G	IP	W-L	ERA	SHO
P	Whitey Campbell	48	243	19–15	2.63	2
P	Dick Ward	20	137	13–4	2.63	2
P	Lou Garland	41	249	21–9	2.67	4
P	Roy Henshaw	38	196	16–4	2.75	4
P	Mike Meola	42	248	20–5	2.90	3
P	Art Mcdougall	23	60	4–2	4.63	0

1935 — Split Season:
1st Place (46–25), 4th Place (52–51) 98–76
Manager — Jack Lelivelt

		G	AB	AVG	HR	RBI
1B	Jim Oglesby	173	678	.350	24	132
2B	Jimmie Reese	155	576	.297	1	66
3B	Gene Lillard	170	642	.361	56	147
SS	Steve Mesner	151	534	.331	13	99
INF	Carl Dittmar	78	215	.260	0	16
INF	Bob Mattick	50	131	.267	0	18
LF	Marv Gudat	176	735	.309	2	65
CF	Jigger Statz	171	716	.330	2	65
RF	Cleo Caryle	173	653	.297	11	100
C	Walt Goebel	95	287	.258	4	36
C	Glyn Gibson	71	180	.194	2	21

		G	IP	W-L	ERA	SHO
P	Mike Meola	39	258	19–8	3.00	3
P	Emmett Nelson	20	121	11–5	3.13	0
P	Lou Garland	36	238	19–11	3.48	4
P	Ralph Buxton	28	134	7–7	3.86	0
P	Glen Gabler	36	151	14–8	4.04	1
P	Whitey Campbell	43	191	13–10	4.15	0
P	Herb Harris	25	100	3–7	4.96	1
P	Newt Kimball	31	169	8–10	5.80	0
P	Keith Frazier	20	71	1–7	6.08	0

1936 — Tied for 5th Place (88–88)
Manager — Jack Lelivelt

		G	AB	AVG	HR	RBI
1B	Don Hurst	155	558	.303	19	113
2B	Jimmie Reese	146	515	.270	0	54
3B	Steve Mesner	176	703	.326	17	132
SS	Carl Dittmar	125	427	.286	1	44
INF	Bob Mattick	73	241	.278	1	30
INF	Glen Russell	73	201	.249	5	33
LF	Cleo Caryle	167	654	.339	3	82
CF	Jigger Statz	158	631	.322	3	62
RF	Wes Schulmerich	142	462	.301	14	85
IOF	Marv Gudat	102	346	.324	1	46
C	John Bottarini	127	393	.295	12	51
C	Jim Steiner	53	129	.202	0	7

		G	IP	W-L	ERA	SHO
P	Jack Salveson	35	251	21–7	2.76	2
P	Fay Thomas	28	206	15–10	3.10	1

		G	IP	W-L	ERA	SHO
P	Joe Berry	32	125	7-7	3.74	0
P	Ray Prim	29	161	13-8	4.47	1
P	Glen Gabler	40	115	7-6	4.69	0
P	Dutch Lieber	34	183	12-12	4.77	1
P	Bob Joyce	33	149	5-13	4.79	0
P	Hugh Casey	19	106	5-8	4.92	1

1937 — 5TH PLACE (90–88)
MANAGER — TRUCK HANNAH

		G	AB	AVG	HR	RBI
1B	Glen Russell	129	407	.278	13	69
1B	Don Hurst	85	284	.271	10	50
2B	Carl Dittmar	72	228	.278	0	17
3B	Steve Mesner	133	505	.329	10	91
SS	Bob Mattick	167	612	.280	2	58
INF	Goldy Holt	82	229	.227	6	36
INF	Kenny Richardson	70	258	.221	7	19
INF	Bill Mcwilliams	54	204	.314	9	31
LF	Marv Gudat	164	621	.332	6	73
CF	Jigger Statz	154	558	.290	2	57
RF	Cleo Carlyle	139	488	.297	7	63
IOF	Bob Hargrave	71	242	.293	3	30
IOF	Murray Howell	46	154	.260	5	26
C	Bob Collins	163	560	.279	13	91

		G	IP	W-L	ERA	SHO
P	Joe Berry	34	266	13-13	2.77	1
P	Jack Salveson	16	73	5-5	3.08	1
P	Fay Thomas	40	294	23-11	3.21	2
P	Ray Prim	39	293	21-14	3.72	2
P	Russ Evans	35	203	11-14	3.99	0
P	Dutch Lieber	38	165	8-10	4.36	0
P	Earl Overman	28	93	5-6	5.32	0
P	Wes Flowers	10	40	2-7	6.53	0
P	Archie Campbell	20	55	1-3	7.85	0

1938 — 1ST PLACE (105–73)
MANAGER — TRUCK HANNAH

		G	AB	AVG	HR	RBI
1B	Glen Russell	178	679	.318	21	114
2B	Eddie Mayo	118	416	.332	5	65
3B	Charlie English	176	709	.303	19	143
SS	Eddie Cihocki	177	646	.248	11	86
INF	Jack Sanford	51	196	.233	2	16
LF	Jack Rothrock	149	516	.287	6	84
CF	Jigger Statz	167	630	.317	2	44
RF	Johnny Moore	140	492	.305	21	86
IOF	Paul Carpenter	91	263	.324	4	35
IOF	Marv Gudat	58	181	.302	2	21
C	Bob Collins	139	484	.253	11	57
C	Hal Sueme	54	139	.176	0	14

		G	IP	W-L	ERA	SHO
P	Dutch Lieber	39	167	10–7	3.18	1
P	Fay Thomas	31	260	18–8	3.29	5
P	Ray Prim	31	230	17–10	3.29	4
P	Joe Berry	39	187	16–10	3.42	3
P	Gene Lillard	29	203	16–10	3.50	2
P	Guy Bush	26	108	8–5	3.93	0
P	Jack Salveson	32	205	12–10	4.13	1
P	Ed Carnett	21	96	3–6	4.15	1
P	Dwight Van Fleet	8	42	2–3	4.64	0
P	Clyde Lahti	13	61	2–3	5.61	1

1939 — 3RD PLACE (97–79)
MANAGER — TRUCK HANNAH

		G	AB	AVG	HR	RBI
1B	Rip Collins	172	586	.334	26	128
2B	Lou Stringer	155	548	.272	16	85
3B	Charlie English	171	660	.279	13	89
SS	Eddie Cihocki	154	564	.280	3	78
INF	Eddie Mayo	127	464	.263	6	61
LF	Jack Rothrock	114	370	.292	5	44
CF	Jigger Statz	145	557	.311	4	62
RF	Johnny Moore	131	491	.301	17	99
IOF	Paul Carpenter	108	340	.229	2	30
IOF	Lou Novikoff	36	135	.452	8	37
C	Bob Collins	144	482	.306	8	52
C	Hal Sueme	58	148	.230	1	19

		G	IP	W-L	ERA	SHO
P	Fay Thomas	35	246	17–13	2.75	5
P	Julio Bonetti	34	238	20–5	3.25	4
P	Dutch Lieber	27	69	4–2	3.39	1
P	Jess Flores	30	173	9–9	3.54	2
P	Ray Prim	39	280	20–17	3.57	2
P	Joe Berry	47	122	8–7	4.43	0
P	Lee Stine	34	208	13–15	5.02	2

1940 — 2ND PLACE (102–75
MANAGER — JIGGER STATZ

		G	AB	AVG	HR	RBI
1B	Rip Collins	174	630	.327	18	111
2B	Lou Stringer	171	638	.263	14	89
3B	Eddie Mayo	162	643	.320	11	85
SS	Eddie Cihocki	141	499	.257	5	56
INF	Peanuts Lowrey	70	216	.250	1	12
LF	Lou Novikoff	174	714	.363	41	171
CF	Jigger Statz	144	453	.289	1	48
RF	Johnny Moore	120	380	.311	9	69
IOF	Paul Carpenter	106	338	.216	4	38
IOF	Wally Carroll	57	125	.304	0	9
C	Chico Hernandez	109	308	.269	6	36
C	Billy Holm	102	281	.231	1	31

		G	IP	W-L	ERA	SHO
P	Joe Berry	53	143	9–5	2.39	1
P	Ray Prim	38	240	18–11	2.59	3
P	Lee Stine	37	257	18–10	2.83	2
P	Bob Weiland	25	164	12–7	3.78	1
P	Julio Bonetti	28	193	14–10	4.28	2
P	Jess Flores	32	132	7–5	4.43	2
P	Jack Fallon	46	141	13–9	4.72	2
P	Fay Thomas	30	161	6–11	4.97	1

1941 — 7th Place (72–98)
Manager — Jigger Statz

		G	AB	AVG	HR	RBI
1B	Phil Weintraub	118	417	.302	18	75
2B	John Stamper	80	286	.238	0	25
3B	Eddie Mayo	109	412	,286	13	72
SS	Len Merullo	81	275	.218	1	17
SS	Bill Schuster	70	261	.257	1	33
INF	Rabbit Warstler	89	276	.254	0	25
LF	Harvey Storey	137	465	.280	2	50
CF	Peanuts Lowrey	165	653	.311	6	65
RF	Johnny Moore	135	474	.331	18	100
IOF	Jigger Statz	74	143	.268	0	21
IOF	Wally Berger	59	141	.241	8	18
IOF	Ralph Samhammer	48	154	.214	0	3
IOF	Tom Tatum	32	106	.245	0	9
C	Gilly Campbell	77	245	.261	0	23
C	Billy Holm	77	198	.197	5	17
C	Bob Collins	59	197	.315	1	30

		G	IP	W-L	ERA	SHO
P	Ray Prim	35	255	16–15	2.85	4
P	Jess Flores	39	223	12–15	3.23	6
P	Julio Bonetti	18	111	7–3	3.24	0
P	Jess Dobernic	13	72	3–7	3.25	0
P	Bob Weiland	17	57	1–4	3.75	0
P	Fay Thomas	28	154	10–13	4.09	1
P	Byron Humphreys	10	69	2–6	5.18	0
P	Joe Berry	52	125	6–10	5.26	0
P	Lee Stine	34	168	9–14	5.41	1
P	Slick Coffman	33	80	1–3	5.73	0
P	Frank Totaro	28	77	3–3	6.19	0

1942 — 2nd Place (104–74)
Manager — Jigger Statz

		G	AB	AVG	HR	RBI
1B	Eddie Waitkus	175	699	.336	9	81
2B	Roy Hughes	166	630	.298	1	61
3B	Eddie Mayo	171	635	.307	12	110
SS	Bill Schuster	179	640	.298	6	78
LF	Fern Bell	67	246	.228	5	21
CF	Barney Olsen	174	645	.302	15	87

		G	AB	AVG	HR	RBI
RF	Johnny Moore	134	487	.347	7	85
IOF	Jigger Statz	100	263	.228	2	22
IOF	Peanuts Lowrey	96	393	.257	5	39
C	Al Todd	122	375	.256	5	44
C	Gilly Campbell	97	249	.201	1	19

		G	IP	W-L	ERA	SHO
P	Ray Prim	39	277	21–10	2.47	3
P	Paul Gehrman	46	196	11–6	2.57	2
P	Jess Flores	37	185	14–5	2.63	2
P	Red Lynn	43	211	12–13	3.11	1
P	Pete Mallory	42	154	10–8	3.21	1
P	Ken Raffensberger	51	242	17–18	3.54	1
P	Peaches Davis	27	61	6–2	4.13	0
P	Red Adams	11	67	6–4	4.16	0
P	Jess Dobernic	36	98	5–5	4.96	1
P	Ed Heusser	9	42	2–3	5.36	0

1943 — 1st Place (110–45)
Manager — Bill Sweeney

		G	AB	AVG	HR	RBI
1B	Wimpy Quinn	157	573	.236	11	80
2B	Roy Hughes	121	461	.323	0	41
3B	Charlie English	157	591	.323	16	98
SS	Bill Schuster	157	618	.275	5	67
INF	Rabbit Mallory	47	159	.346	3	18
LF	John Ostrowski	143	472	.282	21	82
CF	Cecil Garriott	98	286	.255	10	47
RF	Andy Pafko	157	604	.356	18	118
IOF	Johnny Moore	81	217	.290	1	31
IOF	Glen Russell	53	153	.320	7	26
C	Billy Holm	97	271	.292	2	28
C	Bill Sarni	33	83	.229	1	9
C	Harry Land	27	92	.239	0	9

		G	IP	W-L	ERA	SHO
P	Ken Raffensberger	35	244	19–11	2.14	4
P	Paul Gehrman	35	226	20–7	2.43	4
P	Red Lynn	36	248	21–8	2.47	5
P	Don Osborn	30	102	10–1	2.65	0
P	Oren Baker	33	111	10–3	2.84	1
P	Jodie Phipps	33	202	17–5	3.03	4
P	Pete Mallory	34	192	11–8	3.08	4

1944 — 1st Place (99–70)
Manager — Bill Sweeney

		G	AB	AVG	HR	RBI
1B	Reggie Otero	130	421	.306	0	54
2B	Glen Russell	155	585	.315	17	89
3B	Charlie English	88	312	.283	2	44
SS	Guy Miller	156	519	.233	0	47
INF	George Ogorek	50	188	.245	0	14
LF	Ted Norbert	111	363	.289	10	57

		G	AB	AVG	HR	RBI
CF	Cecil Garriott	170	619	.286	13	70
RF	John Ostrowski	124	475	.282	10	67
OF	Ed Sauer	108	392	.293	5	52
IOF	Johnny Moore	84	120	.325	3	30
IOF	Manny Salvatierra	45	122	.246	1	14
C	Ed Fernandes	130	400	.280	5	57
C	Bill Sarni	86	229	.237	5	24

		G	IP	W-L	ERA	SHO
P	Ray Prim	41	286	22–10	1.70	5
P	Pete Mallory	12	73	6–3	2.59	1
P	Jorge Comellas	41	276	18–14	2.61	1
P	Boyd Tepler	11	48	3–4	2.81	0
P	Claude Horton	18	91	9–4	2.87	0
P	Dick Conger	26	169	13–7	2.88	4
P	Don Osborn	42	216	15–13	3.25	1
P	Red Adams	44	186	10–7	3.58	2
P	Irv Stein	25	67	1–4	4.70	0

1945 — 7th Place (76–107)
Manager — Bill Sweeney

		G	AB	AVG	HR	RBI
1B	Mel Hicks	171	606	.299	10	87
1B	Reggie Otero	84	302	.344	0	23
2B	Ray Viers	175	606	.244	2	53
3B	Pete Elko	174	630	.284	4	59
SS	Charlie Brewster	65	261	.284	1	28
INF	Guy Miller	69	158	.203	0	18
INF	Russ Peterson	37	128	.226	0	8
LF	Lou Novikoff	101	390	.310	9	52
CF	Jim Tyack	150	518	.326	8	69
RF	Glen Russell	157	538	.342	14	89
IOF	Leroy Paton	67	247	.247	0	18
IOF	Hal Douglas	45	142	.303	1	9
IOF	Nick Rhabe	45	129	.279	0	12
C	Mickey Kreitner	101	328	.277	0	36
C	Doc Greene	94	223	.247	6	32

		G	IP	W-L	ERA	SHO
P	Don Osborn	41	269	18–13	2.68	3
P	Red Adams	41	298	21–15	2.72	2
P	Charlie Cuellar	38	225	13–17	4.40	3
P	Jorge Comellas	26	156	6–16	4.44	2
P	Ken Hicks	35	134	6–10	5.24	0
P	Paul Lammers	42	119	4–11	5.45	0
P	Warren Merkle	36	88	2–3	5.82	0
P	George Woodend	20	90	3–11	7.50	0

1946 — 4th Place (94–89)
Manager — Bill Sweeney

		G	AB	AVG	HR	RBI
1B	Reggie Otero	127	399	.273	1	46
1B	Wimpy Quinn	62	154	.234	1	20

Appendix C: Individual Batting and Pitching, by Season and Career

		G	AB	AVG	HR	RBI
1B	Jack Richards	29	108	.278	0	7
2B	Albie Glossop	93	284	.250	5	26
2B	Rabbit Mallory	93	279	.219	1	11
3B	George Archie	130	457	.258	4	62
SS	Bill Schuster	176	626	.286	4	69
INF	Stu Martin	79	121	.231	0	17
LF	Loyd Christopher	158	569	.304	26	96
CF	Leon Treadway	126	496	.286	0	27
RF	Ed Sauer	184	685	.273	20	82
IOF	Jim Tyack	100	168	.244	0	16
IOF	Barney Olsen	81	208	.255	3	23
C	Dewey Williams	98	260	,200	2	21
C	Joe Stephenson	74	135	.207	3	9
C	Hal Spindel	57	157	.210	0	6

		G	IP	W-L	ERA	SHO
P	Oren Baker	32	63	4–1	2.14	0
P	Red Adams	17	104	9–4	2.68	4
P	Red Lynn	41	271	17–16	2.79	7
P	Yank Terry	33	152	12–15	2.86	4
P	Cliff Chambers	37	268	18–15	3.02	2
P	Bill Fleming	15	88	9–5	3.17	2
P	Jess Dobernic	46	134	4–5	3.22	0
P	Don Osborn	36	180	10–14	3.38	0
P	Dick Errickson	21	49	2–2	3.49	0
P	Dick Conger	18	116	7–8	3.88	0

1947 — 1st Place (106–81)
Manager — Bill Kelly

		G	AB	AVG	HR	RBI
1B	Larry Barton	166	547	.272	18	83
2B	Lou Stringer	161	548	.292	13	72
3B	John Ostrowski	173	654	.292	24	110
SS	Bill Schuster	174	687	.262	6	70
INF	Albie Glossop	98	239	.264	8	41
LF	Clarence Maddern	129	458	.332	15	83
CF	Cecil Garriott	171	639	.283	22	77
RF	Ed Sauer	150	568	.280	17	86
IOF	Tuck Stainback	87	290	.279	2	34
IOF	Loyd Christopher	70	206	.228	5	23
C	Eddie Malone	146	447	.260	10	72
C	Paul Gillespie	53	100	.250	5	21

		G	IP	W-L	ERA	SHO
P	Cliff Chambers	37	233	24–9	3.13	4
P	Oren Baker	46	132	6–4	3.14	0
P	Red Lynn	42	273	16–16	3.36	2
P	Don Osborn	33	73	6–4	3.45	0
P	Red Adams	34	236	14–12	3.51	0
P	Jess Dobernic	55	141	8–4	3.57	0
P	Bob Mccall	23	119	5–12	3.86	1
P	Russ Bauers	23	147	10–8	3.92	2
P	Bill Fleming	26	131	11–6	4.19	2

1948 — 3rd Place (102–86)
Manager — Bill Kelly

		G	AB	AVG	HR	RBI
1B	Jack Sanford	105	361	.247	6	44
1B	Eddie Lukon	110	296	.257	11	46
2B	Mickey Burnett	92	314	.271	3	40
2B	Don Johnson	70	285	.288	5	28
3B	John Ostrowski	109	397	.295	15	56
3B	Jim Tabor	22	73	.329	4	9
SS	Bill Schuster	151	617	.264	11	60
SS	Len Merullo	48	163	.227	0	10
INF	Albie Glossop	150	474	.281	17	75
LF	Dom Dallessandro	159	514	.397	20	87
CF	Cecil Garriott	164	581	.232	19	55
RF	Ed Sauer	150	571	.305	16	121
IOF	Cliff Aberson	116	389	.329	34	103
C	Eddie Malone	122	385	.268	9	48
C	Rube Novotney	84	256	.270	4	26

		G	IP	W-L	ERA	SHO
P	Dewey Adkins	34	212	17–10	2.25	2
P	Red Adams	32	226	14–11	3.54	1
P	Red Lynn	42	244	19–10	3.73	2
P	Lee Anthony	38	197	16–11	3.93	2
P	Hal Kleine	34	110	6–5	4.01	1
P	Fred Schmidt	15	76	2–5	4.14	0
P	Tom Hafey	34	147	7–9	4.35	1
P	Russ Bauers	32	95	3–9	4.93	0
P	Don Carlsen	25	136	7–6	5.20	0
P	Walt Lanfranconi	29	101	5–5	6.06	1

1949 — 8th Place (74–115)
Manager — Bill Kelly

		G	AB	AVG	HR	RBI
1B	Butch Moran	121	419	.243	8	43
1B	Gordon Goldsberry	52	164	.238	2	15
2B	Wayne Terwilliger	115	432	.278	8	46
2B	Frank Gustine	49	170	.294	4	22
3B	John Ostrowski	129	478	.318	32	90
3B	Lee Handley	33	123	.301	1	15
SS	Bill Schuster	93	349	.226	4	40
SS	Bob Sturgeon	79	294	.269	0	25
INF	Albie Glossop	117	254	.213	5	37
INF	Bob Rhawn	41	156	.267	1	10
LF	Clarence Maddern	129	495	.307	14	83
CF	Cecil Garriott	145	494	.255	10	47
RF	Carmen Mauro	155	500	.292	12	63
IOF	Cliff Aberson	103	313	.230	17	49
IOF	Dom Dallessandro	39	117	.291	8	28
C	Eddie Malone	84	293	.341	6	46
C	Nels Burbrink	80	239	.272	4	28
C	Rube Novotney	47	138	.210	1	7

Appendix C: Individual Batting and Pitching, by Season and Career

		G	IP	W-L	ERA	SHO
P	Booker Mcdaniels	18	113	8–9	4.22	1
P	Bob Kelly	36	205	9–16	4.57	1
P	Don Carlsen	28	135	9–8	4.73	1
P	Don Watkins	47	204	8–11	4.81	0
P	Lee Anthony	47	182	7–19	5.09	1
P	Walt Lanfranconi	17	54	2–5	5.33	0
P	Alan Ihde	57	118	7–6	5.34	0
P	Cal Mclish	29	150	8–11	5.76	0
P	Bryan Stephens	17	102	3–11	6.00	1
P	Red Lynn	16	75	4–7	6.12	1
P	Ken Gables	29	54	5–2	7.17	0

1950 — 7TH PLACE (86–114)
MANAGER — BILL KELLY

		G	AB	AVG	HR	RBI
1B	Elbie Fletcher	155	506	.289	9	72
2B	John Lucadello	108	335	.239	2	33
2B	Lou Klein	97	331	.332	14	76
3B	Leon Brinkopf	88	311	.267	4	40
SS	Gene Baker	100	375	.280	2	16
INF	Albie Glossop	124	341	.217	5	47
INF	Bob Sturgeon	110	342	.202	0	17
INF	Frank Whitman	48	159	.277	0	29
LF	Clarence Maddern	162	573	.283	14	102
CF	Cecil Garriott	151	451	.268	10	53
RF	Frank Baumholtz	172	670	.379	15	89
IOF	Les Layton	154	503	.296	27	96
IOF	Stan Spence	146	438	.228	22	66
C	Rube Novotney	125	393	.254	8	46
C	Ray Cash	66	197	.239	7	30

		G	IP	W-L	ERA	SHO
P	Cal Mclish	42	260	20–11	3.60	3
P	Ralph Hamner	34	225	13–16	3.80	2
P	Bob Muncrief	43	244	15–17	3.84	2
P	Jess Dobernic	21	46	1–4	4.11	0
P	Emil Kush	38	79	1–4	4.67	0
P	Pete Mallory	35	145	4–12	4.78	0
P	Ken Gables	30	54	3–3	5.00	0
P	Herm Besse	35	193	11–14	5.12	3
P	Frank Marino	35	149	9–9	5.13	0
P	Booker Mcdaniels	37	68	3–4	6.49	0
P	Dewey Adkins	28	96	1–6	6.56	0
P	Dick Manville	26	80	2–9	6.98	0

1951 — 3RD PLACE (86–81)
MANAGER — STAN HACK

		G	AB	AVG	HR	RBI
1B	Chuck Connors	98	390	.321	22	77
1B	Dee Fondy	70	274	.376	11	45

		G	AB	AVG	HR	RBI
2B	Jack Hollis	149	561	.283	3	54
3B	Leon Brinkopf	157	530	.279	25	93
SS	Gene Baker	168	666	.278	11	62
INF	Tod Davis	45	109	.275	4	13
LF	Les Layton	144	498	.303	23	100
C	Bob Talbot	159	598	.249	9	51
RF	Max West	138	472	.282	35	110
IOF	Tom Neill	101	293	.273	7	50
C	Les Peden	117	402	.249	11	54
C	Bill Raimondi	52	107	.290	0	8

		G	IP	W-L	ERA	SHO
P	Herm Besse	27	98	8–5	3.67	0
P	Bob Spicer	35	248	17–13	3.70	1
P	Warren Hacker	28	193	8–15	3.87	5
P	Doyle Lade	24	148	8–6	3.89	0
P	Fred Baczewski	37	232	12–10	4.03	3
P	Bill Moisan	31	142	10–8	4.12	2
P	Ralph Hamner	35	105	4–6	4.37	0
P	Jess Dobernic	43	60	6–4	4.56	0
P	Dewey Adkins	22	63	6–3	5.43	0
P	Ed Chandler	34	90	5–7	5.50	0

1952 — 6th Place (87–93)
Manager — Stan Hack

		G	AB	AVG	HR	RBI
1B	Chuck Connors	113	406	.259	6	51
1B/IOF	Max West	149	497	.262	35	91
2B	Jack Hollis	164	609	.250	3	56
3B	Leon Brinkopf	135	450	.238	27	67
SS	Gene Baker	174	696	.260	15	73
INF	Tod Davis	57	184	.228	2	20
LF	Bob Usher	125	461	.293	3	45
CF	Bob Talbot	164	623	.279	6	50
RF	Les Layton	132	400	.240	5	44
IOF	Ron Northey	92	235	.255	11	38
C	Les Peden	153	527	.279	18	71
C	Elvin Tappe	40	114	.211	0	7

		G	IP	W-L	ERA	SHO
P	Joe Hatten	16	104	8–8	2.25	5
P	Ralph Hamner	50	68	2–6	2.25	0
P	Don Watkins	35	77	4–1	2.69	0
P	Walt Dubiel	13	81	6–5	3.22	1
P	Ed Chandler	40	236	16–14	3.51	3
P	Willie Ramsdell	13	89	5–6	3.64	0
P	Cal Mclish	34	212	10–15	3.78	2
P	Bill Moisan	34	238	16–12	3.82	2
P	Bob Spicer	37	114	6–7	3.95	0
P	Doyle Lade	31	171	8–12	3.95	1
P	Bob Zick	39	104	4–2	4.47	0

1953 — 3rd Place (93–87)
Manager — Stan Hack

		G	AB	AVG	HR	RBI
1B	Fred Richards	180	740	.296	26	92
2B	Frank Diprima	147	497	.268	9	60
3B	Bud Hardin	125	425	.261	0	28
SS	Gene Baker	162	595	.284	20	99
INF	Tod Davis	63	204	.294	14	27
INF	Murray Franklin	45	155	.271	1	16
LF	Dick Smith	126	338	.225	12	42
CF	Bob Talbot	180	762	.287	14	70
RF	Bob Usher	169	672	.304	15	90
IOF	Dixie Upright	80	245	.306	12	42
IOF	Max West	38	54	.241	5	15
C	Les Peden	100	340	.268	11	55
C	Al Evans	78	235	.285	2	26
C	Elvin Tappe	38	114	.281	0	16

		G	IP	W-L	ERA	SHO
P	Joe Ostrowski	28	73	3–6	2.97	0
P	Bill Moisan	34	223	10–11	3.03	2
P	Randy Gumpert	36	100	7–9	3.07	1
P	Joe Hatten	42	224	17–11	3.34	4
P	Cal Mclish	35	235	16–11	3.71	2
P	Bob Spicer	45	196	12–10	3.90	0
P	Bill Padget	50	178	11–7	4.30	1
P	Alan Ihde	35	91	4–4	4.34	0
P	Ed Chandler	32	179	7–12	4.48	1
P	Willie Ramsdell	18	56	5–6	5.35	1

1954 — 6th Place (73–92)
Manager — Bill Sweeney

		G	AB	AVG	HR	RBI
1B	Fred Richards	145	497	.227	24	61
2B	Gene Mauch	153	565	.287	11	58
3B	Bruce Edwards	106	393	.298	9	64
SS	Bud Hardin	135	435	.242	2	21
SS	Hank Nasternak	71	211	.237	3	16
LF	Tommy Brown	152	502	.263	14	61
CF	Bob Usher	156	574	.254	13	73
RF	Don Robertson	82	219	.237	7	28
IOF	Dixie Upright	94	235	.234	10	28
IOF	Max West	89	169	.260	12	37
IOF	Vic Marasco	51	134	.254	5	16
IOF	Jacques Monette	51	96	.250	4	10
C	Al Evans	92	269	.268	5	29
C	John Pramesa	93	231	.294	11	37
C	Hal Meek	32	93	.172	1	5

		G	IP	W-L	ERA	SHO
P	Turk Lown	30	73	5–3	2.48	0
P	Bob Spicer	33	231	13–16	3.07	4
P	John Pyecha	28	147	7–7	3.24	1

		G	IP	W-L	ERA	SHO
P	Joe Hatten	41	232	13–17	3.53	2
P	Cal Mclish	37	245	13–15	3.55	3
P	Bubba Church	26	134	11–9	3.89	3
P	Bill Moisan	31	101	1–7	4.09	0
P	Sheldon Jones	19	62	3–6	4.86	0
P	Randy Gumpert	37	64	4–4	4.92	0
P	Tom Simpson	35	62	1–4	5.14	0

1955 — 3rd Place (Tied) (91–81)
Manager — Bill Sweeney, Jack Warner (5-23-55), Bob Scheffing (5-25-55)

		G	AB	AVG	HR	RBI
1B	Steve Bilko	168	622	.328	37	124
2B	Gene Mauch	155	584	.296	8	49
3B	Bus Clarkson	100	316	.294	13	46
SS	Eddie Winceniak	128	415	.248	12	51
INF	Bud Hardin	123	299	.261	0	24
INF	Vern Morgan	28	89	.169	3	6
LF	Hal Rice	142	493	.262	25	78
CF	Gale Wade	101	378	.310	8	27
RF	Bob Usher	128	394	.226	10	46
IOF	Bob Coats	122	336	.276	2	33
IOF	Bob Talbot	48	200	.225	3	14
IOF	Solly Drake	44	161	.261	1	11
Util	Piper Davis	82	253	.244	4	22
C	Jim Fanning	88	284	.226	4	27
C	Elvin Tappe	62	165	.121	0	8
C	John Pramesa	61	164	.262	3	21

		G	IP	W-L	ERA	SHO
P	Turk Lown	61	114	12–5	2.13	0
P	Jim Brosnan	31	228	17–10	2.38	3
P	Ray Bauer	34	42	3–3	3.00	0
P	Don Elston	53	224	17–6	3.06	2
P	Hy Cohen	18	100	5–10	3.59	2
P	Bubba Church	34	143	11–8	3.66	2
P	Joe Hatten	39	138	11–9	3.73	3
P	George Piktuzis	34	188	7–13	4.04	2
P	Bob Zick	40	106	2–7	5.17	0

1st Place (107–61)
Manager — Bob Scheffing

		G	AB	AVG	HR	RBI
1B	Steve Bilko	162	597	.360	55	164
2B	Gene Mauch	146	566	.348	20	84
3B	George Freese	137	474	.291	22	113
SS	Casey Wise	168	705	.287	7	60
INF	Don Lauters	39	100	.260	2	6
LF	Bob Speake	158	580	.300	25	111
CF	Gale Wade	101	383	.292	20	67
RF	Jim Bolger	165	592	.326	28	147

		G	AB	AVG	HR	RBI
IOF	Bob Coats	103	237	.316	0	29
IOF	Piper Davis	64	152	.316	6	24
IOF	Eddie Haas	41	149	.275	4	19
C	Elvin Tappe	100	303	.267	3	36
C	Joe Hannah	93	239	.272	1	33

		G	IP	W-L	ERA	SHO
P	Bob Anderson	70	105	12–4	2.65	0
P	Ray Bauer	49	80	6–1	3.16	0
P	Dave Hillman	33	210	21–7	3.38	3
P	Gene Fodge	44	192	19–7	4.31	2
P	Dick Drott	35	197	13–10	4.39	1
P	Red Adams	15	86	6–2	4.50	0
P	Harry Perkowski	22	84	4–6	4.78	2
P	Bob Thorpe	29	156	7–7	4.86	1
P	Chick Pieretti	38	156	7–9	4.90	0
P	John Briggs	18	80	5–5	5.62	0
P	Hy Cohen	5	30	5–0	5.70	0

1957 — 6TH PLACE (80–88)
MANAGER — CLAY BRYANT

		G	AB	AVG	HR	RBI
1B	Steve Bilko	158	536	.300	56	140
2B	George "Sparky" Anderson	168	619	.260	2	35
3B	Jim Baxes	83	297	.259	16	48
3B	Roy Hartsfield	149	459	.281	7	63
SS	Wally Lammers	132	395	.248	5	36
INF	Bob Dolan	82	200	.260	3	24
LF	Jim Fridley	90	275	.273	13	43
CF	Tom Saffell	135	443	.262	6	30
RF	Bert Hamric	114	357	.291	19	56
IOF	Gale Wade	111	329	.237	7	33
IOF	Bob Jenkins	96	261	.310	13	54
C	Elvin Tappe	79	214	.187	0	12
C	Herb Olson	62	149	.181	5	18
C	Earl Battey	42	143	.252	9	20

		G	IP	W-L	ERA	SHO
P	Connie Grob	13	87	6–3	2.18	2
P	Bill George	59	116	4–1	2.25	0
P	Dick Hanlon	11	71	5–4	3.18	0
P	John Jancse	30	180	9–12	3.74	2
P	Tom Lasorda	29	132	7–10	3.90	1
P	Jim Hughes	45	66	7–6	3.95	0
P	Vito Valentinetti	19	111	9–5	3.96	1
P	Red Adams	9	54	2–5	4.19	1
P	Ralph Mauriello	27	156	11–5	4.21	2
P	Glenn Mickens	61	119	8–8	4.40	0
P	Babe Birrer	24	75	5–6	4.87	0
P	Bob Darnell	22	116	4–11	5.14	0
P	Ron Negray	11	39	1–4	5.35	0

Individual Season Batting Records

Batting Average: .383 **Frank Demaree**, 1934.
Times at Bat: 896 **Dummy Hoy**, 1903; Since 1918: 823 **Jigger Statz**, 1926.
Runs Scored: 190 **Frank Demaree**, 1934.
Hits: 291 **Jigger Statz**, 1926.
Singles: 202 **Jigger Statz**, 1933.
Doubles: 68 **Jigger Statz**, 1926.
Triples: 23 **Harl Maggert** & **Ivan Howard**, 1913; Since 1918: 22 **Dixie Carroll**, 1922.
Home Runs: 56 **Gene Lillard**, 1935; **Steve Bilko**, 1957.
Runs Batted In: 184 **Wally Hood**, 1924.
Total Bases: 463 **Frank Demaree**, 1934.
Stolen Bases: 89 **Harl Maggert**, 1913; Since 1918: 61 **Jigger Statz**, 1934.

Bases on Balls: 131 **Cecil Garriott**, 1947.*
Strikeouts: 150 **Steve Bilko**, 1957.*
Sacrifice Hits: 59 **Jimmy "Ike" McAuley**, 1921.
Most Home Runs in a Game: 3; **Walter Carlisle**—August 18, 1907; **Jack Fournier**—June 17, 1919; **Steve Mesner**—June 5, 1937; **Loyd Christopher**—August 2, 1946; **Chuck Connors**—March 31, 1951; **Max West**—April 1, 1951.
Most Consecutive Games Played: 393 **Marv Gudat**, September 3, 1933 to September 20, 1935.
Hitting Streak: 44 games **Jim Oglesby**, June 11, 1933 through July 22, 1933.
Most Consecutive Hits: 11 **Glen "Rip" Russell**, July 27–29, 1938.

*Records not kept before 1940

Top Ten Angels in Career Batting

1919–1957

Games Played		Times at Bat		Runs	
Jigger Statz	2,790	Jigger Statz	10,657	Jigger Statz	1,996
Carl Dittmar	1,399	Carl Dittmar	4,690	Wally Hood	656
Ray Jacobs	1,121	Wally Hood	3,961	Ray Jacobs	641
John Moore	1,118	Bill Schuster	3,798	Carl Dittmar	637
Wally Hood	1,094	Ray Jacobs	3,727	Marv Gudat	618
Bill Schuster	1,017	John Moore	3,589	Cece Garriott	594
Cece Garriott	925	Marv Gudat	3,417	John Moore	565
Marv Gudat	885	Cece Garriott	3,106	Bill Schuster	545
Glen "Rip" Russell	745	Babe Twombly	2,579	Fred Haney	456
Eddie Mayo	687	Eddie Mayo	2,570	Gene Lillard	436

Hits		Doubles		Triples	
Jigger Statz	3,356	Jigger Statz	597	Jigger Statz	136
Carl Dittmar	1,336	Wally Hood	289	Sam Crawford	49
Wally Hood	1,261	Ray Jacobs	279	Wally Hood	47
John Moore	1,170	Carl Dittmar	240	Babe Twombly	47
Ray Jacobs	1,140	John Moore	239	Dixie Carroll	37
Marv Gudat	1,098	Bill Schuster	204	John Moore	37
Bill Schuster	1,039	Marv Gudat	178	Marv Gudat	35
Babe Twombly	823	Jim Oglesby	165	Ray Jacobs	35
Glen "Rip" Russell	796	Eddie Mayo	144	Carl Dittmar	31
Wes Schulmerich	784	Glen "Rip" Russell	144	John Ostrowski	30

Home Runs		Runs Batted In		Stolen Bases	
Steve Bilko	148	Jigger Statz	1,017	Jigger Statz	466
Gene Lillard	138	Wally Hood	773	Fred Haney	170
Wally Hood	120	John Moore	696	Marv Gudat	146

Home Runs		Runs Batted In		Stolen Bases	
Ray Jacobs	115	Ray Jacobs	657	Wade Killefer	126
John Moore	112	Carl Dittmar	645	Bill Schuster	121
John Ostrowski	102	Jim Oglesby	469	Ed Sauer	101
Max West	87	Gene Lillard	467	Cece Garriott	99
Cece Garriott	84	Marv Gudat	454	Wally Hood	99
Wes Schulmerich	80	Glen "Rip" Russell	448	Babe Twombly	98
Glen "Rip" Russell	77	Steve Bilko	428	Dixie Carroll	84

Individual Season Pitching Records

Most Wins: 39 **Doc Newton**, 1904; Since 1918: 30 **Buck Newsom**, 1933

Most Losses: 28 **Charles "Spider" Baum**, 1905; Since 1918: 27 **Win Ballou**, 1932

Strikeouts: 216 **Dolly Gray**, 1908; Since 1918: 212 **Buck Newsom**, 1933

Bases on Balls: 155 **Dolly Gray**, 1907 and 1908; Since 1918: 127 **Bob Kelly**, 1949

Won-Loss Percentage: .875 **Fay Thomas**, 1934 (28–4) (15 or more decisions)

Shutouts: 7 **Buck Newsom**, 1933/**Red Lynn**, 1946

Wild Pitches: 17 **Tom Hughes**, 1915; Since 1918: 13 **Will Peters**, 1927 and **Ed Baecht**, 1932

Hit Batsmen: 36 **Joe Corbett**, 1903; Since 1918: 26 **Bill Piercy**, 1927

Home Runs Allowed: 25 **Cal McLish**, 1953*

Earned Run Average: 1.70 **Ray Prim**, 1944

Games Pitched: 70 **Bob Anderson**, 1956 (all in relief)

Innings Pitched: 456 **Flame Delhi**, 1911; Since 1918: 364 **Ed Baecht**, 1930

Longest Winning Streak: 15 **Buck Newsom**, 1933 and **Fay Thomas**, 1934

Longest Losing Streak: 11 **Jorge Comellas**, 1945

*Records not kept before 1940

Pitchers with 45 or More Victories (Since 1918)

	W	L	Pct.
Doc Crandall	207	128	.618
Ray Prim	150	97	.607
Fay Thomas	137	84	.620
Red Lynn	89	70	.560
Red Adams	82	60	.577
Win Ballou	70	60	.538
Cal Mclish	68	66	.507
Tom Hughes	64	57	.529
Curly Brown	62	42	.596
Claude Thomas	60	62	.492
Don Osborn	59	45	.567
Joe Berry	59	53	.527
Leroy Herrmann	57	27	.679
Vic Aldridge	53	35	.602
Ed Baecht	52	33	.612
Will Peters	51	52	.495
Clyde Barfoot	50	41	.549
Joe Hatten	49	45	.521
George Lyons	49	47	.510
Bob Spicer	48	46	.511
Charlie Root	46	29	.613

MVPs*

1903–1957

1903	Cap Dillon	1931	Jigger Statz
1904	Doc Newton	1932	Gilly Campbell
1905	Dolly Gray	1933	Buck Newsom
1906	Cap Dillon	1934	Frank Demaree/Fay Thomas
1907	Gavvy Cravath	1935	Gene Lillard
1908	Ted Easterly	1936	Jack Salveson
1909	Bill Tozer	1937	Bob Collins
1910	Ivan Howard	1938	Eddie Mayo
1911	Pete Daley	1939	Eddie Cihocki
1912	Joe Berger	1940	Lou Novikoff
1913	Harl Maggert	1941	Johnny Moore/Peanuts Lowrey
1914	Rube Ellis	1942	Eddie Waitkus
1915	Walter Boles	1943	Bill Schuster
1916	Jack Ryan	1944	Cecil Garriott
1917	Irish Meusel	1945	Red Adams
1918	Jack Fournier	1946	Bill Schuster
1919	Sam Crawford	1947	Jess Dobernic/John Ostrowski
1920	Johnny Bassler	1948	Ed Sauer
1921	Jim Mcauley	1949	(No Selection)**
1922	Art Griggs	1950	Frank Baumholtz
1923	Wally Hood	1951	Leon Brinkopf
1924	Charlie Root	1952	Les Peden
1925	Doc Crandall	1953	Gene Baker
1926	Jigger Statz	1954	Gene Mauch
1927	Art Jahn	1955	Steve Bilko
1928	Charlie Tolson	1956	Steve Bilko
1929	Wally Berger	1957	Steve Bilko
1930	Wes Schulmerich		

*MVP choices prior to 1926 are retroactive selections, announced by Bill Schroeder, the executive director of the Helms Athletic Foundation, in 1943. The Club did not officially select MVPs until 1926.

**In view of the Angels' dismal last place finish in 1949, president Don Stewart decreed that no seraph should be designated as MVP. Clarence Maddern was the unofficial selection.

Appendix D: Managers and Their Records

	Years	W	L	PCT
Clay Bryant	1957	80	88	.476
Frank Chance	1916–17	162	123	.568
Cap Dillon	1903, 1905–15	1,311	1,154	.532
Tim Flood	1904	119	97	.551
Stan Hack	1951–53	266	261	.505
Truck Hannah	1929, 1937–39	297	241	.552
Bill Kelly	1947–50	368	394	.483
Red Killefer	1917–22	559	432	.564
Marty Krug	1923–29	644	648	.498
Jack Lelivelt	1929–36	792	597	.570
Bob Scheffing	1955–56	173	117	.597
Jud Smith	1904	9	4	.692
Jigger Statz	1940–42	278	247	.530
Bill Sweeney	1943–46, 1954–55	477	426	.528
Jack Warner	1955	0	2	.000

Appendix E: Paid Attendance

1919 230,647	1932 143,829	1945 349,917
1920 279,679	1933 222,416	1946 501,259
1921 288,044	1934 129,672	1947 622,485
1922 289,227	1935 153,101	1948 576,237
1923 267,709	1936 128,565	1949 402,089
1924 355,480	1937 196,793	1950 320,757
1925 297,242	1938 188,808	1951 328,294
1926 273,202	1939 224,645	1952 359,161
1927 197,944	1940 186,184	1953 363,818
1928 286,855	1941 162,881	1954 238,567
1929 341,173	1942 271,169	1955 291,732
1930 314,944	1943 236,642	1956 271,982
1931 256,416	1944 362,816	1957 220,547

These figures do not include women who were admitted at no charge on Ladies Day, which began as a regular feature in 1925.

Bibliography

Books

Bauer, Carlos. *The Coast League Doomsday Book*. San Diego: Baseball Press Books, 2001.

_____. *Pacific Coast League Cyclopedia*. San Diego: Baseball Press Books, 2003.

Berger, Walter A., and George M. Snyder. *Freshly Remembered*. Redondo Beach, CA: Schneider/McGurk, 1993.

Dobbins, Dick. *The Grand Minor League: An Oral History of the Pacific Coast League*. Emeryville, CA: Woodford, 1999.

_____, and John Twitchell. *Nuggets on the Diamond: Professional Baseball in the Bay Area from the Gold Rush to the Present*. Emeryville, CA: Woodford, 1994.

Finch, Robert L., L. H. Addington, and Ben Morgan, eds. *The Story of Minor League Baseball*. Columbus, OH: National Association of Professional Baseball Leagues, 1952.

Ginsburg, Daniel E. *The Fix Is In: A History of Baseball Gambling and Game Fixing Scandals*. Jefferson, NC: McFarland, 1995.

Golenbock, Peter. *Bums: An Oral History of the Brooklyn Dodgers*. New York: Putnam, 1984.

Goodale, George. *The 1951 Angels and the All-Time Record Book, 1903–1951*. Los Angeles: Los Angeles Angels, 1951.

Goode, Chris. *California Baseball: From the Pioneers to the Glory Years*. Raleigh, NC: Lulu, 2009.

Johnson, Lloyd, ed. *The Minor League Register*. Durham, NC: Baseball America, 1994.

Johnson, Lloyd, and Miles Wolff, eds. *The Encyclopedia of Minor League Baseball*, 3d edition. Durham, NC: Baseball America, 2007.

Lange, Fred W. *History of Baseball in California and the Pacific Coast League*. N.p.: privately published, 1938.

Mackey, R. Scott. *Barbary Baseball: The Pacific Coast League of the 1920s*. Jefferson, NC: McFarland, 1995.

Mayer, Ronald A. *The 1937 Newark Bears: A Baseball Legend*. East Hanover, NJ: Vintage, 1980.

Mead, William B. *Even the Browns*. Chicago: Contemporary Books, 1978.

Mullins, William H. *The Depression and the Urban West Coast, 1929–1933*. Bloomington: Indiana University Press, 1991.

Obojski, Robert. *Bush League: A History of Minor League Baseball*. New York: Macmillan, 1975.

O'Neal, Bill. *The Pacific Coast League, 1903–1988*. Austin, TX: Eakin Press, 1990.

Runquist, Willie, comp. *Pacific Coast League Almanac, 1938–53*.

Schroeder, W. R. *The Pacific Coast League from 1903 to 1940*. Los Angeles: Helms Athletic Foundation, 1941.

_____. *Pacific Coast League Rosters, 1903–46*. Los Angeles: Helms Athletic Foundation, 1947.

_____. *Who's Who on the Los Angeles and Hollywood Baseball Clubs*. N.p.: privately published, 1930.

Snelling, Dennis. *The Pacific Coast League: A Statistical History, 1903–1957*. Jefferson, NC: McFarland, 1995.

Spalding, John E. *Pacific Coast League Stars: One Hundred of the Best, 1903 to 1957*. San Jose, CA: privately published, 1994.

_____. *Pacific Coast League Stars*, Volume II. San Jose, CA: privately published, 1997.

_____. *Sacramento Senators and Solons: Baseball in California's Capital, 1886 to 1976*. Manhattan, KS: Ag Press, 1995.

Stadler, Ken. *The Pacific Coast League: One Man's Memories, 1938–1957*. Los Angeles: Marbek, 1984.

Sullivan, Neil J. *The Dodgers Move West*. New York: Oxford University Press, 1987.

Waddingham, Gary. *The Seattle Rainiers, 1938–1942*. Seattle: Writers Publishing Service, 1987.

Weiss, Bill, and Marshall Wright. *The Greatest Minor*

League Teams of the 20th Century. Parker, CO: Outskirts, 2006.

Wright, Marshall D. *The American Association: Year-by-Year Statistics for the Baseball Minor League, 1902–1952.* Jefferson, NC: McFarland, 1997.

_____. *The International League: Year-by-Year Statistics, 1884–1953.* Jefferson, NC: McFarland, 1998.

Zingg, Paul J., and Mark D. Medeiros. *Runs, Hits and an Era: The Pacific Coast League, 1903–58* Urbana: University of Illinois Press, 1994.

Zuckerman, Lauren T. *Ballparks of the Pacific Coast League.* San Diego: Baseball Press Books, 2007.

Periodical Articles

Bauer, Carlos. "The 1903 Coast League Season." *Minor League History Journal* 3 (1994): 28–37.

Berman, Jay. "The 1956 Los Angeles Angels." *The National Pastime: A Review of Baseball History* 17 (1997): 81–84.

Doutt, Ronald C. "Catalina, Baseball and the Angels." *WaterLines: A Journal of the Santa Catalina Island Company* (1st quarter, 2003).

Gough, David. "Home Run Derby." *The National Pastime: A Review of Baseball History* 17 (1997): 111–116.

McCue, Andy. "Open Status Delusions: The PCL Attempt to Resist Major League Baseball." *Nine: A Journal of Baseball History and Social Policy Perspectives* 5, no. 2 (spring 1997): 288–304.

Newspapers

Los Angeles Examiner, 1922–1957.
Los Angeles Times, 1918–1957.
Sacramento Bee, 1928–1957.
San Francisco Chronicle, 1918–1957.
The Sporting News, St. Louis, 1918–1957.

Baseball Guides

Pacific Coast Blue Book, 1950–53.
Pacific Coast League Record Book, 1953, 1955, 1956.
Reach's Official Baseball Guide, 1919–40.
Spalding-Reach Official Baseball Guide, 1941.
Spalding's Official Baseball Guide, 1925–40.
The Sporting News Baseball Guide and Record Book, 1942–43.
The Sporting News Official Baseball Guide, 1944–58.

Index

Page numbers in ***bold italics*** indicate photographs. All baseball teams are referred to by their city and team name, e.g., Los Angeles Angels.

Abbott, Pete 191
Abernathy, Chuck 191
Aberson, Cliff ***137***, 137–38, 139, 141, 144, 147, 191
Abstein, Bill 8, 191
Accardo, Tom 191
Adams, Buster 109, 110
Adams, Herb 166, 167, 191
Adams, Jim 191
Adams, Red 108, 118, 120, 121, 123, 126, 129, 130, 134, 136, 138, 139, 142, 143, 191
Adkins, Dewey 136, 138, 139, 141, 150, 154, 155, 191
African American players 146–47, 150, ***164***, 171
Agnew, Jim 191
Akin, Roy 191
Aldridge, Vic 13, 14, 15, 19, 20, 22, 191
Alfano, Don 145, 191
Alston, Tom 172
Always on Sunday (Spalding) 5
American League *see* major leagues
Anderson, Andy 191
Anderson, Bob 176, 178, 181, 182, 191
Anderson, George "Sparky" 186, 191
Andre, John 177, 178, 191
Andrews, Red 191
Angel City Baseball Association 21
Angels *see* Los Angeles Angels
Anheier, Clyde 191
Anthony, Lee 136, 138, 139, 142, 143, 147, 191
Arbogast, Carl 191
Archie, George 98, 125, ***125***, 129, 191
Atchley, Jim 191
attendance: and competition with Hollywood teams 38,
89–90, 126; of female fans 43, 47, 160; game start time effects on 115; and Great Depression 53, 54, 59, 61, 68; radio/television broadcasting impact 140, 146, 148, 160, 165, 168, 179; and World War II 122; by year 240; *see also* season schedule adjustments
Atwell, Dick 83, 191
Atz, John 191
Augustus, Ray 191
Auman, Howard 136, 191

Baczewski, Fred 154, 156, 158, 191
Baecht, Ed 46, 47, 48, 51, 52, ***52***, 53, 59, 63, 191
Baker, Gene 150, 153, 155, 160, 162, 163, ***164***, 167, 191
Baker, Loris 53–54, 191
Baker, Oren 113, 123, 126, 129, 130, 133, 191
Baldwin, Earl "Red" 21, 25, 191
Ballou, Win "Old Pard" 48, 52, 53, 54, 56, 58–59, 64–65, 66, 77, 191
Balser, Ernie 191
Banks, Ernie ***164***
Barbee, Dave 51–52, 54
Barber, Turner 24
Barfoot, Clyde 41, ***42***, 43, 46, 47, 50, 52–53, 191
Barnes, Don 105–6
Barrett, Charlie "Red" 149
Barrett, Dick "Kewpie" 98, 109
Barrett, Red 191
Bartholemy, Al 191
Barton, Carroll 191
Barton, Larry 128–29, 131, 136, 137, 191
Barton, Vince 53, 54, 191
baseball design and quality 67–68, 116, 129, 160
baseball movies 189
Bassler, Johnny 9, 10, 12, 14, 15, 17, 18, 19, 26, 34, 191
Bates, Ray 191
Battey, Earl 191
Bauer, Ray "Moe" ***173***, 178, 181, 182, 191
Bauers, Russ 129, 130, 133–34, 136, 141
Baum, Spider 191
Baumholtz, Frank 149, 151, 191
Baxes, Jim 186, 191
Beall, Johnny 191
Beard, Ted 164, 165
Beck, Clyde 26, 31, 33, 34, 191
Beck, John 191
Beer, Sam 191
Beggs, Joe 73
Bell, Fern 108, 191
Bentley, Jack 72
Berger, Joel 191
Berger, Walter "Wally" 41, 42, 43, 44, 45, 46, ***46***, 48, 102, 191
Bergmann, Fred 191
Bernard, Curt 6, 191
Berra, Yogi 99
Berry, Henry 8
Berry, Joe 80, 82, 84, 86, 88, 89, 91, 97, 98, 100, 108, 191
Bert, Eugene F. 5
Besse, Herm 149, 150, 153, 154, 162, 191
Betts, Harry 191
Bigbee, Carson 41, 191
Bigbee, Lyle 191
Bilko, Steve 77, 171–73, ***173***, 174, 175, 176, 177, 178, ***178***, 179, 180, 185, 186–87, 188, 191
Billings, John 191
Birrer, Werner 191
Bishop, Max 72
Blackburn, Byron 59, 191
Blair, Clarence "Footsie" 58, 191
Bliss, Jack 191

243

Block, Cy 123, 191
Boehler, George 39, 44, 191
Bogart, Ed 19
Boles, Walter 12, 191
Boley, Joe 72
Bolger, Jim 176, 179, 180, 181, 191
Bonetti, Julio 91, 94, 95, 97, 98, 102, 103, 191
Bonneville Park 34
Boone, Ike 38
Bordagaray, Frenchy 74
Borkowski, Bob 185, 186, 191
Borowy, Hank 121
Borton, Babe 17
Boston Braves 162
Bottarini, John 80, 191
Bowman, Frank 191
Bramham, Judge W.G. 103, 104
Brandt, Dutch 191
Brant, Grover 191
Brashear, Kitty 6, 191
Brashear, Roy 191
Brazill, Frank 35, 38, 41, 191
Brenner, Bill 191
Brent (first name unknown) 191
Brewer, Jack 131
Brewster, Charlie 191
Briggs, John 179, 181, 192
Brinkopf, Leon 150, 153, 155, 157, 158, 160, 167, 192
Briseno, Midget 192
Briswalter, Andy 192
Broadbent, Al 192
Brock, Ken 192
Brooklyn Dodgers 146, 176, 183–87
Brooks, Clarence 8, 192
Brosnan, Jim 171, 173, 175, 176, 192
Brovia, Joe 156
Brown, Curly 11, 13, 14, 15, 17, 192
Brown, Mace 192
Brown, Tommy 167, 192
Browne, Harvey 192
Browne, Pidge 192
Browning, Frank 71
Bryant, Clay 185
Buchanan, George 192
Buckley, Walter 192
Buemiller, Al 192
Burbrink, Nelson 142, 153, 192
Burgess, Forrest "Smoky" 144–45, 192
Burke, Speck 192
Burkett, Howard 192
Burnett, Mickey 137, 140, 192
Burns, Bill 192
Burns, George "Tioga George" 55, 58, 192
Burns, Leo 192
Bush, Guy 192
Butler, John 44, 192
Buxton, Ralph 75, 77, 78, 80, 127, 192
Byler, Butch 192
Byrnes, Jim 192
Byrnes, Milt 192

Caffey, Ira 192
Caldera, Leon 192
Caldwell (first name unknown) 192
California State League 5–6
Calvo, Jack 192
Campbell, Archie 83, 84, 192
Campbell, Gilly 53, 58, 60, 67, 75, 83, 102, 108, 192
Campbell, J. Millard "Whitey" 67, 72, 75, 76, 78, 80
Candini, Milo 181, 192
Carleton, Tex 72
Carlisle, Walter 192
Carlsen, Don 130, 136, 138, 142, 143, 146, 147, 192
Carlucci, Cece 165
Carlyle, Cleo 64, 75, 78, 80, 81, 86, 154, 192
Carnes, Fred 192
Carnett, Ed 75, 80, 87, 93, 192
Caro, Jack 185, 186, 192
Carpenter, Paul 89, 93, 94, 96, 100, 192
Carroll, Dixie 19, 21, 22, 192
Carroll, Wally 102, 192
Carson, Clarence 192
Casey, Hugh 78, 80, 192
Casey, Tom 192
Cash, Ray 192
Caster, George 82, 192
Castleton, Roy 192
Catton, Bob 192
Cavaretta, Phil 166
Cecil, Rex 130
Cellar, Emanuel 156
Chambers, Cliff 124, 126, 127, 129, 130, 131, 133, **133**, 135, 192
Chance, Frank 9, 10, 192
Chandler, Ed 154, 157, 158, 159, 160, 162, 163, 192
Chandler, Happy 134
Chase, Hal 6, 192
Chavez Ravine site 185, 187
Chech, Charlie 8, 192
Chesley, Harry 192
Chesnes, Bob 131
Chess (first name unknown) 192
Chicago Cubs: Angels as farm club of 93, 135–36, 151, 161, 171; farm system 112, 120, 147, 153; management changes 166; pre-farm club relationship with Angels 19, 21, 30, 104–5; *see also* major leagues
Chirness, Sidney 103
Chition (first name unknown) 192
Chmiel, Herb 136, 192
Chozen, Myer 192
Christopher, Loyd 123, 124, 126, 129, 136, 154, 192
Church, Bubba 168, 169, 170, 174, 175, 176, 192
Church, Ed 192
Chutes Park 6, 7

Cihocki, Eddie 86, 89, 94, 95, 97, 101, 192
Clarkson, Jim "Bus" 171, 173, 174, 175, 176, 179, 192
Coats, Bob 173, **173**, 174, 176, 179, 185, 192
Cobb, Bob 92, 146, 175
Coffman, Slick 192
Cohen, Hy 174, 175–76, 177, 178, 179, 192
Coleman, George 192
Coleman, Ralph 192
Collins, Bob 83, 86, 94, 95, 96, 102, 192
Collins, Jim "Rip" 93, 94, 97, 100, 101, 192
Colmar, John 192
Colombo, Richie 121, 192
Comellas, Jorge "Pancho" 116, 118, **118**, 119–20, 121, 192
Conger, Dick 116, 118, 123, 124, 192
Connors, Chuck 154–55, 157, 158, 192
Conrad, Otto 192
Cooper, Claude 12, 13, 192
Corbett, Joe 192
Core, John 8, 192
Couch, Johnny 20, 192
Couchman, Bob 192
Cox, Dick 39, 40, 192
Crabb, Roy 192
Cracchiolo, Frank 192
Crandall, Al 39–40, 192
Crandall, Jimmy 40
Crandall, Karl 14, 15
Crandall, Otis "Doc" 9, 10, 11, 12–13, 14, 15, 17, 19, 20, 23, 25, 26, 28, **28**, 31, 35, 37, 38, 119
Crandall, Rufus 192
Crane, Bob 192
Cravath, Gavvy 5, 192
Crawford, Ivan 192
Crawford, Sam 11, 12, 13, 14, 15, 16–17, 19, 22, 62, 192
Criger, Elmer 192
Cronin, Bill 58, 67, 192
Cruise, Walton 27, 192
Cuellar, Charlie 121, 192
Cunningham, Bruce 40, 41, 43, 192
Cunningham, Dave 192
Curtis, Dan 192
Cutting, Ed 192

Dahlgren, Babe 68
Dale, Jean 17, 192
Daley, Pete 7, 8
Dallessandro, Dom 136, **136**, 137, 138, 139, 141, 142, 192
Daly, Tom 22, 192
Damato, Joe 145, 192
Damn Yankees (movie) 189
Daniels, Bill 192
Danning, Ike 192
Dant, Bob 155, 192
Darnell, Bob 186

Davelia (first name unknown) 192
Davenport, Charles 192
Davis, Bill 192
Davis, Bob 192
Davis, Piper 174, 185, 192
Davis, Roy "Peaches" 108, 110, 192
Davis, Tod 162, 163, 192
Day, Clyde 192
Deakins (first name unknown) 192
Deal (first name unknown) 192
Deal, Charlie 22, 23, 24, 25, 192
Dean, Dizzy 63
De Cuir, Eddie 192
Delaney, Art 52, 53, 192
Delhi, Flame 192
Dell, Wheezer 14
Delmas, Bert 192
Demaree, Frank 38, 67, **70**, 70–71, 73, 75, 77, 98, 180, 192
DeViveiros, Bernie 58, 59, 192
Dickshot, Johnny 114
Dillon, Cap 5, 6, 7, 8, 192
DiMaggio, Joe 65, 68, 77
DiPrima, Frank 162, 167, 192
Dittmar, Carl 41, 43, 44, 48, 51, 53, 63, 65, 67, 69, 72, 73, 75, 77, 78, **79**, 84, 91, 192
Dobbins, Dick 5
Dobernic, Jess 108, 110, 112, 126, 129, 130, 131, 133, 136, 139, 150, 192
Dodger Stadium 188
Dodgers *see* Brooklyn Dodgers
Doerr, Hal 192
Dolan, Bob 192
Donald, Atley 73
Donaldson, Gordon 101, 102, 192
Donnelley, Blix 110
Donovan, Elmer 192
Donovan, Maury 124, 192
Dotson, Lew 192
Douglas, Hal 192
Douglas, Ken 192
Downs, Jerry 192
Drake, Solly 175, 192
Dreisewerd, Clem 119
Dressen, Charlie 166
Drinkwater, Vianello 192
Driscoll, Babe 192
Driscoll, Paddy 12, 13–14, 192
Drott, Dick 176, 178, 179, 180, 181, 182, 192
Drysdale, Scott 75
Dubiel, Walt 158, 192
Dulin, Cliff 192
Dumovich, Nick 20, 23, 26, 28, 192
Dunlap, Grant 158, 192
Durst, Cedric 26, 27, 192
Dwyer, Ray 192
Dye, Otto 192
Dykes, Jimmy 126

Eager, Bob 192
Earned Run Average statistic, first calculation of 8

Easterly, Ted 192
Easterwood, Roy 192
Ebbets Field 176, 183–84
Eckhardt, Oscar 68
Eddington, Frank 15
Edmonds Field 165
Edwards, Bruce 167, 169, 192
Ehmke, Howard 192
Eldred, Brick 27
Elko, Pete 120, 192
Ellis, Rube 8, 12, 15, 19, 192
Ellison, Bert 20, 27, 30
Elston, Don 171, 174, 175, 176, 192
Emmerich, Bill 192
Emory (first name unknown) 192
Encoe, Chief 193
English, Charlie 86, 89, 91, 93, 94, 96, 113, 114, 115, 116, 117, 118, 193
Ennis, Russ 193
Epperly, Al 94, 193
Errickson, Dick 193
Essick, Bill 14
Evans, Al 162, 164, 168, 193
Evans, Russ "Red" 83, 84, 86, 193

Fabrique, Bunny 14, 15, 193
Fagan, Paul 147, 156, 165
Fahey, Howard 193
Fain, Ferris 130
Fallon, Jack 72, 97, 98, 100, 193
fan base 105, 135, 148, 172; *see also* attendance; female fans
Fanning, Jim **173**, 174, 193
farm clubs and working agreements *see* Chicago Cubs; Los Angeles Angels; major leagues
Farrell, Eddie "Doc" 53–54, 58, 193
Fausett, Buck 126
Fear, Vern 154, 193
Felderman, Marv 193
female fans and Ladies Day 43, 47, 53, 67, 160, 170
Ferguson, Les 193
Fernandes, Ed 116, 117, 193
Ferree, Elmer 193
Fine, Tommy 137
Fisher, Bob 193
Fittery, Paul 13, 14, 15, 16, 193
Fitzgerald, Ed 127
Fitzhenry (first name unknown) 193
Fitzke, Bob 59, 193
Flater, Jack 193
Flaugher, Will 193
Fleming, Bill 126, 129, 130, 136, 139, 193
Fleming, Dave 67, 77, 80–81, 83, 86, 89–90, 92, 94, 95, 96, 103, 105
Fletcher, Elbie 149, 151, 153, 193
Flood, Tim 193
Flores, Jess 91, 95, 97, 98, 102, 103, 108, 109, 110, 112, 193

Flowers, Ben 193
Flowers, Wes 193
Fodge, Gene 178, 180, 181, 193
Fondy, Dee 154, 155, 157, 172, 193
Foulke, Leon 193
Fournier, Jack 10, 11, 12, 13, 15, 154, 193
Franklin, Murray 163, 164, 165, 193
Frazier, Keith 76, 193
Freese, George 176, 181, 193
Freitas, Tony 109, 110
Frick, Ford 134, 171
Fridley, Jim 187, 193
Friene, Charley 193
Fritsch, Ted 193

Gabler, Glen 41, 42, 76, 77, 78, 193
Gables, Ken 150, 193
Galan, Augie 66
Galatzer, Milt 86, 87, 193
Galloway, Jim 193
Gamble, Bill 193
gambling scandals 17, 103
Gandil, Chick 193
Gantenbein, Joe 193
Gardner, Earle 193
Gardner, Hal 193
Garland, Lou 67, **71**, 72, 75, 76–77, 78, 193
Garner, Tom 193
Garriott, Cecil 114, 115, 116, 118, 120, 128, 131, 132, **133**, 136, 141, 142, 149, 153, 193
Garrity, Rabbit 193
Gazella, Mike 63, 193
Gedeon, Joe 193
Gehrman, Paul 108, 109, 111, 114, 115, 116, 193
George, Bill 186, 193
George, Ron 193
Gettel, Alan 174
Gibson, Glyn 75, 193
Gibson, Sam 77, 116
Gill, Roy 193
Gill, Warren 193
Gillespie, Paul 133, 193
Gilmore Field 92, 164
Glazner, Whitey 35, 193
Gleason, Art 85
Glor, Henry "Hank" 121, 193
Glossop, Albie 125, 133, 136, 137, 140, **140**, 141, 149, 153, 193
Gober, E.E. 193
Gochnaur, John 193
Goebel, Walter 75, 193
Goldsberry, Gordon 193
Goldstein, Izzy 193
Golvin, Walter 26, 27, 193
Gomez, Lefty 47
Goodwin, Bunny 193
Goodwin, Pep 193
Gordon, Joe 73, 155, 156
Goryl, John 193
Graham, Jack 138

Gray, Dolly 6, 193
Gray, Stan 119, 193
Great Depression 53, 54, 57, 59, 61, 68, 74
Green, Cecil 193
Green, Len "Doc" 193
Gregg, Vean 27
Gregory, Howard 193
Gregory, Nick 193
Griffith, Calvin 183
Grigg, Don 193
Griggs, Art 15–16, 17, 19, 22, 23, 24, 26, 193
Grimes, Ray 27, 31, 34, 193
Grimm, Charlie 46, 144
Grindle, Pinkie 193
Grob, Connie 186, 193
Groebling, Frank 193
Grove, Lefty 72
Gudat, Marv 63, 78, **78**, 80, 84, 86, 87, 88, 193
Gumpert, Randy 162, 193
Gunther, Fred 193
Gustine, Frank 146, 193

Haas, Eddie 176, 179, 193
Haas, Ernie 193
Hack, Stan 73, 127, 151–52, 153, 154, 156, 161, 166, 182
Hacker, Warren 153, 155, 156, 157
Hackharth (first name unknown) 193
Hafey, Tom 139, 141, 193
Hahn, Kenneth 184, 185
Hall, Charley 193
Hall, Herb 193
Hall, Rusty 6, 193
Halla, John 193
Hallett, Jack 91, 193
Hallman, Eddie 193
Hamilton, Earl 34, 37, 40, 41, 193
Hamner, Ralph 147, 149, 150, 153, 154, 155, 157, 193
Hamric, Bert 193
Hamrick, Ray 127
Handley, Gene 165, 185
Handley, Lee 143, 193
Haney, Fred 14, 16, **45**, 45–46, 48, 51, 52, 53–54, 55, 57, 59, 60, 146, 193
Hanlon, Dick 186, 193
Hanna, Roy 193
Hannah, J. Harrison "Truck" 34–35, **36**, 37, 41, 45, 49–50, 53, **79**, 81, 83, 85, 86, 90, 94, 95, 193
Hannah, Joe 171, 176, 193
Hanson, Jack 101, 193
Hardin, Bud 163, 164, 167, 168, 173, 193
Hargrave, Bob 193
Harkins, Pat 193
Harper, George 48–49, 193
Harper, Harry 193
Harrell, Ray 118
Harridge, Will 134

Harris, Herb 193
Hartley, Grover 15
Hartsfield, Roy 186, 193
Hatch, Sid 193
Hatten, Joe 158–59, 160, 162, 163, 164, 168, 170, 173, 175, 176, 193
Hausmann, Clem 193
Haynes (first name unknown) 193
Head, Claire 193
Heitmuller, Heinie 7, 193
Hemingway, Ed 34, 35, 41, 193
Henshaw, Roy 67, 72, 75, 193
Herman, Billy 100
Hernandez, Chico 96, 193
Herrmann, Leroy 53, 55, 56, 58–59, 60, **60**, 63, 66, 193
Hess, Bert 193
Heusser, Ed 108, 193
Hicks, Ken 121, 193
Hicks, Mel 120, 193
Hillman, Dave 176, 179, 180, 181, 193
Hinchman, Lorenzo 168, 193
Hitt, Roy 193
Hoag, Oliver 193
Hodges, Gil 154
Hodges, Red 193
Hoffman, Dutch 193
Hoffmeister, Paul 193
Hogan, Happy 193
Hogg, Brad 9, 10, 193
Holland, John 175, 185
Holling, Carl 43, 44, 171, 193
Hollingsworth, H. 193
Hollis, Jack 153, 155–56, 162, 193
Hollywood Sheiks/Stars 34, 38, 77–78
Hollywood Stars 89–90, 92, 135, 146, 187
Holm, Billy 96, 102, 112, 115, 193
Holmes, Les 193
Holmes, Tommy 174
Holt, Goldy 83, 84, 193
Hood, Wally 24, **24**, 26, 27, 31, 32–33, 34, 35, 38, 40, 41, 42, 44, 193
Hood, Wally, Jr. 33
Hooks, Gene 166, 193
Hopkins, John 193
Horan, Joe "Shags" 31, 193
Horne, Berlyn 46, 52, 193
Hornsby, Roger 53
Horton, Claude 193
Hosp, Franz 193
Houck, Byron 14
Howard, Ivan 8, 193
Howard, Robert 193
Howell, Murray "Red" 83, 84, 193
Hoy, Dummy 193
Hricinak, John 178, 193
Hughes, Jim 185, 186, 193
Hughes, Roy 108, 109, 113, 114, 115

Hughes, Thomas J. 193
Hughes, Thomas L. 16, 20, 23, 25, 28, 193
Hunt, Mike 68
Hurlburt, Ed 193
Hurst, Don 78, 81, 84–85, **85**, 193

Iacovetti, Joe 164
Ihde, Alan 142, 144, 147, 162, 163, 193
Intlekofer, John 193
Irvin, Monte 185, 186, 194
Isekite, Floyd 194

Jackson, Charley 194
Jackson, Ransom 142, 194
Jacobs, Art 53
Jacobs, Elmer 34, 35, 37, 38, 194
Jacobs, Jack 194
Jacobs, Ray 25, 26, 27, 31, 33, 34, 41, 44, 47, **47**, 48, 55, 58
Jacobs, Willie 194
Jahn, Art 34, 37, 38, 40, 194
Jakucki, Sig 86, 87–88, 194
James (first name unknown) 194
Jancse, John 186, 194
Jansen, Larry 130
Jasper, Hi 194
Jelincich, Frank 121, 194
Jenkins, Bob 194
Jenkins, Joe 26, 194
Jensen, Forrest "Woody" 40, 41, 194
Johnson, Clayton 194
Johnson, Don 137, 141, 194
Johnson, Ernie 194
Johnson, Everett 194
Joiner, Roy "Pappy" 58, 77, 114, 194
Jolley, Smead 43, 68
Jones, Bob 41, 43, 47, 48, 194
Jones, Oscar 194
Jones, Percy 23, 25, 194
Jones, Sheldon 166, 168, 194
Joyce, Bob 80, 82, 118, 194
Judd, Oscar 194

Kahler, George 194
Kahn, Jack 40, 194
Kamm, Willie 20
Kane, John 194
Kansas City Athletics 170
Keane, Jack 194
Keating, Ray 16, 17, 194
Kelleher, Frank 164, 165
Keller, Charlie 73
Kelly, Bill 127, **128**, 129, 133, 134, 136, 142, 149, 151–52, 194
Kelly, Bob 142, 143, 146, 147
Kemper, Dick 116, 194
Kennedy, John 194
Kenworthy, Duke 10, 12, 13–14, 194
Kerrigan, George 194
Keyser, Lee 50
Kies, Joe 194

Kilduff, Pete 30
Killefer, Wade "Red" 10, 11, 12, 13–14, 15, 16–17, 19–20, 23, 27, 194
Kimball, Newt 75, 76, 78, 80, 83, 84, 93, 194
Kimberlin, Harry 194
Kitsos, Chris 168, 194
Klein, Chuck 70
Klein, Eddie 194
Klein, Lou 149, 194
Kleine, Hal 136, 194
Knapp (first name unknown) 194
Koerner, Phil 194
Koestner, Bob 194
Korndor, Hans 194
Kowalski, Ed 194
Kraus, Jack 194
Kreevich, Mike 57–58, 194
Kreitner, Al 194
Krug, Marty 23–24, 24–25, 26, 28, 30–31, 40–41, 44–45, 49, 95, 194
Kruger, Art 194
Kumulae, Clarence 194
Kuncl, Joe 174, 194
Kush, Emil 94, 147, 150, 153, 194

Lade, Doyle 137, 154, 155, 157, 158, 159, 160, 194
Ladies Day and female fans 43, 47, 53, 67, 160, 170
Lafayette, George 194
Lahti, Clyde 87, 194
Laird, Bill 194
Lammers, Paul 194
Lammers, Wally 185, 194
Land, Harry 112, 194
Landis, Kenesaw Mountain 103
Lane, Bill 33–34, 43, 77–78
Lanfranconi, Walt 136, 139, 143, 194
Lapan, Pete 12, 13, 14, 15, 194
Larner, Bud 194
Larsen, Spike 194
Lary, Al 194
Lasorda, Tom 186, 194
Latshaw, Bob 194
Lauters, Don 194
Lavigne, Ed 158, 194
Lawler, Jack 194
Laws, Brick 156, 165, 166, 177
Layton, Les 147, 151, 153, 154, 155, 157, 158, 160, 162, 194
Lazzeri, Tony 138, 180
Leathers, Hal 194
LeBrand, Deke 194
LeGros, Tom 178, 194
Leguin (first name unknown) 194
Lelivelt, Jack 44–45, 49–50, 52, 54, *56*, 57, 58–59, 77, 78, 80–81, 82, 83, 88, 90, 92, 95, 194
Leonhardt, Elmo 194
Leverenz, Walter 8, 194

Lieber, Dutch 80, 82, 84, 86, 88, 89, 91, 94, 194
Lightfoot, Charlie 194
Lillard, Gene 57, 59, 61, 63, 65, 70, 73, 75–76, 77, 86, 87, *87*, 88, 89, 97, 109–10, 194
Lindimore, Howard 19, 25, 26, 194
Liska, Ad 102
"Lively Ball" era 24
Lloyd, Truck 194
Loane, Bob 194
Lober, Ty 194
Lockhardt, Charlie 23
Lorenz, Howard 85
Los Angeles, aerial views of *169*
Los Angeles Angels team portraits: 1913 *8*; 1926 *37*; 1930 *49*; 1931 *54*; 1933 *62*; 1934 *69*; 1939 *92*; 1940 *96*; 1941 *102*; 1943 *113*; 1944 *117*; 1947 *128*; 1949 *143*; 1950 *148*; 1952 *157*; 1953 *161*; 1954 *166*; 1955 *172*; 1956 *177*
Los Angeles Coliseum *169*, 187
Los Angeles Loo-Loos 5–6
Los Angeles Railway tickets *105*
Love, Slim 8, 194
Lowe, Lloyd 194
Lown, Turk 170, 173, 175, 176, 194
Lowrey, Peanuts 101, 102, 104, 108, 111, 194
Luby, Hugh 131
Lucadello, John 149, 150, 194
Lukon, Eddie 137, 194
Lynn, Red 108, 109, 110, 113, 114, 115, 123, 124, 126, 129, 130, 134, 136, 138, 139, *140*, 141, 142, 143, 194
Lyons, George 20, 23, 25, 26, 194

Mack family 170
Maddern, Clarence 129, 130, 131, 132, *132*, 135, 144, 149, 153, 194
Maggert, Harl 8, 17, 194
Maier, Edward and Fred 6, 23, 25, 34
Major League Executive Committee 123–24
major leagues: draft system 134, 141, 148, 156, 161; farm clubs and working agreements 74, 93, 104–5, 135–36, 146, 147, 177–78; PCL aspirations to join 116, 123–24, 134, 157, 170, 183; players optioned from 161, 166; radio broadcasting in PCL cities 148, 160; West Coast expansion/relocation 134, 141, 162, 165, 170, 171, 176, 183–87, 186, 188; *see also* Brooklyn Dodgers; Chicago Cubs
Malis, Cy 194
Mallory, Pete 108, 109, 113, 116, 149, 150, 194

Mallory, Rabbit 101, 102, 112, 114, 123, 124, 125, 194
Malone, Eddie 127, 136, 142, 143, 145, *145*, 164, 194
Maltzberger, Gordon 194
Mangerina, Henry 194
Mangini, Art 91, 194
Mann (first name unknown) 194
Manning, Ed 194
Manville, Dick 194
Maranville, Rabbit 30
Marasco, Vic 168, 194
Marino, Frank 150, 154, 194
Marks, Fred 194
Marsden, John 194
Marshall, Max 127, 194
Marshall, Ralph 194
Martin, Stu 125, 194
Martinke, Felix 194
Mason, Del 194
Matheson, Bill 131
Mathews, Wid 153, 171
Mattick, Bob 78, 80, *81*, 84, 85, 86, 93, 95, 194
Mattos, Ernie 194
Mauch, Gene 167, 168, 173, 175, 176, 177, 179, 181, 194
Mauriello, Ralph 186, 187, 194
Mauro, Carmen 142, 143, 147, 194
Mayo, Eddie 88, 89, 90, 93, 94, 95, 97, 100, 102, 104, 108, 111, 112, 194
Mazar, Pete 143, 194
McAuley, Jim "Ike" 15–16, 21, 24, 26, 30–31, 34, 194
McCabe, Bill 21, 22, 24, 25, 194
McCafferty, Chas 194
McCall, Bob "Dutch" 129, 130, 131, 194
McCarthy, Bill 17, 25
McCarthy, Joe 45
McClelland, Lou 194
McClelland, Walter 194
McCoy, Paul 194
McDade, Eddie 194
McDaniels, Booker "Cannonball" 146–47, 194
McDonald, Tex 16, 194
McDonnell, Speed 194
McDougal, Art 194
McGinnity, Bugs 194
McKenry, Pete 194
McLarry, Polly 146, 194
McLish, Cal 144, 149–50, 151, 158, 160, 162, 163, 168, 170, 173, 174, 194
McMinn, Glenn 194
McMullen, Hugh 62, 63, 66, 194
McMullin, Fred 194
McQuaid, Herb 194
McQuinn, George 73
McWilliams, Bill 83, 84, 194
Medwick, Joe 99
Meek, Dad 194
Meek, Hal 194
Mene, Joe 75, 194

Menking, Paul 194
Meola, Emile "Mike" 67, 72, 75, 76–77, 78, 194
Merkle, Warren 194
Merullo, Len 101, 102, 137, 194
Mesner, Steve 75, 77, 78, 80, 81, 85, 86, 93, 95, 154, 194
Metzger, George 194
Meusel, Irish 10, 194
Mickens, Glenn 186, 187, 194
Middledorf, Bert 194
Middleton, Charlie 194
Miller, Abe 194
Miller, Dots 24
Miller, Guy 116, 117, 119, 120, 121, 194
Miller, Jack "Dots" 22
Miller, O. 194
Miller, Oscar 194
Miller, Russ 43, 194
Milstead, George 195
Milwaukee Brewers 93
Minner, Paul 147
Mission Club of San Francisco 34, 89–90; *see also* Vernon Tigers
Mitchell, John 34, 37, 40, 195
Mohler, Kid 63
Mohler, Orv 63, 65–66, 195
Moisan, Bill 153, 154, 155, 157, 158, 159, 160, 162, 163, 164, 168, 195
Moncrief, Charlie 59, 195
Monette, Jacques 168, 195
Montgomery, Alvin 195
Moore, Charlie 8, 195
Moore, Dee 195
Moore, Johnny 48–49, 51, 52, 55, 86, 89, 93, 94, 97, 101, 102, 104, 108, 111, 114, 116, 117, 122
Mooty, Jake 195
Moran, Butch 142, *144*, 195
Morgan, Vern 195
Morley, James 8, 14, 195
Moses, Robert 184
Mosolf, Jim 67, 195
Moss, Malcolm 53, 55, 56, 58–59, 195
Moss, Ray 39, 195
Most Valuable Player award 238
Mueller, Ray 109, 110
Mulligan, Eddie 30
Muncrief, Bob 147, 149, 150, 151, 195
Murphy, Herb 195
Murray, Bob 195
Musial, Stan 151
Musser, Paul 195
Myer, Myron 195
Myers, Elmer 26, 28, 195
Myers, Richie 179

Nagle, Walter "The Judge" 6, 7, 195
Nast, Gene 195
Nasternak, Hank 168, 195
National Association of Professional Baseball Leagues 103
National League *see* major leagues
Negray, Ron 195
Neill, Tom 153, 195
Nelson, Emmett 72, 76, 195
Nelson, Lynn 53, 55, 58, 195
New York Giants 185
Newlin, Otto 195
Newsom, Lewis N. "Buck" 62, 64, 66, 195
Newton, Doc 6, 195
Niehoff, Bert 13–14, 15, 16, 19, 195
night baseball games 48, 50–51, 53, 107, 112, 115, 179
Niles, John 195
Norbert, Ted 111, 117, 195
Norgren, Swede 195
Northey, Ron 158, 162
Novakovich, John 195
Novikoff, Lou 94, 95, 97, 98–100, *99*, 101, 120–21, 180, 195
Novotney, Ralph "Rube" 136, 144, 195
Nuggets on the Diamond (Dobbins) 5

Oakes, Rebel 195
Oakland Oaks 165, 177
O'Connell, Jimmy 20
O'Doul, Lefty 20, 115, 131
Oglesby, Jim 59, 61, 65, **65**, 73, 76, 77, 78, 195
Ogorek, George 116, 195
Ograin, Cliff 195
Olsen, Barney 108, 111, 123, 124–25, 127, 195
Olson, Bill 195
Olson, Herb 195
O'Malley, Walter 176, 183–85, 187
O'Neal, Oran 195
Open Classification system 156–57, 160, 170
optioned players from major leagues 161, 166
Orndorff, Jess 195
Osborn, Bob 195
Osborn, Don 113, 116, 118, 120, 121, 123, 124, 130, 133, 195
Ostrowski, Joe 112, 162, 195
Ostrowski, John 114, 115, 117, 118, 121, 129, 130, 132, 135, 137, 138, 142, 143, 145, **145**, 146, 195
Otero, Reggie 117, 120, 122, 123, 125, 128, 195
Overman, Earl 83, 84, 86, 195

Pacific Coast League (PCL): All-Star games 68; batting averages and baseball design 67–68; expansion of 12; Great Depression roster and salary limits 57, 61, 74; major league aspirations 116, 123–24, 134, 157, 170, 183; major league farm clubs and working agreements 74, 84, 135–36, 146, 147; Most Valuable Player 70, 125; optioned players from major leagues 161, 166; origins of 5–6; pitching rules changes 20; player draft 134, 141, 148, 156; playoffs 74, 89; post–1958 changes 187, 189; reaction to Dodger purchase of Angels 185; roster limits 57, 61, 74, 107, 162; season schedule adjustments 13, 16, 21, 54, 74–75, 151, 154, 157, 162, 177; television broadcasting policies 141, 160; World War I and 10–11; World War II and 107, 112, 115
Padget, Bill "Spec" 162, 163, 195
Pafko, Andy 112, 114, 115, 195
Page, Bill 8, 187, 195
Page, Chuck 195
Palica, Ambrose 195
Palmer, George 195
Parker, Art 195
Parker, William 165
Passarella, Al 195
Paton, Leroy 121, 195
Patrick, Joe 21, 25, 28, 34, 38, 45, 52, 67, 95
Paulson, Norris 176
Pawelek, Ted 129, 195
Payne, George 26, 28, 34–35, 195
Paynich, Rudy 195
PCL *see* Pacific Coast League
Peckham, Frank 195
Peden, Les 153, 155, 157, 160, 162, 163, 195
Peek, Steve 137
Pepe, Joe 195
Perkowski, Harry 176, 178, 181, 195
Perritt, Pol 195
Pertica, Bill 11, 13, 15, 19, 195
Peters, Will 41, 43, 44, 51, 195
Peterson, Russ 121, 195
Petty, Jess 53, 55, 56, 58, 195
Philadelphia Athletics 170
Phillips, Elmer 195
Phillips, Pat 195
Phipps, Jodie 113, 114, 115, 195
Piercy, Bill 40, 185, 195
Pieretti, Chick 178, 180, 195
Piktuzis, George 173, 174, 175–76, 177, 179, 195
Pillette, Herman 68
Pillette, Ted 195
Pittenger, Clarke 30, 195
Pitts (first name unknown) 195
playoffs 74, 89
Plitt, Norman 41, 43, 44, 48, 195
Pocatello club (Utah-Idaho League) 41
Ponca City Angels 75, 93
Ponder, Elmer 22, 23, 25, 26, 195

Index

Pontarelli, Mike 195
Poulson, Norris 184, 185
Powell, Bob 101, 195
Powell, Larry 195
Powers, John F. 8, 15, 19, 21
Pramesa, John 166, 173, 195
Prim, Ray 80, 82, 84, 86, 88, 89, 91, 94, 95, 97–98, 100, 102, 103, 108, 109, 110, 111, 112, 116, 118, 119, *119*, 120, 195
Prince, Bill 195
Prout, Len 195
Pyecha, John 168, 170, 174, 179, 195

Quinn, Wimpy 101, 102, 113, 115, 117, 125, 195

Raffensberger, Ken 108, 109, 110, 111, 115, 195
Rager, John 195
Raimondi, Bill 153, 195
Ramsdell, Willard 158–59, 162, 163, 195
Ramsey, Buck 195
Randolph, Red 195
Rapp, Earl 150, 151, 175
Rawlings, John 195
Raymond, Tealy 195
Read, Bert 195
Reams, Babe 195
Reeder, Bill 195
Reese, Jimmie 18, 63, 67, 72, 77, 78, 80, 83, 86, 195
Rego, Tony 195
Reichow, Oscar 21, 34, 38, 51, 52, 85–86, 92
Reinhart, Art 19, 195
relief pitching practices 181–82
Renshaw, Frenchy 103
Reppy, Gaylord 195
Reyes (first name unknown) 195
Reynolds, Carl 195
Rhabe, Nick 195
Rhawn, Bob 146, 195
Rhyne, Hal 30, 41
Rice, Hal 174, 175, 176, 195
Richards, Fred 162, 163, 165, 167, 168, 195
Richards, Jack 124, 125
Richardson, Kenny 75, 84, 85, 195
Rieger, Elmer 195
riots 164–65
Roberts, Red 43, 48, 195
Robertson, Don 168, 171, 173, 185, 195
Robertson, Larry 195
Rogers, Brown 195
Roosevelt Stadium 184
Root, Charlie 26, 28, 30, 35, 195
Ross, Art 195
Rossbach, Henry 195
Rossomondo, Joe 195
roster limits 57, 61, 74, 107, 162
Roth, Bill 195
Rothrock, Jack 86, 87, 89, 94, 195

Rowe, Ralph 195
Rowland, Clarence "Pants" 105, 108, 110, 116, 123, 134, 141, 185
Roybal, Ed 176
Ruby, Harry 195
Ruether, Dutch 195
Rumler, Bill 15, 17
Runge, Ed 160
Runyon, Damon 13
Russell, Glen "Rip" 75, 78, 84–85, 86, 89, 90, 91, 95, 105, 114, 115, 116, 117, 119, 120, 121–22, 126, 195
Ryan, Jack 8, 9, 10, 195

Sacramento Solons 165, 178
Saffell, Tom 186, 187, 195
St. Louis Browns 105–6, 147, 162
salary limits 57
Salt Lake City Bees 33–34
Salvatierra, Manny 117, 195
Salveson, Jack 80, 81–82, 84, 86, 87, 89, 91, 195
Samhammer, Ralph 101, 102, 195
San Diego Padres (formerly Hollywood Sheiks) 77–78
San Francisco Giants 185
San Francisco Seals 165, 177–78, 187
Sandberg, Gus 31, 35, 41, 47, 49, *50*, 195
Sandel, Warren 195
Sanders, Herb 195
Sanford, George 87, 88, 195
Sanford, Jack 86, 137, 141, 195
Santa Catalina Island Company 104, 184
Sarni, Bill 116, 117, 195
Sauer, Ed 117, 118, 120, 123, 124, 126, 129, 131, 136, 137, 138, 139, *139*, 141, 195
Sawyer, Carl 195
Scarsella, Les 139
Schaefer, George 195
Scheel, Karl 195
Scheffing, Bob 174, 182, 185
Schenz, Hank 125, 195
Scherf, Charlie 195
Schick, Maurice 10, 13, 195
Schlafly, Larry 195
Schmidt, Bill 109
Schmidt, Frank 195
Schmidt, Fred 136, 195
Schmidt, Harry 195
Schoor, Ed 195
Schroeder, Bill 37–38
Schulmerich, Wes 41, 42, 43, 46, 47, 48, 52, 78, 80, 83, 142, 195
Schulte, John 53, 58, 195
Schultz, Dick 195
Schultz, Joe 195
Schultz, Toots 195
Schuster, Bill 104, 108, 109, 113, 115, 123, 124, 126, 127, 128, 131, *131*, 132, 136, 138, 141, 145, 195

Scoggins, Jim 195
Scott, "Death Valley" 20
season schedule adjustments 13, 16, 21, 54, 74–75, 151, 154, 157, 162, 177; *see also* attendance
Seaton, Tom 17, 195
Seats, Tom 118
Seattle Indians 23, 27
Seattle Rainiers 91–92
Seerey, Pat 144, 195
Serafini, Mel 110
Sewell, Luke 180
Shealy, Al 53, 195
Sheely, Earl 58, 59, 196
Shellenback, Frank 20, 39–40, 51, 54, 60, 64
Sherry, Larry 196
Shoap, Art 196
Sick, Emil 88, 92, 185
Sigafoos, Frank 48, 51, 53, 196
Simpson, Tom 167, 196
Skaff, Mike 196
Skiff, Bill 49–50, 196
Slagle, Walt 196
Slotter, Joe 121, 196
Smalley, Roy 116, 117, 196
Smith, Al 163, 196
Smith, Bart 196
Smith, Casey 17
Smith, Dick 162, 196
Smith, Elmer 196
Smith, Jud 6, 196
Smith, K. 196
Smith, Red 25, 196
Smith, Walter 196
Snodgrass, Fred 196
Snyder, Ray 104
Sorey, Ray 196
Soria, Lefty 196
Sousa, Henry 196
South, Lynn 75, 196
Spalding, John 5
Spasoff, Pete 196
Speake, Bob 178–79, 181, 196
Speece, Byron 116
Spence, Stan 149, 153, 196
Spencer, Ed 196
Spicer, Bob 153, 154, 155, 156, 157, 158, 162, 163, 168, 170, 196
Spies, Heinie 196
Spindel, Hal 196
spitball (pitch) 20, 39–40
Spores (first name unknown) 196
Stabelfeld, Elvin 196
Stadille, Art 196
Stainback, George "Tuck" 57, 60, 63, 64, 65, 66, *66*, 67, 129, 196
Staley, Gale 34, 41, 44, 196
Stamper, John 104, 196
Stanage, Oscar 19, 21, 196
Standridge, Pete 9, 10, 196
Stanka, Joe 171, 196
Starr, Fay 196
Statz, Arnold "Jigger" 17, 18, 19,

21, 22, 31, 34, 37–38, 39, 44, 45, 46, 48, 52, 53, 60, 67, 73, *73*, 78, 80, 81, 84, 86, 94, 95–96, 97, 100, 110–11, 196
Stefani, Lou 196
Stein, Irv 196
Steiner, Jim 196
Steitz, Chris 196
Stephens, Bryan 196
Stephenson, Joe 123, 124, 196
Stephenson, Walt 196
Sterger, Ted 196
Stewart, Don 116, 146, 147, 171
Stewart, Gabby 196
Stine, Lee 91, 94, 97, 100, 102, 103, 104, 196
Stitzel, Hal 56, 58, 59, 67, 196
Stoddard, Dwight 174, 196
Storey, Harvey 102, 123, 125, 196
Stringer, Lou 93, 94, 95, 97, 100, 101, 127–28, 130, 131, 132, 135, 196
Stroud, Ralph 196
Struss, Clarence 196
Sturgeon, Bob 145, 149, 196
Sueme, Hal 196
Sullivan, Jack 196
Sullivan, John 196
Summa, Homer 53, 58, 59, 196
Swanson, Don 196
Sweeney, Bill 112, 116, 118, 120, 127, 166, 174, 196
Sweetland, Les 58–59, 196

Tabor, Jim 136, 137, 196
Taitt, Doug 196
Talamante, Richard 196
Talbot, Bob 153, 156, 157, 160, 163, 171, 173–74, 196
Tappe, Elvin 179, 181, 185, 196
Tatum, Tom 196
Teck, Eddie 196
Teed, Dick 196
television and radio broadcasting 67, 140–41, 146, 148, 160, 168, 179
Tepler, Boyd 196
Terry, Yank 126, 196
Terry, Zeb 10, 196
Terwilliger, Wayne 142, 143, 146, 189, 196
Thomas, Claude 15–16, 17, 20, 23, 25, 196
Thomas, Fay 61–62, 63, 64, 67, 69, *71*, 71–72, 73, 78, 80–81, 82, 84, 86, 87, *87*, 88, 89, 91, 94, 95, 97, 100, 102, 103, 108, 196
Thompson, Howard 196
Thompson, Lefty 196
Thornton (first name unknown) 196
Thorpe, Bob 179, 181, 196
Thorsen, Bull 196
Tierney, Martin 196
Tindall, Dick 196
Tobey, Dan 196
Todd, Al 108, 196

Tolson, Charlie "Slug" 41, 42, 43, 45, 46–47, 196
Toman, Jim 196
Toren, Roy 196
Totaro, Frank 107, 196
Tozer, Bill 7, 196
Trabous, Manuel 196
Treadway, Leon 126, 196
Treager, Del 196
Tremel, Bill 171, 174, 196
Tucson Padres 189
Turpin, Hal 109
Tuttle, W.C. 103, 116
Twombly, Clarence "Babe" 22, 24, 26, 31, 33, 196
Tyack, Jim 121, 196

Upright, Dixie 163, 167, 168, 196
Usher, Bob 158, 160, 163, 167, 168, 173, 174–75, 196

Valencia, Ralph 196
Valentinetti, Vito 186, 196
Vancouver Mounties 177
Van Dyke, Gordon 196
Van Fleet, Dwight 88, 94, 196
Vann (first name unknown) 196
Vanni, Edo 98
Vaughn, Bob 196
Veeck, Bill 162
Veltman, Art 75, 80, 196
Vernon, Harry 196
Vernon Tigers 23, 25, 34; *see also* Mission Club of San Francisco
Viers, Ray 120, 196
Vusich, John 196

Wade, Ben 147, 196
Wade, Gale 174, 175, 176, 179, 180, 181, 196
Waitkus, Eddie 108, 111, 112, 113, 117, 196
Wakeham, Fred 196
Walby (first name unknown) 196
Wallace, Bob 196
Walsh, Augie 43, 44, 47, 52–53, 196
Walters, John 196
Waner, Paul 30
Ward, Dick 59, 61, 64, 66, 67, 72, 73, 75, 89, 196
Ward, Preston 147
Ware, Andy 196
Waring, Ted 196
Warren, Dallas 50, 196
Warren, Henry 63, 196
Warstler, Rabbit 102, 196
Washington, Kenny 150, 196
Washington Park 7, 14, 28, 29
Washington Senators 183
Waterbury, Frank 196
Watkins, Don 143, 146, 157, 196
Weathersby, Earl "Tex" 40, 41, 196
Webb, Earl 44, 45, 46–47, 196
Weber, Boots 21

Weiland, Bob 97, 98, 100, 102, 103, 196
Weinert, Phil 196
Weintraub, Phil 102, 104, 108, 196
Weis, Art 34, 37, 40, 41, 67, 196
Welsh, Jimmy 52, 53
Werber, Bill 93
West, Hi 196
West, Max 130, 150, 153, 154, 155, 157, 158, 160, 163, 167–68, 178, 196
Wetzel, Buzz 56, 196
Whaley, Bill C. 26, 27, 31, 181, 196
Whaley, Bill F. 196
Whaling, Bob 196
Wheat, Mack 196
Wheeler, George 196
Whitman, Frank 149, 196
Wicker, Kemp 109
Williams, Dewey 123, 124, 196
Williams, Harry 25, 31
Williams, John 196
Willingham, Hugh 196
Wilson, Artie 98
Wilson, Dick 196
Wilson, Harry 196
Wilson, Jake 196
Winceniak, Eddie 171, 173, 196
Windish, Bob 196
Winsell, George 196
Winslow, Bob 196
Wise, Casey 176, 177, 181, 196
Wolf, Al 110
Wolfe (first name unknown) 196
Wolter, Harry 8, 196
Woodend, George 196
working agreements and farm clubs *see* Chicago Cubs; Los Angeles Angels; major leagues
World War I 10–11
World War II: effects on Angels 115, 120, 121; impact on attendance 122; PCL season schedule adjustments during 107; players drafted into armed services 107, 108, 112, 116, 120; and quality of PCL play 115, 123
Wotell, Mike 196
Wright, Bill 196
Wright, Gene 196
Wright, Wayne 35, 37, 40, 41, 42, 196
Wrigley, P.K. 105, 166
Wrigley, William, Jr. 19, 21, 23, 38, 43, 44
Wrigley Field: aerial photographs *28*, *169*; Angels final games at 187; construction, opening and dedication 23, 31–32, *33*; dimensions and power baseball 28; Hollywood teams at 77, 90; improvements to 171; post–PCL use and demolition 188–89; sale to

Dodgers 184; transit and parking issues *105*, 146
Wyman, Rosalind 176
Wyse, Hank 143, 196

Yarrison, Rube 34, 37, 196
Yates, Bob 196

Yerkes, Carroll 51, 52, 196
York, Jim 22
York, Tony 197

Zabel, Zip 197
Zaby, Charlie 197
Zanic, John 197

Zeider, Rollie 16, 197
Zick, Bob 158, 171, 197
Zimmerman, Paul 110, 134
Zoeterman, George 197
Zuber, Bob 197

www.ingramcontent.com/pod-product-compliance
Lightning Source LLC
Chambersburg PA
CBHW081549300426
44116CB00015B/2812